lonely planet

Tasmania

Charles Rawlings-Way, Andrew Bain

CONTENTS

Plan Your Trip

The Guide

The Boathouse (p238), Currie, King Island

Wallaby, Wineglass Bay (p152), Freycinet National Park

Toolkit

Storybook

Bay of Fires (p171), east coast

Acknowledgement of Country

Lonely Planet would like to acknowledge the First Nations throughout this country, who have nurtured and maintained the land since time immemorial. This guide was written on, and is written about, the lands of many diverse nations.

We recognise the unique and ongoing connection that First Nations peoples have to land and waters and thank them for their efforts to preserve them. We pay our respects to Elders past and present and extend this respect to any Aboriginal or Torres Strait Islander people who may be reading this guide.

We also recognise the ongoing efforts of Aboriginal and Torres Strait Islander peoples for reconciliation, justice, and social, cultural and economic self-determination. Sovereignty was never ceded. Australia always was, and always will be, Aboriginal land.

Cultural Sensitivity Warning

Aboriginal and Torres Strait Islander readers are advised that this guide may contain names and images of people who have since passed away.

WILLIAM EDGE/SHUTTERSTOCK

Hobart (p44)

TASMANIA

THE JOURNEY BEGINS HERE

I spent my childhood in Taroona, just south of Hobart, wheeling my BMX between the beach and the bush. It was the '70s, man – Tasmania was a magical, freewheeling place to be a kid. Like so many other islanders, I was lured away in my 20s by the mainland big smoke, but now I'm back in Tasmania with my own family. It's a joy to eat and drink here; to leave our footprints on empty beaches; to hurl snowballs in winter; and to chase the island's art scene as it jumps and sparks in surprising directions. Tasmania is a magical, freewheeling place to be an adult, too.

Charles Rawlings-Way

@crawlingsway

Based in Hobart, Charles writes about travel, cricket, food, education and music – inspired and haunted by Tasmania's history, landscapes and maritime soul.

My favourite experience is looking out across the River Derwent in the evening: colours shift to deep navy and clouds fray as fishing boats return to the **Hobart waterfront** (p56).

WHO GOES WHERE

Our writers and experts choose the places that, for them, define Tasmania.

BJORN SVENSSON/ALAMY

There's something almost ethereal about **Takayna/Tarkine** (p248). As you kayak down the Pieman River (pictured) at dawn, the reflections of the largest temperate rainforest in Australia are so perfect as to be disorienting, and yet one of the wildest stretches of coastline in the country is just a band of trees away. It speaks volumes about the yin and yang of Tasmania – so classically beautiful on the one hand and so wildly wondrous on the other.

Andrew Bain

@bainonbike

Andrew is a travel writer who was drawn to Tasmania almost 20 years by the presence of so many outdoor opportunities.

Flinders Island
An island off an island with hike-worthy peaks (p180)
Bicheno
Idyllic holiday town with salubrious seafood (p162)
Tamar Valley
Tour the vine-striped hillsides of the Tamar Valley (p204)
Derby
MTB mayhem on the Blue Derby trails (p175)
Launceston
Festivale food-and-drink fiesta and Cataract Gorge (p190)
Cradle Mountain
Tackle the 65km Overland Track (p240)
BASS STRAIT
TASMAN SEA
Cape Wickham
Egg Lagoon
Yambacoona
King Island
Sea Elephant Bay
Naracoopa
Currie
Grassy
Seal Bay
Hope Channel
Hunter Island
Three Hummock Island
Hunter Passage
Woolnorth Point
Robbins Island
Perkins Bay
Stanley
The Nut
Montagu
Smithton
Studland Bay
Marrawah
Edith Creek
Arthur River
Arthur-Pieman Conservation Area
Sandy Cape
Wynyard
Burnie
Ulverstone
Devonport
Waratah
Savage River
Corinna
Rosebery
Zeehan
Cradle Mountain-Lake St Clair National Park
Mole Creek
Deloraine
Breona
Poatina
Yingina/Great Lake
Longford
Perth
Launceston
Exeter
Beaconsfield
George Town
Low Head
Noland Bay
Bridport
Scottsdale
Lilydale
Derby
Ringarooma
Gladstone
Eddystone Point
Larapuna/Bay of Fires
St Helens Point
St Helens
Scamander
St Marys
Fingal
Legges Tor (1572m)
Ben Lomond National Park
Douglas-Apsley National Park
Bicheno
Banks Strait
Truwana/Cape Barren Island
Cape Barren
Lady Barron
Whitemark
Flinders Island
Sellars Point
Emita
Babel Island
Cape Frankland
Palana
Stanley Point
Inner Sister Island
Outer Sister Island

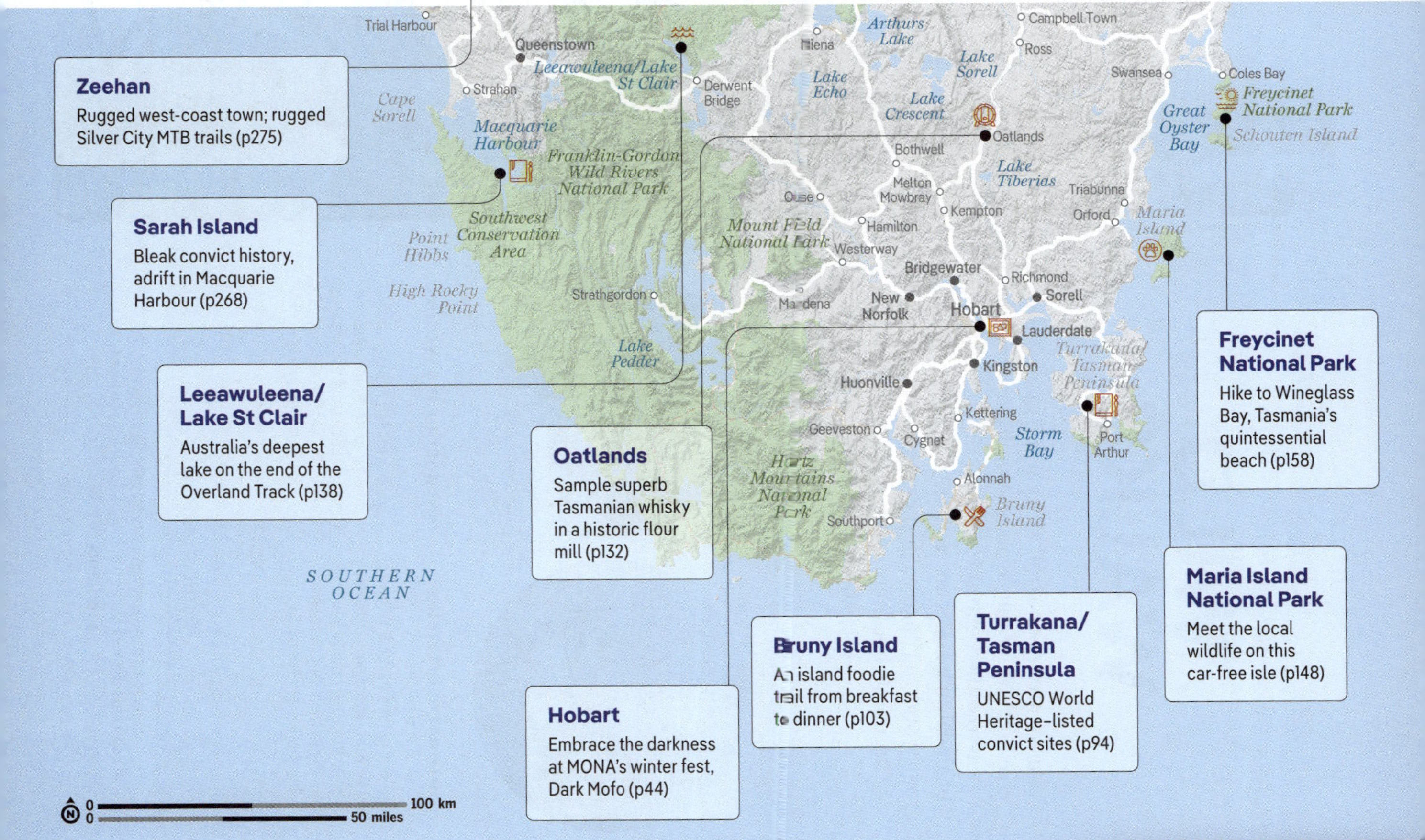
Zeehan
Rugged west-coast town; rugged Silver City MTB trails (p275)
Sarah Island
Bleak convict history, adrift in Macquarie Harbour (p268)
Leeawuleena/ Lake St Clair
Australia's deepest lake on the end of the Overland Track (p138)
Oatlands
Sample superb Tasmanian whisky in a historic flour mill (p132)
Hobart
Embrace the darkness at MONA's winter fest, Dark Mofo (p44)
Bruny Island
An island foodie trail from breakfast to dinner (p103)
Turrakana/ Tasman Peninsula
UNESCO World Heritage-listed convict sites (p94)
Maria Island National Park
Meet the local wildlife on this car-free isle (p148)
Freycinet National Park
Hike to Wineglass Bay, Tasmania's quintessential beach (p158)
Trial Harbour
Queenstown
Strahan
Cape Sorell
Macquarie Harbour
Leeawuleena/Lake St Clair
Derwent Bridge
Franklin-Gordon Wild Rivers National Park
Southwest Conservation Area
Point Hibbs
High Rocky Point
Strathgordon
Lake Pedder
Arthurs Lake
Liena
Lake Echo
Lake Sorell
Lake Crescent
Campbell Town
Ross
Swansea
Coles Bay
Freycinet National Park
Great Oyster Bay
Schouten Island
Oatlands
Bothwell
Lake Tiberias
Triabunna
Orford
Maria Island
Ouse
Melton Mowbray
Kempton
Hamilton
Mount Field National Park
Westerway
Bridgewater
Richmond
Sorell
Maydena
New Norfolk
Hobart
Lauderdale
Turrakana/ Tasman Peninsula
Kingston
Huonville
Kettering
Geeveston
Cygnet
Storm Bay
Port Arthur
Hartz Mountains National Park
Alonnah
Bruny Island
Southport
SOUTHERN OCEAN
0 100 km
0 50 miles
N

WILD WALKS

Take an afternoon stroll along some magnificent coastal cliffs, or tackle an epic multiday traverse across the Central Highlands: Tasmania's bushwalking trails are arguably Australia's best. From World Heritage wilderness to short, accessible nature walks, there's mesmerising scenery everywhere you look.

FROM LEFT: TOM JASTRAM/SHUTTERSTOCK, GARETH GRIFFITHS/500PX, VISUAL COLLECTIVE/SHUTTERSTOCK

60 Great Short Walks

These self-guided **Parks & Wildlife Service** *(parks.tas.gov.au)* hikes range from one hour to a full day – the perfect introduction to bushwalking in Tasmania.

Weathering the Weather

January to March brings stable weather to the Southwest and Highland Lakes, but the snow can blow in any season. Be ready for anything.

Outdoors Shops

Hobart and Launceston's city streets play host to myriad outdoors shops – plenty of options if you need an extra pair of socks.

Cradle Mountain-Lake St Clair National Park (p240)

BEST BUSHWALKING EXPERIENCES

Traverse the highest sea-cliffs in Australia on the spectacular ❶ **Three Capes Track** (p94), delivering you to Cape Hauy.

Explore jagged dolerite peaks, icy mountain tarns and mega-deep Lake St Clair on the famous ❷ **Overland Track** (p244).

Get a taste of the magnificent long-haul South Coast Track on the achievable day walk to ❸ **South Cape Bay** (p122).

Take a break from the city and hike beneath the otherworldly Organ Pipes on ❹ **Kunanyi/ Mt Wellington** (p70).

Hike to the lookout then down to the sand at ❺ **Wineglass Bay** (p158) – an essential Tasmanian experience. And have a swim!

Port Arthur Historic Site (p98)

A DARK HISTORY

Not all of Tasmania's World Heritage Sites are natural wonders. Several of the island's convict ruins feature on the UNESCO Australian Convict Sites list, while many other buildings were constructed using convict labour – in some cases, earning the builders their freedom. Two of Australia's oldest stone bridges (including the oldest) are here too.

Underground Misery

The **Coal Mines Historic Site** (p100) on Turrakana/Tasman Peninsula was a brutal convict workstation – even the cells were underground.

Visions of Country Civility

Take the Convict Trail Walk from the convict-built farm village of **Brickendon** (p201) to the well-kept grounds of **Woolmers Estate** (p201), near Longford.

BEST CONVICT EXPERIENCES

Scare yourself silly on a Ghost Tour at ❶ **Port Arthur Historic Site** (p98) or reflect on the sombre ruins in daylight.

Check out the 186 carved images on ❷ **Ross Bridge** (p129) before inspecting the bleak Ross Female Factory.

Cruise out onto Macquarie Harbour from Strahan and visit ❸ **Sarah Island** (p268) – once home to the 'worst of the worst' convict offenders.

Wander the Hobart Rivulet trail upstream into South Hobart to learn about the hard lives of women convicts at the ❹ **Cascades Female Factory** (p68).

Explore historic Richmond, home to Australia's oldest bridge (1825), then learn about the harsh conditions endured by convicts at ❺ **Richmond Gaol Historic Site** (p83).

MEET THE LOCALS

Tasmania is home to rare birds, migrating whales and rampant marsupials, some of which are extinct on the mainland – including the ubiquitous Tasmanian pademelon *(Thylogale billardierii)* and the eastern barred bandicoot *(Perameles gunnii)*. Carnivorous marsupial predators include the spotted and eastern quolls, and the famously grumpy Tasmanian devil.

FROM LEFT: DAN BROUN, VIA ANIMALS FANDOM WIKI; BIRD DUDE/SHUTTERSTOCK

Freshwater Crays

The Tasmanian giant freshwater crayfish *(Astacopsis gouldi)* – the world's largest freshwater crayfish, growing up to 80cm long – lives in the rivers of Takayna/Tarkine.

Unique Beaks

Twelve Tasmanian bird species are found nowhere else on Earth, including the common 'turbo chook' (Tasmanian native hen; pictured) and the shy and beautiful forty-spotted pardalote.

Love Island

Classified as 'breeding endemics', both the rare orange-bellied parrot and endangered swift parrot return to Tasmania from mainland Australia to breed every spring.

BEST WILDLIFE EXPERIENCES

Watch the rehabilitated devils and feed the kangaroos at the excellent ❶ **Bonorong Wildlife Sanctuary** (p84).

Say g'day to wombats, pademelons, echidnas and potaroos on a ❷ **Maria Island National Park** (p148) bush walk, discovering its diverse menagerie.

Get up close and personal to a posse of feasting Tasmanian devils at Mole Creek's ❸ **Trowunna Wildlife Sanctuary** (p227).

Hunt for wombats and echidnas along the Ronny Creek flats and look for platypuses in the tarns around ❹ **Cradle Mountain** (p242).

Spy passing whales from ❺ **Cape Tourville** (p160) on the East Coast, or get closer on a boat tour with Hobart's ❺ **Pennicott Wilderness Journeys** (p62).

SHRED THE TRAILS

It wasn't so long ago that a lot of small Tasmanian mining and timber towns were in gradual, sleepy decline. Then one fateful day, Derby awoke from its slumber and decided to become a world-class mountain-biking venue. The change in Derby's fortunes has been meteoric and has flowed into other towns and regions – including Zeehan, Maydena, St Helens and Queenstown – as the global MTB boom continues apace.

FROM LEFT: VICTOR LUCAS/ALAMY, FILEDIMAGE/SHUTTERSTOCK, ANDREW BAIN/ALAMY

Suburban MTB

Glenorchy Mountain Bike Park (p79) in Hobart's northern suburbs is a free council mountain-bike park offering a range of trails for all abilities.

One-Stop Shop

Tasmanian Mountain Bike Adventures *(tasmba.com.au)* can organise bike hire, transport, airport transfers and just about anything else you might need on a Tasmanian mountain-biking adventure.

Electro-Flow

Take the sting out of the massive elevation gains on Kunanyi/Mt Wellington's trail by hiring an electric mountain bike (warning: they're hugely addictive).

Bay of Fires trail (p167), St Helens

BEST MTB EXPERIENCES

Ride the wild ❶ **Bay of Fires trail** (p167) from the the mountains to the sea at Larapuna/Bay of Fires near St Helens.

Traverse Kunanyi/Mt Wellington's tree-lined flanks on the ❷ **Pipeline Track** (p69), with bonus walk to Wellington Falls.

Immerse yourself into the Southwest wilderness on the epic gravity tracks at ❸ **Maydena Bike Park** (p118).

Head west for exposed and exciting downhill gravel trails at Queenstown's ❹ **Mt Owen** (p273).

Explore the forested trails of the world-class MTB scene around ❺ **Derby** (p175).

GOURMET BOUNTY

Tasmania and fine produce go together like a knife and fork – with the definition of 'produce' these days extending far beyond apples and seafood. Look for local garlic, truffles, saffron, pork, lamb, cheese, berries, beef, chocolate, bread and mushrooms – much of which can be found in farmers markets, foraged from regional driving tours, or served up in island's best restaurants.

Tapping the Source

Stock up on picnic goodies at Launceston's Saturday Harvest Market (pictured) or Hobart's Sunday **Farm Gate Market** (p50), where island growers sell their produce direct.

The Tasting Trail

Follow the **Tasting Trail** *(tastingtrail.com.au)* from Launceston into the northwest, visiting 40-plus top island farms, producers, cellar doors, distillers and brewers.

Southern Picnic Supplies

Missed the markets? Fear not: the Wursthaus Kitchen just off Hobart's Salamanca stocks a superb selection of the best island produce.

FROM LEFT: NESS VANDERBURGH/LONELY PLANET, MICHAEL R EVANS/SHUTTERSTOCK, YIFEN WU/SHUTTERSTOCK

Oysters, Bruny Island (p103)

BEST FOODIE EXPERIENCES

Devour briny-fresh oysters with a side order of East Coast sunshine at ❶ **Melshell Oyster Shack** (p155).

Team a lobster roll with elevated views of the Gulch at the ❷ **Lobster Shack** (p165) in Bicheno.

Commit to the long-haul set menu showcasing garden produce at New Norfolk's ❸ **Agrarian Kitchen** (p84).

Tour the ❹ **Huon Valley** (p109) and grab a bag of apples to go from a roadside apple stall. Crunch.

Ferry across to bountiful ❺ **Bruny Island** (p103) for an Adventure Bay picnic with delicious local cheese, beer, bread and oysters.

TIME FOR A DRINK?

Tasmania isn't a great place for teetotallers: around every corner there's a craft brewery, cidery or artisanal distillery creating bespoke spirits and winning global awards. And then there are the wineries: from the Huon Valley to Pipers River, the island hillsides are striped with rows of cool-climate grapes. Resistance is futile.

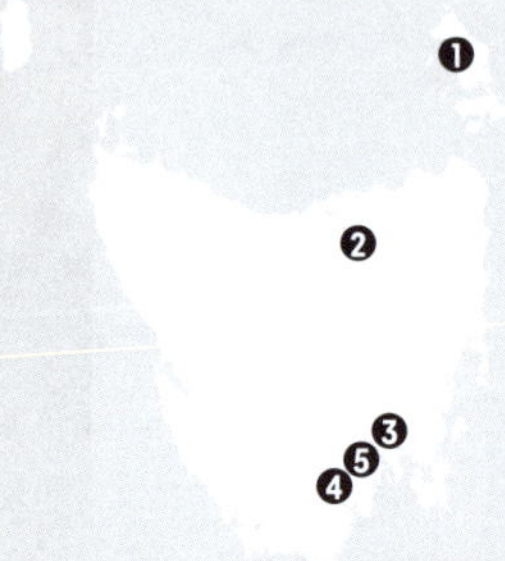

BEST DRINKING EXPERIENCES

Sip on single-malt whisky tinged with maritime influences at the ❶ **Furneaux Distillery** (p184) on remote Flinders Island.

Relax with wood-fired pizza and craft beers at Launceston's ❷ **Du Cane Brewery & Dining Hall** (p198).

Nose your way into some peppy pinot noirs and buttery chardonnays in the ❸ **Coal River Valley** (p82) between Cambridge and Richmond.

Discover another use for all those Huon Valley apples at ❹ **Frank's Cider House & Cafe** (p113) in Franklin.

Rock-out with an icy pint at the ❺ **Longley International Hotel** (p78) beer garden, listening to a touring band turn it up to 11.

FROM LEFT: DAVID GREENE/SHUTTERSTOCK, ELLA MACDONALD/SHUTTERSTOCK

Beer for the Ages

Tasmania has plenty of 'Australia's oldest' things, including its oldest brewery: **Cascade Brewery** (p68) in South Hobart started bottling beer in 1824.

Midlands Whisky

Tasmania's historic Midlands are a great destination for whisky touring, with distilleries in Oatlands, Kempton and Pontville.

Heritage Hops

A mysterious garden of hop vines was discovered on King Island recently, thought to be almost identical to hops grown in 18th-century Kent, England.

KARIN WHEELER/SHUTTERSTOCK

BEST FESTIVAL EXPERIENCES

Check your inhibitions at the door for Tasmania's flagship winter festival. ❶ **Dark Mofo** (p61) is edgy, unexpected and disquieting. Nude Solstice Swim, anyone?

Bring the kids to ❷ **Festivale** (p196) in Launceston's City Park, with live music, creative activities and lots of delicious things to eat and drink in January.

Snap your fingers at the ❸ **Devonport Jazz Festival** (p220), bringing the winter celebrations to the edge of Bass Strait every July.

Soak up some sun and fine wine at ❹ **Great Eastern Wine Week** (p154), along the East Coast Wine Trail, in October.

Join the end-of-year party at ❺ **Taste of Summer** (p63), a family-friendly week of food and live tunes on the Hobart waterfront.

Festivale (p196), Launceston

FAB FESTIVALS

Stop what you're doing and book tickets in advance for Tasmania's top festivals. From Hobart to Launceston, accommodation books out early as visitors surge into the state to experience the island's offbeat arts, edgy music and fine food and drink. Fly solo, or bring the kids – it's a very family-friendly party.

Winter Season

Bucking the national trend, winter in Tasmania is prime festival season: arts, music, whisky and song. Forget about hibernating – pull on a beanie and a 'Tassie tuxedo' (puffer jacket) and get into it.

The MONA Effect

Hobart's **MONA** (p76) isn't just an art gallery – the museum is a prime mover in Tasmania's festival scene, always pushing the boundaries and experimenting with new directions. Don't miss Dark Mofo.

REGIONS & CITIES

Find the places that tick all your boxes.

The Northwest & Cradle Country

GOURMET GOODNESS, WILD COASTLINES AND ALPINE ADVENTURES

South of Devonport, where the big red *Spirit of Tasmania* ferry docks, embark on a foodie road trip around the Great Western Tiers and Cradle Country. Explore quirky coastal towns on Bass Strait, then dial up the action around Mole Creek and Cradle Mountain, starting point for the epic Overland Track.

Launceston & Around

GOURMET LIFE IN A GORGE-SPLIT CITY

Australia's third-oldest city has great architecture and a gorgeous gorge. To the south are convict-built estates and historic towns; to the east are snowy peaks; and to the north along Kanamaluka/Tamar River there are too many wineries for one afternoon (make it two, with a visit to Pipers River Wine Region).

The East Coast

BEACHES, WILDLIFE, WHISKY AND WINE

Beach yourself at Wineglass Bay and Larapuna/Bay of Fires; detour to Maria Island National Park for convict history and wildlife; and take a slow-roaming road trip along the East Coast Wine Trail. Fresh seafood is everywhere – the ideal fuel for your mountain-bike adventures around St Helens and Derby.

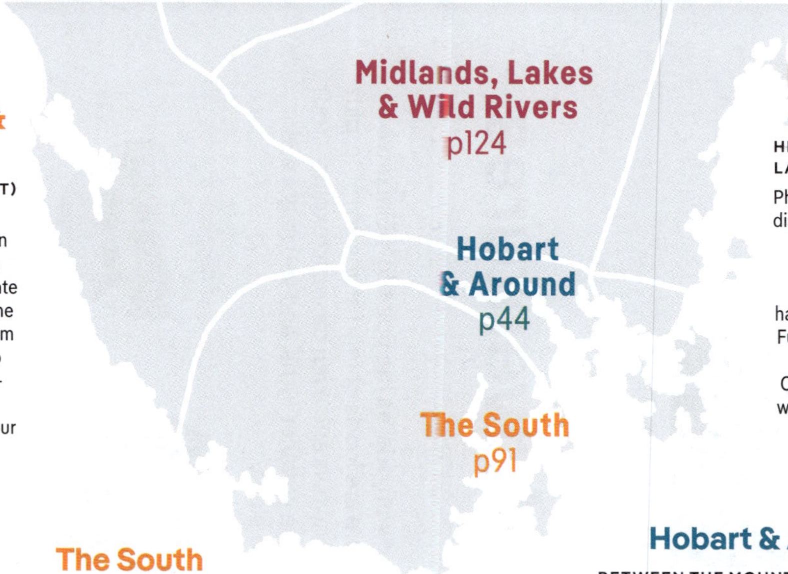

Takayna/Tarkine & the West Coast

RUGGED, REMOTE AND (ALMOST) OFF THE MAP

As wild and remote as anywhere on Earth, this rain-lashed landscape takes you from the sublime temperate rainforests of Takayna/Tarkine to the pounding surf of Marrawah; and from tiny fishing-shack communities to mining towns reborn as mountain-biking must-dos. A cruise from Strahan onto vast Macquarie Harbour is always a good idea.

The South

CONVICTS YESTERDAY, FOOD TODAY, WILDERNESS ALWAYS

From the haunting convict ruins of Port Arthur Historic Site to the Huon Valley's gourmet delights, and from the natural wonders of Bruny Island to the end of the road (literally) at Cockle Creek on the threshold of the magnificent Southwest, the lands below 43°S are a modern explorer's dream.

Midlands, Lakes & Wild Rivers

HISTORIC TOWNS, HIGHLAND LAKES AND UNTAMED RIVERS

Photogenic sandstone towns and distilleries populate the Midlands – rising to vast and desolate Central Highlands, home to a million lakes, wily trout and a hardy crew of diehard fisher-folk. Further west lies World Heritage wilderness, the end of the Overland Track, and Tasmania's wildest river, the fabled Franklin.

Hobart & Around

BETWEEN THE MOUNTAIN AND THE SEA

Insta-worthy Hobart, Tasmania's compact capital, gets rowdy in the pubs and restaurants around historic Salamanca and the Waterfront. The city centre hides funky bars and cheap eats, rolling uphill to the North Hobart 'eat street', with MONA's irreverent arts not far away – all under the watchful gaze of 1271m Kunanyi/Mt Wellington.

TSVIBRAV/GETTY IMAGES

Cape Bruny Lighthouse (p106)

ITINERARIES

Southern Adventures

Allow: 7 days **Distance**: 440km

This is a great route to tackle with kids, as the point-to-point drive times are achievable and there are loads of food stops en route, plus ferries, beaches, picnics, bushwalks and even caves to explore. You're never too far from Hobart if the weather turns, and you might even spot the Aurora Australis one night.

1

BRUNY ISLAND 1 DAY

From Hobart, drive south to yacht-filled Kettering on the D'Entrecasteaux Channel. Ferry across to **Bruny Island** (p102) and forage for lunch – cheese, honey, bread, beer and oysters – and climb to **Truganini Memorial** (p108) for spectacular views. Picnic on the beach at **Adventure Bay** (p106).

Detour: *Couple of free hours? Continue south to* ***Cape Bruny Lighthouse*** *(p106) for incredible ocean views.*

2

CYGNET 1 DAY

Back on the Tasmanian mainland, the coast road tracing the D'Entrecasteaux Channel from Kettering to Cygnet is super-scenic, with excellent views across the water to Bruny Island. Duck into **Peppermint Bay Hotel** (p115) for lunch, and enjoy an afternoon glass at **Mewstone Wines** (p116). Hippie-chic **Cygnet** (p113) has excellent cafes, craft shops and local cider.

3

FRANKLIN 1 DAY

Dart through Huonville to historic **Franklin** (p113) on the Huon River for a Turkish-inspired breakfast at **Cinnamon & Cherry** (p112). Explore the sweet-smelling **Wooden Boat Centre** (p113), then retire to **Frank's Cider House & Cafe** (p113) for some apple juice for grown-ups.

Detour: *The small village of* ***Ranelagh*** *is worth a trip for the excellent* ***Summer Kitchen Bakery*** *(p112).*

FROM LEFT: MICHAEL R EVANS/SHUTTERSTOCK, PAULKEMPVIDEO/SHUTTERSTOCK, TIMOX14, VIA WIKIMEDIA COMMONS

4 DOVER 1 DAY

Keep trucking south along the Huon River downstream to photo-perfect **Dover** (p117) for lovely swimming beaches and languid vibes, perfect for dangling a line off the jetty.

Detour: *From Geeveston en route to Dover, jag west into the alpine* ***Hartz Mountains National Park*** *(p115) on the edge of the Tasmanian Wilderness World Heritage Area (TWWHA) for a day walk.*

5 SOUTHPORT 1 DAY

Sleepy **Southport** (p117) at the end of the Huon Hwy has a cool water tank-turned-coffee shop near the jetty (pictured), and Australia's most southerly pub. The beaches here are seemingly designed for doing not very much at all. Excellent.

Detour: ***Hastings Caves & Thermal Springs*** *(p116) are just off the main road, with subterranean depths and a hot-springs pool to dunk yourself in.*

6 COCKLE CREEK 2 DAYS

You've reached the end of the road: the most southerly point of the Australian continent that you can get to in a car. On the edge of Southwest National Park, **Cockle Creek** (p123) offers low-key waterside camping and bushwalking, before your Hobart return.

Detour: *Take the well-marked trail into Southwest NP to meet the thundering Southern Ocean at* ***South Cape Bay*** *(p122).*

FROM LEFT: XAVIER HOENNER/SHUTTERSTOCK, GAVIN WAKERELL PHOTOGRAPHY/GETTY IMAGES, ASHLEY WHITWORTH/SHUTTERSTOCK

MARK WARDLE/ALAMY

Salamanca Place (p56), Hobart

ITINERARIES

Lakes, Cities & Midlands

Allow: 7 days **Distance**: 690km

This super-circuit from Devonport's ferry terminal takes in both Hobart and Launceston, as well as the Highland Lakes and the gourmet Coal River Valley. Visit Australia's deepest freshwater lake (Leeawuleena/Lake St Clair) and check out the waterfalls at Mt Field National Park and cross two of Australia's oldest bridges.

1

MIENA 1 DAY

Trundle south from Devonport through arty Deloraine and ascend into the rugged, snowy Highland Lakes region. Tiny **Miena** (p133) sits on the shores of vast Yingina/Great Lake, surrounded by fishing shacks (pictured) and jumping trout. Hook up with a guide to show you how to cast a line and snare your dinner.

2

LEEAWULEENA/LAKE ST CLAIR 1 DAY

The southern terminus of the epic Overland Track, **Leeawuleena/Lake St Clair** (p138) is Australia's deepest freshwater lake (215m) and the headwaters of the River Derwent. Take a nature walk or chill out on the lake's silvery shores.

Detour: *Drive west from Derwent Bridge to the lookout atop* ***Donagyhs Hill*** *for a glimpse of Tasmania's fabled Southwest wilderness.*

3

MT FIELD NATIONAL PARK 1 DAY

Delve into the dense temperate rainforest cloaking the lower reaches of **Mt Field National Park** (p85) on the trail of a series of gorgeous waterfalls.

Detour: *Follow the winding unsealed road up to* ***Lake Dobson*** *(p86) on the exposed alpine plateau for more challenging hikes, and to witness the 'turning of the fagus' deciduous autumn spectacle.*

FROM LEFT: SANDRA JOHNSTONE/SHUTTERSTOCK, IAN WOOLCOCK/SHUTTERSTOCK, MRFOREVER/SHUTTERSTOCK

4

HOBART 2 DAYS

Wheel into Hobart for **MONA** (p76), **Salamanca Market** (p57) and the bars and restaurants around the historic waterfront. Explore **Battery Point** (p64; pictured) on two feet, then hit the North Hobart pubs and eateries.

Detour: *Drive to the summit of 1271m* ***Kunanyi/Mt Wellington*** *(p70) for an incredible view of the city and the River Derwent (or perhaps an otherworldly whiteout inside a cloud).*

5

ROSS 1 DAY

Walk around the compact Georgian village of **Ross** (p129) after a day of gourmet delights in the Coal River Valley, Richmond and the Midlands distilleries. **Richmond Bridge** (p82) is Australia's oldest, but **Ross Bridge** (p129; third-oldest; pictured) has more carvings (186). Reflect on Tasmania's historical deprivations at the **Ross Female Factory Historic Site** (p130) and **Old Ross Burial Ground** (p131).

6

LAUNCESTON 1 DAY

Lonnie (p190) is a UNESCO City of Gastronomy, awash with craft-beer and dazzling dining, plus well-preserved architecture and the world's largest collection of **Salvador Dalí** (p198) drawings! The splendour of **Cataract Gorge** (p194; pictured) awaits on the edge of town, as do the Kanamaluka/ River Tamar wineries.

Detour: *Take an afternoon to weave around the cellar doors of the* ***Tamar Valley Wine Region*** *(p204) north of Launceston.*

FROM LEFT: CRBELLETTE/SHUTTERSTOCK, JANELLE LUGGE/SHUTTERSTOCK, DAVID STEELE/SHUTTERSTOCK

ITINERARIES

East Coast Explorer

Allow: 7 days **Distance**: 680km

This route links Hobart and Launceston airports via the East Coast, where it's all sunshine and seaside towns, breezy beaches, wonderful wineries, prolific wildlife and show-stopping coastal scenes. Distances are short(ish), so there's plenty of time to explore, get sidetracked, and discover a seldom-seen winery or an out-of-the-way cabin.

Cape Barren geese, Maria Island National Park (p148)

1 TURRAKANA/TASMAN PENINSULA 1 DAY

Explore the wonders of **Turrakana/Tasman Peninsula** (p94), home to Australia's tallest sea cliffs and the rugged Three Capes Track, plus the sombre ruins of World Heritage–listed **Port Arthur Historic Site** (p98). Also world-class are the local sea-kayaking and scuba-diving opportunities.

Detour: *Take a stroll along lonely, windswept* ***Seven Mile Beach*** *(p80), only five minutes from Hobart Airport.*

2 MARIA ISLAND NATIONAL PARK 1 DAY

Car-free **Maria Island** (p148) is an ace place to camp and meet some Tasmanian wildlife, including wombats, wallabies and Cape Barren geese. Discover curious coastal features like the **Painted Cliffs** (p150) and the World Heritage–listed convict relics around Darlington – or if you really want get exploring, bring a mountain bike over on the ferry.

3 BICHENO 2 DAYS

Bicheno (p168) makes an excellent base to spend a few days exploring nearby **Freycinet National Park** (p158; of iconic **Wineglass Bay** fame), as well as its own enticements, including wine, oysters, whisky and lobster rolls. Local wildlife-viewing opps include Tasmanian devils and penguins (not together!), and there are plenty of coastal walking trails and some beaut beaches. Holiday perfection.

FROM LEFT: MARK ODWYER/SHUTTERSTOCK, FILEDIMAGE/SHUTTERSTOCK

4 ST HELENS 1 DAY

Spend the day on MTB trails in the forests near fishing-town **St Helens** (p167). Or stock up with picnic supplies and explore gorgeous **Binalong Bay** (p174) at the southern end of Larapuna/Bay of Fires.

Detour: *Up in the hills behind St Helens, Pyengana's interesting diversions include cheese at the* ***Pyengana Dairy*** *(p169) and the vertiginous* ***St Columba Falls*** *(p170).*

5 DERBY 1 DAY

Derby (p175) is a town devoted almost entirely to mountain biking – ground zero for serious shredders. But even if cranks and chains aren't your thing, it still deserves a night, especially after a day exploring Larapuna/Bay of Fires and the old tin-mining towns of the northeast. Don't miss the floating sauna and a few local craft beers.

6 EVANDALE 1 DAY

Historic **Evandale** (p201) is only a five-minute drive from Launceston Airport, but it's centuries away in mood and architectural vibes – the perfect wind-down town after a hard session on the MTB gears.

Detour: *Alternatively, check out the fab wineries around the* ***Pipers River wine region*** *(p204) for some perfect pinot, a cheeseboard and/or bottle of bubbly.*

SHUANG LI/SHUTTERSTOCK

The Nut and Stanley (p254)

ITINERARIES

West Coast Wilds

Allow: 8 days **Distance**: 1110km

Take the road less travelled between Launceston and Hobart airports, on a journey to the 'Edge of the World' (or so the sign says at Gardiners Point on the wild-and-woolly west coast). You'll see Cradle Mountain, a Tasmanian essential; plus historic Stanley with its knobbly Nut, and traverse the largest expanse of temperate rainforest in the country.

1 MOLE CREEK 1 DAY

Tracking west from Launceston Airport, amble along **Deloraine Riverbank Walk** (p224) then head for **Mole Creek Karst National Park** (p227) where the kids will enjoy subterranean delights, plus the quolls, devils and wombats at nearby **Trowunna Wildlife Sanctuary** (p227; pictured).

Detour: *If dripping caves fill you with ungodly dread, consider overnighting in the 'Town of Murals' –* ***Sheffield*** *(p225) – instead.*

2 CRADLE MOUNTAIN 2 DAYS

World Heritage–listed wilderness awaits at the northern end of the eternally popular **Cradle Mountain-Lake St Clair National Park** (p242). Take your time to explore the tarns, peaks and wildlife, encircled by eye-popping alpine scenery. The famed Overland Track heads south from here to the finish line at Leeawuleena/Lake St Clair (pack your boots).

3 STANLEY 2 DAYS

Picture-postcard **Stanley** (p254; pictured), with its rows of heritage houses and chunky geologic **Nut** (p254), makes an ace base for further northwest explorations, including Table Cape, Boat Harbour Beach and **Rocky Cape National Park** (p235) along the Bass Strait coast.

Detour: *Jag west to check out* ***Marrawah*** *(p262), a far-flung farming town with huge surf rolling in from the open ocean.*

FROM LEFT: -JKB-, VIA WIKIMEDIA COMMONS, CATHERINE SUTHERLAND/LONELY PLANET, SHUANG LI/SHUTTERSTOCK

4

CORINNA 1 DAY

Superbly remote, little **Corinna** (p264) on the edge of the Takayna/Tarkine wilderness is the place to turn off and unplug (no reception – bring a book). Take a cruise on the **Pieman River** (p265; pictured) to one of Tasmania's wildest beaches, or tackle one of the rainforest walks radiating out from the village. Overnight in a cabin behind the pub.

5

STRAHAN 1 DAY

It's tempting to just sit, eat and drink in **Strahan** (p267), but a cruise across Macquarie Harbour, up the Gordon River and out to Sarah Island is must-see Tasmania. That steam whistle you can hear belongs to the **West Coast Wilderness Railway** (p271; pictured).

***Detour:** From Zeehan, drive to the trailhead for the 104m **Montezuma Falls** (p276), one of Tasmania's highest.*

6

MAYDENA 1 DAY

Boot it southwest past **Leeawuleena/Lake St Clair** (p138) (Australia's deepest lake) to the timber town of Maydena, now home to **Maydena Bike Park** (p118; pictured), one of Tasmania's top MTB parks, with gravity runs aplenty. Continue down the Derwent Valley to New Norfolk (make time for a luxe late lunch at the **Agrarian Kitchen**; p84) before rolling into Hobart Airport.

FROM LEFT: XAVIER HOENNER PHOTOGRAPHY/GETTY IMAGES, ANGRYBIRDPRODUCTIONS/SHUTTERSTOCK, CHRIS PUTNAM/SHUTTERSTOCK

WHEN TO GO

There's no denying it: Tasmania gets cold. Embrace winter with whisky, warm pubs and open fires, or come back for summer's fab festivals and beachy vibes.

Raked by the Roaring 40s winds, and with Antarctica the next stop south, Tasmania's climate isn't like anywhere else in Australia. Snow can happen any time of year around the Highland Lakes, and occasionally descends to sea level in Hobart.

December to January is peak season down south, with Australians on holidays: festivals, beach days and mega-deck cruise ships. Coastal and lakeside camp sites fill up quickly, as do walking trails. February to March is less hectic, with lovely stable weather. Southern days linger long into the evening, and the sea is still warm(ish).

April to May (autumn) and September to November (spring) deliver lower prices and less-crowded trails, campsites, hotels and restaurant tables. Autumn is also harvest season, bringing fresh produce and the turning of the fagus (deciduous beech). Expect snow in the Highlands and Southwest over winter – also prime time for local oysters and Tasmania's offbeat winter festivals, which warm everyone's hearts.

I LIVE HERE

WINTER DARK

Meg Worby is a transplanted South Australian English teacher who's become a winter convert. *@megworby*

In the Tasmanian winter I rug up in a favourite jacket and keep an excited eye on snow levels on Kunanyi/Mt Wellington. In the late-afternoon dusk, Dark Mofo's Winter Feast is packed but accessible, the waterfront food hall illuminated by red neon crosses and long, candlelit tables. Winter swim? I set a personal record running *out* of the 10°C River Derwent – but never felt better afterwards.

Dark Mofo (p61), Hobart

FROM LEFT: XAVIER HOENNER/SHUTTERSTOCK, STEVE WATERS/LONELY PLANET

RAIN SHADOW

Surprisingly, given its chilly rep, Hobart is Australia's second-driest capital (after Adelaide) – in part due to massive 1271m Kunanyi/Mt Wellington catching the clouds and casting a rain shadow across the city. Huonville, just 30km south, receives 11.7 more centimetres of rain each year.

Weather Through the Year (Hobart)

JANUARY	FEBRUARY	MARCH	APRIL	MAY	JUNE
Avg. daytime max: **23°C**	Avg. daytime max: **22°C**	Avg. daytime max: **21°C**	Avg. daytime max: **18°C**	Avg. daytime max: **15°C**	Avg. daytime max: **13°C**
Days of rainfall: **5.3**	Days of rainfall: **5**	Days of rainfall: **6.2**	Days of rainfall: **6.6**	Days of rainfall: **7.1**	Days of rainfall: **6.6**

COLD CLIMES

Tasmania's coldest recorded temperature was -14.2°C in 2020 at Liawenee in the lofty Central Highlands. Kunanyi/Mt Wellington behind Hobart plunged to -9.1°C in 1993, yet the wind chill often makes it feel much colder up here, with gusts regularly topping 100km/h. Brrr...

Main Events

Sydney to Hobart Yacht Race (p61) Hobart's waterfront is party central as wind-weary boat crews cross the finish line of one of the world's oldest and toughest open-ocean yacht races. **December/January**

Taste of Summer (p63) Hobart cranks up the summertime vibes with this week-long celebration of Tassie's gastronomic prowess over the New Year. Lots of live music and a New Year's Eve party to boot. **December/January**

Festivale (p196) Launceston rocks-out to three days of quality booze, fab food and big-name music acts in City Park – with decidedly family-friendly vibes. **February**

Dark Mofo (p61) Winter be damned! Get thee out and socialising under Hobart's blood-red lamps. It's MONA's potent Gothic cocktail of the sublime, the unhinged and the downright ludicrous. **June**

Regional Raves

Cygnet Folk Festival (p113) Embrace your inner hippie at this earthy celebration of folk music, poetry, dance, food and local cider over three summer days in the Huon Valley. **January**

Devonport Jazz Festival (p220) Brightening up winter on the northwest, this four-day festival fills venues and stages around town with all things bee-bop, trad, Dixieland, big-band and free-form jazz. **July**

The Unconformity (p273) Edgy biennial arts festival with a touch of the MONAs, messing with your mind against the lunar backdrop of far-flung Queenstown. Take the trip. **October in odd-numbered years**

Bicheno Food & Wine Festival (p154) Sunshine in the sky and by the bottle in beachy Bicheno, over one fun springtime day. Lots of great seafood and live tunes into the night. **November**

I LIVE HERE

SUMMER BEACHES

Holly Ward is taking a gap year after finishing school in Hobart. *@h.ollyward*

Hidden in Hobart's suburbs are some unique beaches, tucked away for the locals. I might have a summer dip and some cheeky fish-and-chips at Bellerive Beach, or wander along beautiful Kingston Beach or Hinsby Beach in Taroona, where city life dissolves into wild and quiet nature. Each beach offers the chance to swim, stroll, catch up with friends, or just find a quiet moment in Hobart's busy summer schedule.

Kingston Beach (p87)

SHIVERY SEAS

Around the island, average sea temperatures peak in February. In Hobart, this means a coolish 17°C – fresh enough to scare off most mainlanders. A dunk in the brine isn't too bad from December to March, but outside these months it's heading south of 15°C.

JULY	AUGUST	SEPTEMBER	OCTOBER	NOVEMBER	DECEMBER
Avg. daytime max: **13°C**	Avg. daytime max: **14°C**	Avg. daytime max: **16°C**	Avg. daytime max: **17°C**	Avg. daytime max: **19°C**	Avg. daytime max: **21°C**
Days of rainfall: **7.8**	Days of rainfall: **8.8**	Days of rainfall: **8**	Days of rainfall: **8.4**	Days of rainfall: **7.6**	Days of rainfall: **7.3**

FROM LEFT: PIXDELUXE/GETTY IMAGES, EVERETT COLLECTION INC/ALAMY

GET PREPARED FOR TASMANIA

Useful things to load in your bag, your ears and your brain.

Clothes

Layers Be prepared for wintry gusts or warm sun any time of year. Layer up or down as required.

Puffer jacket Standard issue: can be worn to any occasion, including work. Aka the 'Tassie tuxedo'.

Fleece A versatile mid-layer (often a vest) that will keep you warm even when you're wet.

Windjacket When the sea breeze picks up, an insulated soft-shell jacket is your new best friend.

Sunglasses Coming in low and sharp across the water, the southern sun makes a good pair of polarising lenses essential.

Walking shoes Comfortable hiking shoes are great for city streets and day walks. Save your heavy boots for gnarlier ground.

Beanie A woolly hat is the most useful item of clothing you can pack...or buy a local knit to keep as a memento.

Manners

Invited to dinner? If you're going to someone's house for a meal or BBQ, bring a bottle of wine, some cheese or a dessert.

Your shout When someone buys you a drink at the pub, they've 'shouted' you. Never leave before returning the 'shout' (buying the next round).

Greetings Total strangers will often say 'good morning' in Tasmania. Don't be alarmed: suspend cynicism and return the greeting.

READ

Death of a River Guide (Richard Flanagan; 1994) The Man Booker prize winner's surreal first novel, set on the Franklin River.

Thylacine (David Owen; 2003) Poignant recounting of the tragic demise of the Tasmanian tiger.

Butterfly Man (Heather Rose; 2005) What if runaway alleged murderer British Lord Lucan was alive and well and living in Hobart?

For the Term of His Natural Life (Marcus Clarke; 1874) Classic account of convict life at Port Arthur. Take or leave the 1983 TV adaptation...

Words

'A bit how ya going' Average, dodgy or sub-par.
'Arvo' Afternoon, as in 'this arvo'.
'Barbie' Not a blonde plastic doll but a BBQ.
'Beer o'clock' Stop working, it's time for a beer.
'Bogan' Inherently uncouth person.
'Fagus' Deciduous beech *(Nothofagus gunnii)*. The 'turning of the fagus' is a big deal in autumn, when fagus leaves put on a colourful show.
'Flannelette Curtain' Imaginary socioeconomic line heralding the start of Hobart's northern suburbs.
'Footy' Australian Rules football (AFL nationally; local leagues in Tasmania).
'Garbo' Garbage bin or the person who empties it.
'G'day' Universal greeting: 'G'day mate'.
'Gone for a paddle' Could be kayaking, sea kayaking or rafting.
'Hydro' The Hydro Electric Commission, as in 'hydro bill' meaning electricity bill.
'Lonnie' Launceston.
'Lutruwita' Tasmania
'Mate' Universal term to address someone you know, don't know, or can't remember their name. 'Old mate' is a generic bloke (mildly patronising).
'NoHo' North Hobart.
'Palawa' Tasmanian Aboriginal person.
'Shout' Buy a round of drinks: 'It's your shout, mate'.
'SoHo' South Hobart.
'Tassie tuxedo' Down-filled puffer jacket, essential in winter.
'Thongs' These go on your feet, nowhere else.

WATCH

Deadloch (Kate McCartney/Kate McLennan; 2023–) Dark, quirky comedy in pursuit of a small-town serial killer. Filmed in Cygnet and Kingston Beach.

The Hunter (Daniel Nettheim; 2011) Willem Defoe goes hunting for the last Tasmanian tiger.

Rosehaven (Luke McGregor/ Celia Pacquola; 2016–21; pictured) Real-estate comedy series set in a fictional Tasmanian town (filmed in Geeveston, New Norfolk and Oatlands).

The Giants (Laurence Billiet/ Rachael Antony; 2022) A celebration of Tasmania's forests and their most famous protector, Dr Bob Brown.

LISTEN

Lutruwita/Tasmania (Denni Proctor; 2022) Sung in palawa kani, the reconstructed Tasmanian Aboriginal language. Mesmerising, stripped-back vocals.

Music Tasmania (musictasmania.org/ listen; 2025) Eclectic repository of Tasmanian aural offerings, from podcasts to folk, hip-hop, country and rock.

A Night at the Mirage (208L Containers; 2022) Bizarre concept album based on comedian Andrew Denton's public hunt for '90s villain Christopher Skase.

Sometimes I Sit and Think, and Sometimes I Just Sit (Courtney Barnett; 2015) Debut art-school rock from ex-Hobart local Barnett, with disarmingly comic lyrics.

NESS VANDERBURGH/LONELY PLANET

Local dishes at Timbre Kitchen (p210), Tamar Valley

THE FOOD SCENE

With bountiful fresh island produce, spectacular seafood and sublime cool-climate wines, Tasmania is the promised land for foodies.

Tasmania's farmers markets serve up a dizzying array of edible delights from small growers and producers: everything from dark, nutty truffles to gins flavoured with beachcombed botanicals, and wallaby salami to fresh unshucked oysters and art-worthy boxes of bizarrely shaped mushrooms. Maybe it's the clean air, fertile soil and regular rains that make Tasmania such fertile terrain – or the necessary productivity that comes with island life. Maybe both. Either way, the end result is exceptionally fine food and drink sought by chefs across Australia and overseas.

Hobart and Launceston restaurants are keen to showcase all this delectable produce. Beyond the two main cities, a taste for fine food has spread along island tourist routes, via pubs and wineries, food trucks and night markets. Seafood features prominently. Vegetarian? Relax. You're just as likely to find roast cauliflower and tahini on the menu as you are pan-fried scallops.

Eating out (even takeaway) is expensive compared to the mainland: self-catering from markets and roadside stalls will ease the pain.

Wine, Cider & Spirits

Tasmanian vintners bottle up excellent cool-climate wines: pinot noir, chardonnay, riesling and pinot gris/grigio are the mainstays, though you'll also find world-class sparkling wine (especially around Pipers River – don't dare call it 'champagne') and the odd merlot. The main wine regions

Best Tasmanian Dishes

APPLES
It ain't known as the Apple Isle for nothing!

CURRIED SCALLOP PIES
Scallops baked in a creamy curry sauce inside a pie. Yes!

MEAT
Cape Grim beef, Scottsdale pork or saltgrass lamb?

are the Tamar Valley and Pipers River in the north, along the east coast between St Helens and Swansea (especially around Bicheno), and the Coal River, Derwent and Huon Valleys in the south around Hobart.

Most cider production is concentrated in the south around the apple- and pear-growing Huon Valley, with boozy overflow into the nearby Derwent and Coal River Valleys. In the north there are several producers in the Devonport–Deloraine–Tamar triangle.

Whisky and gin are also big business here, with classy distillery tasting rooms across the state. Farmers markets usually stock the best local bottles.

Craft Beer

At last count the island was home to around 30 craft breweries. There's been a move away from the typical 'brew pub' into industrial conversions and sheds with food trucks, wood-fired pizzas or outdoor fire pits. Many breweries only open a few days per week; some smaller breweries don't even have a cellar door (though their fluid fare can often be found in nearby pubs).

Vegetarians & Vegans

Dedicated veg-only restaurants are rare in Tasmania, with a handful around Hobart's city centre catering to office workers. But these days most savvy cafes, restaurants and pubs have a good selection of veg options and cheerily accommodate other dietary requirements. Fine-dining 'feed me' menus will always have a veg option. At the other end of the fiscal scale, cheap South and Southeast Asian cafes catering for veg-centric local students are solid choices.

Craft beer

Taste of Summer (p63)

FOOD & DRINK FESTIVALS

Taste of Summer (p63; *tasteofsummer.com.au; December/January*) The island's premier foodfest rocks Hobart's waterfront with a zillion tasting stalls.

Festivale (p196; *festivale.com.au; February*) Launceston's chance to shine with sensational food and wine, cooking classes and live tunes over three family-friendly days.

Stanley & Tarkine Forage Festival (p254; *stanleyandtarkineforagefestival.com.au; May*) Sample the best of the northwest seafood, beef, cheese and gin.

Great Eastern Wine Week (p154; *eastcoastwinetrail.com.au/event; October*) Four days of celebrations at over 40 east-coast wineries and venues.

Winter Feast (p61; *darkmofo.net.au; June*) Dark Mofo's midwinter food fest drags Hobartians out of their burrows for nights of red-tinged debauchery and excess.

CHEESE	FISH AND CHIPS	OYSTERS	RASPBERRIES	TRUFFLES
Rich and flavoursome, from King Island to Bruny Island.	Ubiquitous; get some close to the docks!	The east coast drips with briny goodness. Best in winter.	Sharply tangy and sweet, hanging heavy on the summer canes.	*Oui! Les truffes ici sont magnifiques!*

Local Specialities

From the Sea

Scallops Pan-seared, char-grilled or in the iconic curried scallop pie; scallops are in season from Easter to July.

Mussels Australian blue mussels are grown in Spring Bay in cold, clear waters several kilometres offshore.

Abalone Both black- and green-lipped varieties are readily available in Tasmania.

Crayfish Technically it's southern rock lobster (but don't get too uptight about it). They're in season from November to April. Bass Strait lobster is highly prized.

Oysters Flavoursome Pacific oysters are grown along the east coast from St Helens to Bruny Island, while local angasi oysters, sometimes marketed as 'Tassie gold', are harder to find.

Blue-eye trevalla Firm, tasty white fish caught in deep ocean waters, readily found in five-star restaurants and local fish-and-chippers.

Scallops

Trout Highland lakes and rivers are full of both brown and rainbow trout, just waiting to be caught and pan-fried with butter.

From the Land

Wallaby A lean and flavourful meat, sweeter and less gamey than kangaroo. Can appear as steaks, in burritos and salamis, and as a less-fatty lamb substitute.

Truffles East-coast walnut farms are ground zero for funky truffles, aromatic fungi that grow underground, sniffed out by truffle hounds and shaved sparingly into your dinner.

MEALS OF A LIFETIME

Aløft (p61) Exquisite chef's menu with crisp, clear flavours, tastefully paired drinks and the best view on the Hobart waterfront.

Agrarian Kitchen (p84) With a holistic approach to food, the lengthy set-menu lunches showcase the best of its New Norfolk garden and local producers.

Stillwater (p191) Launceston's historic flour mill raises the bar (and keeps it there) for seasonal fine dining in the north.

Callington Mill Distillery (p128) Innovative food in Oatlands featuring fresh-caught seafood, local meats and vegetables. Not to mention the whisky...

Get Shucked Oysters (p105) A dozen freshly shucked oysters on the deck, with a glass of island sparkling and a Bruny Island sunset. Sublime.

THE YEAR IN FOOD

SPRING

Asparagus (pictured) hits the markets and salads are everywhere. Trout season opens and there are plenty of Pacific oysters to be had. Apples and pears are young, fresh and crisp.

SUMMER

Berries, cherries and stone fruit populate roadside stalls, and fresh southern rock lobster (aka crayfish) is on the menu. BBQ season is here: think marinated lamb backstrap, local sausages, craft beer and riesling.

AUTUMN

It's harvest time as the vine rows burn deep red and golden and drop their leaves. New-season apples (pictured) and pears are back, and pumpkins show off their colours. Peak season for blue-eye.

WINTER

Winter roasts and hearty root vegetables, beets and Brussels sprouts, sluiced down with island stout, whisky and red wine. Dark Mofo's Winter Feast is a must-do, and oysters are at their best.

TOP: EYEOFPAUL/SHUTTERSTOCK; FROM LEFT: OLENA RUDO/SHUTTERSTOCK, DRAGOS ASAFTEI/SHUTTERSTOCK, ALECTRUSLER2015/SHUTTERSTOCK, WILLOWTREEHOUSE/SHUTTERSTOCK

STEVE LOVEGROVE/SHUTTERSTOCK

Abalone

HOW TO... Eat Tasmanian Seafood

'I'm on a seafood diet. I see food, then I eat it.' Jokes aside, seafood is a menu mainstay in Tasmanian restaurants – especially oysters, scallops, abalone and salmon. The trick with the local shellfish is getting your seasonal timing right, and knowing how to crack into their exo-defences.

How to Eat Oysters

Buy Tasmanian oysters either 'shucked' (cracked open and ready to eat, with the flesh separated from the shell), or 'unshucked' (straight off the racks, unopened). Shucked oysters usually arrive on a tray by the half-dozen or dozen, with a couple of wedges of lemon. You'll pay around $20 a dozen at an oyster farm. Squeeze on the lemon and slurp them down. Unshucked oysters are a cheaper takeaway option: take them home and shuck them yourself with an oyster knife, attempting not to impale yourself in the process. Going high-end? In a restaurant you'll pay three or four times as much per dozen, with garnishes that are complex (gin, caviar and grilled seaweed butter, anyone?) but undeniably tasty. Oysters are at their best in winter, when they're lean and firm; in the summer spawning season they can sometimes be a bit fatty and creamy (but still delicious).

How to Eat Abalone

Black-lip and green-lip abalone are prized Tasmanian shellfish, levered off rocks by scuba divers, risking sharks and freezing waters and paying an absolute fortune for a licence to do so. The abalone shell is about the size of your hand, stuck to the rock by the muscular abalone itself. The flesh can be tough and chewy if not tenderised or if cooked too much: try some in a restaurant with a chef who knows what they're doing. Pan-fried with butter and a few herbs is the way to go: keep it simple, so the natural flavour prevails (somewhere between scallops and squid in texture and taste). Cost may be a barrier (there's a reason abalone licences are so expensive: the Asian market is mega-lucrative, reflected in local prices). But hey, you're on holiday, right? Enjoy yourself.

How to Eat Scallops

Scallops are another bottom-dwelling mollusc, generally sold and served minus their shells. Some diners find the orange roe part of the scallop too rich, and focus solely on the white muscle flesh. As per abalone, scallop cooking time is critical: just long enough to seal the surface will suffice. If that's all too difficult, you can order a creamy, spicy curried scallop pie for about $10 in takeaway shops pretty much anywhere in the state. Scallop season runs from Easter to July; you'll pay about $50 per kilogram in a supermarket.

TASMANIAN SALMON: YES OR NO?

Farming Atlantic salmon on an industrial scale isn't new: Norway, Canada, Chile and Scotland have been doing it for decades. But the environmental impact of salmon farming in Tasmania's estuaries has become a real hot-button issue. Fish welfare and harm to marine ecosystems are the key issues – leading some restaurants to ban local salmon, suggesting that it's akin to fast food. Others say the industry is good for the economy. No one is short of an opinion, including Booker Prize–winning Tasmanian author Richard Flanagan, whose book *Toxic* is a damning exposé of the industry – one side of this very divisive local story.

Tasmanian devil

TRIP PLANNER

TASMANIAN WILDLIFE

Like most things in Tasmania, the mammals here are similar to mainland versions but a bit different: they're smaller, darker and in some cases a distinct sub-species. Koalas are absent altogether, though both monotremes (echidnas and platypuses) call the island home. Tasmania also has 12 endemic bird species not found anywhere else on Earth.

Meet Some Mammals

MACROPODS

All Tasmanian marsupials carry their young in a pouch; the most common are the macropods (kangaroos, wallabies and pademelons). The **Forester kangaroo** is the largest, though they're mostly restricted to the east coast. You're more likely to see the smaller and darker **Bennett's wallaby**, while the **Tasmanian pademelon** has extended its terrain to pretty much everywhere, including Hobart's suburbs. The smallest Tasmanian macropods are the **Eastern bettong** and **long-nosed potoroo**, both found nosing around on Maria Island.

QUOLLS & DEVILS

You'll probably hear **Tasmanian devils** before you see them: their screech is an unearthly howl in the dark. Ferocious scavengers, they sometime approach huts along the Overland Track, but they're fundamentally shy of humans. Sadly, Devil Facial Tumour Disease (DFTD) has decimated devils in the wild, but breeding programmes on offshore islands are seeking to create reserves of tumour-free devils.

Tasmania has two species of **quoll**: the **spotted-tail** and the **eastern** (also covered in spots, but not on its tail!). You might spy one sniffing around camp sites along the South Coast or South West Cape tracks.

MARINE MAMMALS

Bass Strait once had four species of seal, of which three were hunted to local extinction. Now only the **Australian fur seal** breeds in the Strait. The **long-nosed** (previously New Zealand) **fur seal** breeds in low numbers off the south coast and is considered threatened in Tasmania.

Southern right and **humpback whales** cruise along the east coast during their annual migration north, then back south (May to October). Pods of **common** and **bottlenose dolphins** hang around the bays and estuaries and ride the stern wave of the *Spirit of Tasmania* ferry as it crosses to/from the mainland.

OTHER MARSUPIALS

Instantly recognisable by their compact stocky shape (and compact stocky droppings), the common **wombat** is found all over the island. There are several species of **possums**, from tiny **sugar gliders** and **pygmy possums** up to the large **brushtails**. **Bandicoots**, **antechinus** and **marsupial mice** also live here, though you'll be hard-pressed to see any outside of a zoo.

MONOTREMES

Shy, egg-laying **platypuses** inhabit rivers and creeks but are notoriously difficult to see. Amazingly, you've got a good chance of spying one in the Hobart Rivulet. The best viewing times are dawn and dusk: perch on a riverbank and you might be lucky. **Echidnas** (erroneously labelled 'spiny anteaters'), on the other hand, are quite common and, depending on the season, might just bumble across a track right in front of you. When disturbed, they curl into a ball of spikes...but if you wait them out, they're likely to resume their business of digging up tasty ants.

Echidna

ENDEMIC BIRDS

Tasmania is home to 12 bird species that you won't find anywhere else.

Tasmanian native hen The flightless 'turbo chook' is found by grassy watercourses across the island.

Forty-spotted pardalote Small, rare and beautiful bird restricted mostly to Maria and Bruny Islands.

Yellow wattlebird The world's largest honeyeater is found in urban gardens, coastal heaths and eucalypt forests.

Yellow-throated honeyeater Territorial honeyeater with a dislike for other birds.

Black-headed honeyeater This distinct black-headed scrub bird has an insatiable craving for insects.

Strong-billed honeyeater Similar to black-headed but separate in range, preferring tall mountain-ash forests.

Dusky robin Small brown, widespread bird known for a distinctive 'melancholy' call.

Tasmanian thornbill Small bird similar to the brown thornbill but with white underwings.

Scrubtit Tiny hard-to-see bird preferring dense, wet forests. Has a distinctive cream throat.

Tasmanian scrubwren Small brown bird of the forest understorey.

Black currawong Similar to mainland currawongs, this large black bird is found across the island.

Green rosella The largest rosella has a yellow belly, blue throat and a red spot above its beak. Widespread.

The following 'breeding endemics' return to the island to reproduce:

Orange-bellied parrot A rare tiny parrot that wings into Melaleuca to breed every summer.

Swift parrot Endangered due to habitat loss, this small parrot breeds in the southeast forests.

FROM LEFT: ANDREW BAIN/GETTY IMAGES, SLOW WALKER/SHUTTERSTOCK

Rafting, Franklin River (p137)

THE OUTDOORS

Tasmania is a wild place: temperate rainforests, snow-capped peaks, lonely beaches and soaring sea cliffs. Get amongst it!

Tasmania attracts hikers from across the country and overseas to experience unique wilderness along multiday trails. The island has also carved out a niche as a world-class mountain-biking hub. Surfers flock to the wild west-coast swells (and warmer waves out east), while the lakes of the Central Highlands are the promised land for fly-fishers. Divers, kayakers and snorkellers explore Turrakana/Tasman Peninsula and south- and east-coast beaches – but the biggest adrenalin buzz of all is rafting the majestic Franklin River, still wild, still running free.

Bushwalking

Tasmania delivers the best bushwalking in Australia, from long-haul epics to spectacular day walks – especially during summer when it's too hot to hike on the mainland. There are walks for all levels, regardless of age, fitness and experience: the Parks & Wildlife Service's **60 Great Short Walks** *(parks.tas.gov.au/things-to-do/60-great-short-walks)* is the perfect place to start.

Tracks on the east coast and Turrakana/Tasman Peninsula are generally easier, with lower elevations, better access and predictable weather. But for show-stopping scenery, head for the mountains and tarns of the Tasmanian Wilderness World Heritage Area (TWWHA), including Cradle Mountain-Lake St Clair, Walls of Jerusalem, Franklin-Gordon Wild Rivers, Hartz Mountains, Mt Field and Southwest national parks. Here you can walk for a week and not see a road, and be blissfully phone-free.

Mountain Biking

Tasmanian mountain biking took off in the northeast tin-mining town of Derby in 2015, and has never looked back. The town's Blue Derby trails (around the craggy Blue

Other Outdoor Adventures

SURFING
Carve up some gnarly cold-water surf at the west-coast breaks around **Marrawah** (p262).

KAYAKING
Paddle the coastline of **Freycinet National Park** (p161) and check out the Hazards and Honeymoon Bay from the water.

SKIING
Strap on the cross-country skis for a trip out the back of **Mt Mawson** (p86) or maybe a downhill run or two at **Ben Lomond** (p202).

FAMILY ADVENTURES

Dangle from the chairlift at **Cataract Gorge** (p194) in Launceston and spy some peacocks.

Meet some devils, quolls and wombats and learn how they're rehabilitated at **Bonorong Wildlife Sanctuary** (p84).

Ride a bike around car-free **Maria Island National Park** (p148), with its convict ruins, easygoing trails and curious wildlife.

Climb aboard for a **West Coast Wilderness Railway** (p271) ride through remote rainforest and gorges.

Go underground at **Mole Creek Karst National Park** (p227) in the northwest, or **Hastings Caves & Thermal Springs** (p116) in the south.

Watch Little Penguins waddle back to their nests in the dunes at sunset at **The Neck** (p103) on Bruny Island.

Drive to the top of **Kunanyi/Mt Wellington** (p70) in Hobart for awesome views, rock-hopping and winter snowballs.

Tier plateau) are revered worldwide, with long forest runs for all styles and skill levels. Aprés-shred activities include plenty of beers and cafes and a unique floating sauna.

Over on the east coast, St Helens has its own forest scene and lays claim to the legendary 42km Bay of Fires ride from the mountains to the sea.

Hobart's Kunanyi/Mt Wellington is a family-friendly option, with straightforward access and a good selection of easy and intermediate runs, like the excellent North–South Track.

In the Southwest, Maydena could be rivalling Derby for sheer forest-shredding fun-factor, except the town's amenities haven't quite caught up with the bike park. Yet.

Out west, Queenstown's denuded Mt Owen offers a totally different MTB experience: you can actually see where you're going on the rocky, treeless slopes. The Silver City trails at nearby Zeehan are a new addition, offering more of the same.

There are also MTB trails in the north around Penguin, Latrobe, George Town and Hollybank near Launceston. Where do you want to start?

ACTION AREAS
See p40

Surfing near Hobart (p44)

Rafting

If you're really craving some adventure and chasing the essence of Tasmania, a rafting trip down the fabled Franklin River is for you. The river was made famous by a long and eventually successful environmental campaign to prevent it being dammed in the early 1980s. This is a true wilderness experience: once you paddle out into the flow, you're committed to at least a week of being wet, weary and downright exhilarated, until you finally emerge into the lower Gordon River.

Queenstown's King River offers a different rafting experience, with day trips through a deep gorge and the promise of a hot shower and a beer at the end.

FLY-FISHING
The **Highland Lakes** (p133) are brimming with brown and rainbow trout, just begging to leap into your frying pan.

SCUBA DIVING
Explore a subterranean cathedral beneath the dolerite cliffs of **Turrakana/Tasman Peninsula** (p102).

CYCLE TOURING
Tackle the 480km **Tasmanian Trail** (p135) from Devonport to Dover, with camping spots and/or accommodation every 30km or so.

SNORKELLING
Discover the strange underwater locals along the reefs of the **Tinderbox Marine Reserve** (p87) south of Hobart.

Walking/Hiking
1 Overland Track (p244)
2 Three Capes Track (p94)
3 Kunanyi/Mt Wellington (p70)
4 Frenchmans Cap (p140)
5 Wineglass Bay (p158)
6 South Coast Track (p121)
7 Strzelecki Peaks (p183)
National Parks
1 Cradle Mountain-Lake St Clair (p240)
2 Tasman (p95)
3 Freycinet (p158)
4 Maria Island (p148)
5 Mt Field (p85)
6 Ben Lomond (p202)
7 Southwest (p118)
BASS STRAIT
Cape Wickham
Egg Lagoon
Yambacoona
King Island
Sea Elephant Bay
Naracoopa
Currie
Grassy
Seal Bay
Hunter Passage
Hope Channel
Hunter Island
Three Hummock Island
Woolnorth Point
Robbins Island
Perkins Bay
Stanley
The Nut
Montagu
Studland Bay
Smithton
Marrawah
Wynyard
Burnie
Edith Creek
Arthur River
Arthur-Pieman Conservation Area
Sandy Cape
Waratah
Savage River
Corinna
Rosebery
Zeehan
Ulverstone
Devonport
Port Sorell
Beaconsfield
Low Head
George Town
Exeter
Cradle Mountain-Lake St Clair National Park
Mole Creek
Deloraine
Breona
Poatina
Yingina/Great Lake
Longford
Perth
Launceston
Noland Bay
Bridport
Scottsdale
Lilydale
Derby
Ringarooma
Gladstone
Legges Tor
Mathinna
Ben Lomond National Park
Douglas-Apsley National Park
St Helens
Scamander
St Marys
Bicheno
Eddystone Point
Larapuna/Bay of Fires
St Helens Point
Inner Sister Island
Outer Sister Island
Palana
Stanley Point
Cape Frankland
Babel Island
Emita
Flinders Island
Sellars Point
Whitemark
Lady Barron
Franklin Sound
Truwana/Cape Barren Island
Cape Barren
Banks Strait
Cape Portland
Swan Island

ACTION AREAS

Where to find Tasmania's best outdoor activities.

Mountain Biking

1. Derby (p175)
2. St Helens (p167)
3. Maydena (p118)
4. Queenstown (p273)
5. Zeehan (p275)
6. George Town (p204)

Animals/Wildlife

1. Bonorong Wildlife Sanctuary (p84)
2. The Neck (p103)
3. Maria Island National Park (p149)
4. Narawntapu National Park (p212)
5. Trowunna Wildlife Sanctuary (p227)
6. Stanley (p257)
7. Cradle Mountain (p240)

Beaches

1. Kingston Beach (p87)
2. Seven Mile Beach (p80)
3. Bicheno (p162)
4. Marrawah (p260)
5. Boat Harbour Beach (p235)
6. Cockle Creek (p122)

TASMANIA

THE GUIDE

Chapters in this section are organised by hubs and their surrounding areas. We see the hub as your base in the destination, where you'll find unique experiences, local insights, insider tips and expert recommendations. It's also your gateway to the surrounding area, where you'll see what and how much you can do from there.

Trowutta Arch (p263), Tarkine Wilderness

VISUAL COLLECTIVE/SHUTTERSTOCK

Researched by
Charles Rawlings-Way

Hobart & Around

BETWEEN THE MOUNTAIN AND THE SEA

Revel in the natural, cultural and culinary pleasures of Australia's best-looking capital city.

With a cinematic location and temperate maritime airs, Nipaluna/Hobart lies on Muwinina land. The English sailed their convict boats into Sullivans Cove in 1804, and Australia's second-oldest city was born. From the shores of one of the world's deepest natural ports, the fledgling colony climbed the leafy flanks of Kunanyi/Mt Wellington, a 1271m plateau edged by dolerite cliffs. Hobartians find reassurance in the mountain's solid presence: when all else is changing, Kunanyi is a constant.

CURIOSO.PHOTOGRAPHY/SHUTTERSTOCK

Down at the harbour, the world rushes in on the tide, bringing influences from afar and leaving the locals buzzing. Hobart has this buzz: old pubs rub shoulders with craft-beer bars, arty cafes, museums, festivals, top-flight dining and bespoke distilleries, all of it washed in history and sea-salty charm. The hyperactive Salamanca Market is here too, drawing thousands of people every Saturday morning (even more if there's a cruise ship in town). When the market winds up, Salamanca reverts to its usual unhurried tempo, locals and visitors drifting between galleries, bars and good places to eat.

Heading north, Elizabeth St rolls uphill from the CBD into North Hobart, home to the city's more bohemian restaurant and bar scene. Cafes, an art-house cinema, pubs, craft-beer breweries, multicultural eats, live music – it's all here. Keep trucking north and you'll reach MONA, Australia's edgiest art gallery, sitting on a saucepan-shaped headland jutting into the River Derwent. Delve into the underground galleries (the architecture is astonishing) and be delighted, amused, appalled and entertained – then kick back with some fine food and wine in the sunshine.

Indeed, on a sunny summer afternoon, Hobart can be downright pleasant. But there are dark undercurrents here, too. On a winter morning, gusts of icy wind whip down the face of the mountain, thin feathers of cloud race across the high sky, and moody foothills hump down to the slate-grey River Derwent. Hobart can feel far-flung and forlorn sometimes.

But embrace Hobart's Gothic charm. The Dark Mofo winter fest is unmissable, and it's these inexorable ties to nature – all that cold water and all that mountain – that give Hobart its unique appeal.

THE MAIN AREAS

CENTRAL HOBART
Sassy bars, cheap lunches, outdoor gear. **p50**

SALAMANCA & THE WATERFRONT
Historic buildings, restaurants, nocturnal fun. **p56**

BATTERY POINT, SANDY BAY & SOUTH HOBART
Colonial heritage, restaurants, Kunanyi/Mt Wellington. **p64**

NORTH HOBART
Eat street, live tunes, MONA. **p74**

BEYOND HOBART
Beaches, history, accessible wilderness. **p80**

For places to stay in Hobart and around, see p88

ANGRYBIRDPRODUCTIONS/SHUTTERSTOCK

Left: Apples at Salamanca Market (p56); Above: The Waterfront (p56) and Central Hobart (p50)

Find Your Way

Compact Hobart begins at the waterfront and nearby Salamanca, flows uphill through the city centre and continues north, all below Kunanyi/Mt Wellington. Keep Kunanyi on your left for North Hobart; on your right for Battery Point, Sandy Bay and South Hobart. And if you can't see the mountain, head indoors!

FROM THE AIRPORT
Hobart Airport is 18km east of the city centre – about a 25-minute drive. SkyBus coaches meet every flight and pick up/drop off at six central and waterfront locations ($22/38 single/return). Budget $38 to $48 for a rideshare to Salamanca.

WALK
The easiest way to explore Hobart is on two legs. Most of the wine-and-dine options are strung out between Salamanca and North Hobart: you could cab it, but an amble between the Whaler and the Republic Bar takes 30 minutes, tops. And there are views everywhere.

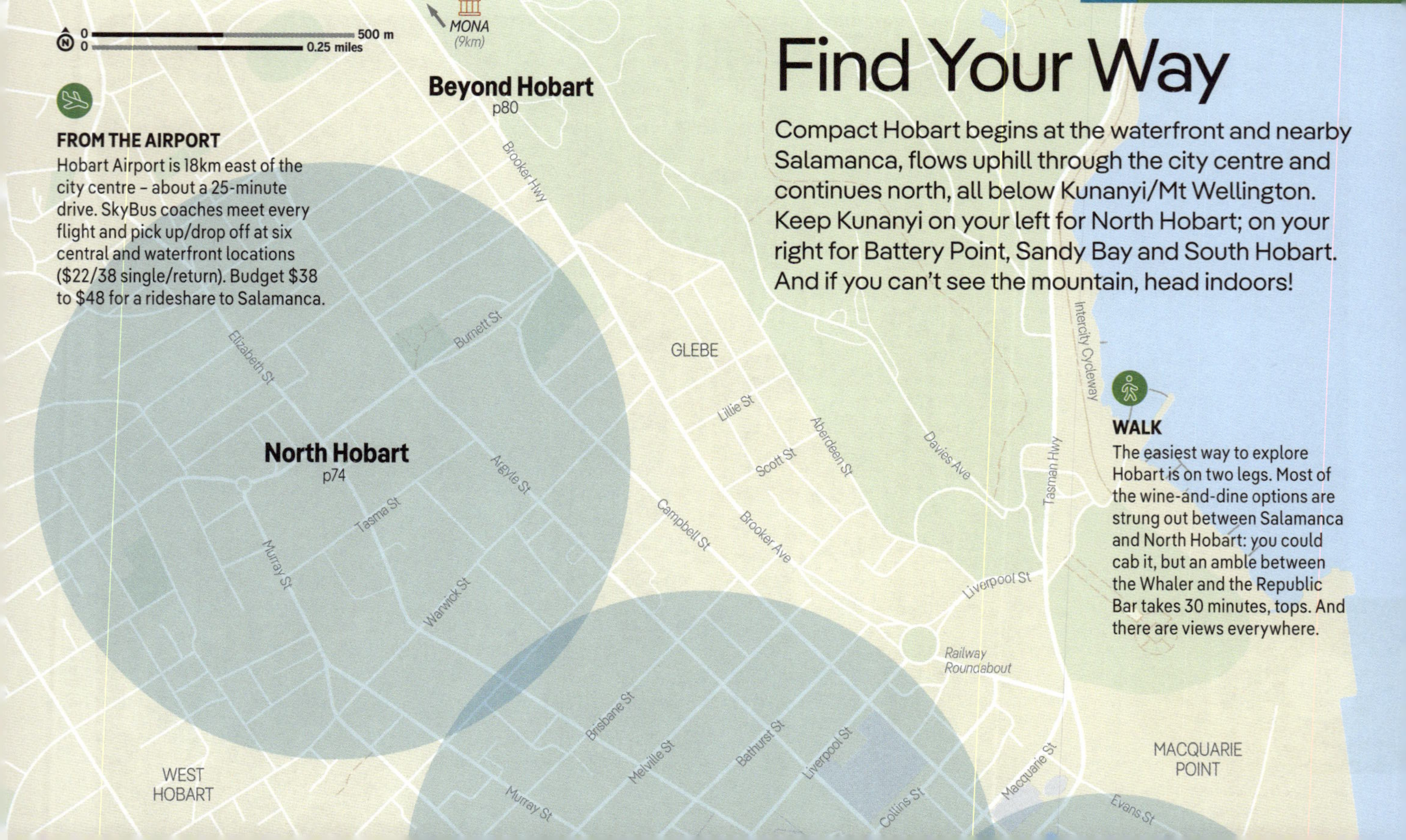

BICYCLE

Cycling is popular in this outdoorsy city – there are plenty of bike paths, bike shops, bike hires and dedicated bike parking. Hobart is hilly, though, so e-bikes can be handy: they come in all styles and configurations, both to rent or to buy.

E-SCOOTER

The quickest way around town is on a purple Beam e-scooter that you'll find outside Hobart's entertainment hot spots. Scan the QR code, download the app and strap on a helmet. It's legal to ride on the footpath, but check exclusion zones.

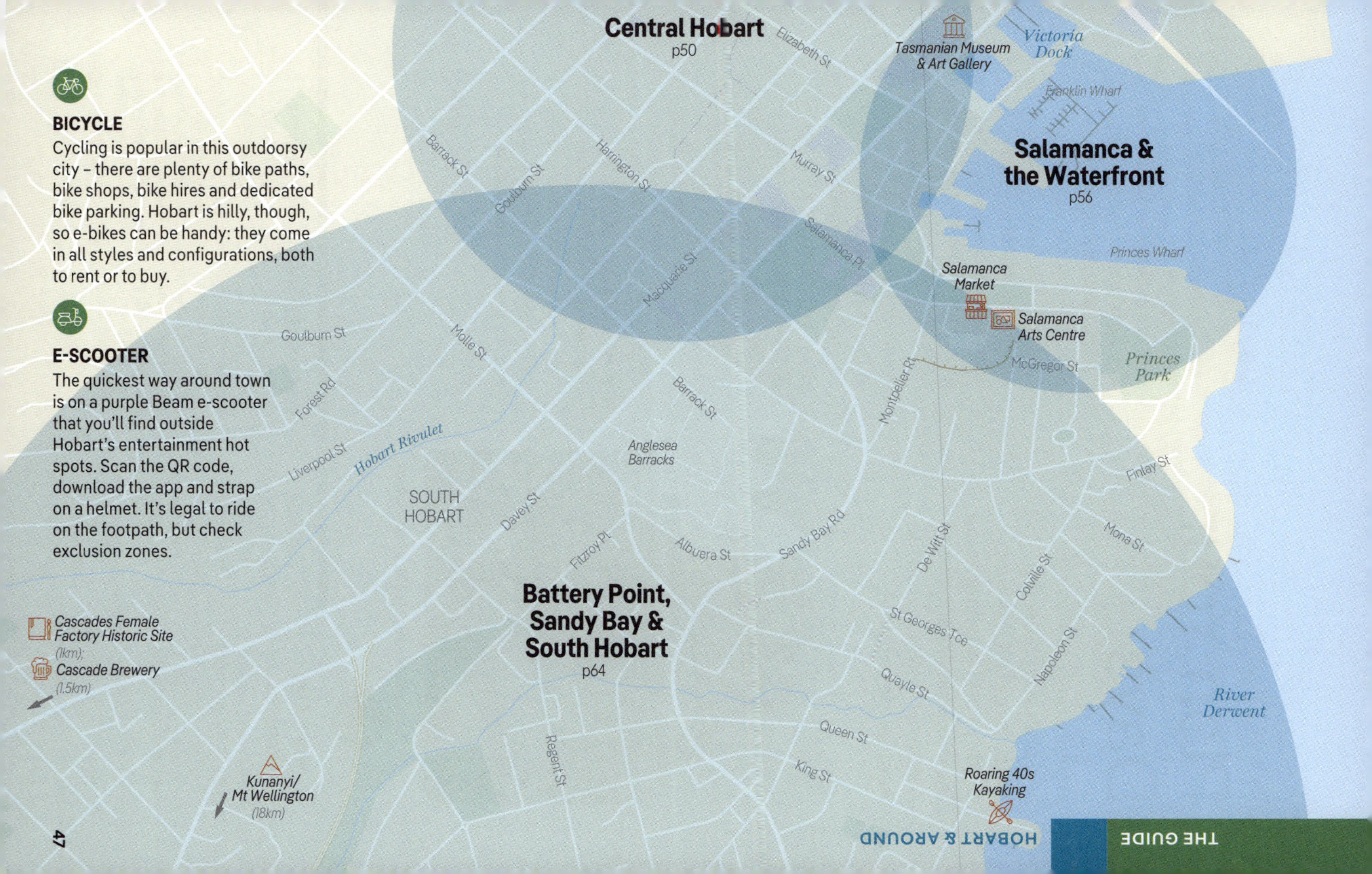

Plan Your Days

Muster some cleverness and plan your time: the markets and MONA have set days and opening hours. Trips to Bruny Island and Kunanyi/Mt Wellington are weather-dependent.

DOUGLAS CLIFF/SHUTTERSTOCK

Cascade Brewery (p68), South Hobart

Day 1

Morning

- Grab a croissant from **Jackman & McRoss** (p66) at Battery Point, then take **Kelly's Steps** (p66) down to Salamanca Place. If it's a Saturday, lose track of time at **Salamanca Market** (p57); on other days, check out Salamanca's galleries, bars and eateries.

Afternoon

- Take the **MONA ROMA** (p62) ferry for a cruise up the Derwent. Have a bite at **Moorilla Wine Bar** (p77) before descending into the **MONA** (p76) galleries. Have a drink on the lawn before the return ferry (hot tip: book the 'Posh Pit').

Evening

- Munch fish and chips from **Flippers** (p62) on Constitution Dock, then wander to Salamanca for a whisky at the **Whaler** (p60) and live tunes at **Jack Greene** (p78).

You'll Also Want to...

Now you've got the hang of Hobart, you'll want to spread your wings (and legs) further on nearby day trips.

EXPLORE TURRAKANA/ TASMAN PENINSULA

Explore the convict ruins at **Port Arthur** (p98) and **Coal Mines** (p100) historic sites, and marvel at incredible sea-cliffs on a hike to **Cape Hauy** (p95).

DISCOVER BRUNY ISLAND

Chug across on the ferry, climb the lookout at **the Neck** (p103), then picnic on **oysters** (p105), **honey ice cream** (p108) and **cheese and beer** (p105) at Adventure Bay.

FOLLOW THE DERWENT UPSTREAM

Look forward to fine food, hops, books and antiques in **New Norfolk** (p84) and the bucolic Derwent Valley, 35 minutes' drive from Salamanca.

Day 2

Morning

- Sunday? Complement your coffee with a bao bun from **Farm Gate Market** (p50) and score some lunch provisions, before driving to the **Springs** (p73) halfway up **Kunanyi/Mt Wellington** (p70).

Afternoon

- Hike to the **Organ Pipes** (p73) and pick a spot with a view for your picnic lunch. Or keep driving all the way up to the **Pinnacle Lookout** (p71) for jaw-dropping views over Hobart and beyond.

Evening

- Enjoy a quiet ale at the **New Sydney Hotel** (p54) in the city, before wandering up to the **State Cinema** (p74) in North Hobart for a film and a well-earned curry at **Annapurna** (p78).

Day 3

Morning

- Hot-foot it back to NoHo for breakfast at **Room for a Pony** (p78), then drive out to meet some Tasmanian devils at **Bonorong Wildlife Sanctuary** (p84). At nearby Richmond, stretch your legs and assess historic **Richmond Bridge** (p82) for structural integrity.

Afternoon

- Sip a glass of top **Pooley Wines** (p85) product before some Coal River Valley grazing at **Puddleduck Vineyard** (p85), **Coal River Farm** (p84) and **Frogmore Creek** (p85) and/or a whisky tasting at **Sullivans Cove** (p84).

Evening

- Grab dinner and beers at **Cascade Brewery Bar** (p69), then walk it off in the long twilight along **Nutgrove Beach** (p67) in Sandy Bay, or windswept **Seven Mile Beach** (p80) near the airport.

DAY-TRIP TO THE HUON VALLEY

Buy bags of fresh apples from roadside stalls as you roam between farmy **Huonville** (p112), hippie **Cygnet** (p113) and the gorgeous **D'Entrecasteaux Channel** (p114).

PADDLE SOUTHERN SHORES

Whether it's a morning city paddle or a day trip discovering the southern coast, **Roaring 40s Kayaking** (p66) has got you covered.

WANDER TO WATERFALLS

Get a taste of Tasmania's lush southwest wilderness on rainforest ambles to hidden waterfalls at **Mt Field National Park** (p85).

HANG OUT AT KINGSTON BEACH

Hike the **Alum Cliffs Track** (p87) from Taroona, swim at Kingston Beach, then hit the **Salty Dog** (p87) pub for ciders and Sunday afternoon tunes.

Central Hobart

SASSY BARS, CHEAP LUNCHES AND OUTDOOR GEAR

TOP TIP

The city centre is a great place for a cheap lunch: Elizabeth St Mall and Collins St (particularly near Harrington St) are prime terrain for noodles, rice and curries. Less obvious are the arcades: try the Bank of Us Centre on Collins St or Bank Arcade off Liverpool for sushi, dumplings and further curries.

On a busy weekday, Hobart's city centre is heaving with office workers and tourists bouncing between cheap lunch spots and buying gear for their next wilderness adventure. By late afternoon the sea breeze has stiffened, lunch cafes have shut up shop and the stores are closing. As dusk falls on Kunanyi/Mt Wellington, roller shutters rise as bars and restaurants get ready for another evening's frivolities.

Hobart's low-rise city centre – dominated by the Royal Hobart Hospital and a scattering of squat office blocks and UTAS buildings – is bisected by Elizabeth St. This main drag heads north from the bus interchange at Franklin Sq and the GPO, momentarily becomes Elizabeth St Mall lined with shoe shops and department stores, then welcomes back traffic as it rolls uphill past the outdoor shops towards North Hobart.

Buried beneath it all is Hobart Rivulet, the city's *raison d'être,* unloved and unheralded (but it's nice to know it's there).

Farm Gate Foraging

Get it straight from the growers

A Sunday morning stroll down Bathurst St between Murray St and Elizabeth St is a weekly Hobart ritual. The excellent

GETTING AROUND

Downtown Hobart's one-way street system, expensive all-day parking and heartless parking inspectors mean it's better to save the car for out-of-town excursions or a trip up Kunanyi/Mt Wellington. Fortunately, Central Hobart is compact and easily navigated on foot, with Salamanca, Battery Point and North Hobart all within easy walking distance. Rideshares are quick and cheap compared to mainland standards. Buses are only useful if you're staying beyond the city centre or waterfront areas: you'll need a Greencard from the Metro Shop on the Mall, or the correct change.

HIGHLIGHTS
1 Farm Gate Market
2 Tasmanian Museum & Art Gallery

SIGHTS
3 Maritime Museum of Tasmania

ACTIVITIES
4 Glazed & Confused
5 Rock It Climbing
6 Takara Nipaluna

SLEEPING
7 Alabama Hotel
8 Astor Private Hotel
9 Hadley's Orient Hotel
10 Hobart Central YHA
11 Old Woolstore Apartment Hotel
12 Vibe Hotel Hobart

EATING
13 Criterion Street Cafe
14 Fico
15 Ja and Jon
16 Pigeon Whole Bakery
17 Pilgrim Coffee
18 Pot Sticker Dumpling House
19 Sawak Cafe
20 Scholé
21 Still Thai
22 Urban Greek

DRINKING & NIGHTLIFE
23 Grinners Dive Bar
24 Hope & Anchor
25 In the Hanging Garden
26 Lucinda Wine Bar
27 Mountain Culture
28 New Sydney Hotel
29 Rude Boy
30 Shamrock Hotel

ENTERTAINMENT
31 Altar Bar
32 Pablo's Cocktails & Dreams
33 Theatre Royal

SHOPPING
34 Cat & Fiddle Arcade
35 Centrepoint Arcade
36 Cool Wine
37 Eumarrah
38 Fullers Bookshop
39 Mountain Creek Outdoors
40 Tommy Gun Records

TOP SHOPS

Fullers Bookshop: In this UNESCO City of Literature, Fullers leads the way. Australia's oldest independent bookshop (1920) has a lovely cafe and great staff.

Cool Wine: An excellent selection of cool-climate Tasmanian wine (plus a few global interlopers, if they're good enough).

Tommy Gun Records: For all your vinyl, secondhand CD, studded-leather wristband and heavy-metal T-shirt requirements.

Mountain Creek Outdoors: The best of the outdoors shops clustered around the corner of Elizabeth St and Bathurst St. Go wild.

Eumarrah: Follow Hobart's many hippies into this excellent whole-foods shop. Spices, nuts, teas and buckets of grains to go.

Farm Gate Market *(farmgatemarket.com.au; 8.30am-1pm)* offers sustainably produced mushrooms, bespoke pasta, artisanal loaves, crumbly cheeses and expertly cured salamis. A jaunty selection of food vans serves interesting breakfasts of bao buns, *murtabaks* (pan-fried flatbreads), wallaby burritos and congee...although not everyone needs a gin-tasting at 8.30am. A sunny seat with a coffee and a sourdough doughnut might be more your speed? Either way, stock up on picnic provisions for your Sunday drive.

Hobart History

TMAG is an essential Hobart museum

In a sprawling complex of colonial-era buildings between Davey St and Macquarie St, the **Tasmanian Museum & Art Gallery** *(TMAG; tmag.tas.gov.au; free)* is quintessentially Hobart, zeroing in on Tasmanian history, art, culture and natural science. Learn about the ill-fated thylacine (Tasmanian tiger) and the Black War between the colonists and Tasmania's Aboriginal people. Come to grips with Hobart's inexorable ties with Antarctica; and learn some words of palawa kani, Tasmania's reconstructed Aboriginal language. Free 40-minute tours run Friday to Sunday and cover art gallery highlights (11am), TMAG's historic buildings (noon) and museum highlights (2pm). Lots of kid-focused exhibitions and a cool courtyard cafe. Closed Mondays April to December.

What the Sea Wants, the Sea Shall Have

Explore the Maritime Museum Tasmania

Behind TMAG, the sea-salty **Maritime Museum Tasmania** *(maritimetas.org; adult/child $16/free)* captures the role the sea has played in Hobart history, from convict transportation and whaling to modern-day port operations, naval history and shipwrecks (of which Tasmania has more than 1000). Old sea dogs with a spare hour to fill can look forward to lots of interesting photos, paintings, models and relics. Try to resist ringing the huge brass bell from the *Rhexenor*. Moored across

EATING IN CENTRAL HOBART: CAFES & ASIAN EATS

Pilgrim Coffee: Exposed bricks, timber beams and distressed walls. Expert coffee. *6.30am-3pm Mon-Fri, to 1pm Sat & Sun* $

Criterion Street Cafe: Enduring downtown favourite: a short menu on a short street. Order the corn fritters. *7am-3pm* $

Pigeon Whole Bakery: Beaut baguettes, breads and biscuits. Sit in the window with your coffee and watch the city scenes. *7.30am-3pm Mon-Fri, to 1pm Sat & Sun* $

Westside Laundry: This reinvented laundromat does bagels and sandwiches by day, morphing into a NYC-inspired bar by night. *7.30am-3pm Wed-Mon, 5-9pm Thu-Sun* $

Pot Sticker Dumpling House: This old-time dumpling and stir-fry joint is on every Hobartian's list. Great vegetarian. *11.30am-8.45pm* $

Sawak Cafe: See students on the run from the books, slurping prawn laksa and *char kway teow* (stir-fried flat noodles). *11.30am-2.30pm & 5-9pm Mon-Sat* $

Ja and Jon: The queue out the door at lunchtime is a sure-fire indicator: these are the best banh mi in town. *9am-8pm* $

Still Thai: Long-running Thai does all the classics with friendly aplomb. Don't bypass the green chicken curry. *11.30am-2.30pm Tue-Fri, 4.30-8.30pm Mon-Sat* $$

DICKLYON, VIA WIKIMEDIA COMMONS

Hobart Rivulet from Collins Street

the road is a key piece of the collection, *Westward,* the only Tasmanian yacht to twice win the Sydney to Hobart Yacht Race, and now being restored by the museum.

Rivulet Meandering

Trace Hobart's original water supply beneath the city streets

Flowing down from Kunanyi/Mt Wellington, the **Hobart Rivulet** was a critical water source for colonial Hobart. Over time it became horribly polluted and the city section was covered and rerouted. Today you can play hide-and-seek with the waterway, heading upstream through the city.

Meet the creek in its concrete culvert below the Royal Hobart Hospital on Collins St. Get another glimpse at the northern end of Elizabeth St Mall, where a pavement peephole reveals the flowing waters beneath a colonial-era bridge.

TIPS FROM THE LORD MAYOR

Rt Hon Cr Anna Reynolds, the Independent Lord Mayor of Hobart, was elected in 2018, only the third woman to ever hold the position. *@annareyno*

Hobart is such a vibrant, creative and down-to-earth small city, set in a stunning landscape ranging from alpine country to sandy beaches.

Street Eats @ Franco: On a Friday night in summer, it's a lively mix of everything Hobart.

Stagg Midtown: Serves my favourite coffee in a thriving part of the city centre.

Institut Polaire: A celebration of Hobart's connection to Antarctica, with great food and drinks.

Organ Pipes: On Kunanyi/Mt Wellington, get up close to the 'face' of Hobart, with views rivalling the Pinnacle. A Hobart favourite for over 100 years (p73).

EATING IN CENTRAL HOBART: DECADENT DINNERS

Templo: Unpretentious but classy, Templo is a Hobart treasure. Just 20 seats, so book in advance. *noon-2pm Fri-Sun, 5.30-9pm Wed-Sun* $$

Urban Greek: You'll smell the charcoal seafood before you see it. Succulent Mediterranean dishes and good Greek beer. *5-9pm Wed-Mon* $$

Scholé: Groundbreaking local chef Luke Burgess has transformed this skinny, heritage shopfront into his latest restaurant-wine bar. *4-8pm Tue, 5.30pm-midnight Wed-Sat* $$

Fico: Amazing Italian. Paired wines take the flavours of the 'feed me' menu to another planet. *6-8pm Thu-Sat, noon-1.30pm Sun* $$$

STEVE LOVEGROVE/SHUTTERSTOCK

Theatre Royal

Enter 1960s **Cat & Fiddle Arcade** and walk through to Murray St. In the early 1800s this was seamy Cat & Fiddle Alley, home to inns, brothels and drunken sailors along the Rivulet's muddy banks.

The 1970s **Centrepoint Arcade** is next, also built over the Rivulet, before it sees sunlight again behind Village Cinemas on Collins St. Beyond Barrack St, the Rivulet becomes (almost) beautiful, with its some of its natural geology resuming.

From Molle St, the jogger-filled, wheelchair-accessible 2.5km **Riv 5 walking trail** *(hobartcity.com.au; free)* follows the Rivulet (now open-air and certainly beautiful – with resident

DRINKING IN HOBART: OLD PUBS & COOL BARS

New Sydney Hotel: Open fires, creative food, live-music jams, a dozen craft beers and ciders and no screens. Winner. *noon-10.30pm Mon-Sat, 4-10pm Sun*	**Shamrock Hotel:** Old-school downtown boozer with hefty meals, all-comer vibes and zero posturing. Change is overrated. *11am-10pm*	**Hope & Anchor:** Australia's oldest continually licensed pub (1807), the Hope & Anchor has suitably refused to gentrify. Nautical mood, cold beer. *noon-9pm*	**Mountain Culture:** Backed by investor Pat Cummins, the Australian Test cricket captain, this craft-beer hall is a post-work paradise. *noon-9pm Wed, Thu & Sun, to midnight Fri & Sat*
Lucinda Wine Bar: Gorgeous, candlelit Lucinda is just begging you to come inside. French small plates, fine wine and conversation. *4pm-late Tue-Sat*	**Grinners Dive Bar:** Loud rock, craft beer, tacos and late-night street tables. Fun! *4pm-midnight Sun & Mon, noon-midnight Tue-Thu, noon-4am Fri & Sat*	**In the Hanging Garden:** Multi-level laneway complex infused with greenery, performance spaces and hole-in-the-wall eats. *11am-9pm Sun-Thu, to midnight Fri & Sat*	**Rude Boy:** Fried chicken and cocktails. Ramp up the rowdiness with rum BBQ sauce and cherry sour beer. Reggae rules. *4pm-midnight Tue-Sat*

platypuses!) all the way to Cascade Brewery (p68) in South Hobart. Beer o'clock?

Takara Nipaluna

Uncover a different history

Time-travel to colonial-era Nipaluna/Hobart on these immersive, impactful 90-minute **walking tours** *(blackledtours.com/takara-nipaluna; from $70)*. The tours retrace the route of the Aboriginal resistance group who walked into Hobart Town in 1832 in pursuit of a treaty to end the Black War. What happened next reshaped their future forever, with the forced deportation of Tasmania's remaining Aboriginal people to Flinders Island (p180) in the Bass Strait. Operating hours can be irregular; book in advance.

Convict Heritage in the City Centre

Explore Hobart's original gaol

The courtrooms, cells and gallows at the **Hobart Penitentiary** *(nationaltrust.org.au/places/penitentiary; tours from adult/child $35/20)*, aka 'the Tench', had a hellish reputation in the 1800s. Most of Tasmania's 75,000 convicts passed through here. The barracks and main yard are long gone, replaced by Hobart's rather stylish 1980s ambulance HQ – but the Penitentiary's beautiful red-brick 1834 chapel remains solidly intact. Visits are by 90-minute 'Unshackled' tours; book well ahead. Not spooky enough? Sign up for a 90-minute Ghost Tour. Outside along Campbell St are remnants of the old sandstone prison wall: amazingly high where it connects to the chapel, and continuing in fragments all the way to Bathurst St.

Royal Performances

Catch a show at Australia's oldest theatre

Hobart's endearing **Theatre Royal** *(theatreroyal.com.au; tours adult/child $20/10)* is Australia's oldest still-functioning theatre, where thespians have been treading the boards since 1837. Seating 700, it's still the centre of Hobart's performing-arts scene, hosting contemporary drama, comedy, dance and live music. Jump online and see who's playing, or take a 75-minute guided tour and hear stories of the theatre's chequered past, including the resident ghost 'Fred' and 1984 fire that ravaged the building. Enter via the impressive new Hedberg UTAS performing arts centre next door; the box office is here too.

WHERE'S WAPPING?

Hobart's lost suburb of Wapping once occupied the muddy flatlands where the Hobart Rivulet emptied into Sullivans Cove – today, roughly between the Theatre Royal on Campbell St and the Grand Chancellor Hotel on Davey St. This swampy, tidal, disease-ridden area was where no one wealthy wanted to be – it was left to the sailors, whalers, ex-convicts and women of the night to occupy. Development through the 1800s was unchecked, and untenable whenever the Rivulet flooded – and when a huge fire tore through the 'hood in 1890, Wapping was levelled, built over and lost to history. Wander down Sackville St behind the Theatre Royal and imagine lowbrow life here in 1830 (keep one hand on your wallet).

Salamanca & the Waterfront

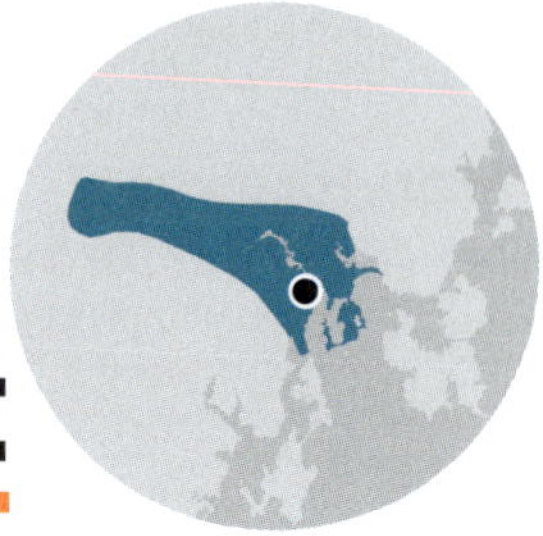

HISTORIC BUILDINGS, RESTAURANTS AND NOCTURNAL FUN

TOP TIP

The airport SkyBus stops at Grand Chancellor Hotel (Stop 1) and Brooke St Pier (Stop 2) are handy for the waterfront and Salamanca. The MONA ferry, Red Decker, Kunanyi/Mt Wellington Explorer and Gray Line tourist buses all drop-off at Brooke St Pier.

Ground zero for most Hobart visitors, the waterfront's broad concrete apron skirts Sullivans Cove and is dotted with excellent restaurants, floating fish punts, yachting berths, piers, high-end hotels and apartments – some visitors don't get much further!

The 19th-century sandstone warehouses along Hunter St, largely a former jam factory, now house upmarket hotels, restaurants and the UTAS School of Creative Arts. Expect a cruise ship most summer days at adjacent Macquarie Wharf. Constitution Dock hosts bobbing fish-and-chippers, while Victoria Dock is home to Hobart's working fishing fleet, supplying the many waterfront seafood restaurants.

Along Sullivans Cove's southern flank is Salamanca Place, an improbably well-preserved, 500m-long row of 1840s sandstone warehouses. Once used to store wool, whale oil, seal fur, wheat and apples, the buildings now house a buzzing collection of galleries, cafes, restaurants, pubs, bars and live-music venues. Salamanca Market has been happening here every Saturday morning since 1972. Busy!

Salamanca Market Mayhem

Great food and even better people-watching

What started out as a couple of hippies selling raspberries in 1972 has evolved into a kilometre-long frenzy of food and

GETTING AROUND

The easiest way to negotiate the waterfront and Salamanca area is on foot: it's dead flat and rather parking-unfriendly. There are plenty of e-scooters lying around, but most people use them for novelty value rather than any real transport need. The main access routes into this area are Kelly's Steps from Battery Point (avoid if you have knee or mobility issues), St David's Park (for central hotels), Murray St (ditto) and Elizabeth St. The Intercity Cycleway comes straight into the waterfront from Hobart's northern suburbs.

SCOTTI13/SHUTTERSTOCK

Salamanca Market

commerce that consumes all of Salamanca Place every Saturday morning (8.30am to 3pm), rain, hail or shine – it's Tasmania's number 1 tourist attraction. With thousands of people here every week, **Salamanca Market** *(salamancamarket.com.au; free)* is something to behold: give yourself at least a few hours to wander its length and back again, a slow-shuffling circuit down one side of the stalls then back up the other. The cafes overflow, the buskers are in fine voice and (even when it's cold and wet) the atmosphere is downright convivial. Don't miss it.

Artfully Salamanca

Lose a few hours at the Salamanca Arts Centre

As with many of Tasmania's architectural treasures, the Salamanca Place warehouses only survived the 20th century because no one here had the money to knock them down. Thank goodness! Indeed, these chunky stone walls would take some shifting: step into the **Salamanca Arts Centre** *(salarts.org.au; free)* for an up-close look. Running since 1975, the SAC is a vital hub of Hobart's artistic life, maintaining a hectic programme of launches, events and performances – always as progressive and socially inclusive as they are creative. There are dozens of commercial artists' studios, retail spaces, cafes and galleries here too. Don't miss **handmark** for exquisite ceramics, glass, jewellery, paintings and sculpture; the **Salamanca Wool Shop** for nice knits; the **Kudelka Shop**, home to works by mildly anarchic local cartoonist Jon Kudelka; and a coffee at Tricycle Cafe & Bar.

SHIFTING SHORELINES

It's hard to imagine now, but Salamanca's warehouses were once a lot closer to the water than they are today. No, the warehouses haven't moved – but the shoreline has: the broad concrete apron encircling the whole of Sullivans Cove is largely built over reclaimed land. Merchants were once able to sail their ships right up to a beach in front of the warehouses to offload/load their goods with ease. On the other side of the Cove, Hunter St is built on top of Hunter Island, once connected to the rest of Hobart via a narrow causeway. Look for the brass discs set into the concrete road tracing the line of the causeway below.

EATING AT SALAMANCA & THE WATERFRONT: CAFE SCENES

Retro Cafe: Masterful breakfasts, salads and burgers, plus laughing staff, jazz and the whirr of the coffee machine. *7.30am-4pm Mon-Fri, from 8am Sat & Sun* $

Daci & Daci: Slick bakery-cafe that's a hit with the local parliamentarians. Take your cake to the streetside deck. *7am-5pm* $

Tricycle Cafe & Bar: Artful nook inside the Salamanca Arts Centre serving cafe classics (ace muffins) and local wines. *8.30am-4pm Mon-Sat* $

Machine Laundry Cafe: Washing machine, killer coffee and plates of spicy potato hash. Live like a Uni student in Salamanca Sq. *7.30am-3pm* $

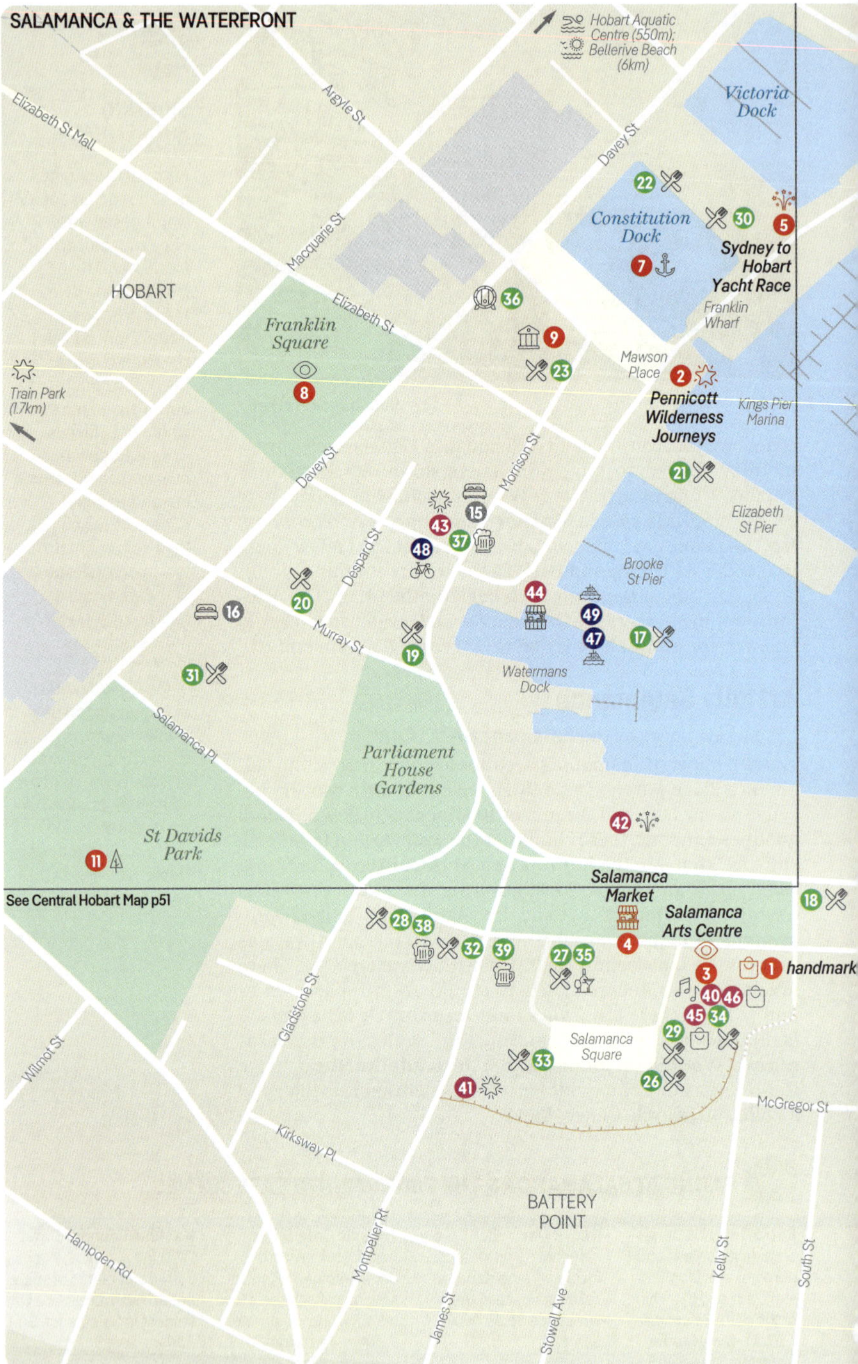
SALAMANCA & THE WATERFRONT
Hobart Aquatic Centre (550m); Bellerive Beach (6km)
Victoria Dock
Elizabeth St Mall
Argyle St
Davey St
22
Constitution Dock
30
5
Sydney to Hobart Yacht Race
7
Macquarie St
HOBART
Elizabeth St
36
Franklin Wharf
Franklin Square
9
Mawson Place
Train Park (1.7km)
8
23
2
Pennicott Wilderness Journeys
Kings Pier Marina
Morrison St
21
Davey St
15
Elizabeth St Pier
43
37
Despard St
48
Brooke St Pier
20
44
16
49
Murray St
47
17
19
31
Watermans Dock
Salamanca Pl
Parliament House Gardens
42
St Davids Park
11
Salamanca Market
See Central Hobart Map p51
18
28
38
Salamanca Arts Centre
32
39
27
35
4
3
1
handmark
Gladstone St
40
46
45
34
29
Salamanca Square
Wilmot St
33
26
41
McGregor St
Kirksway Pl
BATTERY POINT
Montpelier Rt
Hampden Rd
Kelly St
South St
James St
Stowell Ave

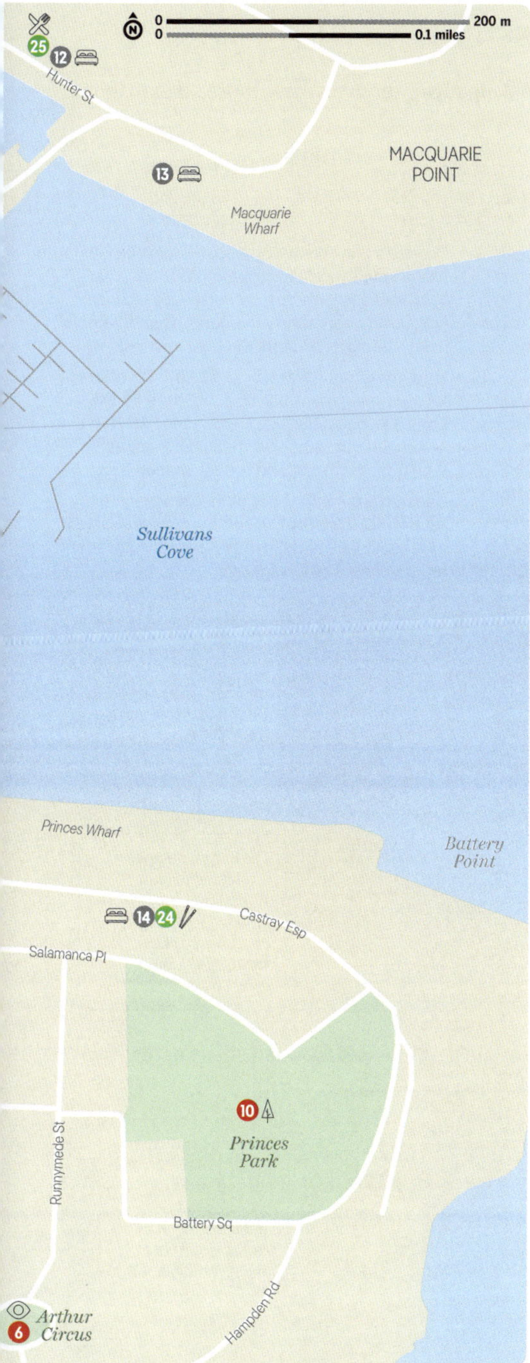

HIGHLIGHTS
1 handmark
2 Pennicott Wilderness Journeys
3 Salamanca Arts Centre
4 Salamanca Market
5 Sydney to Hobart Yacht Race

SIGHTS
6 Arthur Circus
7 Constitution Dock
8 Franklin Square
9 Mawson's Huts Replica Museum
10 Princes Park
11 St David's Park

SLEEPING
12 Henry Jones Art Hotel
13 MACq 01
14 Salamanca Wharf Hotel
15 Sullivans Cove Apartments
16 Tasman

EATING
17 Aløft
18 Blue Eye
19 Customs House Hotel
20 Daci & Daci
21 Fish Frenzy
22 Flippers
23 Frank
24 Kosaten Hobart
25 Landscape
26 Machine Laundry Cafe
27 Maldini
28 Manky Sally's
29 Mezethes
30 Mures
31 Peppina
32 Retro Cafe
33 Suzie Luck's
34 Tricycle Cafe & Bar

DRINKING & NIGHTLIFE
35 Jack Greene
36 Lark Distillery
37 Telegraph Hotel
38 Waterman's Hotel
39 Whaler

ENTERTAINMENT
40 Rektango
41 Society
42 Taste of Summer
43 Telegraph Hotel

SHOPPING
44 Hobart Twilight Market
45 Kudelka Shop
46 Salamanca Wool Shop

TRANSPORT
47 Derwent Ferries
48 Hobart Bike Hire
49 MONA ROMA

WHO'S UP FOR A DRINK?

Hobart has always been a hard-drinking town – and nowhere more so than the waterfront. When in Rome...

START	END	LENGTH
Whaler	Hobart Brewing Co	1.5km; 2hr

Start with a pint at the rollicking, unpretentious 1 **Whaler**, which has been pouring ales under various names since 1829 (mention 'Knopwood's Retreat' and older Hobartians tend to smile). The crew here is an egalitarian mix of tourists, tradies and suits – come as you are.

Next up is the colonial-era 2 **Customs House Hotel**, dating from around 1846, with an old-school public bar and a scattering of outdoor tables with water views. Keeping your left hand on the shopfronts, shamble into the 3 **Telegraph Hotel**, a swanky Art Deco drinking hole on the next street corner, reborn a few years ago with a rooftop bar, live music and good-looking drinkers.

Craving a bite? Weave around to Brooke St Pier (via the mildly exciting Watermans Dock water-level walkway), where a corned beef sandwich (OK, and a pepperberry margarita) from 4 **Rosie in My Midnight Dreams** will right your rudder.

Next, make a quick detour to 5 **Lark Distillery** for a warming dram, before onwards to 6 **IXL Long Bar** inside the luxe Henry Jones Art Hotel. Watch the sun sink slowly behind Kunanyi/Mt Wellington with jazz and further libations.

Decamp around the back of the art school to 7 **Hobart Brewing Co**. This big red shed serves excellent beers and the outside fire pits (mostly) repel Hobart's chilly night air.

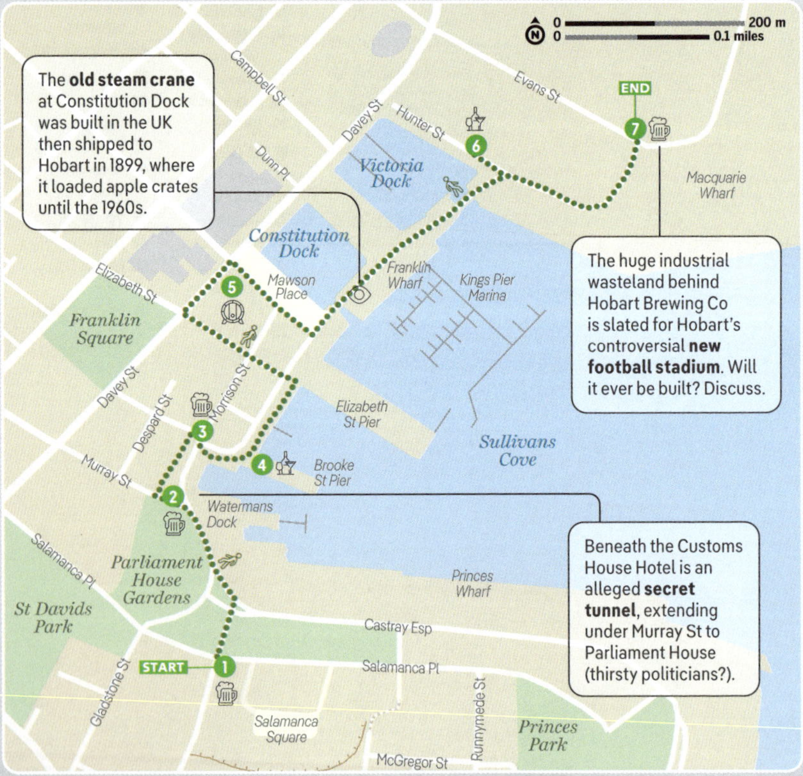

In the Winter Dark

Get loose at Hobart's decadent midwinter festival

The brainchild of the twisted minds out at MONA (p76), **Dark Mofo** *(darkmofo.net.au; prices vary)* is a winter arts-and-culture fest held in June each year. Focused on the waterfront, Dark Mofo revels in all things unhinged, Gothic and blood-red, and attracts visitors from around the world. Everything from the Tasman Bridge to Salamanca's warehouses are bathed in red light, with glowing red crosses studding the city. There's nonstop live music and performance art – shocking, sublime and downright weird. There's a new lineup every year, but three events are constant: the indulgent multi-night **Winter Feast** at Princes Wharf 1; the **Burning of the Ogoh-Ogoh**, a ritualistic bonfire of fears; and the festival-closing **Winter Solstice Nude Swim** at Long Beach (p67) in Sandy Bay. Book tickets in advance; leave your inhibitions elsewhere.

Recreating Antarctica

Life inside Sir Douglas Mawson's hut

Hobart is a major gateway for researchers and scientists heading to the frozen continent – the Australian Antarctic Division HQ is in Kingston, south of town. On the waterfront next to Constitution Dock, **Mawson's Huts Replica Museum** *(mawsons-huts-replica.org.au; adult/child $15/5)* is a model of one of the huts that Sir Douglas Mawson's Australasian Antarctic Expedition team, which set sail from Hobart, hunkered down in from 1911 to 1914. The replica is painstakingly exact (Mawson's tiny keyboard, a sledge and an ice axe are actually originals) and a knowledgeable guide is on hand to answer your Antarctic inquiries. Imagine 18 men living here, surviving on penguin stew. The original hut is still at Commonwealth Bay in Antarctica.

Yacht Rock

Experience the Sydney to Hobart Yacht Race

Arguably the hardest open-ocean yacht race in the world, the **Sydney to Hobart Yacht Race** *(rolexsydneyhobart.com; free)* has been running since 1945, departing Sydney every Boxing Day and finishing at Hobart's **Constitution Dock** several days later. The city is abuzz with anticipation from 27 December onwards, as sails materialise in the River Derwent

BEST FOR KIDS

Kids always get a buzz out of TMAG (p52), but here are a few other handy diversions.

Rektango: All-ages live-music shindig every Friday evening in the Salamanca Arts Centre Courtyard. Free.

Rock It Climbing: This back-lane climbing gym in the city centre has knobbly walls for all ages.

Glazed & Confused: Next door to Rock It, this pottery studio runs courses for kids and grown-ups.

Hobart Aquatic Centre: Pools of all lengths and depths.

Playground crawl: Try the playgrounds at Princes Park (p64), Long Beach (p67) and **Train Park** on for size.

EATING AT SALAMANCA & THE WATERFRONT: CLASSY DINNERS

Aløft: Hobart's best? Aløft occupies an lofty eyrie atop floating Brooke St Pier. Set-price menu, service, view... all excellent. *5.30-10pm Tue-Sat* **$$$**

Landscape: Inside the Henry Jones Art Hotel, moody, stone-walled Landscape headlines local meats (Cape Grim beef, Lenah Valley wallaby) and fine wines. *6-9.30pm* **$$$**

Frank: South American–inspired flavours designed for sharing, from empanadas to small plates. Sensational steaks. *noon-9.30pm* **$$$**

Peppina: Within the Tasman hotel, super-chef Massimo Mele plates-up divine modern Italian (try the *paccheri* pork-and-fennel sausage pasta). *7-10.30am daily, 5.30-8.30pm Mon-Sat* **$$$**

LGBTIQ+ HOBART

Telegraph Hotel: Wednesday night's Drag Trivia is a hoot down on the waterfront. *7-9pm Wed*

Society: Divine cocktails, late-night pizzas and raucous Drag Bingo at this glitzy Salamanca speakeasy. *6.30-9.30pm Thu twice monthly*

Altar Bar: In the city centre, 'Judy's' is an LGBTIQ+ dance party at this late-night lurker. Bust out the sequins. *9pm-late last Sat of the month*

Boodle Beasley: Queer-friendly bar in North Hobart, inside a gorgeous old shopfront on the Elizabeth St strip.

Shambles Brewery: Drag Bingo nights in North Hobart, with your irrepressible host Rosa Rita. *5-7pm last Sun of the month*

ALEX FONDA/SHUTTERSTOCK

Taste of Summer festival

and the waterfront bars start heaving with sunburned sailors. For landlubbers, the classic Sydney to Hobart experience is to promenade slowly (with ice cream) past the moored yachts, ooh-ing at expensive equipment and dreaming of the open-ocean glories. Or just head to the effervescent **Race Village** hub near Constitution Dock and have a beer instead.

Messing About in Boats

Derwent discoveries: sea cliffs, caves and a historic lighthouse

From the waterfront, there are a few ways to get out onto the Derwent and have a look around: catch the **MONA ROMA** ferry out to MONA (p76) for great views of the sci-fi-like Nyrstar zinc factory; shunt over to Bellerive on the eastern shore with Derwent Ferries; take a sea-kayak tour (p66); or sign up for a trip with **Pennicott Wilderness Journeys** *(pennicottjourneys.com.au; tours from adult/child $145/125).* The latter's 2½-hour boat tour takes you down-river offshore from Battery Point, Sandy Bay and Taroona; past sea cliffs and caves to Kingston Beach and Blackmans Bay; then out to the convict-built Iron Pot Lighthouse at the head of the

The best calamari in Hobart.

EATING AT SALAMANCA & THE WATERFRONT: SUPER SEAFOOD

Mures: A dockside regular. Upstairs is high-end; downstairs has oysters, ice-cream cones to go and the best seafood chowder in town. *8am-9pm* $$

Blue Eye: Seafood linguine, char-grilled octopus, sashimi, garlic-butter abalone – all sluiced down with Tasmanian wines and beers. *noon-10pm Tue-Sat* $$$

Fish Frenzy: Family-friendly fish and chips, inside and outside Elizabeth St Pier. Seagulls loiter with intent. *11.30am-8pm* $$

Flippers: Fish-shaped Flippers is the pick of the floating fish punts in Constitution Dock, serving fresh, sea-salty fish and chips. *9.30am-9pm* $

estuary – the oldest lighthouse in Australia (1832). Expect lots of local history, corny gags and maybe a dolphin or two.

What Does Summer Taste Like?

Hobart's end-of-year food festival

Coinciding with the arrival of the Sydney to Hobart Yacht Race fleet, the **Taste of Summer** *(tasteofsummer.com.au; free)* festival runs between Christmas and the first week of January, celebrating fine Tasmanian food, drink and music. Waterfront streets are blocked off as local restaurants, breweries, wineries and distilleries set up stalls in and around Princess Wharf 1 near Salamanca. It's free to get in, then you buy your food and drink. Shoot for a table in the sun and tune in to the live music (usually a big-name act on New Year's Eve).

Shore to Shore

Ferry over to Hobart's eastern shore for a look around

After Hobart's Tasman Bridge was hit by the hefty ship *Lake Illawarra* and collapsed in 1975, there were ferries all over the River Derwent, shuttling people between the eastern shore and the city. When the bridge was rebuilt, the ferries disappeared, until a **commuter ferry** *(derwentferries.com.au; one way adult/child $2/1)* between Brooke St Pier and Bellerive was reintroduced in 2021. And people loved it! Enjoy the ride to the 'sunny side of the river' (as eastern-shore locals never grow weary of telling you) and wander along the boardwalk, ogle some shiny hulls at Bellerive Yacht Club, munch some fish and chips, mooch along **Bellerive Beach**, have a pint at the old pub, then chug back across the river. Derwent Ferries fares are just a couple of bucks each way: pay by cash, card or Metro 'Greencard'. See the website for timetables.

Fridays by the Water

Hobart Twilight Market at Brooke St Pier

The enthusiastic congregation of food and drink vans at the **Hobart Twilight Market** *(hobarttwilightmarket.com.au; free)* operates rain, hail or shine year-round in front of Brooke St Pier. There's live music and plenty of booze flowing. Hot tip in a cold town: bring an all-weather jacket and a beanie for the outdoor tables. The market usually happens on the third and fourth Friday of each month: check the website for confirmed dates. Also at Long Beach (p67) in Sandy Bay over summer.

PARKLIFE

Too many people for a Saturday morning? Sidestep Salamanca Market and chill out in a nearby park.

St David's Park: Shady park (formerly a cemetery) behind Salamanca, with a heritage bandstand and dazzling autumn colours.

Princes Park: Atop Battery Point's namesake gun emplacement, with daisy-studded lawns and a fab playground.

Franklin Square: A big fountain, mature trees, lawns and a giant chess set, right in the middle of town.

Napoleon St Playground: Adjacent to the historic Battery Point Slipyards, with mesmerising River Derwent views.

Arthur Circus: Improbably cute circular park in Battery Point, ringed by historic Georgian cottages.

EATING AT SALAMANCA & THE WATERFRONT: MULTICULTURAL EATS

Maldini: Enduring Italian. Some say it's unadventurous; we say, 'If it ain't broke, don't fix it.' Fab risottos. *noon-2.30pm Wed-Fri, 5-9pm daily* $$

Kosaten Hobart: Darkened Japanese bunker in an old stone ordnance store. Sushi train, cold Asahi, good vegetarian. *11.30am-3pm & 5-8.30pm* $$

Mezethes: Tried-and-true Greek. Classics (moussaka, souvlaki, lamb, fish, saganaki, baklava) and indulgent seafood platters. *6-9pm Tue-Sun* $$

Suzie Luck's: Sublime Southeast Asian. Order the vegan yellow curry, the mushroom dumplings and a bangin' cocktail. Big on veg. *noon-10pm Mon-Fri, 4-11pm Sat, 5-9pm Sun* $$

Battery Point, Sandy Bay & South Hobart

COLONIAL HERITAGE, RESTAURANTS AND KUNANYI/MT WELLINGTON

This broad southern swathe encompasses two of Hobart's defining landmarks – the looming 1271m Kunanyi/Mt Wellington; and Battery Point, Hobart's first suburb and host to a photogenic clutch of historic houses. You could easily spend a day wandering little streets, ducking into galleries and pubs and catching unexpected water glimpses here. The Hampden Rd cafes and restaurants are great – but after dark, the Asian-inspired restaurant strip in affluent Sandy Bay has more of a pulse. The main UTAS campus is in Sandy Bay, too.

Kunanyi/Mt Wellington also demands a full day to explore its hike/bike trails and lookouts (wow!). At the foot of Kunanyi, with the mountain's main access roads, historic South Hobart hosts two of Hobart's key sights – Cascade Brewery and the Cascades Female Factory Historic Site. There are some decent cafes along Macquarie St, but again, once night falls, it'll only be the shadow of the mountain keeping you company.

GETTING AROUND

Battery Point is a five-minute shuffle uphill from Salamanca. Street parking is free here, but tightly time-limited – leave your wheels elsewhere. Metro bus services run along Sandy Bay Rd, and upper Macquarie St in South Hobart. The Red Decker Tourist hop-on, hop-off bus service connects all three suburbs. Walking from Sandy Bay into Battery Point? Expect a stiff climb up either Napoleon St, or the aptly named Nanny Goat Lane or Billy Goat Lane.

TOP TIP

Battery Point is only a five-minute walk up Kelly's Steps from Salamanca – though an equally interesting route follows Castray Esplanade then climbs through Princes Park to Runnymede St and the geometrically perfect Arthur Circus, with its curves of quaint Georgian cottages.

The Buried Battery

Take a walk down Hampden Rd

Beyond the Hampden Rd cafes, **Princes Park** is where Battery Point's gun battery once stood, built in 1818 to protect Hobart from the imagined threat of invading fleets of Americans, Russians, French, Dutch... The invasion never happened, the cannons are long gone, and Princes Park is now a peaceful spot for a picnic or a snooze in the sun, although you can still see the entrance to the old underground magazine (ammunition storage vault) on Castray Esplanade, where local blokes gambled and drank until the archway was sealed in 1934.

Away from the Fray

Discover Battery Point's secret places

Away from Hampden Rd, Battery Point is awash with hidden places and beguiling finds.

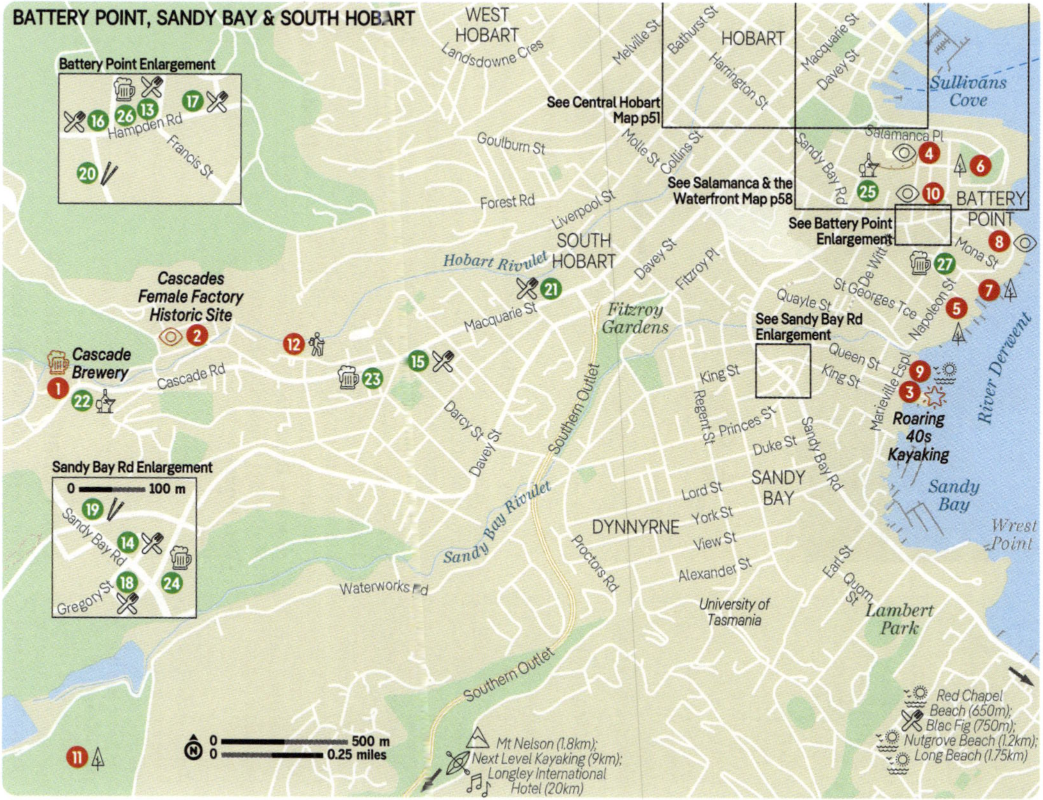

HIGHLIGHTS
1 Cascade Brewery
2 Cascades Female Factory Historic Site
3 Roaring 40s Kayaking

SIGHTS
4 Kelly's Steps
5 Napoleon St Playground
6 Princes Park
7 Purdon Featherstone Reserve
8 Secheron House
9 Short Beach
10 South Street
11 Waterworks Reserve

ACTIVITIES
12 Riv 5

EATING
13 Da Angelo
14 Don Camillo
15 Ginger Brown
16 Jackman & McRoss
17 Magic Curries
18 Metz
19 Suminato
20 Three Japanese
21 Vanidol's

DRINKING & NIGHTLIFE
22 Cascade Brewery Bar
23 Cascade Hotel
24 Mayfair
25 Preachers
26 Prince of Wales Hotel
27 Shipwrights Arms Hotel

ANDREW BALCOMBE/SHUTTERSTOCK

Sea-kayakers at Long Beach, Sandy Bay

HOBART'S ARCHITECTURAL HERITAGE

Fred Ward, director of 1+2 Architecture, shines a light on Hobart's historic buildings. *@l+2architecture*

Hobart has largely preserved its architectural heritage, avoiding the widespread 20th-century demolition experienced by other Australian cities. Notable treasures include the cottages of **Battery Point**, one of Australia's most intact Georgian suburbs; and the early-19th-century stone **warehouses and factories** around Sullivans Cove. Many of these have been thoughtfully repurposed into modern businesses, blending historical integrity with contemporary design. A great example is the former IXL Jam Factory on Hunter St, now the **UTAS School of Creative Arts**. Other highlights include the **Tasmanian Museum and Art Gallery** (TMAG; p52) and the exquisitely restored **Theatre Royal** (p55).

Skinny little **South Street**, off Hampden Rd, is crowded with historic timber and stone cottages that aren't particularly consistent or in particularly good condition. But South St just oozes maritime soul – the essence of Battery Point.

At the bottom of adjacent Kelly St, the foot-worn 1840 **Kelly's Steps** are named after one-time Hobart harbourmaster James Kelly and traverse the formerly impassable quarry face between Battery Point and Salamanca.

Another hidden gem is the little waterside **Purdon Featherstone Reserve** at the foot of Trumpeter St near Battery Point's last remaining slip yards. National Trust–listed **Secheron House** is tucked away nearby, Battery Point's grandest manor (1831).

But sometimes it's transient occurrences that give Battery Point its character: a little pile of seashells on a doorstep; or a graffiti poem on a pub wall: *'Three flag-swept days/Ships monstrous and transitory/Heroes I could not captain'*.

See Hobart from the Sea

Sea-kayak into Sullivans Cove

Clear, calm mornings on Sullivans Cove are perfect for sea-kayaking – especially if you've got zero experience! **Roaring 40s Kayaking** *(roaring40skayaking.com.au; tours adult/*

EATING IN BATTERY POINT: OUR PICKS

Jackman & McRoss: Famous Battery Point bakery-cafe: breakfast, brunch, breads and baked delights. Footpath tables when it's warm enough. *7am-5pm* $

Da Angelo: This classic ristorante packs out each night (book ahead). Pastas, pizzas and Carlton Football Club fandom. *noon-2.30pm Fri, 5-9.30pm daily* $$

Three Japanese: Atmospheric Japanese: try the pork belly charcoal skewers. Scary sake selection. *5.30-9pm Tue-Sun* $$

Magic Curries: Sip a cold Kingfisher beer in these magically coloured interiors and await your face-meltingly hot beef vindaloo. Excellent vegetarian, too. *5-9.30pm* $$

child $140/85) runs a 2½-hour paddling trip most mornings between October and April, suitable for all skill levels and kids over seven. The put-in is at Sandy Bay's Short Beach, then the trip heads north around Battery Point into Sullivans Cove. You'll paddle right into Constitution Dock for a floating fish-and-chip lunch. Day trips and multi-day trips also available.

New to kayaking and want a lesson? Contact **Next Level Kayaking** *(nextlevelkayaking.com.au; lessons from $110)* at Kingston Beach just south of Hobart.

Sandy Bay Sand

Beaches, long and short

Sandy Bay has a string of interesting urban beaches that improve the further south you head. **Short Beach** on Marieville Esplanade is barely 150m in length, where the Sandy Bay Rivulet meets the River Derwent. Famous Tasmanian actor Errol Flynn swam here as a callow lad. The '1909' sign commemorates his birth year.

Super-secret **Red Chapel Beach** is accessed through a gate at the bottom of its eponymous park on Sandy Bay Rd. Further south again, **Nutgrove Beach** is a longer, breezy expanse, often dotted with small sailing skiffs – but it's **Long Beach** around Sandy Bay Point that's the best spot for a dip. Swim out to the pontoon and survey the scene. Around the southern headland is an old lighthouse and a musty abandoned gun bunker to explore.

Lakeside Serenity

Chill out at Waterworks Reserve

In the valley between Sandy Bay and South Hobart at the top of Waterworks Rd, bushy **Waterworks Reserve** *(hobartcity.com.au; free)* surrounds two historic reservoirs that still supply much of Hobart's drinking water. Undiscovered by tourists, these grassy slopes host a scattering of heritage buildings, BBQs, picnic tables, playgrounds and rampant native wildlife. Sit in the sun and read your trashy airport novel, or hike/bike the rugged Pipeline Track (p69) to Fern Tree.

Hobart's Smaller Mountain

River views from not-so-mountainous Mt Nelson

Got wheels? Drive up the Southern Outlet highway, or tackle 'the Bends' – aka Nelson Rd, with its six switchback hairpin

CAPTAIN BLOOD

Legendary swashbuckling actor Errol Flynn was born in Battery Point, first showing his handsome, future-moustachioed face at the Queen Alexandra Hospital on Hampden Rd on 20 June 1909. Flynn lived in Hobart, where his father was a professor of biology, until he was sent to school in London at the rather pivotal age of 14. Flynn went on to become a dashing Hollywood superstar, lighting up the screen in films like *Captain Blood* (1935), *The Charge of the Light Brigade* (1936) and *The Adventures of Robin Hood* (1938). A notorious drinker and philanderer (his bedroom antics inspiring the phrase 'In like Flynn'), he expired prematurely while visiting Canada in 1959, aged just 50. Listen to Australian Crawl's 1981 song 'Errol' for further insights.

EATING IN SANDY BAY: OUR PICKS

Metz: All-day bar-bistro on the Sandy Bay strip, in a reinvented heritage house. Sicilian eggs and a breakfast Bloody Mary? *10.30am-9.30pm Mon-Thu, 8am-10pm Fri-Sun* $$

Suminato: Modern Japanese using top local produce. Slick interior design and lots of veg and gluten-free offerings. *noon-2.30pm Tue-Sun, 5-9pm daily* $$

Don Camillo: Quite possibly Hobart's oldest restaurant (1965), with a tight menu of classic pastas, risottos and meat dishes. No pizza! *5-8pm Tue-Sun* $$$

Blac Fig: Part providore, part cafe and part gelato shop, Blac Fig is an essential pit stop in Lower Sandy Bay. Lovely staff. *7am-7pm* $

ON THE TOWN

A common misconception about female convicts transported from England, Ireland and Scotland to Tasmania is that they were mostly sex workers being punished for their profession. Convict ship records would label a prisoner as 'On the Town' if indeed they had been a sex worker – but the term was also applied to vagrant transportees who'd been living on church handouts. Indeed, so grim was life in England for unmarried, uneducated, impoverished young women that many deliberately committed crimes in order to be sent to the other side of the planet, hoping that their lives would somehow improve – could they be any worse? Unfortunately, for many who ended up at the Female Factory, the answer was 'yes'.

corners – to the lookout atop 352m **Mt Nelson** *(parks.tas.gov.au; free)*. It's more of a hill than a mountain, but the views over Hobart and the River Derwent estuary are excellent. The 1811 **Mt Nelson Signal Station** here was once a semaphore link between Hobart and Port Arthur penal colony. You can also walk to the top via the 90-minute return **Truganini Track** from Cartwright Reserve off the Channel Hwy in Sandy Bay.

Australia's Oldest Beers

Tour Cascade Brewery and sample the good stuff

Standing in startling Gothic isolation next to the Hobart Rivulet, **Cascade Brewery** *(cascadebreweryco.com.au; brewery tour $38, historic tour adult/child $23/12)* is Australia's oldest brewery (1824) and is still pumping out superb beers. Daily one-hour tours dive into the beer-making process, with a tasting paddle at the end (try the pale ale). Under-18s aren't permitted on the main brewery tour (take the family-friendly Historic Tour instead); and brewery machinery might not be running if you're here on a weekend (brewers have weekends too). Wear flat, closed-toe shoes. Want to skip straight to the liquid stuff? Cascade Brewery Bar is across the road.

Notorious Strumpets & Dangerous Girls

Experience the haunting Cascades Female Factory Historic Site

The UNESCO World Heritage–listed **Cascades Female Factory Historic Site** *(femalefactory.org.au; adult/child admission $35/20, 1hr tour $40/22)* in South Hobart was where female convicts were incarcerated and put to work in vile conditions. Around 12,500 women were transported to Tasmania, and during its peak years of operation between 1828 and 1856, the Female Factory could hold up to 1200 women. Children suffered here, too: convict women sent to work on settlers' farms would often return pregnant, give birth to their illegitimate children – then lose them to orphanages. Admission includes a 45-minute guided tour of the hauntingly spare yards with their interpretive installations; or book a one-hour themed **Notorious Strumpets and Dangerous Girls** tour, telling the tales of seven resilient convict women. See the website for tour times; kids' tours also available.

Try the Killer Raspberry fruited sour ale.

DRINKING IN BATTERY POINT & SANDY BAY: BEST FOR BEERS

Mayfair: Enduring Sandy Bay pub with live music, craft beers and vegan bar snacks. *3-10pm Mon-Thu, noon-11pm Fri & Sat, noon-10pm Sun*

Shipwrights Arms Hotel: 1846 'Shippies' near the old Battery Point shipyards has had a slick makeover, but the front bar is still sea-salty. *noon-11pm*

Prince of Wales Hotel: Battery Point's POW is an architectural poke in the eye, but it does cracking pub food and ice-cold local lagers. *11am-10pm Sun-Thu, to midnight Fri & Sat*

Preachers: Uphill from Salamanca, this backstreet beer garden (complete with old bus) has beaut brews and burgers. *noon-midnight*

SUE BURTON PHOTOGRAPHY/SHUTTERSTOCK

Cascades Female Factory Historic Site

Ride the Pipeline

Tackle a classic Hobart mountain-bike trail

This classic 36km-return trail makes for a rewarding MTB ride. From Waterworks Reserve (p67) behind Sandy Bay, crank the gears uphill through dry eucalypt forest, joining the **Pipeline Track** *(wellingtonpark.org.au/bike-riding; free)* to Halls Saddle. Follow Huon Rd to the far end of Fern Tree Park, where the track continues, hemmed by tall trees. From Silver Falls Junction, continue through damp forest to Pipeline Track Hut, one of many shelters (official and unofficial) on Kunanyi/Mt Wellington. At Wellington Falls Track, lock your bike for the 80-minute return walk to Wellington Falls. The return ride is good fun – all downhill! No bike? Try **Hobart Bike Hire** *(hobartbikehire.com.au; bike hire per day from $44).*

WHALES IN THE DERWENT

In the 1830s Hobartians joked about walking across the River Derwent on the backs of whales, and complained about being kept awake at night by whales cavorting offshore. A glance across the river from Sandy Bay might reveal any number of spouting blowholes and splashing flukes. In typical Tasmanian style, the ensuing whaling boom was catastrophic, driving local populations of southern right and humpback whales to near extinction. Though still rare, the occasional forgiving whale returns to the Derwent during their June–July northbound and October–November southbound migration. If you spy one, call the Parks & Wildlife Service whale hotline on 0427 WHALES (0427 942 537).

EATING & DRINKING IN SOUTH HOBART: OUR PICKS

Cascade Brewery Bar: At the foot of Kunanyi/Mt Wellington, with heritage gardens and brewery views. Tasting paddles and classic pub grub. *11am-9pm*

Vanidol's: Modern Asian, with a Thai twist. Try the *namtok* warm BBQ chilli-beef salad. *11am-2pm & 5-8.30pm Tue-Sat* $$

Ginger Brown: The pick of the Macquarie St cafes. Great baked eggs and coffee; kid- and cyclist-friendly. *7.30am-3pm Mon-Fri, from 8.30am Sat & Sun* $

Cascade Hotel: There were a dozen pubs in South Hobart once; Cascade Hotel (1846) is the last one. Super seafood, schnitzels and Cascade beer. *10am-9pm*

TERRY SZE/SHUTTERSTOCK

Kunanyi/Mt Wellington lookout

TOP EXPERIENCE

Kunanyi/Mt Wellington

Majestically sky-high or mysteriously shrouded in cloud, 1271m-high Kunanyi/Mt Wellington is so large it generates its own weather patterns. Criss-crossed by walking and mountain-biking trails and dappled with winter snow, Kunanyi is Hobart's beacon, its protector, its playground and its weather barometer...and the views from the top are awesome! A drive to the wind-lashed summit is a defining Hobart experience.

DON'T MISS

- The view from the top
- Hiking to the Organ Pipes
- Winter snow
- Mountain-bike trails
- Coffee at Lost Freight
- Warming up at Fern Tree Tavern
- Lost World

The Summit

Assess the city far below from the lofty top of Kunanyi/Mt Wellington. The sealed 12km Pinnacle Rd from the hippie 'hood of Fern Tree to the summit was the brainchild of Albert Ogilvie, premier of Tasmania in the 1930s. When the Great Depression hit hard in Hobart, Ogilvie deemed that all those unemployed hands would be best engaged in doing something constructive for the community. After several years of back-breaking labour, Pinnacle Rd opened in 1937. Initially very visible from the city and not entirely popular, the road became know as 'Ogilvie's Scar'. These days the road has mostly been

PRACTICALITIES

● wellingtonpark.org.au ● free

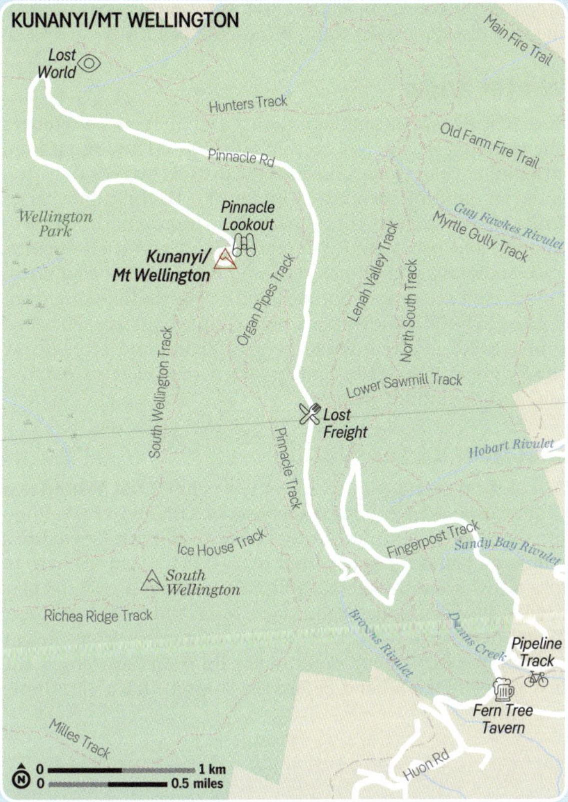

TOP TIPS

- The Springs is a handy spot to jump on several mountain-biking tracks, including Radfords Track and the 11km North–South Track to Glenorchy.
- Notorious escaped convict/bushranger Rocky Whelan, who murdered 12 men, lived in Rocky Whelan's Cave, a short walk below the Springs off Fingerpost then Fern Glade tracks.
- **Lost Freight** is a shipping-container cafe at the Springs, with strong coffee, hot pies, wraps and brownies. Most welcome!
- Full of hikers and mountain-bikers, earthy **Fern Tree Tavern** at the base of Pinnacle Rd is a top spot for a cold beer, a hot lunch and a roaring fire.

obscured by trees; much more visible are the two huge transmission towers at the peak. At the summit car park, put on every layer of clothing you own and dash to the curvy-roofed **observation shelter**, in which you can hide from the wind and check out the eye-popping views. Don't be deterred if the sky looks overcast from sea level: often the summit rises above the gloom, and the view from the top extends across a magical sea of cloud-tops.

Hiking & Biking

The mountain is criss-crossed by a web of hiking paths, bike tracks, horse-riding trails and fire roads, some well-trodden and wide, some overgrown and intriguing. Popular tracks include the Radfords Track, Pinnacle Track, Fern Glade Track, Pipeline Track (p69), the steep Zig Zag Track and the Organ Pipes Circuit (p73), looping below Kunanyi's trademark dolerite cliffs. Check out greaterhobarttrails.com.au for detailed track and planning info. At any time of year on the mountain, expect rapid and extreme weather shifts: this ain't no walk in the park (well, it is, but you know what we mean – be

CHARLES DARWIN CLIMBS KUNANYI

In February 1836, esteemed English naturalist Charles Darwin sailed into Hobart and climbed Kunanyi/Mt Wellington. Darwin was intrigued by the mountain's geology and flora, vividly describing the sunny day he spent here in his book *The Voyage of the Beagle*. Darwin stayed in Hobart for two weeks, before setting sail for Western Australia (no, not Darwin – he never actually visited his eponymous city).

prepared). Take warm clothes and wet-weather gear on even the shortest mountain walk. Wind-chill is a killer.

Winter Snow

Sure, Canberra has sub-zero nights and Melbourne requires one to don a woolly hat occasionally, but do any Australian cities other than Hobart have access to ACTUAL SNOW!? 'No', is the resounding response. Kunanyi/Mt Wellington wears a white cloak regularly throughout the winter months (June to August, and occasionally in late autumn and early spring), with snowfalls sometimes reaching down into the suburbs. Skiing isn't an option, but local kids grow up knowing what it's like to build a snowman and hurl snowballs at each other. Pinnacle Rd is often closed before, during and after heavy snows: check hobartcity.com.au for live road closure updates, and a nifty summit webcam.

Discover a Lost World

A real local secret (not so secret now, eh?), **Lost World** is a dramatic boulder field near the peak of Kunanyi/Mt Wellington, backed by a miniature version of the Organ Pipes. Rock climbers, boulder-hoppers and bushwalkers venture here to lose a few hours in surreal solitude, scan the views, or play hide-and-seek among the massive fractured hunks of stone. To get here, take the little track heading north from the car park at 'Big Bend', 9km up Pinnacle Rd from Fern Tree – the last major hairpin bend before the summit. It's a 45-minute walk one way.

BOY_ANUPONG/GETTY IMAGES

Snow on Kunanyi/Mt Wellington

HIKE THE ORGAN PIPES CIRCUIT

This half-day walk below the towering Organ Pipes on Kunanyi/Mt Wellington (p70) passes historic huts, bushland, rocky slopes and mesmerising lookouts.

START	END	LENGTH
The Springs	The Springs	9.2km; 4hr

From 1 **The Springs**, the trail heads into dense myrtle forest, just far enough below Pinnacle Rd to feel like you're in the wilds. About 30 minutes in, 2 **Sphinx Rock** is a sandstone outcrop with views sweeping across the city and south. Beyond a couple of small creeks, 3 **Rock Cabin** (built from rocks) is right on the trail and has sheltered many a storm-stuck hiker.

Track downhill to a bush clearing and chunky stone 4 **Junction Cabin**. Scoff some chocolate inside then head uphill on Hunters Track. Looming above the trail, lofty 5 **Crocodile Rock** packs a surprise punch. Explore the small caves here (are you in there Elton John?) then continue uphill. A vast open 6 **scree slope** soon emerges – a slow cascade of fractured boulders tumbling inexorably down the mountainside. Continue ever upwards, turning left onto the Old Hobartians Track and rising to Pinnacle Rd.

If you haven't had lunch, 7 **The Chalet** hut awaits, an even kilometre above the River Derwent below. Behind the Chalet, the trail delivers more show-stopping views, then tracks across the base of the 8 **Organ Pipes**. Soaring 120m high and visible from the city, this wall of huge hexagonal dolerite columns is rock-climbing nirvana. Truck downhill (passing crimson waratah blooms in spring) to the peculiar UTAS 9 **Cosmic Ray Observatory** as you approach the Springs.

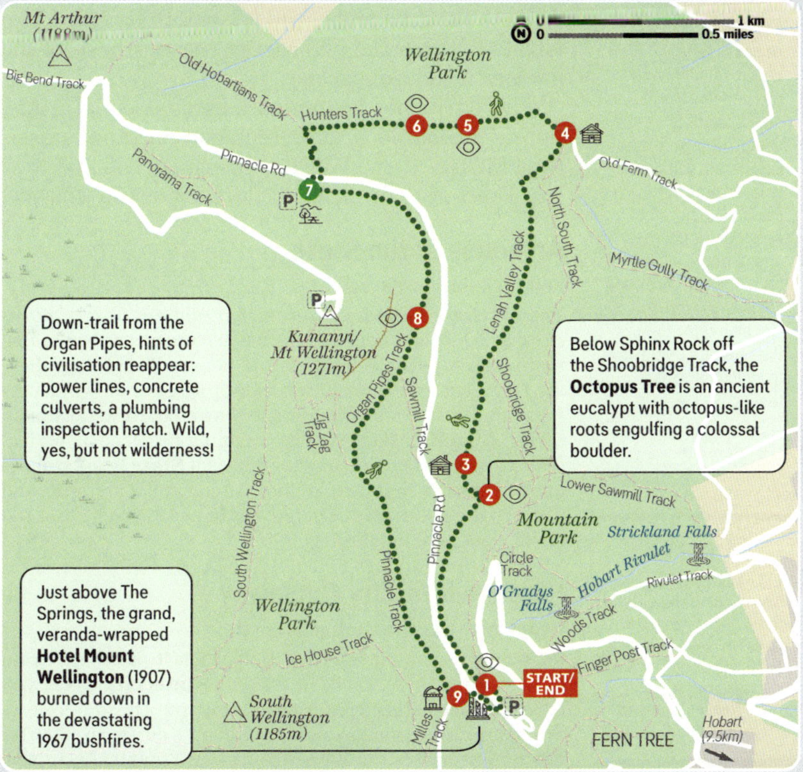

North Hobart

EAT STREET, LIVE TUNES AND MONA

Bohemian North Hobart ('NoHo' to those with a sense of humour) is a recipe for a fun night out. Roughly bounded by Federal St to the north and Burnett St to the south, the buzzy Elizabeth St restaurant strip serves up everything from Indian, Italian, Thai, Middle Eastern and Korean to burger joints, kebab shops, bakeries, cafes, patisseries and espresso nooks. Add craft-beer pubs, classy bars and Hobart's best (only) arthouse cinema and staunchest live-music room to the mix, and NoHo is a potent package. The vibe here is relaxed and earthy, the antithesis of the flashier waterfront scene.

A short drive north is one of Hobart's essential attractions – the fabulous, irreverent, enriching and unsettling MONA, David Walsh's Museum of Old and New Art. Don't even think about skipping out on this one.

GETTING AROUND

The main North Hobart strip, between Burnett St and Federal St, is a 20-minute walk up Elizabeth St from the city centre. Parking, as usual, tends to be a royal pain. Any bus heading north on Elizabeth St should get you there. E-scooters will get you as far as the Republic Bar. Ubers abound – you'll need one to get to MONA, 10km further north, or catch the ferry! You can also ride along the Intercity Cycleway to MONA, if you're feeling perky.

Arthouse at the State

Fellini, Kubrick, Marvel

The old **State Cinema** *(statecinema.com.au; tickets adult/child $22/17)* dates back to 1913, when it opened as one of Tasmania's first purpose-built picture houses. These days there are 11 screens here (including a rooftop screen), showing films from the latest three-hour epics to shaky handheld documentaries. **Angelika Bar**, with its warming fireplace, is perfect for a pre-movie martini; and the adjacent **State Bookstore** is one of Hobart's best (art, architecture, travel, biography and film are the mainstays). There's a **cafe** out the back, too. You could exist here indefinitely.

TOP TIP

Eat early if you're going to an evening show at the State Cinema midweek. As hip as NoHo is, it's mostly tumbleweeds and crickets on Elizabeth St after 9pm. Weekends are less subdued.

Bike the Intercity Cycleway

Pedal your way into Hobart's north

Following a disused rail line (Hobart's last passenger train clicked along these tracks in 1978), the **Intercity Cycleway** *(hobartcity.com.au; free)* runs 15km from the waterfront, around the hilly Domain and into Hobart's northern suburbs. En route it passes the Royal Tasmanian Botanical Gardens,

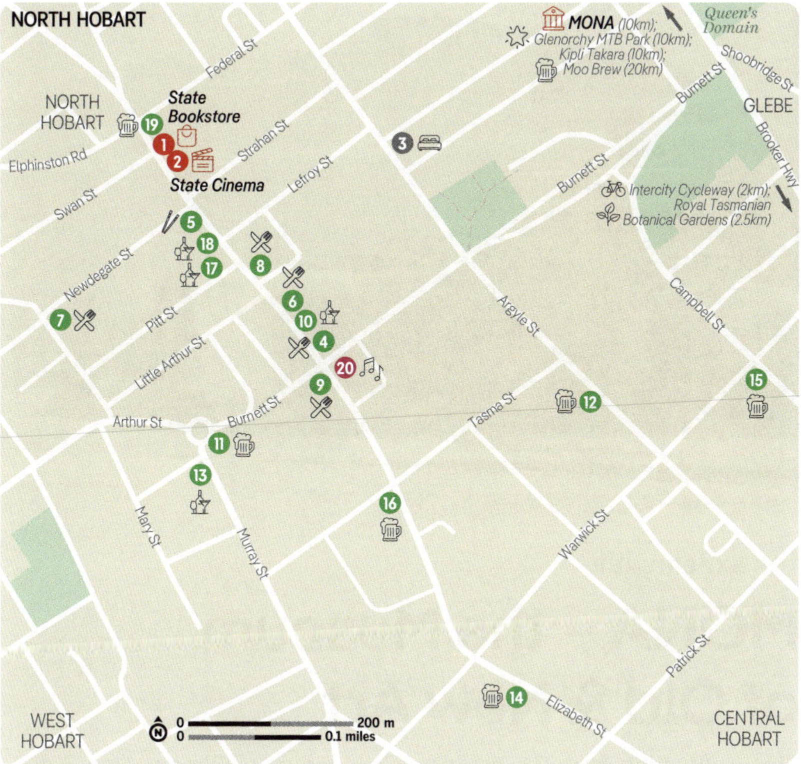

HIGHLIGHTS
1 State Bookstore
2 State Cinema

SLEEPING
3 Waggon & Horses

EATING
4 Annapurna
5 Kalbi
6 Kebab Rehab
7 Providence
see 5 Raincheck Lounge
8 Renown Milk Bar
9 Room for a Pony

DRINKING & NIGHTLIFE
see 2 Angelika Bar
10 Boodle Beasley
11 Crescent Hotel
12 Deep South Brewing Co
13 Ogee
14 Shambles Brewery
15 Tasmanian Inn
16 T-Bone Brewing Co
17 Voodoo Lounge
18 Willing Bros
19 Winston

ENTERTAINMENT
20 Republic Bar

ducks under the Tasman Bridge, then reaches Cornelian Bay, with its sports grounds, boatsheds and cemetery. From here the Cycleway cuts inland though groovy Moonah and edgy Glenorchy, before reaching the river again near MONA (p76). Hire some wheels from Hobart Bike Hire (p69).

Botanic Royalty

Wander through Australia's second-oldest botanical gardens

Over the leafy Domain from North Hobart, the lush, sloping **Royal Tasmanian Botanical Gardens** *(rtbg.tas.gov.au; free)* are Australia's second-oldest (1818) – 14 hectares of local

continued on p78

CHAMELEONSEYE/SHUTTERSTOCK

TOP EXPERIENCE

MONA – the Museum of Old & New Art

Think, eat, drink, feel. The provocative Museum of Old and New Art (MONA) at Berriedale is David Walsh's crazed ode to his hometown – simultaneously delivering a magnificent 'up yours' to the art-world establishment. Explore the challenging, the rare, the ancient, the horny and the downright disgusting as you wander through dim-lit stone galleries cut into a promontory above the River Derwent.

DON'T MISS

Snake

MONA Confessional

Chamber of Pausiris

Amarna

Cloaca Professional

Drinking in the dimness

Live music

The Backstory

MONA mastermind David Walsh grew up in nearby Glenorchy and turned his mathematical genius to professional gambling – and made a pile of money. An avid art collector, he originally bought the on-site **Moorilla Estate** winery, then launched MONA in 2011. MONA is now the largest private art gallery in the southern hemisphere, and has boosted tourism and Tasmania's general self-esteem immeasurably – the so-called 'MONA effect'. The ever-expanding MONA world also includes **Moo Brew** brewery (off-site); **Manky Sally's** bar in Salamanca (Moo Brew's public face – try the pilsener); the

PRACTICALITIES

● mona.net.au ● non-Tasmanian adult/child $39/free, Tasmanian adult/child $5/free ● 10am-5pm Thu-Mon fabulously unhinged Dark Mofo (p61) winter festival; luxury accommodation and even a recording studio. Visionary and rogue in equal measure, Walsh isn't short on ideas or ambition.

Must-See MONA

It's hard to know where to start at MONA. Perhaps the best approach is to suspend preconceived ideas of a 'plan', wander through the subterranean galleries, and see what kind of fun comes your way.

There are, of course, some must-sees in the vast collection here. Don't bypass **Snake** by Sidney Nolan, a 46m-long array of 1620 panels exploring the connections between myth and modernity; and the **Chamber of Pausiris**, containing the coffin and mummy of a 2000-year old Egyptian.

Other essentials include the very cathartic **MONA Confessional**, in which you can broadcast your sins anonymously to random listeners far above; James Turrell's above-ground archi-light installation **Amarna**, active at sunrise and sunset (stick around); and every kid's favourite, the aromatic **Cloaca Professional** poo machine. The machine gets fed in morning; the poo comes out around 2pm.

Then there are the regularly rotating, head-tripping guest exhibitions. Lost in time, space, art and darkness, three hours can pass at MONA and you still won't know how to get back to daylight.

Fine Wine, Fine Food

There are some ace places to eat and drink at MONA – it's all part of the experience.

Heavy Metal Kitchen Indulgent burgers, grilled meat sandwiches, charred cauliflower and hot chips for lunch on the lawn. Rock on.

Moorilla Wine Bar Moorilla winery was here for ages before MONA showed up. Outside the museum entrance, it's share plates, coffee and drinks in the sun. Plenty of vegan; open all day.

Void Bar Gasping for a Manhattan and some crunchy jalapeno corn? Follow the live music into the half-light, 17m underground. Museum admission applies.

Faro Bar + Restuarant Fine-dining in a light-filled space, with massive glass windows overlooking the river. The menu changes constantly: high-end and superb. Lunch and dinner, too.

The Source Five-star lunch service in an immaculate restaurant, with river views and top Tasmania ingredients (ooh, oysters). Fixed-price menus or à la carte.

Architecture as Art

Once you've ogled the art and eaten and drunk your fill, kick back on the lawn and check out mona.net.au/museum/architecture. Along with David Walsh's take on the colourful Pharos wing, there's an entertaining interview with architect James Pearce from designers Fender Katsalidis, explaining the thinking behind the architecture and the museum's amazing site. Then head back to the bar.

EMBRACE THE O

To make any sense of MONA's labelless artworks, you'd be well advised to download the 'O' app to your phone – a marvel of geospatial programming that reveals all you ever needed to know about the artwork you're standing in front of. And probably a few things you didn't. It's also useful for finding the exit. BYO headphones (there's audio).

TOP TIPS

- You can drive to MONA, but the ferry is much more fun. Book the Posh Pit for champagne and canapes.
- For most people, a decent half-day at MONA is plenty.
- For some exhibits (eg *MONA Confessional*), you need to queue up via the O. When it's your turn, the O will let you know.
- Tasmanians get into MONA for free, but still have to book and pay a $5 deposit. Bring ID.
- Bike it to MONA from Salamanca in 50 minutes, along the Intercity Cycleway (p74).
- Some of MONA's exhibits are, well, pervy. If you blush easily, ask which rooms to avoid. Ditto if you're strobe-averse.

BEST LIVE MUSIC

Big-name bands hit MyState Bank Arena in Glenorchy or the city-centre Odeon. Sold out? Go here:

Republic Bar: North Hobart mainstay for singer-songwriters, open-mic nights, covers bands and touring rock interlopers.

Pablo's Cocktails & Dreams: Hidden, atmospheric, late-night jazz bunker off Harrington St in the city.

Altar Bar: Touring and local metal, alt-rock and dance acts in the city centre.

Jack Greene: A few Salamanca bars have live acoustic troubadours; Jack Greene is the pick of the bunch.

Longley International Hotel: Pub over the back of Kunanyi/Mt Wellington, attracting surprisingly big names (no neighbours to annoy).

continued from p75
and cool-climate exotic plants, some more than 200 years old. Wander between the Subantarctic Plant House, the endemic Tasmanian Collection, and collections of Chinese and Japanese plants – or just snooze on the lawns. Near the main entrance is the site of the **former Beaumaris Zoo**, where the last captive thylacine (Tasmanian tiger) died in 1936; a couple of dilapidated enclosures linger in the weeds. Driving here is easiest – or from the city it's a 30-minute stroll (or a 10-minute cycle) along the Intercity Cycleway.

Bush Tucker Tours

Taste traditional Tasmanian Aboriginal foods

Forage for seasonal bush tucker on these fantastic 90-minute Palawa-run **Kipli Takara** *(palawakipli.com/kiplitakara*

EATING IN NORTH HOBART: OUR PICKS

Room for a Pony: Wood-fired pizzas and heated tables outside; beer and nachos inside. *7am-2.30pm Mon & Tue, to 9pm Wed, Thu & Sun, to midnight Fri & Sat* $$	**Raincheck Lounge:** Conversation and boho vibes flow freely at this pioneering North Hobart cafe-bistro-bar. Kid-friendly, too. *7am-3pm* $$	**Providence:** Perfect backstreet cafe with newspapers, great coffee and a reading room! Order the sweet potato rosti and turn some pages. *7am-3pm* $	**Renown Milk Bar:** One of Australia's oldest milk bars (1920s), Renown does super shakes, smoothies, coffees and jars of chocs and lollies. *10am-9pm* $
Annapurna: The best curry joint in North Hobart (there are a few). Try the balti prawns, tandoori lamb cutlets or veggie thali. *5-9.30pm* $$	**Kalbi:** Superbly spicy Korean soups, fried chicken and *pa jeon* (green onion pancakes). Gets busy – book ahead. *noon-2pm Thu-Sat, 5-9pm Tue-Sun* $$	**Ogee:** Part moody restaurant, part wine bar in an appealing old red-brick corner shopfront. Come for a pinot, stay for the tagliatelle. *noon-2.30pm Fri-Sun, 5-9.30pm Wed-Sun* $$$	**Kebab Rehab:** Late night? Improve your tomorrow morning with a salty lamb kebab, loaded with hummus, tahini and chilli. *11am-midnight* $

KIRSTEN COVINGTON/SHUTTERSTOCK

Japanese Garden, Royal Tasmanian Botanical Gardens (p75)

-bushtucker-tours; adult/child $90/25) guided tours at Piyura Kitina/Risdon Cove, across the river from Glenorchy on Hobart's eastern shore. Tours explain how these foods still play an important part in modern Palawa culture, and finish with a tasting of local ingredients, including wallaby, mutton bird, scallops, pepperberry, kunzea, lemon myrtle and wattleseed. DIY transport; book online.

MTB in the Burbs

Go with the flow at Glenorchy Mountain Bike Park

The council-run **Glenorchy MTB Park** *(www.gcc.tas.gov.au; free)* backs onto Kunanyi/Mt Wellington at the end of the 11km North–South Track from Fern Tree. There are 13 trails here, ranging from easy to extremely difficult, including loops and out-and-back, cross-country and downhill runs. Fun! Access via Tolosa St.

TANGLES

Legendary Australian cricketer and all-round good guy Max Walker (1948–2016), nicknamed 'Tangles' for his zany (but highly effective) bowling style, grew up in North Hobart. Max senior ran the big red-brick Empire Hotel – now the Republic Bar – where Max junior was a regular annoyance underfoot. Tangles was also a trained architect, a writer (14 books!), a TV presenter, a public speaker, a professional footballer and father of five. Raise a glass to Tangles – an irrepressible Tasmanian character – as you catch a live band at the Republic today. Conversation starter at the bar: 'How many Test matches did Tangles play, and how many wickets did he take?' Answer: 34 and 138, at an average of 27.47, ahead of other greats like Mitchell Johnson and Jeff Thomson. Impressive!

DRINKING IN NORTH HOBART: PUBS & BARS

Crescent Hotel: Faux-Tudor exteriors disguise everybody's favourite local inside, with good Guinness and a rooftop terrace. *noon-10pm Sun-Thu, to midnight Fri & Sat*	**Winston:** Raffish corner pub with craft beer, a pool table and US-style eats (don't skimp on the Carolina Reaper chilli mayo). *4-10.30pm*	**Tasmanian Inn:** A few blocks away from the Elizabeth St fray, the Tas Inn is all honky-tonk, hipster and rainbow. *4-11pm Tue-Sat*	**Shambles Brewery:** Shamble into Shambles, down Elizabeth St en route to the city, for a pint of the house pale. *4-10pm Wed & Thu, noon-midnight Fri & Sat, to 8pm Sun*
Deep South Brewing Co: Camouflaged as a warehouse. Flat Witch XPA, wood-fired pizzas, occasional live tunes. *4pm-10.30pm Tue-Thu, from noon Fri & Sat*	**T-Bone Brewing Co:** Down on the corner, T-Bone's quirky ales should impress. Love the barrel-aged stout. *4-9pm Wed, 2-9pm Thu, 2-11pm Fri & Sat, 2-8pm Sun*	**Voodoo Lounge:** Wacko, kitsch, Goth...all of the above. Open the coffin door behind Pancho Villa and order a cold Mexican lager. *6-11pm Thu-Sat*	**Willing Bros:** Cosy wine bar with a fantastic vino selection and sophisticated share plates. Classy, classy. *4.30-10pm Wed-Sat*

Beyond Hobart

BEACHES, HISTORY AND ACCESSIBLE WILDERNESS

Places

Right next to Hobart Airport is achingly deserted Seven Mile Beach – 7 miles of sandy, safe swimming. Craft beer, oysters and superb whisky aren't too far away, while the wineries and gastronomic pleasures of the Coal River Valley beckon on the run up to historic Richmond, with its streets of restored Georgian buildings and much-photographed bridge.

A string of beaches runs south from Hobart to Taroona, where the sheer Alum Cliffs mark a divide before the seductive arc of Kingston Beach. Pack your snorkel and your wetsuit to meet the underwater locals at Tinderbox.

Heading northwest from Hobart, the fertile fields around New Norfolk and the Derwent Valley are striped with hops and vines, while Mt Field National Park offers a taste of true wilderness: waterfalls, fagus and alpine tarns.

TOP TIP

Plan your moves: getting from A to B can take longer than you think here. Taroona, Kingston Beach and Tinderbox are an easy afternoon; give Mt Field National Park a full day. Seven Mile Beach, Richmond, the Coal River Valley and Cambridge are closer to the airport: save them for last if you're flying out.

Seven Mile Beach

TIME FROM HOBART: **25MIN**

Out near the airport, a short drive through back-street beach shacks, then a short walk through the dunes, delivers you to one of Tasmania's most underrated beaches, the aptly named **Seven Mile Beach** (yep – it's 7 miles long), with safe swimming and an occasionally surfable point break. A walk here is guaranteed to blow out the cobwebs; chances are it'll just be you and a few dog walkers.

Cinematic views from Single Hill

On the western end of Seven Mile Beach is the formidable **Single Hill** *(greaterhobarttrails.com.au; free)*. At just 200m high it ain't alpine, but the ascent is a real workout! The 5.3km return track zigzags up the slope, with increasingly eye-popping views. Catch your breath at the top and survey

GETTING AROUND

You will need your own vehicle to fully explore this area. Public buses from Hobart also run to Seven Mile Beach; to Taroona, Kingston Beach and Blackmans Bay; to Richmond via Cambridge and the Coal River Valley; and to New Norfolk, several times daily. Day tours run to Richmond and Mt Field National Park (there's no public transport here), while minivan booze tours hit the wineries, distilleries and breweries in the Derwent and Coal River Valleys.

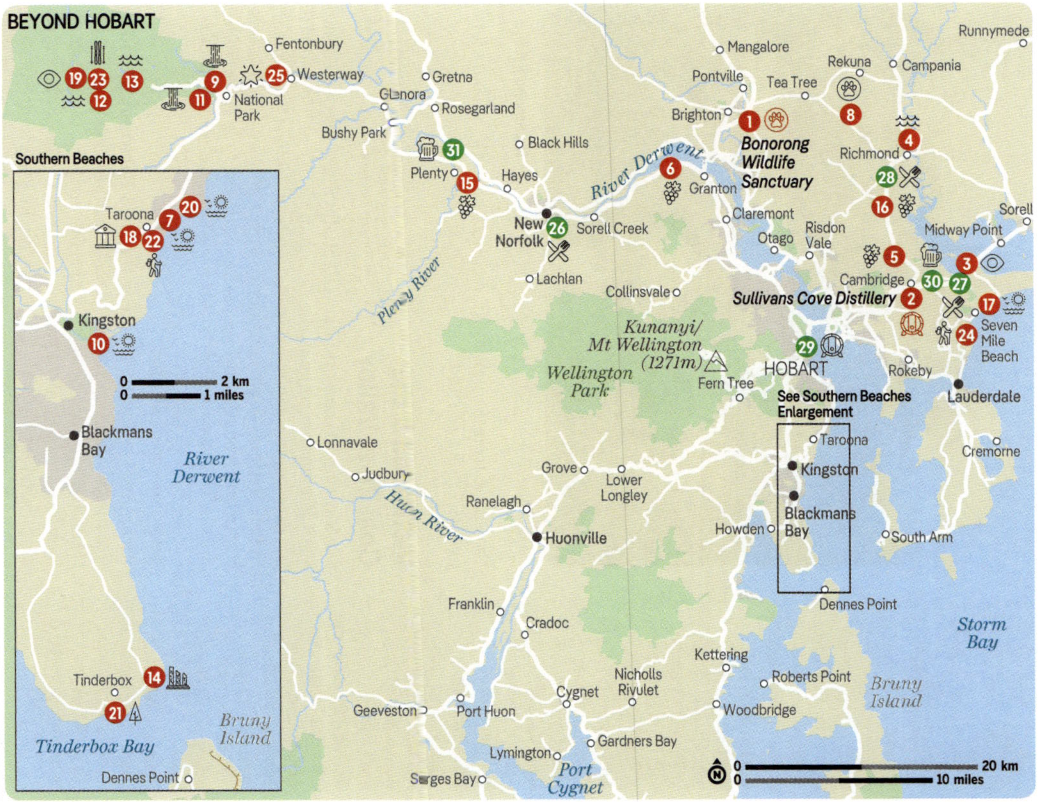

HIGHLIGHTS
1 Bonorong Wildlife Sanctuary
2 Sullivans Cove Distillery

SIGHTS
3 Barilla Bay Oysters
4 Coal River
see 4 Courthouse
5 Craigow Vineyard
6 Derwent Estate
see 5 Frogmore Creek
7 Hinsby Beach
8 Hobart Zoo & Aquarium
9 Horseshoe Falls
10 Kingston Beach
11 Lady Baron Falls
12 Lake Dobson
13 Lake Fenton
14 Piersons Point
15 Plenty Cider
see 4 Pooley Wines
16 Puddleduck Vineyard
see 4 Richmond Bridge
see 9 Russell Falls
17 Seven Mile Beach
18 Shot Tower
see 9 Tall Trees Nature Trail
19 Tarn Shelf Track
20 Taroona Beach
21 Tinderbox Marine Reserve

ACTIVITIES
22 Alum Cliffs Track
23 Mt Mawson
24 Single Hill
25 Westerway Raspberry Farm

EATING
26 Agrarian Kitchen
see 17 Beaches
see 10 Boho
see 5 Coal River Farm
see 10 Eb+Flo
see 4 Richmond Bakery
27 Tasmanian Gourmet Seafoods
28 Wicked Cheese Co

DRINKING & NIGHTLIFE
see 26 Bush Inn
29 Lark Distillery
30 Last Rites Brewing
see 4 Richmond Arms Hotel
see 10 Robbie Brown's
see 10 Salty Dog
31 Two Metre Tall

INFORMATION
see 9 Mt Field National Park Visitor Centre

COAL RIVER VALLEY BOOZE TOURS

North of Seven Mile Beach, the Coal River Valley wine scene is booming. Wine time!

Coal River Wine Hopper: Hop-on, hop-off Coal River Valley winery tours, with hourly pick-ups at liquid hot spots.

Aging Barrel: Winery tours to the Coal River, Derwent and Huon Valleys (and combos thereof), including lunch.

Drink Tasmania: Whisky, wine, cider and beer across the Huon, city and Coal River Valley.

Derwent Experience: 'Ultimate Tasmanian Tasting Tour' of the Derwent and Coal River Valleys: gins, ales, wines and ciders, plus a cheesy lunch.

Boutique Wine Tours: Combine Coal River Valley wineries with a MONA visit, returning on the ferry.

MATT MAKES PHOTOS/SHUTTERSTOCK

Richmond Bridge

the scene from Kunanyi/Mt Wellington to the airport, and across 7 miles of sand.

Richmond & the Coal River Valley

TIME FROM HOBART: **25MIN**

Looking for all the world like a Kentish village teleported into the Tasmanian farmland, the Georgian village of Richmond is a visitor-centric day-trip destination from Hobart (so popular, in fact, that you might consider visiting midweek). Rolling into Richmond from Cambridge to the south, the Coal River Valley makes for a decadent drive (or even better, a minivan tour).

Bridging two centuries

Richmond's defining feature is the 1823 **Richmond Bridge** *(ccc.tas.gov.au; free)*, the oldest still-functioning bridge in Australia. Built by convicts, it's a massive structure that doesn't look like it's going anywhere, anytime soon. The golden stone, manicured lawns and Coal River ducks are picture-perfect, although, in typical Tasmanian style, the bridge has a dark history too: it's purportedly haunted by the 'Flagellator of Richmond', George Grover, murdered here in 1832.

EATING & DRINKING AROUND SEVEN MILE BEACH: OUR PICKS

Tasmanian Gourmet Seafoods: Surprise! Right beside Hobart Airport, this seafood shack serves delicious oysters, crays, scallops and cooked seafood. *11am-7pm* **$$**

Beaches: Nooked behind Seven Mile Beach is this breezy bar-restaurant, serving pizzas, burgers and a kickin' chilli prawn salad. *12.30-8pm Tue-Sat* **$$**

Barilla Bay Oysters: Overlooking Barilla Bay near the airport, plating-up bivalves, fresh from the bay. Takeaways, too. *11am-2pm Thu-Mon, 5-7.30pm Thu-Sat* **$$**

Last Rites Brewing: You might need someone to read your last rites after a few Dead Man's Revenge black IPAs. *2pm-10pm Fri*

RICHMOND RIVERSIDE RAMBLE

The main street in Richmond is heaving with shops and attractions (and people). See it, then unearth some historic backstreet gems.

START	END	LENGTH
Richmond Bridge	Richmond Bridge	2.5km; 1hr

From the Richmond Bridge car park, admire the six sandstone arches of handsome 1 **Richmond Bridge**, Australia's oldest still-functioning bridge (1823). Cross the Coal River and veer left. The elegant, elliptical 2 **Old Courthouse** (1825) by the village green is a hark-back to Richmond's penal past.

Thirsty? Duck into the sandstone 3 **Richmond Arms Hotel** (p84; 1888 – formerly the 1827 Commercial Hotel), then cross the road to the former 4 **Congregational Church** (1875), now private accommodation. Pass noble, symmetrical 5 **Oak Lodge** (1842), fronted by twin oaks and now a National Trust history room. Turn left down Blair St, then zigzag past heritage houses to Torrens St and the sombre 6 **Pioneer Cemetery** (1845), with its 40-plus graves.

Next up is Norman-style 7 **St Luke's Anglican Church** (1834), Australia's oldest Anglican church, where the convict carpenter's handiwork earned him his freedom. At the end of Bathurst St, the unrestored 8 **Richmond Gaol Historic Site** is a sobering reminder of the inhumane treatment of convicts in Tasmania. Wander down to the shallow, reedy 9 **Coal River** and follow the pathway back to Richmond Bridge. The timber platform over the water marks the optimal photo-op. Back at the car park, if you still have gas in the tank, wander up the hill to 10 **St John the Evangelist Church**, the oldest Catholic church in Australia (1836).

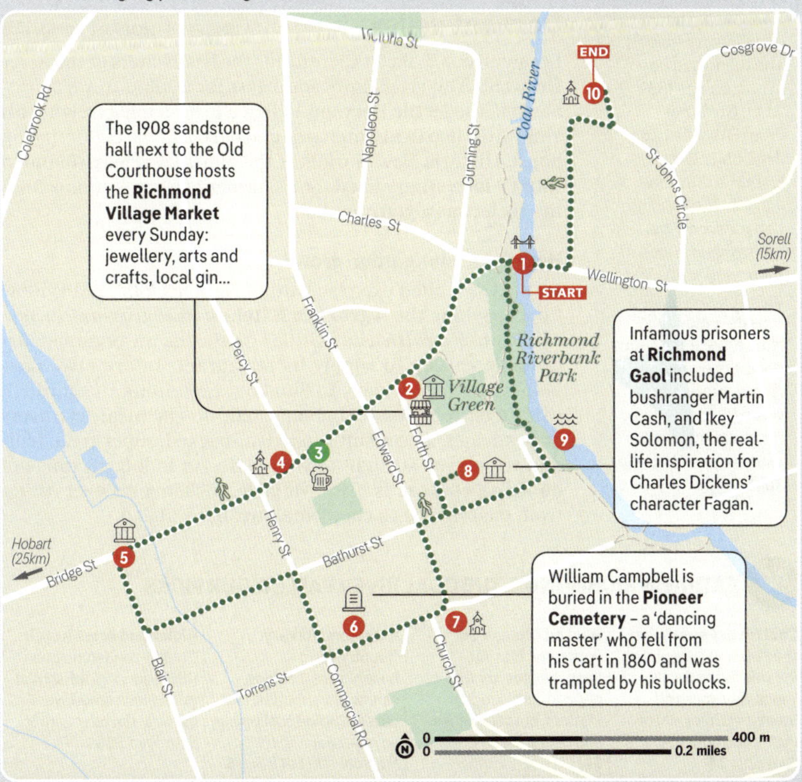

WHISKY HISTORY

With misty highlands, abundant barley, clean-running water...even peat, Tasmania has all the hallmarks of Scotland, the home of fine single-malt whisky. It's little wonder that whisky-making has taken off here, with spectacular results. But it wasn't until 1992 that Bill Lark, the godfather of Tasmanian whisky and founder of Lark Distillery (p60), successfully lobbied to have an archaic law banning backyard distilling overturned. The ruling had been in place since 1839 when Governor Franklin's wife Lady Jane objected to Hobart's drunken ways. In the ensuing decades, only the odd moonshiner (some of them very odd) would dare distill anything remotely alcoholic. Now there are 70-plus distillers on the island, producing winning whisky, gin, rum – even sheep's whey vodka. Oh Lady Jane...

Wildlife, local and imported

Fifteen minutes from Richmond, **Bonorong Wildlife Sanctuary** *(bonorong.com.au; adult/child $35/20)* is a 24/7 wildlife rescue and rehabilitation centre. Bonorong is not a zoo, but it's a great place to see some wildlife: Tasmanian devils, quolls, bettongs, pademelons and kangaroos. Tours and animal encounters run regularly.

Closer to Richmond, **Hobart Zoo & Aquarium** *(hzaa.com.au; adult/child $37/21)* offers a more traditional zoo experience (on a Hobart scale), with a couple of imperious lions, snakes, exotic birds, monkeys, meerkats and a room of aquarium tanks. Kids love the enthusiastic keeper talks.

The best whisky on Earth

The industrial backblocks of Cambridge aren't necessarily where you'd expect to find the world's best whisky. But **Sullivans Cove** *(sullivanscove.com; tours/tastings $70/30)* is exactly that. Inside this black-box building, passionate distillers bottle up the world's best single-malt whisky (2014) and the best single-cask single malt (2018 and 2019), as adjudged at the World Whiskies Awards – the first distillery outside of Scotland or Japan to wear the 'Best Single Malt' crown. Book a 90-minute tour (2pm daily) or a 30-minute tasting (10am daily) in the rather stylish bar.

Derwent Valley

TIME FROM HOBART: **35MIN**

Leeawuleena/Lake St Clair forms the headwaters of the River Derwent. The river flows southeast for 200km towards Hobart via the fertile Derwent Valley, a fecund fold strewn with vineyards, hop fields, orchards and old oast houses (for drying hops). Historic New Norfolk is the main town here (founded 1807) – long stigmatised for its former asylum, but now finding its feet as a gourmet hub.

How does your garden grow?

Inside the walled exercise yard of New Norfolk's old Willow Court asylum, the **Agrarian Kitchen** *(theagrariankitchen.com; tours adult/child $30/15)* cultivates an organic, sustainable garden to supply its restaurant. Informative one-hour tours run Fridays to Sundays, explaining the garden's workings: recycled and composted; no chemical fertilisers or pesticides. The result is nutrient-packed, super-fresh fruit and veg served straight to your plate. An indulgent range of **cooking classes** is also available, focusing on everything from charcuterie to cheesemaking. Book ahead.

EATING IN RICHMOND & THE COAL RIVER VALLEY: OUR PICKS

Coal River Farm: Valley cheeses and chocolates: the washed rind will knock your socks off. Breakfasts, pies, share plates and coffee, too. *9am-5pm* **$$**

Wicked Cheese Co: Puts some bite into their cheeses: try the pepperberry cheddar. Platters, burgers, wines and beers. *10am-4.30pm* **$$**

Richmond Bakery: Country-town bakery: pies, pastries, sandwiches, muffins and cakes. Curried scallop pie, anyone? *6am-5pm Mon-Fri, from 7am Sat & Sun* **$**

Richmond Arms Hotel: Chunky sandstone pub (1888) serving old-school grub. Steak time. Live music in the beer garden. *8am-9pm* **$$$**

STEVE WATERS/LONELY PLANET

Agrarian Kitchen, New Norfolk

DIY berries

At tiny, evocatively named Westerway, en route to Mt Field National Park, is **Westerway Raspberry Farm** *(lanoma.com.au; berries from $18/kg)*. Stop by for a berry ice cream, or wander into the fields with a bucket and pick your own strawberries, raspberries, blackberries, boysenberries and blackcurrants – straight from the bushes. Open December to February.

Mt Field National Park

TIME FROM HOBART: 1½HR

The equal-oldest national park in Tasmania (along with Freycinet, founded in 1916), Mt Field is part of the vast Tasmanian Wilderness World Heritage Area (TWWHA) – an accessible introduction to the wild southwest, just 90 minutes from Hobart. There are some great walks here, from short shuffles to epic alpine adventures.

Waterfalls and wilderness

Around the **Mt Field National Park Visitor Centre** *(parks.tas.gov.au; day pass per person/vehicle $24/48)* are damp groves of temperate rainforest: tree ferns, moss, myrtle beech and towering mountain ash. Hidden in the greenery are a series of exquisite waterfalls. A wheelchair-accessible 1.4km return track leads to the park's big-ticket attraction, the multitiered,

POETIC JUSTICE

Mt Field National Park is named after Barron Field (1786–1846), a dispute-prone English lawyer, scholar and poet. In 1817, Field arrived in Sydney to take up a posting as judge of the Supreme Court of NSW. In 1819 he presided over the first sitting of the Supreme Court of Van Diemen's Land, as Tasmania was then known – but he's better known for publishing Australia's first book of poetry that same year, the 12-page *First Fruits of Australian Poetry*. Sundry disagreements led to Field's recall to England in 1824, followed by further postings (and squabbles) in Ceylon and Gibraltar – none of which extinguished his poetic fires. In 1841 he published another book of poems, *Spanish Sketches*.

DRINKING IN RICHMOND & THE COAL RIVER VALLEY: BEST WINERIES

Frogmore Creek: Quality dining and cool-climate wines in a mod space that can get busy (best to book). Try the iced riesling. *10am-5pm*

Puddleduck Vineyard: Relaxed escape revolving around a duck pond, with zesty vinos (try the 'Bubbleduck') and kid-friendly eats. *10am-5pm*

Pooley Wines: Sip top Coal River pinots inside the heritage cellar door or outside by the vines. Wood-fired pizzas, too. *10am-5pm, pizzas noon-3pm Fri-Sun.*

Craigow Vineyard: Unpretentious and low-key with a farm-cottage cellar door, Craigow bottles up brilliant whites. *11am-4pm Sat & Sun, by appointment Mon-Fri*

QUEEN MARY OF TAROONA

Taroona's most famous ex-resident is Mary Elizabeth Donaldson, the present Queen of Denmark. The classic Cinderella story goes something along the lines of: 'The Crown Prince of Denmark walked into a bar...' The rest is history. The bar was Sydney's Slip Inn during the 2000 Sydney Olympics: Mary was having a drink with a girlfriend when in popped Frederik André Henrik Christian, first in line to the Danish throne. A secret courtship ensued, before the couple married in Copenhagen Cathedral in 2004. Mary learned Danish, had four children, and when Frederik's mum abdicated in 2024, the royal couple ascended the throne. Back in the day she went to Taroona High School and lived on Morris Ave – a very long way from Copenhagen.

STEVE WATERS/LONELY PLANET

Hinsby Beach, Taroona

photogenic **Russell Falls**. For a longer, more challenging circuit (two hours, 6km) continue up to **Horseshoe Falls**, a pair of twin falls deep in the forest; and **Lady Baron Falls**, a set of gentle cascades. Don't miss the short **Tall Trees Nature Trail** in a copse of mountain ash on the way.

For a closer encounter with the TWWHA, take the 30-minute twisting drive up unsealed Lake Dobson Rd from the Visitor Centre to **Lake Dobson**. Here on park's high exposed moorlands, the 12km, full-day **Tarn Shelf Track** takes you into the wilds. Australia's most southerly ski field is here too: the very low-key **Mt Mawson** *(mtmawson.info; day pass adult/child $50/25)*. Rope tows run on weekends and school holidays when there's enough snow.

The turning of the fagus

There aren't many deciduous native trees in Australia – Tasmania's deciduous beech, *Nothofagus gunii,* is one of them. It's a straggly, gnarly shrub found only above 800m elevation in high-rainfall, alpine areas like Mt Field National Park. In autumn, its leaves turn a riot of yellow, orange and russet red, and catching the 'turning of the fagus' creates a buzz on the socials. Head up twisty Lake Dobson Rd within the

DRINKING IN THE DERWENT VALLEY: BEER, CIDER, WINE & WHISKY

Two Metre Tall: Farm brewery producing small-batch, hand-pumped ales and ciders. BYO picnic; on-site BBQs. Is brewer Ashley actually 2m tall? *noon-4.30pm Fri-Sun*

Plenty Cider: There's plenty of hazy, small-batch cider at this cidery in Plenty, using valley fruits. Love the apple + cherry. *11am-4pm Sat & Sun*

Derwent Estate: Sample a dozen wines in Derwent's 1820s cottage tasting room. The Shed restaurant is here too. *11am-5pm*

Bush Inn: Who wouldn't want to drink a beer in Tasmania's oldest continually licensed pub? Nobody, that's who. In New Norfolk. *11am-10pm*

national park to the Tarn Shelf and **Lake Fenton** to witness the spectacle. The fagus does its thing any time from March to May, with the colours lasting several weeks.

Southern Beaches

TIME FROM HOBART: **20MIN**

South of Sandy Bay, the sandy vibes continue. The laid-back residential beach 'burb Taroona is next. In the 1970s there was a real sense of community here, since eroded by the closure of the shopping centre, the petrol station, the newsagent and (especially) the pub. But Taroona Beach and Hinsby Beach are unchanging delights. Over Bonnet Hill, Kingston Beach is a gem, with safe swimming and some great places to eat and drink. Blackmans Bay is the next arc of sand, before diminutive Tinderbox proves that good things come in small packages.

Hike the Alum Cliffs Track

From **Taroona Beach**, with its BBQs, playground and boat ramp, follow the foreshore track south to hidden little **Hinsby Beach**, a perfect patch of sand at the base of the impressive Alum Cliffs. From the far end of the beach, pick up the 8km (return) **Alum Cliffs Track** *(greaterhobarttrails.com.au; free)*. Initially heading inland, the track climbs through coastal scrub and a few back streets to the **Shot Tower** *(parks.tas.gov.au; adult/child $10/4)*. Built in 1870, this 58m circular tower (still one of the tallest buildings in Tasmania!) was designed to create ammunition: molten lead shot pellets were dropped from the top, forming perfect spheres as they fell to cool in a cold cauldron below. Take the creaky 259 steps to the top, scan the horizon, then hit the tearoom. From here, the track heads around the clifftops to handsome **Kingston Beach**. Swim out to the pontoon, then retreat for some fish and chips and a beer at the pub.

Explore the Tinderbox Marine Reserve

Follow the coast road 10km south from Blackmans Bay to sweet little Tinderbox. The small reserve at **Piersons Point** offers up a WWII bunker, a lunar-lander-looking lighthouse and excellent views across to Dennes Point on Bruny Island. Follow the coast road down to Tinderbox Beach, strap on your snorkel and explore the underwater trail along the reefs of **Tinderbox Marine Reserve** *(parks.tas.gov.au; free)*. There are usually plenty of fish here – wrasse, leatherjackets, seahorses and crayfish – although the trail's original submerged plaques are now somewhat hard to read.

WHY I LOVE KINGSTON BEACH

Charles Rawlings-Way, Lonely Planet writer

In the Victorian era, Kingston Beach was a hidden holiday village, a day's journey from Hobart by horse and cart. The old ferry pier and double-storey waterfront hotel are long gone, but a precious cache of heritage houses remains – along with some quality places to eat and drink. It's hard to believe that somewhere this idyllic – with its beautiful beach, swimming pontoon, clifftop trails, backstreet football oval and bird-filled marshes – is just 15 minutes from the centre of an Australian capital city. I won't always call Kingston Beach home, but for the past three years, this place has been some kind of paradise. Can you find the secret pathway to Boronia Beach?

EATING & DRINKING IN KINGSTON BEACH: OUR PICKS

Salty Dog: This 1960s waterfront tavern has been reborn, Miami-style, serving up refined dishes and old faves. Live beer-garden bands on Sundays. *8am-9pm* $$

Robbie Brown's: Beachfront wine bar serving tasty brunches then share plates and pub-style dinners. Order the rosti Benedict. *8am-4pm Sun-Tue, to 9.30pm Wed-Sat* $$

Boho: Bohemian style in the gift shop, extending through to a leafy courtyard cafe. Kid-friendly, killer coffee, wine, open fire, happy days. *7.30am-3pm* $

Eb+Flo: Bright water-facing cafe serving simple soups and sandwiches. The takeaway coffee window does a roaring trade. *7am-4pm* $

Places We Love to Stay

$ Budget $$ Midrange $$$ Top end

Central Hobart

MAP p51

Astor Private Hotel $ Old-world charm in a classic 1922 red-brick guesthouse on Macquarie St. Clean rooms, shared bathrooms, on-site steakhouse.

Alabama Hotel $ Clean, compact private rooms (a former pub) with shared bathrooms, Art Deco style and a cool on-site terrace bar, bang in the middle of town.

Hobart Central YHA $ Safe and secure, maze-like YHA. Same-sex and mixed dorms not far from the waterfront, all with attached bathrooms. En suite doubles also available.

Vibe Hotel Hobart $$ Impressive midrange operator, with swimming pool, views and slick corporate style.

Old Woolstore Apartment Hotel $$ Converted warehouse close to the waterfront with decent rooms and the SkyBus stop right outside.

Hadley's Orient Hotel $$$ Not your everyday sterile five-star, Hobart's 'grand dame' (1834) has well-appointed, heritage-style rooms and super-helpful staff.

Salamanca & the Waterfront

MAP p58

Waterman's Hotel $$ Stylish hotel above ground-zero Salamanca (read: not super-quiet). Rooms go heavy on the old timbers and exposed sandstone.

Customs House Hotel $$ Excellent location across from the waterfront, this historic pub (p60) has a choice of mod renovated rooms upstairs, the best with water views.

Henry Jones Art Hotel $$$ In the restored IXL Jam Factory overlooking Victoria Dock, you'll keep company with revolving art exhibitions. Rooms are suitably extravagant.

Tasman $$$ High-end Hobart at its height: fabulous rooms, from Art Deco to heritage to up-to-the-second contemporary. Bars and eats on site.

Salamanca Wharf Hotel $$$ Down the quieter end of Salamanca, these modern rooms overlook Castray Esplanade and the UTAS Antarctic Studies (IMAS) building.

MACq 01 $$$ Built to resemble an ageing maritime sea chest, the hotel's views across Sullivan Cove and towards Kunanyi/Mt Wellington are show-stopping.

Sullivans Cove Apartments $$$ Several waterfront locations. Historic Gibson's Flour Mill rooms are the most interesting, with exposed beams and a killer location.

Battery Point, Sandy Bay & South Hobart

MAP p65

Montacute $ Boutique backpackers with a choice of small dorms, mixed or same-sex, in a lovely Battery Point building. Shared bathrooms.

Shipwrights Arms Hotel $$ Clean en suite doubles in a characterful old Battery Point pub (p68), or cheaper 'budget' rooms with shared bathrooms.

Grosvenor Court Apartments $$ On a demure Sandy Bay backstreet, this tidy enclave has various apartments over three levels, built in the 1970s but recently rejuvenated.

Lenna of Hobart $$$ Lenna has an old bit (1870s) and a new bit (1970s), but all rooms are thoroughly contemporary. Water views and a top Battery Point/Salamanca location.

De Witt Apartment $$$ Three-bedroom, artfully renovated shopfront in the heart of Battery Point; perfect for small groups or families.

Grande Vue Hotel $$$ Bespoke rooms in a brick Queen Anne manor, loaded with antiques and stained glass. Some water views; super-quiet location.

Islington $$$ South Hobart luxury boutique hotel, dripping in opulence and quiet sophistication. Art by the big names; no kids.

North Hobart

MAP p75

Waggon & Horses $$ Upstairs at the renovated Waggon & Horses pub are lovely designer rooms with huge beds, a far cry from the old pub digs. Great food downstairs.

MONA Pavilions $$$ Expect lots of glass, crazy angles, cavernous beds, spa views, offbeat art, Derwent solitude – and MONA right next door.

Corinda $$$ Gorgeous renovated Victorian mansion, high on the Glebe hillside a short (steep!) walk from NoHo or the city. Each room is different, or there are garden cottages.

Seven Mile Beach

BIG4 Hobart Airport Tourist Park $ Plane-spot from your cabin or caravan at this big, clean and grassy park beside Hobart Airport.

Travelodge Hobart Airport $$ Early flight? Flight cancelled? Either way, you're guaranteed a tidy corporate-style sleep here. Shuttle bus to the departure gate.

Richmond & the Coal River Valley

Daisy Bank Cottages $$ Two cosy cottages with loft bedrooms inside a 1830s sandstone barn on a sheep farm, just outside the village.

Richmond Coachmans Rest $$ When all else is colonial and twee, head for this no-fuss, tidy row of three motel-style units on the main street.

Aquila Eco Retreat $$$ Glamping tents and eco-pods, not omitting any of the fineries (nice linen, decent kitchens, outdoor baths and privacy). Brisk walk to town.

Derwent Valley

New Norfolk Caravan Park $ Idyllically situated on a quiet stretch of the Derwent, with shady sites and a clutch of self-catering cabins.

Shingles $$ Take your pick of four modern New Norfolk riverside units, ranging from a studio to a two-bedroom house. The larger options have kitchens.

Explorers Lodge $$$ Lovely weatherboard B&B on the north bank of the Derwent, with four double rooms and a light breakfast. Just the right amount of cottage style.

Mt Field National Park

Government Huts $ Five rustic 1940s wooden cabins just before Lake Dobson, each sleeping six. Wood heaters; shared toilets. Book through parks.tas.gov.au.

Mt Field National Park Campground $ Powered and unpowered sites along the pretty Tyenna River, within easy reach of the Visitor Centre.

Duffy's Country Accommodation $$ The two cabins in Westerway – one family, one couple-sized – are excellent, with equally excellent veranda views.

Southern Beaches

Hobart Bush Cabins $ These basic cabins at the Lea Scout Centre, midway between Hobart and Kingston, sleep up to six. Full kitchens.

Hobart Hideway Pods $$ Two stylish, eco-designed tiny houses (one fully accessible) in Kingston, with huge windows and verandas with Derwent views.

Tinderbox Peninsula Chalets $$ Birdsong and Frogsong are two mod, open-plan, self-catering cabins for couples on a rural property on the Howden side of Tinderbox.

STEVE WATERS/LONELY PLANET

Customs House Hotel

For places to stay in the south, see p123

CATHERINE SUTHERLAND/LONELY PLANET

Above: Cape Raoul (p95), Turrakana/Tasman Peninsula; Right: Tessellated Pavement (p95), Eaglehawk Neck

Researched by
Charles Rawlings-Way

The South

CONVICTS YESTERDAY, FOOD TODAY, WILDERNESS ALWAYS

The convicts thought this was the end of the world. For you, it's the start of something good.

The lands below 43°S fill you with end-of-land vibes and maritime soul. Kayak along Turrakana/Tasman Peninsula and you'll discover a jagged coastline that's much the same as it was when Abel Tasman sailed past in 1642. In this wild corner of a wild island, settlements are sparse. Tourist coaches decant visitors into the sombre ruins of Port Arthur Historic Site; others find inspiration in the peninsula's natural splendour.

DANIEL KARFIK/SHUTTERSTOCK

Across the D'Entrecasteaux Channel from Kettering, beguiling Bruny Island offers foodie delights and yet more gorgeous coastline. Just over the hill, apples, pears and cherries burgeon in the orchards of the Huon Valley, also home to fine wines and ciders in equal measure. Fishing, farming and forest villages string themselves out along the slow-roaming Huon River, interspersed with inlets and beaches and backed by distant snowy peaks – an impossibly beautiful scene.

You can access Southwest National Park from Cockle Creek, beyond the Huon on the end of the most southerly road in Australia – but to fully engage with the Southwest, head beyond Mt Field National Park and mountain-bike-mad Maydena to drowned Lake Pedder. One of the most scenic and underrated drives in Australia passes raw dolerite peaks, dense temperate rainforest and buttongrass plains. Long-distance walking tracks head into the remote ranges of the Tasmanian Wilderness World Heritage Area (TWWHA) – as wild as wild can be.

THE MAIN AREAS

TURRAKANA/ TASMAN PENINSULA
Convict history and cinematic coastlines.
p94

BRUNY ISLAND
Super scenery and foodie delights.
p103

HUON VALLEY
Waterways and Tasmania's apple heartland.
p109

THE SOUTHWEST
Wilderness, walking and glorious isolation.
p118

Find Your Way

This region fans out from Hobart like a peacock's tail: Turrakana/Tasman Peninsula to the east, Bruny Island to the southeast, the Huon Valley to the south and (predictably) the Southwest to the southwest.

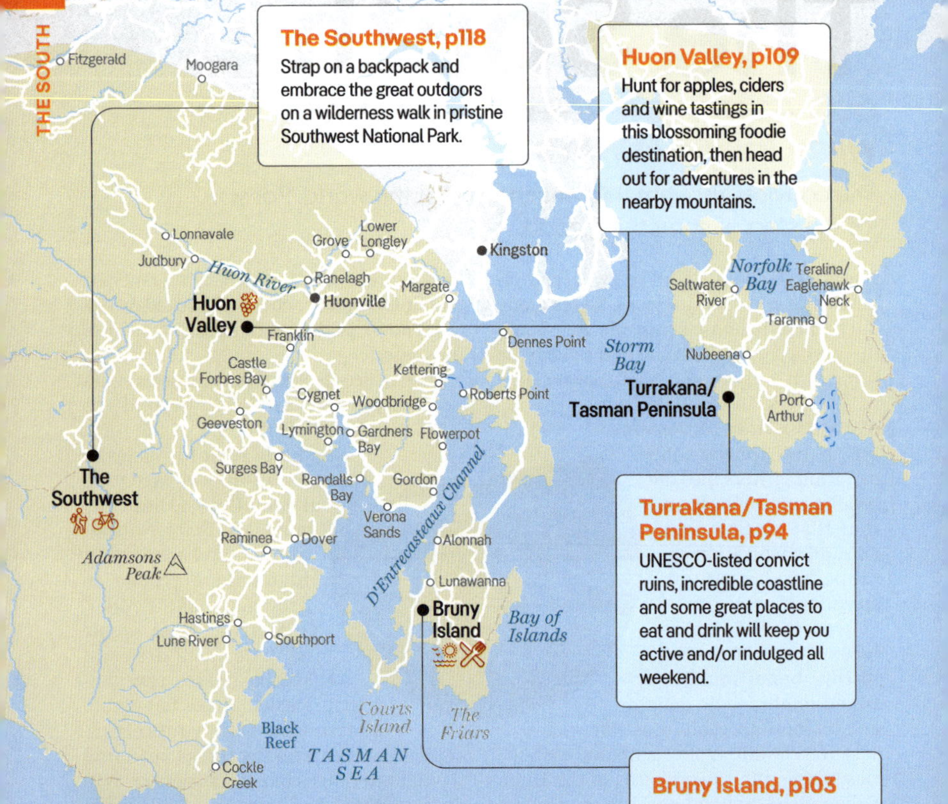

The Southwest, p118

Strap on a backpack and embrace the great outdoors on a wilderness walk in pristine Southwest National Park.

Huon Valley, p109

Hunt for apples, ciders and wine tastings in this blossoming foodie destination, then head out for adventures in the nearby mountains.

Turrakana/Tasman Peninsula, p94

UNESCO-listed convict ruins, incredible coastline and some great places to eat and drink will keep you active and/or indulged all weekend.

Bruny Island, p103

Ferry over to laid-back Bruny for a scenic foodie road-trip and beautiful white-sand beaches with a long history.

CAR

Bring your own vehicle: there's no public transport on Bruny Island, and it thins out south of Huonville. There are also plenty of day tours from Hobart to Turrakana/Tasman Peninsula, and to Bruny Island.

BICYCLE

Throw your bike in the car: cycling is an excellent choice for getting around Bruny Island, Turrakana/Tasman Peninsula and the Huon Valley. For long-haul bikers and hikers, Dover is the southern terminus of the epic Tasmanian Trail.

DANIEL KARFIK/SHUTTERSTOCK

Remarkable Cave (p100), Turrakana/Tasman Peninsula

Plan Your Time

All of these places can be visited as day trips from Hobart, but why rush it? Turrakana/Tasman Peninsula can also be included in an East Coast tour; and the Southwest visited en route to/from the West Coast.

Tight for Time

- Leave Hobart early and catch the Bruny Island ferry from Kettering. Grab some **oysters** (p105), **cheese** (p105), bread and beer for a beach picnic at Adventure Bay, stopping at **the Neck** (p103) en route. Back on the mainland, trace the coast to Cygnet for afternoon tea at **Red Velvet Lounge** (p115). Continue onto Huonville for an evening ale at the **Lost Captain** (p113).

Weekender

- Head to Turrakana/Tasman Peninsula via the **Tessellated Pavement** (p95) at Teralina/Eaglehawk Neck, then check out **Tasman Arch** (p95) and the **Devil's Kitchen** (p95). Spend the afternoon at **Port Arthur Historic Site** (p98), then breathe some sea spray at **Remarkable Cave** (p100). Overnight in Taranna, then drive into Fortescue Bay and day-walk to **Cape Hauy** (p95), the most impressive of the Three Capes.

Seasonal Highlights

SPRING
Wildflowers bloom, fruit trees are budding and the coast looks inviting, though you're likely to have four seasons in one day.

SUMMER
Stable summer weather is prime time in the great outdoors: hiking, camping, kayaking, boating or just lazing around at the beach.

AUTUMN
Harvest time: local markets are overflowing with produce. Fewer visitors means easier driving and some good accommodation deals.

WINTER
Clear winter nights are best for spotting the elusive Aurora Australis: the further south you are, the better your chances.

Turrakana/ Tasman Peninsula

HISTORY | COASTAL SCENERY | OUTDOOR ADVENTURES

TOP TIP

Short on time/money? Dramatic Cape Hauy, the third cape on the multiday Three Capes Track, can be accessed as a four-hour, 9km return day walk. Start at Fortescue Bay and walk in the opposite direction to the main hike. National park fees apply.

Just an hour from Hobart are the staggering coastal landscapes and historic sites of Turrakana/Tasman Peninsula. Bushwalking, sea-kayaking, diving, surfing and rock-climbing opportunities abound – all good reasons to extend your visit beyond a hurried day trip from Hobart.

Protected by Tasman National Park are the peninsula's legendary 300m-high sea cliffs – the tallest in the southern hemisphere. Within the park, the iconic Three Capes Track entices hikers from across the planet to experience this amazing landscape.

Waiting portentously at the end of Arthur Hwy is the amazing, World Heritage–listed Port Arthur Historic Site, an infamous 19th-century convict colony. Today, kids kick footballs and families picnic on the lawns – but it's impossible to totally blank out the tragedy of this place, both historically and more recently.

Development on the peninsula is low-key. There's plenty of accommodation here, but there's not a lot of depth to the food scene: self-catering is a solid option.

Hike the Three Capes Track

One by boat, two by boot

Designed for people who like a modicum of comfort with their wilderness, the 48km, four-day **Three Capes Track** *(parks.tas.gov.au; adult/child $625/495)* meanders along the

GETTING AROUND

Turrakana/Tasman Peninsula is an hour's drive from Hobart, heading out past the airport then through Sorell: a car is your best option for exploring. Several tour companies offer one-way or return trips from Hobart to Port Arthur Historic Site – handy if you're walking the Three Capes Track. There are plenty of day tours that take in the other sights as well, circling around the peninsula. Tassielink buses run once daily in each direction between Hobart and Nubeena, via Teralina/Eaglehawk Neck and Port Arthur.

SUMMIT ART CREATIONS/SHUTTERSTOCK

Sea cliffs, Tasman National Park

spectacular sea cliffs within Tasman National Park. Nights are spent in comfortable, architect-designed cabins, achievable distances apart. The one-directional walk kicks-off at Port Arthur Historic Site, with a cruise to **Cape Raoul** (the first cape) before the walking starts at Denman Creek. Views along the way are phenomenal, especially at **Cape Pillar** and **Cape Hauy** (pronounced 'hoy'). The track ends at photogenic **Fortescue Bay**: celebrate with a swim before the bus takes you back to Port Arthur. The track is walkable year-round – book well in advance. Several companies run fully guided tours, staying in luxury private lodges at fully luxurious prices.

Remarkable Coastline

Coastal curiosities in Tasman National Park

At the northern end of Pirates Bay, a short trail leads to a rocky coastal terrace, the **Tessellated Pavement** – curiously eroded into what looks like tiled paving. Just south of Teralina/Eaglehawk Neck, follow the signs through Doo Town (p102) to the **Blowhole**, where sporadic bursts of sea-spray bloom into the air. Nearby, within **Tasman National Park** *(parks.tas.gov.au; day pass per person/vehicle $24/48)*, short walks lead to **Tasman Arch** (a cavern-like natural bridge) and **Devil's Kitchen** (a rugged 60m-deep cleft). From here, the one-hour, 3.4km return Waterfall Bay Walk traces the clifftops to **Waterfall Bay Lookout**, with magical views of the area's towering sea cliffs.

continued on p100

MAKING WAVES

Into dangerous big-wave surfing? Near Cape Raoul within Tasman National Park is one of the world's most respected (feared) waves – **Shipstern Bluff**. When the weather conditions are right (a large south-southwesterly swell and offshore winds from the north), the Southern Ocean butts heads with an offshore reef here and jacks up into a muscular, barrelling, 10m-high wave – the legendary 'Shippies'. Further complicating matters are the local great white sharks, and a bulging 'step' water formation that appears mid-wave, seemingly designed to dislodge any surfers who make it this far. Pro surfers and their film crews boat it in here from afar; mere mortals can walk in from the end of Stormlea Rd, near Nubeena. It's a four-hour, 16km return hike to the clifftops.

EATING ON TURRAKANA/TASMAN PENINSULA: OUR PICKS

Lanterns: Surprising Dunalley cafe, with good coffee, cheese-and-chive scones and beaut baguettes. Wall of providore goodies. *7.30am-3pm* $

Cannery: Don't muck around – order a seafood platter on the deck at this Dunalley gem. *11am-8pm Mon-Sat, to 4pm Sun* $$

Port Arthur Lavender: Thankfully, not everything at this cafe comes with lavender; try the spiced sweet potato bowl. *10am-4pm* $$

On the Bay: Classy dining attached to Stewarts Bay Lodge at Port Arthur. Big on local wines and produce. *8-10am & 5-9pm Tue-Sat* $$$

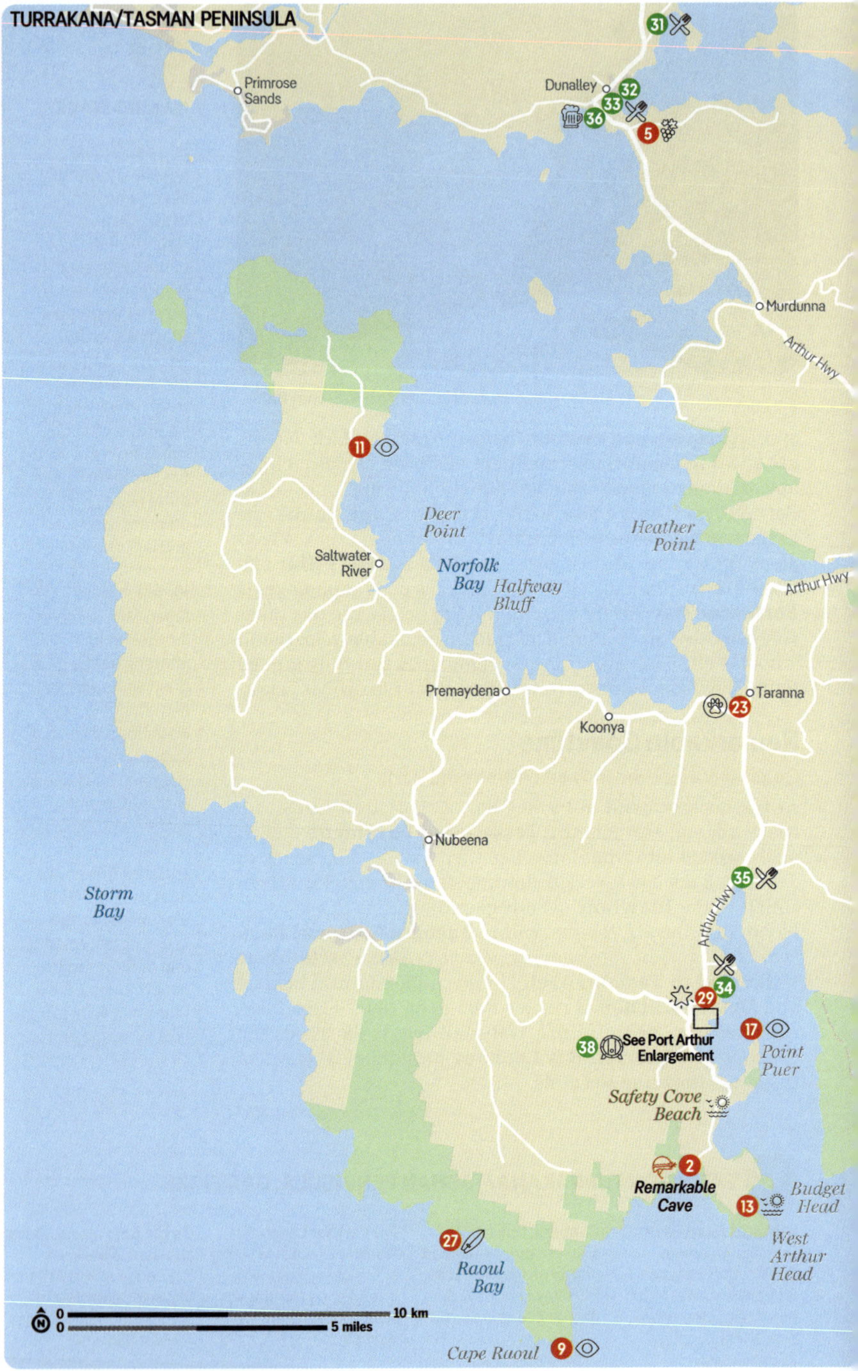
TURRAKANA/TASMAN PENINSULA
Primrose Sands
Dunalley
31
32
33
36
5
Murdunna
Arthur Hwy
11
Deer Point
Heather Point
Saltwater River
Norfolk Bay
Halfway Bluff
Arthur Hwy
Premaydena
Koonya
Taranna
23
Nubeena
Storm Bay
35
Arthur Hwy
34
29
17
38
See Port Arthur Enlargement
Point Puer
Safety Cove Beach
2
Remarkable Cave
13
Budget Head
West Arthur Head
27
Raoul Bay
0
10 km
0
5 miles
9
Cape Raoul

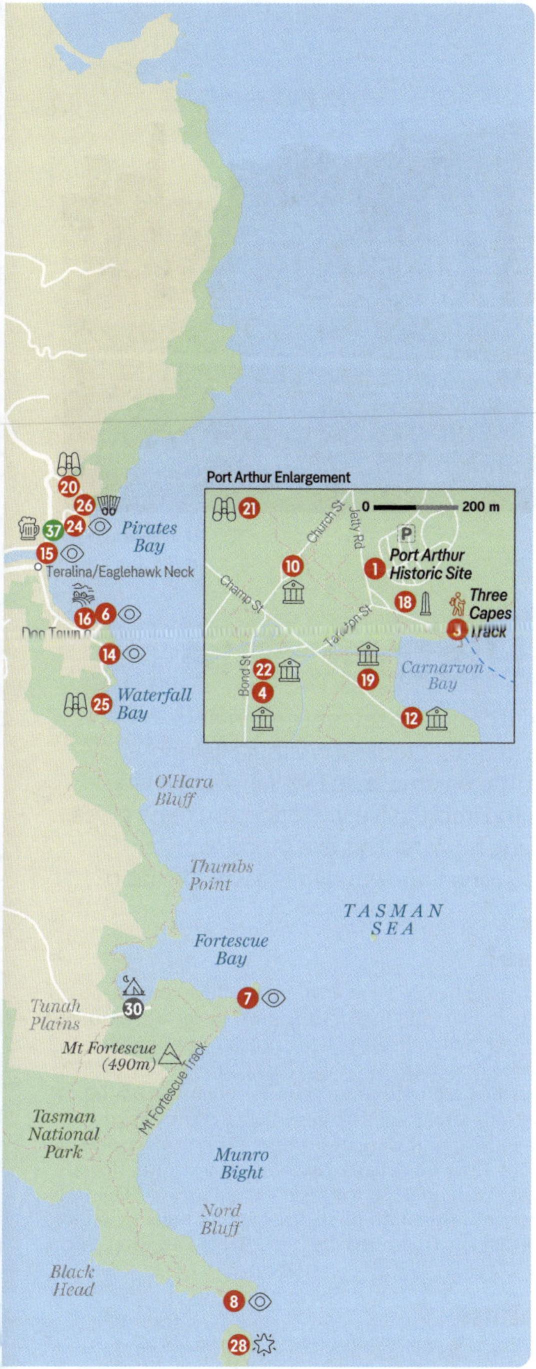

HIGHLIGHTS
1 Port Arthur Historic Site
2 Remarkable Cave
3 Three Capes Track

SIGHTS
4 Asylum
5 Bangor Vineyard Shed
6 Blowhole
7 Cape Hauy
8 Cape Pillar
9 Cape Raoul
10 Church
11 Coal Mines Historic Site
12 Commandant's House
13 Crescent Bay
14 Devil's Kitchen
15 Dog Line
16 Doo Town
17 Isle of the Dead
18 Memorial Garden
19 Penitentiary
20 Pirates Bay Lookout
21 Scorpion Rock
22 Separate Prison
see 14 Tasman Arch
see 14 Tasman National Park
23 Tasmanian Devil Unzoo
24 Tessellated Pavement
25 Waterfall Bay Lookout

ACTIVITIES
26 Eaglehawk Dive Centre
see 1 Ghost Tour
27 Shipstern Bluff
28 Tasman Island
29 Tasman Island Cruises

SLEEPING
30 Fortescue Bay Campground

EATING
31 Blue Lagoon Oysters
32 Cannery
see 20 Cubed
see 6 Doo-Lishus
33 Dunalley Bakery
see 33 Lanterns
34 On the Bay
35 Port Arthur Lavender

DRINKING & NIGHTLIFE
36 Dunalley Hotel
37 Lufra Hotel
38 McHenry Distillery

STEVE WATERS/LONELY PLANET

The Penitentiary

TOP EXPERIENCE

Port Arthur Historic Site

Nowhere does Tasmania's grim convict past feel so tangible than at the atmospheric, World Heritage–listed Port Arthur Historic Site. Green lawns and neat cottages create an English-village vibe between the ruins – but even the impressive visitor centre can't gloss over historical, and more recent, horrors. This is a place to show human reverence and respect, for a time when these were in short supply.

DON'T MISS

- The Penitentiary
- The Commandant's House
- The Separate Prison
- The Church
- Boat tour to the Isle of the Dead
- Free talks
- Scorpion Rock lookout

Why Here?

The British established a small timber-milling settlement at Port Arthur in 1830 and began transporting their unwanted criminals here by the boatful. This process continued until transportation ceased in 1853, the prison finally closing in 1877. Port Arthur had a harsh reputation: miscreants from other colonial prisons often ended up here. Port Arthur was considered escape-proof, as it was cut-off from the rest of Tasmania by narrow Teralina/Eaglehawk Neck, where fierce guard dogs and tales of shark-infested waters deterred escape. The site was abandoned in the late 1890s. Despite its redemption as a major tourist site (the ruins are undeniably amazing), Port

PRACTICALITIES

● portarthur.org.au ● adult/child/family $53/26/117 ● 9am-5pm

Arthur remains a sombre place. Compounding this mood are memories of April 1996, when a deranged young gunman murdered 35 people here and injured 19 more. UNESCO World Heritage status was assigned to Port Arthur in 2010, along with four other Tasmanian convict sites.

Explore the Main Buildings

Most visitors head first to the **Penitentiary**, the massive stand-alone sandstone facade that was once a flour mill, yet ended up housing 484 prisoners. The well-preserved **Commandant's House** is nearby; the refinement and comfort on display a poignant counterpoint to the squalor afforded to the convicts. The well-preserved **Separate Prison** and adjacent **Asylum** are mute reminders of punishment ideology; after being subjected to the psychological torture of the former, prisoners often ended up in the latter. On higher ground, away from the prison buildings, the **Church** indicates the role religion played in prisoner reformation.

Between the Ruins

The Historic Site covers 136 hectares, gently sloping down to tranquil Carnarvon Bay. Several formal gardens appear as you wander around, including the **Civil Officer's Gardens** below the Church, and the hedged **Government Gardens**, complete with fountain. The **Officers Gardens** extend behind **Trentham Cottage**, with a fine example of an English cottage garden. The most poignant garden, though, is the small **Memorial Garden**, commemorating those who lost their lives in the 1996 massacre.

Isle of the Dead

The final destination for many Port Arthur inmates – the oddly tranquil **Isle of the Dead**, a small island in Carnarvon Bay – was the penal colony's cemetery. The majority of the 1100 graves here are unmarked. The boat trip included in your ticket goes out to the island, but you can't get off unless you've paid for the additional **tour** *(adult/child $30/15)*. The isle is just off Point Puer, site of the first boys' prison in the British Empire.

Tours & Talks

To get the most out of your visit, listen to the experts. Free talks are held at various times throughout the day outside the Penitentiary, Commandant's House, Church and Separate Prison; check times online. Other value-added guided tours are available for an additional cost, including the after-hours **Ghost Tour** *(adult/child $35/18)*. For 90 minutes a noir figure carrying a lantern leads you through the ruined buildings, relating tall tales and true.

PYDAIRRERME PEOPLE

Port Arthur lies on the lands of the Pydairrerme people of the larger Paredarerme language group, centred on Oyster Bay. Middens and artefacts have been found here and across the peninsula, even on formidable, cliff-wrapped Tasman Island. Following an all-too-familiar pattern, European contact proved deadly for the Pydairrerme and only one name was ever recorded – Poetigwerlayde, sent to Wybalenna on Flinders Island, fate unknown.

TOP TIPS

- Climb up to **Scorpion Rock** lookout on the path behind the Church for an excellent view over the entire site.
- Your entrance ticket is valid for two days – so don't feel rushed to see it all at once.
- Take the Isle of the Dead tour for a 40-minute guided walk around the cemetery island.
- Is the classy 1830 restaurant open again? It was closed when we visited, but the cafe was doing a roaring trade.
- Don't miss Remarkable Cave (p100) nearby; or to really blow away the sombre vibes, take the four-hour return walk to timelessly beautiful Crescent Bay (p100).

continued from p95

Further south beyond Port Arthur, also within Tasman National Park, descend 115 steps to **Remarkable Cave**, a remarkably long tunnel eroded from the base of a collapsed gully, under a cliff and out to sea. The waves surge through the tunnel and fill the gully with sea spray (and sometimes seawater – watch out!). From the car park here, a four-hour, 9km return walk delivers you to **Crescent Bay** – a magical arc of white sand, seemingly undiscovered on the edge of the world.

Convict Heritage, off the Beaten Track

Explore the Coal Mines Historic Site

The amazing Port Arthur Historic Site gets all the attention – and rightly so. But for a less-visited, low-key convict encounter, detour to the **Coal Mines Historic Site** *(coalmines.org.au; free)*, 28km north of Port Arthur. The state's first operational mine, excavation began here in 1833. Convicts worked in abominable conditions, before the mine closed in 1848 on 'moral and financial grounds'. Walking tracks loop through the ruins: the crumbled sandstone barracks, overlooking the water, is particularly evocative; the solitary confinement cells are torturously small and dark. To get here, from the town of Premaydena, take the signposted turn-off (the C341) 13km northwest to Saltwater River.

Kayak the Coast

The paddle of a lifetime

Roaring 40s Kayaking *(roaring40skayaking.com.au; tours from $280)* runs full-day kayaking expeditions along the wild Turrakana/Tasman Peninsula coastline, exploring sea caves, Cape Hauy, a shipwreck and seal colonies along the ridiculously high sea cliffs. Look forward to lunch in a deserted cove, with perhaps a peregrine falcon keeping you company. Join the tour at Fortescue Bay (national park fees apply), or ex-Hobart.

Crossing the Dog Line

Can you escape from Teralina/Eaglehawk Neck?

Beyond Dunalley, **Teralina/Eaglehawk Neck** is the second isthmus you'll cross heading south to Port Arthur, this one connecting the Forestier Peninsula to Turrakana/Tasman Peninsula. In convict days, the 100m-wide Neck had a row of ornery dogs chained across it to prevent convicts from escaping – the

SOUTHERN KAYAKING

Ewan Blyth, wilderness adventure guide, shares his favourite paddling locales. *@ballaghblyth*

Turrakana/ Tasman Peninsula: With sea caves, fur-seal colonies, white-bellied sea eagles, deserted beaches and the tallest sea cliffs in the southern hemisphere, this is the paddle of a lifetime. Launch from Fortescue Bay; for experienced sea kayakers.

Franklin: For a more serene experience, slide your kayak onto the mirror-like Huon River at Franklin at dawn. Glide silently along glassy waterways and get up close to Tasmania's unique native birdlife at Egg Island Reserve.

Blackmans Bay: South of Hobart, paddle past aptly named Fossil Cove to the Tinderbox Marine Reserve and Tinderbox Beach (8km) where you can put-out or return the same way. Great for newbies; pack a mask and snorkel.

DRINKING ON TURRAKANA/TASMAN PENINSULA: OUR PICKS

Bangor Vineyard Shed: On a hilltop at Dunalley is this excellent vineyard, the cellar door doubling as an oyster-focused restaurant. Fab riesling. *10am-5pm*

McHenry Distillery: Bush distillery near Port Arthur creating classic gins, whiskies and beers, with interesting seasonal variations. Tours and accommodation, too. *noon-4pm*

Dunalley Hotel: Roadside red-brick 1866 pub en route to the main attractions, with a sit-and-sip veranda. Pool table gets busy. *11am-9pm Sun-Thu, to 11pm Fri & Sat*

Lufra Hotel: Grab a cold beer and head for the terrace at this chowder-coloured, all-comers pub overlooking Teralina/Eaglehawk Neck. *8.30am-9pm*

TURRAKANA DAYTRIPPER

If you only have a day on Turrakana/Tasman Peninsula, here's a hit list of essential experiences.

START	END	LENGTH
Dunalley	Remarkable Cave	60km; 1 day

Low-key 1 **Dunalley**, strung along the Dennison Canal, marks the junction between the Forestier Peninsula and the rest of Tasmania. The hand-dug canal opened in 1905 and shaved days from the sea voyage to/from Hobart. Cross the canal and head up to 2 **Bangor Vineyard Shed** for morning fortifications (some oysters – save the wine till later).

Continue south to 3 **Pirates Bay Lookout**, a spectacular viewpoint high above Teralina/Eaglehawk Neck, the narrow isthmus between the Forestier Peninsula and Turrakana/Tasman Peninsula. In convict times, the notorious 4 **Dog Line** was strung across the isthmus, barking at convict escapees from Port Arthur.

Continue through 5 **Doo Town** (p102; any amusing new house names?) to check the ocean swell at the 6 **Blowhole** (p95); then head uphill into Tasman National Park to eyeball the cavernous 7 **Tasman Arch** (p95) and adjacent 8 **Devil's Kitchen** (p95). Further south, the dramatic convict ruins of 9 **Port Arthur Historic Site** (p98) are one of Tasmania's big-ticket lures. The excellent guided tours here will help you to come to grips with the sadness and savagery of the early 1800s.

At the end of a long day, calm yourself with the timeless beauty of Turrakana at 10 **Remarkable Cave**. Here at the end of the road, the waves keep time, surging in and out, same as it ever was.

TASMAN ISLAND

Named (obsequiously) by Abel Tasman's navigator in 1642, the mysterious, cliff-ringed **Tasman Island** guards the entrance to Storm Bay and the River Derwent. Australia's highest lighthouse sits 276m above the waves: read John Cook's *The Last Lighthouse Keeper* for an account of life here in the 1970s. Much further back in time, wild seas and gale-force winds didn't stop Tasmanian Aboriginal people from hunting on the island, with discovered artefacts suggesting that fur seals were on the menu. Both Australian and New Zealand fur seals still breed around the island's rugged shores, along with gaggles of fairy prions. Get an up-close look with **Tasman Island Cruises** *(tasmancruises.com.au; adult/child/family $180/110/560).*

infamous **Dog Line** *(eaglehawkneck.org; free).* Timber platforms sat in narrow Eaglehawk Bay to the west, stocked with yet more angry dogs to prevent convicts from wading around the Dog Line. To discourage swimming, rumours told of shark-infested waters. Remarkably, despite these measures, several convicts made successful bids for freedom. Today you can check out a ferocious-looking **dog sculpture**, without much bite.

Looking for Something to Doo?

Detour to Doo Town

No one is really sure how it all started – the tradition arcs back almost 100 years – but the raggedy collection of fishing shacks at **Doo Town** *(eaglehawkneck.org; free),* 3km south of Teralina/Eaglehawk Neck on the way to the Blowhole, all contain the word 'Doo' in their names. There's the provocative 'Doo Me'; the approving 'We Doo'; the Beatles-esque 'Love Me Doo'; the rather resigned and disappointed 'Make Doo'; and (our favourite) the melancholic 'Doo Write'. We doo hope the new breed of architecturally adventurous beach houses here maintain the tradition. Definitely worth a dootour. Don't miss the Doo-Lishus takeaway fish-and-chip caravan at the Blowhole car park.

This Isn't a Zoo

Visit the Tasmanian Devil Unzoo

Drive-through Taranna's prime attraction is the **Tasmanian Devil Unzoo** *(tasmaniandevilunzoo.com.au; adult/child/family $60/35/150),* an unfenced enclave of beautiful native bushland where the local wildlife is free to come and go. Species you might encounter include native hens, wallabies, quolls, eagles, wattlebirds, pademelons and, of course, Tasmanian devils. The devils *do,* however, have sizeable enclosures: you can see them being fed six times a day.

Diving the Cathedral

A world beneath the waves

Beneath the waterline at Waterfall Bay are some of the most spectacular sea caves in Australia, including the incredible **Cathedral Cave**. **Eaglehawk Dive Centre** *(eaglehawkdive.com.au; boat dives from $140)* runs dive tours here, passing through smaller caves and interconnected canyons with apt descriptions like the **Catacombs**, the **Devils Tonsils** and **Skull Cave**. First-time and full PADI dive courses are also available.

EATING ON TURRAKANA/TASMAN PENINSULA: QUICK EATS

Doo-Lishus: Tasmania's best fish and chips? Unexpected caravan at the Doo Town Blowhole. *10am-5.30pm* $

Cubed: Enjoy views with your coffee at this restored, solar-powered 1957 caravan at Pirates Bay Lookout. Good biscuits. *9am-3pm Thu-Mon* $

Blue Lagoon Oysters: No sign of Brooke Shields at this blue lagoon – but there are plenty of oysters. From $17 a dozen. *10am-3pm Mon & Tue, to 4pm Wed-Sun* $

Dunalley Bakery: Old-school highway-side bakehouse, with egg-and-bacon rolls and fried delights. *6am-6pm Mon-Fri, to 4pm Sat & Sun* $

Bruny Island

WILD COASTLINE | HISTORY | FOODIE TRAIL

Known as Lunawanna-Alonnah to the Nuenonne people, Bruny was (mis)-named after French explorer Bruni d'Entrecasteaux who 'discovered' the channel separating Bruny from the rest of Tasmania. Bruny's original name is kept alive in two of the island's largest settlements.

A popular day tour or weekend getaway from Hobart, Bruny is basically two islands joined by 'the Neck', a long sandy isthmus barely 100m wide. North Bruny has some great foodie distractions, but it's largely low-key and agricultural: most tourists head to South Bruny, with its sparkling beaches and bays, towering sea cliffs and further fine food. Development is refreshingly small scale, mostly clustered around Lunawanna, Alonnah and Adventure Bay, with most of the southern coastline protected by South Bruny National Park.

Sure, you can do Bruny in a day – but if you can handle the peace and quiet, stay a few days. Bruny Island takes hold slowly, then tends not to let go.

TOP TIP

Time-poor visitors can tick off most of Bruny's must-sees in a long day. If you're planning on staying a while, book camping and accommodation well in advance – see brunyisland.com.au or brunyisland.org.au for a list of rental houses. Bring all your groceries with you, as supplies are limited (nonexistent on North Bruny).

Merry Isthmus

Climb the dunes for Bruny's famous hourglass view

Climb to the top of the highest dune on **the Neck**, the skinny isthmus connecting North and South Bruny. Several hundred

GETTING AROUND

There is no public transport on Bruny Island. From Kettering, bring your car across on the **Bruny Island Ferry** *(sealink.com.au/bruny-island; car/motorcycle return $56/8)*, which runs every 20 minutes between 6.10am and 7pm. You can book a ticket in advance, but you'll still have to queue up at the terminal. Or you can buy a ticket when you arrive. The ferry takes 20 minutes to chug across the D'Entrecasteaux Channel. Check rental-car clauses, as most Bruny roads are unsealed, apart from the B66 from the ferry pier to Lunawanna, and the C630 offshoot to Adventure Bay.

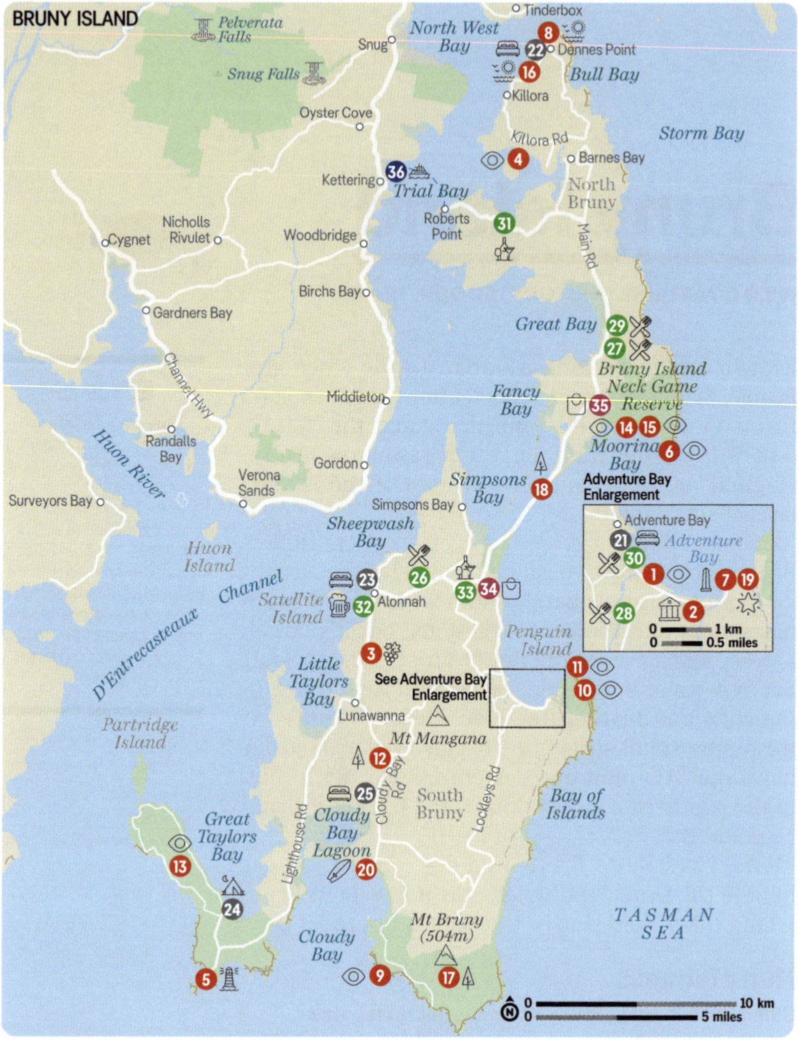

● **SIGHTS**

1 Adventure Bay
2 Bligh Museum of Pacific Exploration
3 Bruny Island Premium Wines
4 Bruny Island Quarantine Station
5 Cape Bruny Lighthouse
6 Cape Queen Elizabeth
7 Captain Cook Plaque
8 Dennes Point Jetty
9 East Cloudy Head
10 Fluted Cape
11 Grass Point
12 Inala Jurassic Garden
13 Labillardiere Peninsula
14 Mars Bluff
15 Moorina Bay
16 Nebraska Beach
17 South Bruny National Park
18 The Neck
see 18 Truganini Memorial

● **ACTIVITIES**

19 Bruny Island Cruises
see 5 Bruny Island Lighthouse Tours
20 Cloudy Bay

● **SLEEPING**

21 43 Degrees
22 Bruny Beach House
23 Bruny Boathouse
24 Jetty Beach Campsite
25 Saintys Creek Cottage

● **EATING**

26 Bruny Baker
27 Bruny Island Cheese Co
28 Bruny Island Raspberry Farm
29 Get Shucked Oysters
see 8 Jetty Cafe
30 Mari Bruny

● **DRINKING & NIGHTLIFE**

31 Bruny Island House of Whisky
32 Hotel Bruny
33 Izzy Bar

● **SHOPPING**

34 Bruny Island Chocolate Co
35 Bruny Island Honey

● **TRANSPORT**

36 Bruny Island Ferry

TOM JASTRAM/SHUTTERSTOCK

The Neck (p103)

steep wooden steps rise to the summit and, once you catch your breath, you'll recognise the view from all the tourism brochures: the hourglass effect of churning oceanic Adventure Bay to the east, and calm shallow Isthmus Bay to the west is utterly photogenic. There's also a poignant Truganini Memorial (p108) at the top – she was born on the island. Come back at dusk for the chance to see little penguins and short-tailed shearwaters return to their burrows in the dunes.

Deserted Headlands & Rolling Surf

Explore South Bruny National Park

South Bruny National Park *(parks.tas.gov.au; day pass per person/vehicle $24/48)* wraps around the bottom of Bruny and captures a separate area east of Adventure Bay. There are some prime bushwalking trails here, alive with birds and wildflowers. In the eastern section, a moderate 4km circuit walk leads out to **Grass Point**, site of an old whaling station, then continues onto the magnificent dolerite columns of **Fluted Cape**. In the southern section, an 18km route circumnavigates the **Labillardiere Peninsula** along beaches and low headlands. Keep an eye out for migrating southern right and humpback whales en route. Cape Bruny Lighthouse is here too.

From **Cloudy Bay**, a 12km-return walk leads along the beach then through scrub to **East Cloudy Head**, from where you

BEST BRUNY TOURS

Bruny Island Cruises: Excellent three-hour Pennicott Wilderness Journeys trips following the cliffs and sea stacks from Adventure Bay to Tasman Head.

Bruny Island Lighthouse Tours: Climb to the top of the 114m, 1836 lighthouse and learn about its history. The sunset tours are awesome.

Bruny Island Safaris: Day trip from Hobart includes oysters and cheese, a pub lunch and a lighthouse tour.

Tasmanian Walking Company: Luxurious three-day glamping guided walk covers East Cloudy Head, Cape Queen Elizabeth and plenty of oysters.

Inala Nature Tours: Twitchers rejoice! Three-hour tours inside a private nature reserve, home to 90-plus species.

EATING ON BRUNY ISLAND: CAFES & LUNCHES

Get Shucked Oysters: Fuel for love: sit on the deck overlooking Great Bay and wolf down a briny dozen. Drive-through takeaways. *9.30am-4.30pm* **$**

Bruny Island Cheese Co: Sensational cheese and beer: try the prosciutto-wrapped Otto washed down with an Oxymoron Dark Ale. *10am-4pm* **$$**

Jetty Cafe: Cafe-providore-gallery serving fab pizzas, fish and chips and weekend breakfasts. North Bruny; book ahead. *hours vary* **$$**

Mari Bruny: The best bet for a bite in Adventure Bay, serving pastas, burgers, curries, eggs Benedict and good coffee. *9am-6.30pm* **$$**

WHY I LOVE NEBRASKA BEACH

Charles Rawlings-Way, Lonely Planet Writer

Becalmed Nebraska Beach near Dennes Point is special – and not only because a wandering uncle mailed me a pair of yellow pyjamas from the US when I was eight, with UNIVERSITY OF NEBRASKA printed across the front. And not just because famous Tasmanian author Richard Flanagan used to live around the corner. Mostly the appeal is conceptual: you could quite feasibly live in one of the heritage beach shacks here, run your little motorboat (or kayak) across the narrow D'Entrecasteaux Channel to Tinderbox every morning, climb in your waiting car and drive into Hobart for work – before returning the same way in the evening. What a beautiful commute! It doesn't hurt to dream.

can gaze back to see Kunanyi/Mt Wellington behind Hobart. Cloudy Bay itself has the most reliable surf on the island, working best with an offshore northerly breeze, and the best view from a public toilet in Australia!

A Historic Light

Climb to the top of Cape Bruny Lighthouse

Designed by colonial architect John Lee Archer, the stout 1836, 13m-high **Cape Bruny Lighthouse** *(capebrunylighthouse.com; tours $25)* watches over the rugged coast within South Bruny National Park. It was Australia's longest-serving lighthouse – 158 years – when it was decommissioned in the 1990s. On guided tours, climb the cast-iron spiral stairs and step into the wind at the top. Clear-day views extend to distant Pedra Branca sea stack, a legendary big-wave surf spot. Book online; national park fees apply.

Northern Reaches

Learn about the history of Dennes Point

Bruny's northern tip is **Dennes Point**, just a few kilometres across the D'Entrecasteaux Channel from Tinderbox on the Tasmanian mainland. **Nebraska Beach** extends southwest from here, with it's endearing collection of boat sheds and heritage beach shacks. Heading north from the Jetty Cafe (p105), an easygoing, 1.5km **heritage trail** with 15 interpretive panels illuminates the natural, Aboriginal, colonial-explorer and early settler history of the area. To get here from the ferry, turn left onto the unsealed C625 instead of right to South Bruny.

Walk to Cape Queen Elizabeth

Birds, bluffs, beaches and bays

Often overlooked, the excellent, bird-busy **Cape Queen Elizabeth Track** *(brunyisland.org.au; free)*, kicks off across the road from Bruny Island Honey (p108) on North Bruny, skirting several lagoons en route to the sea at **Moorina Bay**. The route passes **Mars Bluff**, with its much-photographed stone arch, before a white-sand walk along Miles Beach and a final climb through coastal heath to **Cape Queen Elizabeth**. From the cape, a rocky knoll serves up views of a sea stack called the Houndstooth, **Adventure Bay** and Fluted Cape (p105). Give yourself four hours for the 14km return effort.

DRINKING ON BRUNY ISLAND: OUR PICKS

Hotel Bruny: Unpretentious, come-as-you-are pub in Alonnah, with cold beers, sunset views and good seafood. *noon-9pm*

Bruny Island House of Whisky: Head back to the ferry early for a tasting flight from 150-plus Tasmanian single-malt whiskies. *10am-5pm*

Bruny Island Premium Wines: Swing into the cellar door at Australia's most southerly vineyard. Pinot noir and chardonnay rule the roost. Food too. *11am-4pm*

Classy farm-to-fork daily lunches and Saturday dinners.

Izzy Bar: Quirky, sporadically open wine bar on South Bruny, stocked with Tasmanian wines, beers and ciders. Try your luck. *hours vary*

BRUNY ISLAND FOOD TOUR

Bruny Island is a gorgeous natural realm of beaches and sea-cliffs...or forget all that and enjoy an indulgent foodie day trip.

START	END	LENGTH
Bruny Island Ferry	Bruny Island Ferry	100km; 1 day

Roll off the ferry and follow the main road to 1 **Get Shucked Oysters** (p105). Grab a shucked dozen from the drive-through or sit on the deck and slurp in the sun. Not far away, pull into 2 **Bruny Island Cheese Co** (p105) for some outstanding cheese, beer and sourdough. Settle in for a lazy lunch, or continue to 3 **Bruny Island Honey** (p108) for tastings, a scoop of honey ice cream and a jar to go.

Keep heading south to 4 **the Neck** (p103) and burn off some calories on the steep steps to the 5 **Truganini Memorial** (p108), with dazzling isthmus views. Approaching Adventure Bay, take your pick from sumptuous chocs at 6 **Bruny Island Chocolate Co** (p108), or a punnet of juicy raspberries at 7 **Bruny Island Raspberry Farm** (p108). Maybe both.

Backtrack and head for Alonnah. Pull over to see if the 8 **Bruny Baker** (p108) has filled his retro roadside fridges with his daily sourdough loaves. Leave some coins and keep rolling. In Alonnah, prime yourself for a cold beer, a hot local cider and some fish and chips at 9 **Hotel Bruny**; or continue to Lunawanna for 10 **Bruny Island Premium Wines**.

Weave your way back to North Bruny for a final snifter of Tasmanian whisky at the 11 **Bruny Island House of Whisky**, then roll back onto the ferry.

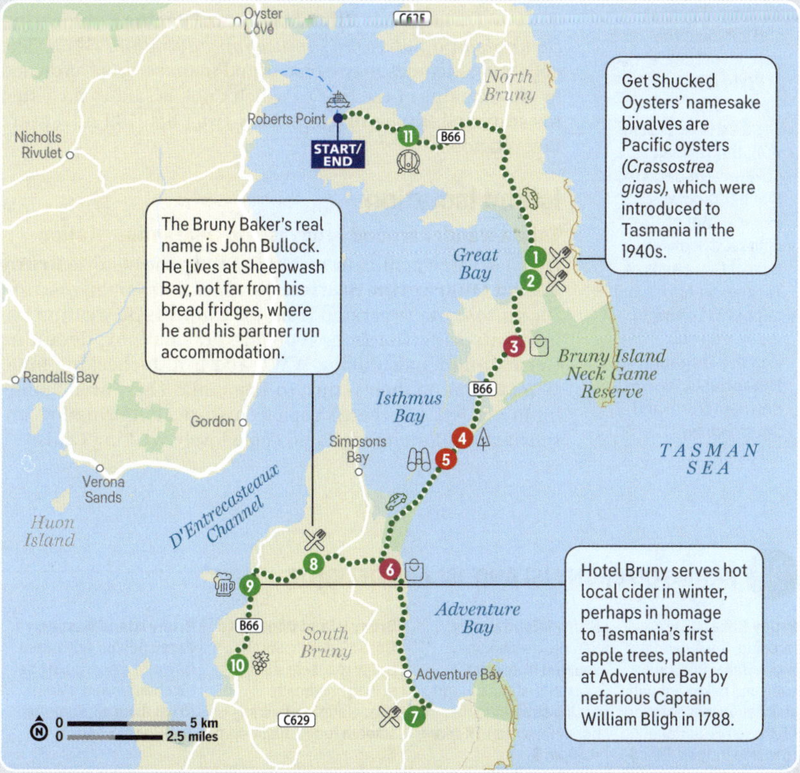

TRUGANINI

One of the last 'full-blooded' Tasmanian Aboriginal people, Truganini lived through the white invasion of Lutruwita: her death has become a symbol of the attempted genocide of her people. Truganini was born on Bruny Island in 1812, the daughter of Mangana, chief of the Nuenonne. She left Bruny to travel with George Robinson, tasked with 'conciliating' the Tasmanian Aboriginal people, and survived the derelict settlements at Wybalenna and Oyster Cove. When she died in Hobart in 1876, the Tasmanian government declared that her race was extinct – but of course, there are tens of thousands of Tasmanian Aboriginal people in Lutruwita today. You can visit the **Truganini Memorial** at the Neck between North and South Bruny.

Ancient Plants & Birdlife

Count bird species in a Gondwanaland garden

Encircled by 600 hectares of private nature reserve on South Bruny, **Inala Jurassic Garden** *(inalanaturetours.com.au; adult/child $10/5)* is a homage to the plants of Gondwanaland. The 750 species here trace their roots back to the ancient supercontinent – 'living fossils' that can be compared to actual fossils in the accompanying museum. The focus is on science and conservation; pick up a map and go exploring. Guided and bird-watching tours also available.

Adventurous History

Explore the exploration museum at Adventure Bay

The first English person to arrive at broad Adventure Bay was Tobias Furneaux (1773), onboard the HMS *Adventure*. Furneaux was accompanying James Cook's second voyage, though Cook didn't anchor in the bay until his third voyage in 1777, leaving his initials carved into a tree. A small **roadside plaque** commemorates JC's early graffiti, though the tree is long gone. A third notable English seafarer, William Bligh, visited the bay several times. Bligh planted Tasmania's first-ever apple trees here (also long gone).

For further insights into all this and more, visit the curio-crammed, windowless **Bligh Museum of Pacific Exploration** *(brunyisland.net.au/blighmuseum; adult/child $4/3)*. The collection includes maps, charts and manuscripts – crowned by the remains of the tree to which Cook is said to have tied his ship, and Bligh's original diary from his 1792 Adventure Bay pit stop.

Island Isolation

Take a wander around Bruny Island Quarantine Station

On an isolated peninsula on North Bruny, the historic **Bruny Island Quarantine Station** *(facebook.com/brunyquarantinestation; free)* operated from 1884 until 1919, treating immigrants suffering from typhoid and smallpox, detaining German nationals during WWI, and health-checking 9000 WWI troops on their return to Tasmania. There aren't many buildings left, but there's copious historical information, enthusiastic volunteer staff and some lovely walking trails.

EATING ON BRUNY ISLAND: ISLAND DELIGHTS

Bruny Baker: Every morning, the legendary Bruny Baker fires up his oven and bakes enough sourdough loaves to fill these two vintage roadside fridges. *24hr* $

Bruny Island Honey: Sample divine honey sourced from from seasonal island blooms, or skip straight to the honey ice cream. *9.30am-4.30pm* $

Bruny Island Chocolate Co: Smart little South Bruny roadside shop selling handmade chocolates and silky-smooth fudge. *10am-4pm* $

Bruny Island Raspberry Farm: Behind Adventure Bay, pick a punnet of ripe raspberries and try not to eat them all. *9am-4pm Tue-Sun Nov-Apr* $

Huon Valley

FAMED FRUIT | CIDER & WINE | SOUTHERN BAYS

Still harbours, heritage villages and misty valleys – the Huon Valley is a nonstop visual delight. The apple-producing heartland of the Apple Isle, this fertile area now also produces cherries, pears, apricots, wine, mushrooms and, of course, cider! The wide, tea-coloured Huon River remains the region's lifeblood. Courtesy of these cool southern latitudes, the Huon also serves up dazzling rainbows and auroras.

As you track south, the valley's fruity hillsides offset the sparkling inlets and fishing towns of the D'Entrecasteaux Channel, with Bruny Island just offshore. Hartz Mountains National Park and Hastings Caves aren't far inland and, further south, magnificent Recherche Bay sits on the doorstep of Southwest National Park.

All sounding a bit gallic? French explorers Bruni d'Entrecasteaux and Nicolas Baudin charted much of this convoluted coastline in the 1790s and early 1800s, a good decade before the Brits hoisted the Union Jack at Piyura Kitina/Risdon Cove near Hobart in 1803.

TOP TIP

It's a straight two-hour drive from Hobart to Cockle Creek if you put your foot down. But why hurry? Much of the appeal of the Huon Valley is peeling off the main roads and exploring orchard-lined back roads and detours to hidden bays and beaches.

GETTING AROUND

Tassielink buses regularly connect Hobart to Huonville and Ranelagh, with less frequent services to Cygnet and south to Geeveston and Dover. Your own vehicle is still the best option for exploring the hinterland, including Hartz Mountains National Park and Hastings Caves. Day tours from Hobart also run to Tahune Adventures and Hastings Caves; winery day tours also run to the Huon Valley vineyards. Cycling between Huonville, Ranelagh and Cygnet is certainly an option, although roads south of here and along the D'Entrecasteaux Channel are skinny and wiggly with not a lot of shoulder space to retreat to when traffic overtakes.

HUON VALLEY
Lonnavale
Grove
Willie Smith's Apple Shed
Ranelagh
Huon River
Huonville
Sherwood Hill Conservation Area
Franklin
Cradoc
Castle Forbes Bay
Glaziers Bay
Cygnet
Arve Rd
Geeveston
Petcheys Bay
Lymington
Port Cygnet
Huon Hwy
Surges Bay
Huon River
Hartz Mountains National Park
Hartz Mountains National Park
Police Point
Dover
Raminea
Strathblane
Huon Hwy
Southwest National Park
Adamsons Peak
Hastings Caves State Reserve
Recherche Bay (13km);
Catamaran (14km);
Cockle Creek Campground (17km);
South Coast Track (17km);
Southern Right Whale Sculpture (17km);
Fishers Point (20km);
South Cape Bay (23km)
Hastings
Southport
Southport Lagoon Conservation Area

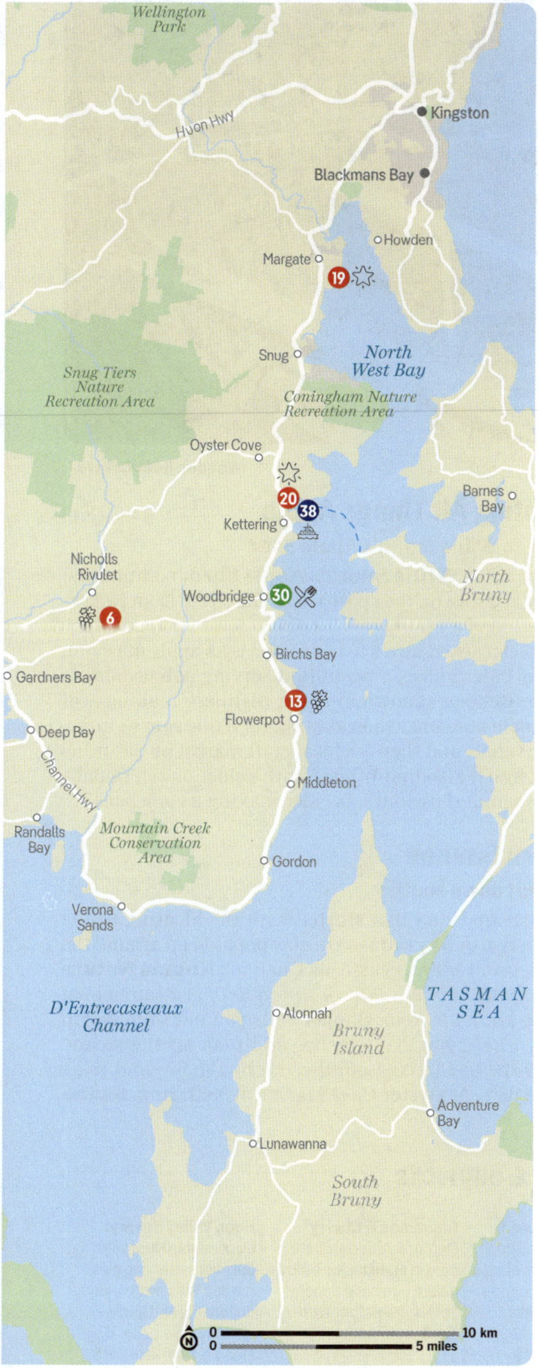

HIGHLIGHTS

1 Hartz Mountains National Park
2 Willie Smith's Apple Shed

SIGHTS

3 Arve Falls
4 Hartz Pass
5 Hartz Peak
6 Hartzview Vineyard
7 Home Hill Wines
8 Ida Bay
9 Kate Hill Wines
10 Lake Esperance
11 Lake Osborne
12 Lune River
13 Mewstone Wines
14 Waratah Lookout
15 Wooden Boat Centre

ACTIVITIES

16 Elsewhere Sauna
17 Farmhouse Kitchen
18 Hastings Caves & Thermal Springs
19 Kuuma Nature Sauna
20 Sauna Boat Tasmania
21 Tahune Adventures

SLEEPING

22 Abbey on Main
23 Cygnet Old Bank
24 Driftwood Holiday Cottages
25 Huon Valley Caravan Park
26 Roundhouses
27 Valley Campground

EATING

28 Botega Crippa
see 22 Cinnamon & Cherry
see 28 Huon Valley Bakery
29 Masaaki's Sushi
see 29 Old Bank Of Geeveston
30 Peppermint Bay Hotel
see 23 Poolish & Co
see 23 Porthole Cafe
see 23 Red Velvet Lounge
31 rocket@The-EndOfTheRoad
32 Summer Kitchen Bakery
33 Wild Bird

DRINKING & NIGHTLIFE

see 15 Frank's Cider House & Cafe
see 28 Lost Captain
34 River Run Lodge Tavern
35 Southport Hotel

SHOPPING

see 23 Cygnet Market
see 22 Franklin Market
36 Geeveston Market
see 2 Grove Market
37 Judbury Market

TRANSPORT

38 Bruny Island Ferry

JEAN-MICHEL HUON DE KERMADEC

Born into French naval royalty in 1746, de Kermadec served in the American War of Independence before joining Bruni d'Entrecasteaux on a 1785 voyage to the Far East on the *Resolution*. He again accompanied D'Entrecasteaux in 1791 as second-in-command, on a voyage to find the missing French explorer La Perouse and his ships *L'Astrolabe* and *Boussole*. Given command of the *Esperance*, he arrived together with D'Entrecasteaux (on the *Recherche*) in 1792 at what is now Recherche Bay (p117) near Cockle Creek. Here they carried out surveys and scientific experiments and even planted a small garden. Huonville, the Huon River, Huon Valley and Huon pine, and the village Kermandie near Geeveston, are all part of Kermandec's local legacy.

ANDREW BAIN/ALAMY

Wooden Boat Centre

Celebrating All Things Apple

Pay a visit to Willie Smith's Apple Shed

It's hard to miss **Willie Smith's Apple Shed**, right on the Huon Hwy at Grove on the approach to Huonville from Hobart – a celebration of all things *Malus domestica* (the good ol' domestic apple). Packed into one large shed is an apple museum, a rollicking cider house, a restaurant serving pub favourites (go for the Reuben sandwich) and a distillery making – of course – apple liqueurs. On Friday nights Willie's turns into a live-music venue, and there's a local craft market on Saturday mornings. You'll also find Willie Smith's cider on tap in pubs across Tasmania these days: is cider making a comeback?

Southern Saunas

Sweat it out down south

Surfing a steam cloud that started with the Floating Sauna (p177) in Derby, quirky saunas are now popping up around the Huon Valley and D'Entrecasteaux Channel. **Kuuma Nature Sauna** *(kuuma.com.au; 90min sauna $80)* is a sauna boat moored at Margate. Your skipper sails you out onto North West Bay, where you drop anchor and soak up the steam. Jump into the bay to cool off, then sit by the fire and relax with some jazz. At Oyster Cove Marina at Kettering, **Sauna**

EATING AROUND HUONVILLE: OUR PICKS

Summer Kitchen Bakery: On the Ranelagh crossroads, the pies and sourdough loaves here are legendary. *7.30am-4pm Mon-Fri, from 8am Sat & Sun* $

Botega Crippa: Superb fresh pasta arranged in neat swirls, plus jars of ragu and ready-to-eat focaccia and pizza in Huonville. *9am-3pm Tue, to 5.30pm Wed-Fri, to 2pm Sat* $

Cinnamon & Cherry: Detour to this excellent cafe in Franklin for Turkish baked eggs and punchy coffee. *9am-3pm Wed-Sat* $

Huon Valley Bakery: Dependable Huonville bakehouse serving pies, pasties, rolls, wraps, vegan doughnuts and family-sized fruit pies. *6am-3pm Mon-Fri, from 7am Sat* $

Boat Tasmania *(saunaboattasmania.com.au; 1hr sauna $59)* offers a similar set-up, although the boat stays moored in the marina. At secretive Drip Beach 15km south of Cygnet, **Elsewhere Sauna** *(elsewheresauna.com; 1hr sauna $50)* is a mobile, beautifully built five-person trailer that makes the most of its locations. You can book all of these saunas exclusively, or share a communal experience.

Get Folked

Book a camp site at the Cygnet Folk Festival

The second weekend in January sees the small arts-and-crafty town of Cygnet resound to the sounds of acoustic guitars, mandolins and duelling banjos. The three-day **Cygnet Folk Festival** *(cygnetfolkfestival.org; day/weekend $132/240)* is heavily community-driven – an earthy celebration of folk, roots and world music, poetry, dance, performing arts, food, cider and wine. Cygnet is inundated with visitors from far and wide, most choosing to camp (extra fee) – it's all kinds of wholesome, inclusive, rainbow-tinged, family-friendly fun.

Let's Cook!

Cucina Pugliese at the Farmhouse Kitchen

Guiliana White shares her passion for the flavours of her Puglian homeland in these immersive Italian cooking classes, held at her beautiful **Farmhouse Kitchen** *(thefarmhousekitchen-tas.com; classes $85-300)* in the hills above Cygnet. Full- and half-day classes explore different seasonal dishes using Huon Valley produce, including pasta, pizza and bread, vegetable and meat-lover recipes. At the end of each session you're invited to sit down to a shared meal and enjoy what you've created. Joy!

Woodworking Magic

Tour the Wooden Boat Centre in Franklin

Marvel at the carpentry skills on display at the **Wooden Boat Centre** *(woodenboatcentre.com; tours adult/child/family $15/5/35)* on the Huon riverbanks in Franklin. Inside, exquisite boats are produced using salvaged, recycled and sustainable Tasmanian timbers, each one a work of art. Take a 40-minute tour for an in-depth appreciation of the centre's place in the local community: a volunteer guide will walk you through the workshop, where you can watch boats being cobbled together and catch a glorious whiff of Huon pine.

BEST HUON MONTHLY MARKETS

Cygnet: First and third Sundays at the Town Hall. Eclectic mix of hippie arts and crafts, bric-a-brac, plants and live tunes.

Judbury: Second Sunday. Every local's favourite, with clothes, produce, arts and crafts and good burgers at Calvert Park.

Grove: Every Saturday at Willie Smith's Apple Shed. Local produce, gourmet condiments, honey, meats, ceramics, leather, baked stuff and wooden things.

Franklin: Fourth Sunday, inside the old Palais Theatre. A celebration of all things locally grown, picked and produced.

Geeveston: First Thursday evening in the Town Hall. A melange of DIY creativity and green-thumbed goodness.

DRINKING IN THE HUON VALLEY: BEST BEER & CIDER

Lost Captain: Huonville taphouse-restaurant in a beautiful riverside homestead. Order a pint of the Huon River Brown Ale and head for the brazier. *noon-9pm*

Frank's Cider House & Cafe: Family-run cider house in Franklin, with Huon heritage dating back to 1836. Live music on Sundays. *10am-5pm, to 4pm Jun-Aug*

River Run Lodge Tavern: At Strathblane near Dover, River Run has cosy hunting-lodge vibes, cold beer and fab waterside tables. *4-11pm Fri & Sat*

Southport Hotel: Duck in for a beer, if only to say you've enjoyed one in Australia's most southerly pub. Pool tables and shoeless fishermen. *noon-9pm*

DRIVING THE CHANNEL

Take the slow road into the Huon Valley along the super-scenic Channel Hwy, tracing the D'Entrecasteaux Channel from Kingston to Cygnet.

START	END	LENGTH
Kingston	Cygnet	66km; 4hr

First stop south of Kingston is Margate: pull over to check out the shops and cafes in the marooned ❶ **Margate Train**. A bit further south, the excellent ❷ **Channel Heritage Centre** zeroes in on D'Entrecasteaux Channel history. Or maybe the floating ❸ **Kuuma Nature Sauna** (p112) at Margate Jetty is more your speed? Beyond Electrona and snug little Snug, the photogenic yacht-filled marina at Kettering is where the ❹ **Bruny Island Ferry** (p103) sets sail. Chug over to the island for a few days, or keep trucking south.

The road meanders between hills and water to the pretty village ofWoodbridge, famous for its school where students grow their own vegetables and learn about organic gardening, and the flashy-but-still-earthy ❺ **Peppermint Bay Hotel**. At Birchs Bay, ❻ **Grandvewe** offers sheep's cheese tastings and spirits from its sister distillery Hartshorn. Time for sheep's whey vodka?

The Channel Hwy continues like a country lane through Flowerpot – pull into ❼ **Mewstone Wines** (p116) for a tasting – then Middleton and Gordon, where there's a granite ❽ **monument to Bruni d'Entrecasteaux** down by the jetty.

The ❾ **beach** at sleepy Verona Sands on the Huon Estuary is good for a moody stroll on a rainy Channel afternoon, before the road, originally heading south, veers north and winds through Deep Bay and Gardners Bay into folky/foodie Cygnet. Cafe time!

NICOLE KWIATKOWSKI/SHUTTERSTOCK

Hartz Mountains National Park

A Taste of Southwest Wilderness

Alpine walks in Hartz Mountains National Park

From Geeveston, take the Arve Rd then partly unsealed Hartz Rd into the 121 sq km **Hartz Mountains National Park** *(parks.tas.gov.au; day pass per person/vehicle $24/48)*, an alpine wilderness that's part of the Tasmanian Wilderness World Heritage Area. The park protects jagged peaks, glacial tarns, gorges and alpine moorlands, where fragile cushion-plant communities hunker down in the cold, misty airs.

There are some great hikes and isolated, sit-and-ponder-your-existence viewpoints here. **Waratah Lookout** is an easy five-minute shuffle from the road. Other well-surfaced short walks include **Arve Falls** (20 minutes return) and **Lake Osborne** (40 minutes return). The steeper **Lake Esperance** walk (1½ hours return) takes you into beautiful high country. You'll need to be fit and experienced to tackle the steep, rougher track that leads to **Hartz Peak** (1254m; four hours return), which is poorly marked with no boardwalks beyond **Hartz Pass** (two hours return). From the Pass it's a scramble to the rocky summit where (on a clear day) the 360-degree views are incredible, sweeping across Southwest National Park to the coast.

There's no camping within the park – just day facilities, including toilets, shelters, picnic tables and barbecues at the

FAST FOOD

All along the Huon Valley roadsides, particularly the B68 between Huonville and Cygnet, you can pull over and buy farm-fresh produce from makeshift (or sometimes sophisticated, illuminated and refrigerated) roadside apple stalls. These usually take the form of tin sheds out the front of farms, stocked with bags of whatever is in season: pears, apricots, peaches, blueberries, blackberries, raspberries, boysenberries, strawberries, potatoes, peas, beans, bottled juice and, of course, apples. It's an honesty system – grab your bag, drop some coins in the box (or often, scan a QR code to pay) and drive off brimming with vitamin C. As a rough guide, a bag of fresh apples sells for about $4. Bargain!

EATING IN CYGNET & THE CHANNEL: OUR PICKS

Poolish & Co: Irresistible sourdoughs, croissants, fruit tarts and other baked delicacies. Perfect Cygnet picnic fodder. *8.30am-3pm Thu-Sun* $

Porthole Cafe: Cakes, tarts (lots of GF and vegan), milkshakes and all-day toasties and fries. Outdoor tables by Cygnet paddocks. *8.30am-3pm Wed-Sun* $

Red Velvet Lounge: Cygnet's favourite coffee-and-cake hangout; plus pizzas, pasta, salads and pies. Live music Fridays. *8am-4pm Mon-Thu, to 8pm Fri & Sat, 9am-3pm Sun* $$

Peppermint Bay Hotel: Classy reimagining on an old Channel-side pub in Woodbridge that hasn't lost its charm. *10am-8pm Thu-Sat, to 4pm Sun* $$

CHASING AURORAS

The Aurora Australis, the southern hemisphere's answer to the Northern Lights, often manifests over southern Tasmania on clear winter nights. Produced by an interaction between solar activity and the Earth's magnetic field, it's usually more visible the further south you go – though it can appear anywhere in Tasmania, especially when solar activity peaks every 11 years. 2024 and 2025 were peak years, with technicolour auroras regularly lighting up the skies over Hobart. In less active years, low-light places like Mt Field National Park, Turrakana/Tasman Peninsula and South Bruny are a better bet. The eerie shimmering lights often look best when recorded by a camera (bring your phone). See sws.bom.gov.au/aurora for the official aurora forecast.

FILEDIMAGE/SHUTTERSTOCK

'Airwalk', Tahune Adventures

main trailhead, 26km from Geeveston. Rapid weather changes bluster through – bring waterproofs and warm clothing.

Airwalk in the Wilds

High above the Huon River with Tahune Adventures

Deep in the old-growth forests along the Arve Rd west of Geeveston, **Tahune Adventures** *(tahuneadventures.com.au; adult/child/family $35/18/38)* offers a spectacular raised steel walkway passing through tall trees to a platform suspended 50m above the Huon River. The devastating 2018–19 bushfires swept through here: the 'Airwalk' escaped with a scalding, but the surrounding forest was not so lucky. The forest has been slow to recover – but that doesn't mean you shouldn't visit, as the views over the muscular, swirling flow of the Huon are truly spectacular. Better yet, the Airwalk is wheelchair-accessible. Other activities include a beautiful riverside loop walk over a couple of suspension bridges, and the **Eagle Hang Glider**, a hang-glider attached to a fixed zip line that soars you across the river and back.

An Amazing Cave

Go underground at Hastings Caves & Thermal Springs

Around 15km from Southport is **Hastings Caves & Thermal Springs** *(parks.tas.gov.au; adult/child $24/12, pool only $5/2.50)*, a state reserve where you can descend into the half-light below conical Adamsons Peak on a 45-minute guided tour

DRINKING IN THE HUON VALLEY: WINERY CELLAR DOORS

Mewstone Wines: At stylish Mewstone in Flowerpot alongside the D'Entrecasteaux Channel, the Hughes brothers create resplendent riesling. *11am-4pm Fri-Sun*

Kate Hill Wines: In a lovely 1880s cottage at Huonville, Kate Hill is big on chardonnay and pinot noir. Low-key, relaxed, kid-friendly. *11am-4pm Wed-Sun*

Home Hill Wines: In Ranelagh, this stylish, rammed-earth winery crafts superb pinot noir, chardonnay and dessert wines. Upmarket restaurant, too. *10am-5pm*

Hartzview Vineyard: High on the hill between Cygnet and Woodbridge, Harzview does fruit liqueurs, ports and peppery pinot noir. Reduced winter hours. *10am-4pm Mon-Sat*

through Newdegate Cave – the largest (publicly accessible) dolerite cave in the country. There are around 500 steps to negotiate (and a few head-bump hazards), but it's an amazing series of caverns, laced with spectacular, dripping stalactites and bulbous stalagmites (don't miss 'Jabba the Hutt'). Cheerful guides fill you in on the local history and geology. Tours run hourly from 11am to 3pm on a first-come, first-served basis. The kids will love it.

Once you emerge blinkingly into daylight, return to the visitor centre for a dip in the thermal pool, filled with naturally heated 28°C water from a spring (admission included with your cave ticket). It's amazing to swim here, surrounded by towering eucalyptus forest a long way from civilisation. The kids will love this, too (maybe more than the cave). A couple of good short walks weave off into the forest.

Drive to the Bottom of Australia

That's it – there's no more road

A wonderful feeling of remoteness becomes palpable the further south you drive from Huonville. The Huon Hwy (A6) ends at Southport, but the asphalt continues onto Hastings, where the C636 begins its lonely journey south to the bottom of Australia. This is epic country, studded with clouded mountains, sigh-inducing beaches and (best of all) hardly any people. Tiny communities crop up along the way – first **Lune River** then **Ida Bay**, where the asphalt runs out. **Catamaran** is a loose affiliation of fishing shacks alongside the soft-lulling waves of **Recherche Bay**, before you cross Cockle Creek into Southwest National Park...and there's no more road. You're as far south as you can get in Australia without a boat or a backpack.

A grand grid of streets was once planned for Cockle Creek, but dwindling coal seams and whale numbers poured cold water on that idea. These days, you can walk to Adams Point (five minutes), where there's a large bronze sculpture of a **southern right whale**. An easy trail follows the coast for another hour to **Fishers Point** for sweeping views back to Bruny Island. The remains of 1843 pilot station here are worth poking through. And of course, Cockle Creek is also the end (or start) of the 85km, week-long **South Coast Track** from/to Melaleuca in Southwest National Park. You can walk the final/first stage of the track from Cockle Creek to South Cape Bay (p122; four hours return) – Australia's most southerly day walk. You might even pass people carrying surfboards.

FRENCH CONNECTIONS

Accompanying D'Entrecasteaux on his 1791 search for La Perouse was naturalist Jacques Labillardière, a friend of Joseph Banks, Cook's famous botanist. When the expedition anchored at Recherche Bay, Labillardière collected many plant specimens. His were the first European descriptions of blue gum *(Eucalyptus globulus)* and pink heath *(Epacris impressa)*, now the floral emblems of Tasmania and Victoria respectively. French explorers often established European gardens on their voyages: Labillardière planted one at the northern end of Recherche Bay. It didn't survive, but the boundary stones were uncovered by environmentalists in 2003 and used as leverage in a push to prevent wide-scale logging in the area, an action that was ultimately successful.

EATING IN GEEVESTON, DOVER & SOUTHPORT: OUR PICKS

rocket@TheEndOfThe-Road: Whacked-out water tank at the end of the Huon Hwy in Southport selling excellent coffee and muffins. *9am-3.30pm seasonal* $

Old Bank Of Geeveston: Local cafe (yes, an old bank) serving excellent coffee, cakes, pastries and artful breakfasts and lunches. Eat on the deck. *11am-3pm Tue-Sat* $

Wild Bird: Progressive, pocket-sized Dover cafe serving breakfast burgers, pumpkin-and-pesto toasties and good coffee. *8am-2pm Thu-Sat, 10am-1pm Sun* $

Masaaki's Sushi: In Geeveston, Japanese chef Masaaki boxes up Tasmania's best bentos. Takes a winter break. *noon till it's gone Sat* $$

The Southwest

UNIQUE WILDERNESS | HIKING | MOUNTAIN BIKING

GETTING AROUND

A car is certainly your best option for accessing the Southwest – via Cockle Creek at the bottom of the Huon Valley, or via the B61 road to Strathgordon beyond Mt Field National Park – as there is no public transport. Bushwalker shuttles can be arranged to drop-off/pick-up at various trailheads, but they don't come cheap. Par Avion flies into the bush strip at far-flung Melaleuca (population zero), which is the go-to option for South Coast Track walkers.

TOP TIP

Don't underestimate drive times on the twisting B61 to Strathgordon or Scotts Peak Dam Rd. Online bushwalking forums like bushwalk.com can be handy for arranging rides to the trailheads, and it bears repeating: be prepared for any kind of weather here, at any time of year.

Blanketing the southwest corner of Tasmania is a primeval wilderness of jagged peaks, bogs, buttongrass plains, temperate rainforest and impenetrable scrub – protected as the Southwest National Park. Facilities here are minimal and mobile-phone reception is nonexistent: visitors need to be self-sufficient. The only sealed road, between Maydena and Strathgordon, is one of Australia's most scenic and wonderfully lonely drives. Similarly far-flung is Cockle Creek, the park's southeastern entry point, at the bottom end of the Huon Valley.

A short hop west from Mt Field National Park, Maydena is a small logging community reinventing itself as a mountain-biking hub and your last chance for food and fuel. Nearby, the Styx Valley of the Giants looms large, before the main road traverses magnificently wild country before passing drowned Lake Gordon and Lake Pedder. Finally, after the small hydro hub of Strathgordon, the road ends at vertiginous Gordon Dam. Beyond here it's nothing but wilderness. Are you out there, thylacine?

MTB Rainforest Trails

Mountain biking at Maydena Bike Park

Carved into the forest on the side of a mountain, **Maydena Bike Park** *(maydenabikepark.com; full-access day pass adult/child $120/100)* offers over 85 mountain-bike trails catering for all skill levels, from rank amateur to hard-tailed pro (plus lessons if you're in the former category). Over 100km of trails include plenty of gravity runs – though there are some climbs for the masochistic, and adventure runs with river crossings. Shuttle buses 'uplift' riders to several different drop-off points, and there's a dizzying array of access-pass options. There's a cafe-bar here too, plus repair ships, bike-wash booths and a classy mountaintop restaurant for summer sunset dinners. Wilderness ATV tours are another option if you prefer adventures on more than two wheels. Takes a winter break.

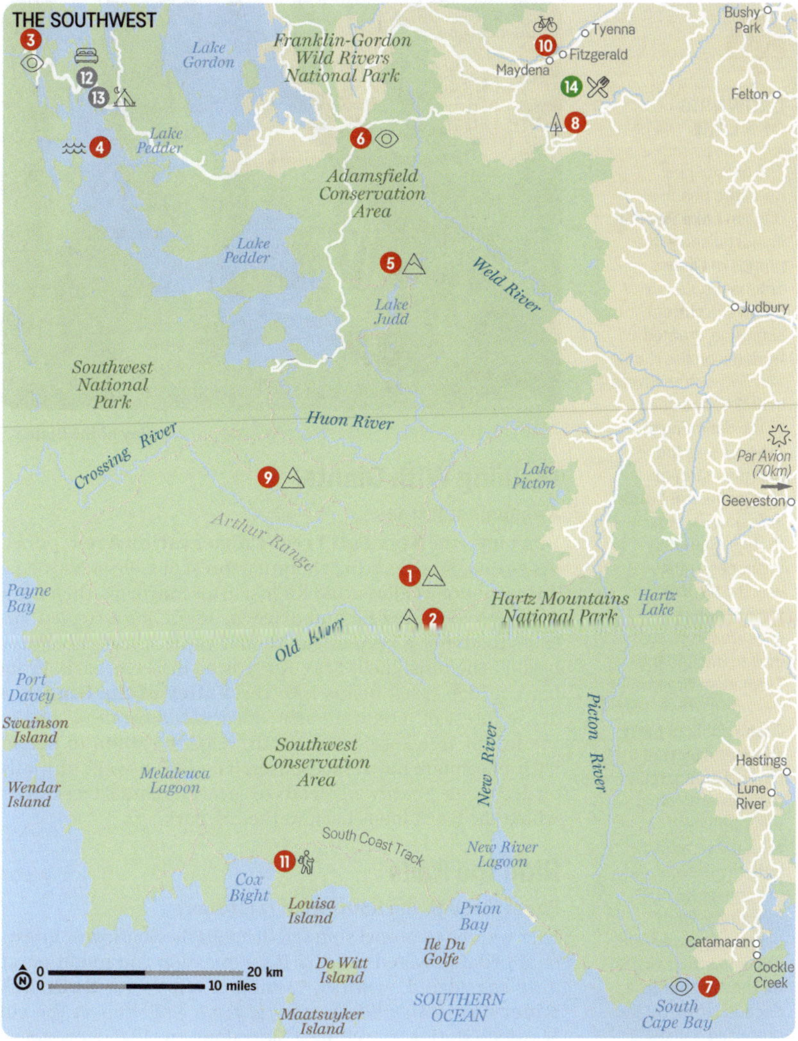

SIGHTS
1 Eastern Arthurs
2 Federation Peak
3 Gordon Dam
4 Lake Pedder
5 Mt Anne
6 Scotts Peak Rd
7 South Cape Bay
8 Styx Tall Trees Conservation Area
9 Western Arthurs

ACTIVITIES
10 Maydena Bike Park
see 10 Railtrack Riders
11 South Coast Track

SLEEPING
see 10 Giants' Table & Cottages
12 Pedder Wilderness Lodge
13 Ted's Beach Campground
see 10 Trails End House

EATING
see 10 Maydena Eats
14 Summit Restaurant
see 12 Twelvetrees Bar & Restaurant

DRINKING & NIGHTLIFE
see 10 Patio

DROWNING OF A LAKE

The unique pink quartzite beach of original **Lake Pedder**, immortalised in the photos of Olegas Truchanus, lies 15m below the current waterline, created by dams on the Huon and Serpentine Rivers in 1972. Opposition to the damming at the time was the first mainstream environmental battle in Tasmania, and though ultimately unsuccessful, it was the birth of the Australian conservation movement and the Tasmanian Greens, the world's first Green political party. The battle alerted the rest of Australia to the beauty of the Southwest wilderness, and both the Greens and the conservation movement were better organised (and ultimately successful) for the next battle, a decade later over the proposed damming of the Franklin River.

STEVE WATERS/LONELY PLANET

Valley of the Giants

Walking With Giants

Awesome tall trees

Don't miss the **Styx Tall Trees Conservation Area** *(parks.tas.gov.au; free)* deep in primordial forest outside of Maydena. Turn right onto Florentine Rd just after Maydena, then right onto unsealed Styx Rd and drive for 16km. It's a rugged forestry road, but a regular car should cope. A few kilometres beyond the (unsigned) Styx River is a small car park. From here, a loop track heads into the **Valley of the Giants**, a dense forest of mountain ash *(Eucalyptus regnans)*, one of the tallest tree species on Earth, reaching 100m in height with enormous buttressed bases. The 600m walk, initially on accessible boardwalk, leads to several colossal trees, after which the track loops back to the car park

Ride the Rails

Pedal through the Southwest rainforest

Ever wanted to propel yourself through the Southwest forests on a pedal-powered railcar? It's a question you might never have considered... Quirky, 75-minute trips with **Railtrack Riders** *(railtrackriders.com.au; from $88)* depart the old Maydena station, travelling 2.5km along an old narrow-gauge

Best coffee in the Southwest.

EATING & DRINKING IN THE SOUTHWEST: OUR PICKS

Twelvetrees Bar & Restaurant: The bar-restaurant at Strathgordon's Pedder Wilderness Lodge is the only sign of life after 6pm. *7.30-9.30am Thu-Sun, noon-3pm daily, 6-8pm Wed-Sat* $$

Maydena Eats: Take a seat at the Giants' Table & Cottages diner in Maydena for pub-style dinners and beers on tap. *5-9pm Wed-Sun* $$

Patio: Maydena Bike Park has an on-site bar-cafe: breakfasts, burgers and beers. *8.30am-7pm Thu & Sun, to 8pm Fri & Sat* $$

Summit Restaurant: MBP's 1100m-high Summit Restaurant is open sporadically over summer: book ahead. *hours vary* $$$

railway line to Florentine station. Ogle the historical displays before pedalling back to Maydena.

Drive to Strathgordon

A lonely road into the Southwest

The tiny town of **Strathgordon** is a 72km, one-hour drive beyond Maydena – a spectacular journey past craggy peaks, forests and lunar-like buttongrass plains. Built in 1969 to house 2000 Hydro Electric Commission (HEC) employees during the construction of the Gordon Dam, Strathgordon remains the base for power station workers today. Pedder Wilderness Lodge (aka the pub) is the centre of the known universe.

About 2km past the town is a lookout over Lake Pedder – the 242-sq-km artificial version of the original 10-sq-km lake, flooded when the Gordon Dam was built. The history of Lake Pedder is divisive, but even in its drowned format it's beautiful. A further 10km west is **Gordon Dam** itself, an incredible concrete arc, 198m long and 140m high, completed in 1974. From the car park, walk down around 200 steps then out along the perfect curve of the dam wall – a spectacular and slightly scary experience.

Reach the Beach

Tackle the epic South Coast Track

The best-known walk in the Southwest is the 85km **South Coast Track** *(parks.tas.gov.au; national park fees apply)*, running along the wild southern edge of Tasmania between Melaleuca and Cockle Creek at the southern end of the Huon Valley. It's a well-marked trail without any alpine sections, but with beautiful Southern Ocean beaches to keep you company. There are no facilities here – it's totally DIY, and the weather can be truly foul. Allow six to eight days to reach Cockle Creek. **Par Avion** *(paravion.com.au)* flies bushwalkers into/out of Melaleuca, and there's vehicle access to Cockle Creek. If you don't have a spare week at your disposal, the last (or first) day of the South Coast Track makes a brilliant four-hour return walk from Cockle Creek to South Cape Bay (p122) and back.

Misty Mountaintops

Southwest wilderness for experienced hikers

Hard-core hiker? Read on... **Scotts Peak Dam Rd** provides access to several of Tasmania's wildest walking tracks to truly remote mountaintops. There are no facilities here: walkers must be totally self-sufficient, good at navigation and prepared for atrocious weather. You'll also need a good head for heights on the **Mt Anne** circuit, a superb three- to five-day route over the Southwest's tallest peak (1423m). The **Western Arthurs** range warrants a four- to six-day commitment; double that if extending to the **Eastern Arthurs** and **Federation Peak**, the Tasmanian bushwalkers' Holy Grail. Progress here is measured in hours not distance, due to continuous climbing and descending – but the rewards of this World Heritage wilderness are immeasurable.

MELALEUCA & DENY KING

Way out in the Southwest is tiny Melaleuca, more of a location than a town. The airstrip here sees plenty of bushwalkers arrive to tackle the South Coast Track and Port Davey Track – but it was once a tin-mining hub, established by the King family in the 1930s. Deny King, a legendary Tasmanian outdoorsman, lived here until he died in 1991. King and his wife Margaret lived comfortably on their mining profits, raising their daughters and tending an elaborate garden. Always welcoming to bushwalkers, the Kings became a beacon in the Southwest: Deny built walkers' huts and the airstrip, and was awarded a Member of the Order of Australia (AM) in 1975 for his efforts.

SOUTH CAPE BAY WALK

Within Southwest National Park, Australia's most southerly day walk delivers you to one of the planet's last wild frontiers.

START	END	LENGTH
Cockle Creek	Cockle Creek	16km; 4–5hr

The trail begins at the tail end of the Huon Valley, near the rangers' hut across the bridge over ❶ **Cockle Creek,** a divine pocket of dunes and lagoons on the southern end of Recherche Bay. Sign the walkers' logbook, pay your park fees and stride out.

The rocky trail rises steadily though dry forest (watch for fantails and glossy black cockatoos), before descending to a narrow boardwalk across the broad ❷ **Heathers Creek marshland**.

Skirt along the top of a deep gulch, before descending into ❸ **lush gully** alongside a chuckling creek. Keep an eye out for foraging lyrebirds. The final push climbs through bracken and bottlebush, the sound of breaking waves becoming ever louder. A ❹ **spectacular view** opens up from atop the final dune – a genuine 'Wow!' moment on a clear-day, with views sweeping along South Cape Bay to Lion Rock. Follow the cairns across the crumbling grey-shale clifftops (watch your step) to the steep steps down to ❺ **South Cape Bay**. Redbill oyster catchers and oceanic gulls patrol the shore, a jumble of battered logs and knotted kelp strewn across the sand.

Before you retrace your steps, pause to consider your position: between here and Antarctica is nothing but 2500km of freezing Southern Ocean. On an increasingly crowded planet, finding yourself alone on this frontier is a humbling and magical experience.

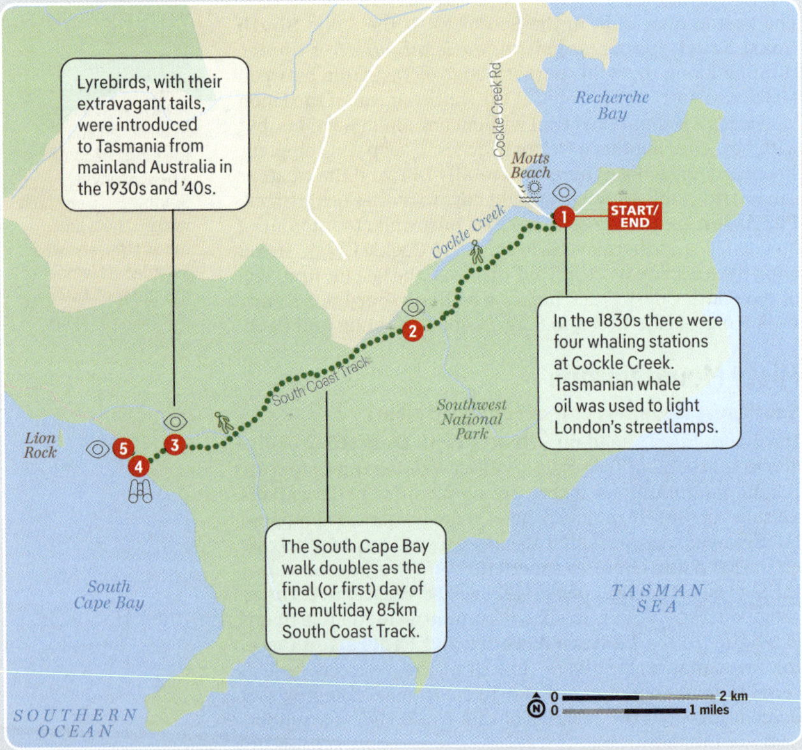

Places We Love to Stay

$ **Budget** **$$** **Midrange** **$$$** **Top end**

Turrakana/Tasman Peninsula

MAP p96

Fortescue Bay Campground $ Roomy bush sites under the trees behind the wide white beach. Hot shower tokens available. National park fees apply.

Lufra Hotel & Apartments $$ This old naughty-weekender (1949) is an icon in this neck of Teralina/Eaglehawk Neck. Newer apartments too. Pirates Bay views and pub.

Abs by the Bay $$ Bricky, affordable self-catering option in Taranna with a backyard sunset over Norfolk Bay. One- and two-bedroom options.

Nautilus Cabin $$$ This shell-shaped, off-grid timber house on 20 hectares at Teralina/Eaglehawk Neck is a sanctuary for nature lovers. Sleeps two.

Stewarts Bay Lodge $$$ Self-contained log cabins at Port Arthur: different sizes (sleeping up to six), with bush or water views. On-site restaurant to boot.

Bruny Island

MAP p104

Jetty Beach Campsite $ Low-key bush camp sites just behind north-facing Jetty Beach inside South Bruny National Park on the D'Entrecasteaux side. National park fees apply.

Bruny Beach House $$ High above Nebraska Beach on North Bruny is this lovely, good-value, woody beach house sleeping four. BYO supplies; two-night minimum stay.

Saintys Creek Cottage $$$ Cosy wooden cottage near Cloudy Bay Lagoon in South Bruny will suit bushwalkers, kayakers and nature lovers. Bonus bird hide.

43 Degrees $$$ Unique 'aircraft-hanger' spa studios at the northern end of Adventure Bay beach, all with verandas and impeccable eco credentials.

Bruny Boathouse $$$ Overlooking Satellite Island in Alonnah, this bright, stylish option sleeps four in two bedrooms. Pub and coastal trail nearby (choose your destiny).

Huon Valley

MAP p110

Huon Valley Caravan Park $ On Mountain River, walking distance to Ranelagh, with grassy powered/unpowered sites and kayaking on the nearby Huon.

Valley Campground $ Drive-in grassy sites alongside the chuckling Crabtree Rivulet, with fire pots and eco loos. Five kilometres north of Grove.

Cockle Creek Campground $ Several areas behind the dunes near the visitor centre, all a short stroll to the sand. National park fees apply.

Cygnet Old Bank $$ On the main drag, three period-style rooms with private bathrooms in what was, funnily enough, the old bank. Cafe downstairs.

Driftwood Holiday Cottages $$ Tidy, self-contained studios overlooking Dover's Port Esperance. Perfect for some waterfront veranda lounging.

Roundhouses $$ Eco-luxe circular straw-bale cottages near Cygnet, with a zero-carbon-footprint attitude. One for guests, one for the owners. Stylishly sustainable.

Abbey on Main $$$ Tastefully renovated 1859 Methodist church in Franklin, with a lovely cottage garden and full kitchen. Sleeps four.

The Southwest

MAP p119

Ted's Beach Campground $ Free campground near Strathgordon, with toilets, BBQs and shelters. Tucked into the scrub by the namesake white beach.

Giants' Table & Cottages $$ A cluster of lovingly restored, self-contained workers' cottages in Maydena, near a pond frequented by platypus. Maydena Eats diner (p120) is here too.

Pedder Wilderness Lodge $$ Stylishly upgraded motel-style accommodation at Strathgordon in a former hydro-workers' lodge. Twelvetrees Bar & Restaurant (p120) on site.

Trails End House $$$ Group accommodation, made by mountain bikers for mountain bikers. There's secure bike storage and tools, fireplaces and up to 11 beds.

Researched by
Charles Rawlings-Way

Midlands, Lakes & Wild Rivers

HISTORIC TOWNS, HIGHLAND LAKES AND UNTAMED RIVERS

Venture into Tasmania's less-travelled heartlands and discover alpine wilderness, trout-filled lakes, whisky distilleries and colonial-era villages.

The Midlands are the genteel, cultured heartland of rural Tasmania, with a string of old garrison towns that are time capsules of Georgian-era architecture and the Victorian-era crafts of whisky distilling and knitting yarns (this is sheep country). You can blow through from Launceston to Hobart in a couple of hours – but detour off the Midland Hwy and these towns spill secrets from harsh, cruel convict times.

CHAMELEONSEYE/SHUTTERSTOCK

Heading west into the Highlands, unsealed tracks lead to idyllic lakeside camp sites on the tarn-studded Central Plateau. This starkly beautiful, sparsely populated region in the centre of Tasmania is home to fragile flora, wily trout and sodden fishers. Access from the Midland Hwy is via Scots-tinged Bothwell in the Clyde River Valley; or from the Lyell Hwy to the southwest via Bronte Park (although the lonely, unfenced road from Ouse to Bothwell is much more scenic).

Continuing west, the windy, single-lane Lyell Hwy drops in and out of gorges populated with hydropower stations, their pipes tumbling vertiginously down mountainsides. Derwent Bridge is a windswept highway stop – the jumping-off point for Leeawuleena/Lake St Clair, the southern terminus of the heralded Overland Track. Entering the Tasmanian Wilderness World Heritage Area (TWWHA) and two of Tasmania's wildest and most magnificent national parks, you'll cross the famed Franklin River and the lonely wilderness track heading southwest to lofty Frenchmans Cap.

THE MAIN AREAS

THE MIDLANDS
A string of historic towns. p128

HIGHLAND LAKES
Cast into a fly-fishing paradise. p133

WILD RIVERS
World-heritage watery wilderness. p137

For places to stay in Midlands, Lakes and Wild Rivers, see p141

ANDREW BAIN/GETTY IMAGES

Left: Fly-fishing (p133); Above: Rafts along the Franklin River (p137)

Find Your Way

The trout-filled lakes of the lofty Central Plateau occupy the middle of Tasmania, with the historic agricultural Midlands towns to the east. To the southwest lies enigmatic Leeawuleena/Lake St Clair and the island's untamed wild rivers.

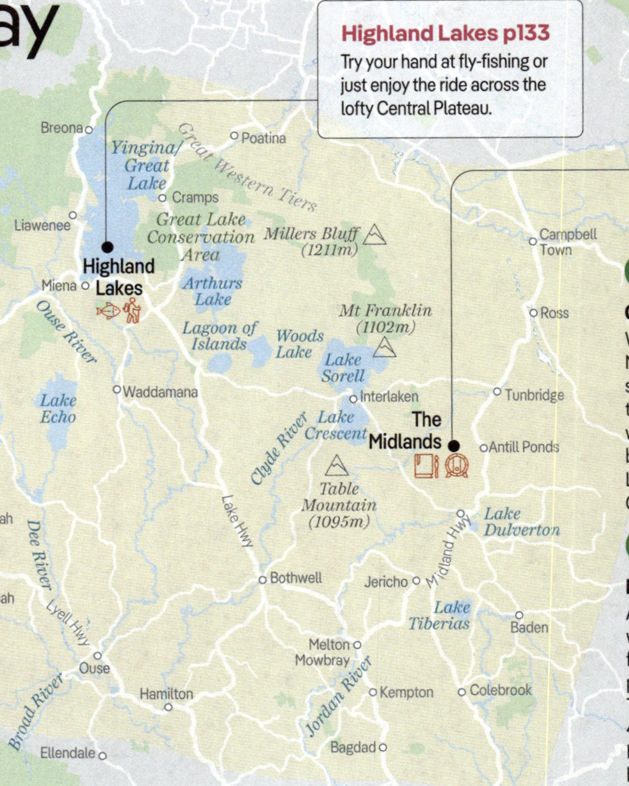

Highland Lakes p133

Try your hand at fly-fishing or just enjoy the ride across the lofty Central Plateau.

The Midlands p128

Wander well-preserved Georgian streets and uncover the harsh history of convict days.

Wild Rivers p137

Raft the mighty Franklin or hike into the Southwest wilderness, trekking to Frenchmans Cap.

CAR & BUS

While intercity buses connect the Midlands to Hobart and Launceston several times daily, and Derwent Bridge twice weekly, you'll need your own wheels to explore this region fully. Pre-booked shuttles can be arranged to/from Leeawuleena/Lake St Clair, handy for Overland Track pick-ups.

BICYCLE

Avoid the busy Midland Hwy on two wheels, but a free-wheeling alternative for those with time and energy is bike-packing the long-distance Tasmanian Trail, bisecting the Central Plateau on its 480km journey from Dover to Devonport. Hikers and horse-riders also use the trail, but a mountain bike is a great way to go.

TRABANTOS/SHUTTERSTOCK

Callington Mill Distillery (p128), Oatlands

Plan Your Time

Decide if historic towns or raw wilderness is your thing. West of the Midlands, travel time is longer, as the hilly narrow roads are notoriously slow going (more time to admire the scenery!).

A Quick Wild Look

- Driving between Devonport and Hobart? Take the scenic and adventurous Highland Lakes Road (A5) south from Deloraine, climbing onto the snowy (even in late spring) **Central Plateau** (p133), past Yingina/Great Lake and through **Miena** (p134) and historic **Bothwell** (p135) before joining the Midland Hwy just north of **Kempton** (p128). It might take you 30 minutes longer than the main route, but wow, what a place!

Lakes & Midlands

- From Launceston, head south into the Midlands through historic **Campbell Town** (p130), **Ross** (p130), **Oatlands** (p132) and **Kempton** (p128). Don't miss a whisky or two at **Callington Mill Distillery** (p128) in Oatlands and **Old Kempton Distillery** (p128) – plus **Lawrenny Estate** (p136) in Ouse after you jag west towards **Franklin-Gordon Wild Rivers National Park** (p137). Don't miss a walk at atmospheric **Leeawuleena/Lake St Clair** (p138), Australia's deepest lake.

Seasonal Highlights

SPRING
Get into a lake; trout are calling. Hike the Overland Track to **Leeawuleena/Lake St Clair** (p138) before summer permits kick in.

SUMMER
Dusky evenings beguile in the Midlands towns, while lakeside camp sites are at a premium. Long days and fine weather.

AUTUMN
There's a nip in the air as summer crowds melt away. The fagus is turning around Leeawuleena/Lake St Clair.

WINTER
Avoid the blizzards raking the Central Plateau and enjoy a warming fireside dram and cosy hospitality down in the Midlands.

The Midlands

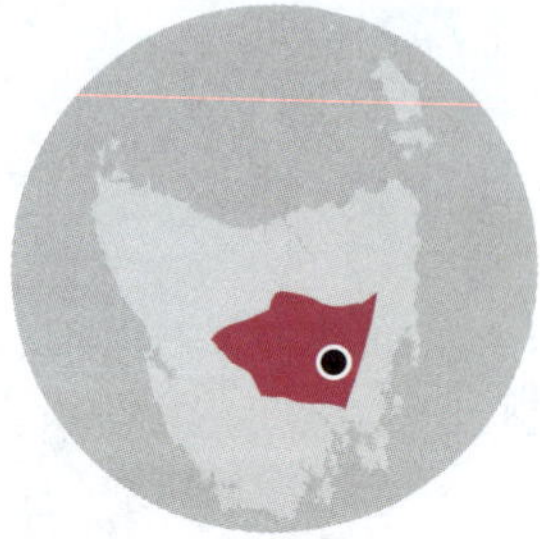

GEORGIAN ARCHITECTURE | WHISKY DISTILLERIES | CONVICT HERITAGE

GETTING AROUND

Intercity buses running between Hobart and Launceston cruise the well-trafficked Midland Hwy (A1) and stop at the main towns four times daily in each direction, reducing to two or three services on Saturday and Sunday. Your own wheels are a better bet, and give you the freedom to explore. Cycling here isn't a great option: unless you're heading west into the Highlands or east to the coast, there's really only one road from A to B, and it's an extremely busy one.

TOP TIP

Ross, more or less in the middle of the Midlands, makes a good overnight base from which to explore the other towns as it has good accommodation and eating options and several excellent convict sights, and is compact enough to wander about on foot.

Straw-coloured plains, hawthorn hedgerows, rows of poplars, grand homesteads – Tasmania's Midlands have a distinctly English countryside feel. This is old-school Tasmania, tracing the route between Hobart and Launceston hammered out by convict gangs in the early 1800s. As the road rolled itself out, sandstone garrison towns and pastoral properties appeared: the Midlands soon became the food factory of Van Diemen's Land.

The current course of the Midland Hwy, Tasmania's main north–south route, has strayed from its original path – a few meandering detours are required to explore the old towns here. Kempton, Oatlands, Ross and Campbell Town all have well-preserved clusters of Georgian architecture, built with convict skill – quiet towns that offer intriguing, and at times harrowing, insights into early colonial life.

These days travellers can take a break from the highway traffic in welcoming pubs and cosy accommodation, and at some sublime artisanal whisky distilleries.

Time for a Wee Dram?

Whisky tasting in the Midlands

Around 30km north of Hobart at Pontville, **Lark Distillery** *(larkdistillery.com)* occupies the historic 1830s Shene Estate, some 16 hectares of fields and heritage buildings the size of a small village. The distillery is open for tastings from 10am to 4pm, with tours at noon and 2pm daily.

Why settle for a bottle when you can own your own cask? **Old Kempton Distillery** *(oldkemptondistillery.com.au)* in the grand old 1842 Dysart Manor house is where you can sample whisky flights, take a tour (11am and 1.30pm daily), grab a cafe feed or purchase a 20L, 50L or whopping 100L tub of sunshine.

The windmill-fronted **Callington Mill Distillery** *(callingtonmill.com.au)* in Oatlands produces world-class single malt whiskies using cutting-edge, innovative technology. Come for a guided tour (noon daily), a whisky flight, lunch in the excellent

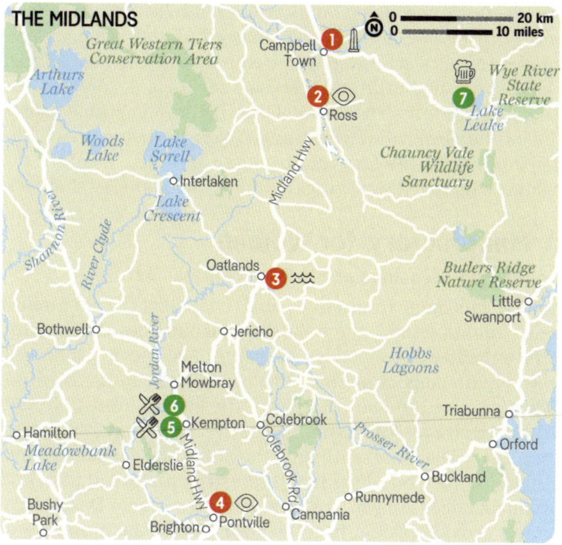

SIGHTS
1 Convict Brick Trail
2 Four Corners of Ross
3 Lake Dulverton
4 Lark Distillery
see 3 Oatlands History Room
see 1 Red Bridge
see 2 Ross Bridge
see 2 Ross Female Factory Historic Site

EATING
see 3 Bunch
5 Huntington Tavern
see 1 JJ's Cafe Campbell Town
see 3 Kentish Hotel
6 Mood Food
see 3 Oatlands Pancake & Crepe Shop
see 2 Ross Hotel
see 2 Ross Village Bakery
see 1 Sweet Brew

DRINKING & NIGHTLIFE
see 3 Callington Mill Distillery
7 Lake Leake Inn
see 5 Old Kempton Distillery

restaurant or a chance to blend your own signature whisky. Even if you don't like whisky, it's worth a wander here: the owners have spent millions restoring the 1837 windmill, stables and old cottages on the estate. There's a great kids' playground adjacent, and the glass-and-steel distillery building itself is a stunner.

Australia's Third-Oldest Bridge

Magnificent convict masonry at Ross

The oft-photographed **Ross Bridge** *(visitross.com.au)* over the Macquarie River is the third-oldest bridge in Australia

THE FATHER OF TASMANIA

Strung-out Kempton, 50km north of Hobart and bypassed by the main highway, was founded in 1838, making it one of the state's earliest settlements. Originally known as Green Ponds, it was later renamed after one-time resident and notorious rabblerouser Anthony Fenn Kemp. Kemp was a charismatic dude: one-half egotistical bankrupt with scant moral fibre and one-half progressive patriot who was critical in Tasmania's evolution from convict dump to independent colony. Fleeing debts in England, he became a dedicated pastoralist, merchant and political sabre rattler. Never far from controversy, he made as many friends as enemies, and left behind more than a dozen children – a fact that has seen him dubbed the 'Father of Tasmania'.

EATING & DRINKING IN THE MIDLANDS: OUR PICKS

Mood Food: The original and best Mood Food (a Tasmanian roadhouse franchise) is on the highway north of Kempton. Burgers, truckers and country music. *24hr* $

Bunch: The pick of the Oatlands cafes, serving pizzas, soups and deli-style sandwiches. Beer and wine; sunny footpath tables. *8.30am-4pm* $

Kentish Hotel: Oatlands' last pub is hanging in there, with beer-garden burgers and an adjunct coffee shop. *9am-10pm Wed-Sat, to 3pm Sun* $$

Old Kempton Distillery: Hearty Midlands fare to augment the single malt: soups, beef-and-whisky pie, sausages and sticky date pudding. *10am-4pm* $$

THE KING OF ICELAND

Jorgen Jorgensen (1780–1841) of Ross Bridge fame was a versatile chap: explorer, sailor, writer, whaler, convict...and self-proclaimed King of Iceland. Born in Denmark, he left for the high seas at 15, arriving in Van Diemen's Land to help establish the colony in the early 1800s. In 1809 he spent time in Iceland, proclaiming the country's freedom from Danish-Norwegian rule and installing himself as king, for which he was imprisoned in England. When he got out in 1812, he became a British spy in the Napoleonic Wars, but was transported back to Tasmania for theft. Pardoned in 1835, he married Irish convict Norah Corbett in 1831 and died in Hobart 10 happy years later.

(1836). Designed by colonial architect John Lee Archer, it was built by two convict stonemasons, James Colbeck and Daniel Herbert, who were granted pardons for their efforts. Herbert chiselled the 186 intricate carvings decorating the arches, including Celtic symbols, animals and notable people (including Governor Arthur and Anglo-Danish convict Jorgen Jorgensen, the farcical ex-king of Iceland). At night the bridge is lit up – the carvings shimmer with spooky shadows.

A 'Manufactory' for Women

Count your blessings at the Ross Female Factory

Deriving its name from a historical twisting of the old English word 'manufactory', the windswept **Ross Female Factory Historic Site** *(parks.tas.gov.au)* was once one of Tasmania's four female-convict prisons. The others were in Launceston, George Town and South Hobart – the latter now a UNESCO World Heritage–listed site. Memories have lingered longer than the bricks here, with only the Superintendent's Cottage still standing – but it's full of interesting historical info, and archaeological excavations have revealed much. Descriptive panels provide insight into the hard lives of the hundreds of women (and their many children) who were imprisoned here from 1847 to 1854. Most of the buildings were demolished in 1897: wander the lawns out the back and imagine the church, workrooms, nurseries, morgue and solitary confinement cells that once stood here.

The Four Corners of Ross

Choose your destiny

Feeling a bit aimless? Life lacking direction? Get some guidance down at the **Four Corners of Ross**. Here at the Church St and Bridge St crossroads, your soul can choose from four directions: 'Damnation' (the old jail, now a private residence), 'Recreation' (the Town Hall), 'Salvation' (the Catholic Church) and 'Temptation' (the pub). For most visitors, it's not a very challenging decision to make.

Red Bricks of Campbell Town

One convict-built bridge, hundreds of convict stories

The convict-built bridge across the slow-moving Elizabeth River at Campbell Town was completed in 1838, making it almost as venerable as the Ross Bridge. Locals call it the **Red**

EATING & DRINKING IN THE MIDLANDS: OUR PICKS

Sweet Brew: Top Campbell Town coffee, plus fat blueberry muffins, toasties and spinach-and-fetta *börek* (Balkan pastry). *7.30am-2pm* $

Ross Village Bakery: Towering slabs of vanilla slice, pies and sourdough baked in an 1860 oven. Courtyard and inside or footpath tables. *8.30am-3pm Wed-Sun* $

Ross Hotel: In the process of culinary reinvention when we visited: pizza in the beer garden will suffice. *11.30am-10pm Wed, Thu & Sun, to 11pm Fri & Sat* $$

Callington Mill Distillery: Exquisite menu showcasing the best Tasmania has to offer: super steaks and even better pulled-lamb ravioli (p128). *10am-5pm* $$$

SUCCUMB TO TEMPTATION

Take a walk around the Ross streets and riverbanks and discover the town's key historic sites.

START	END	LENGTH
Four Corners of Ross	Ross Hotel	3km; 1hr

From the 1 **Four Corners of Ross**, head south past the 1891 2 **Town Hall** (aka 'Recreation') uphill to the 1885 3 **Uniting Church**, with heaven-sent country views. Truck back downhill past the 4 **Tasmanian Wool Centre** (buy a beanie), then turn left to reach 5 **Ross Bridge** (p129) and its 186 intricate carvings (how many animals can you spot?).

Follow the trail south along the Macquarie River, passing some interesting churchyard ruins, to arrive at the 6 **Ross Female Factory**. Check out the Superintendent's Cottage and the bleak yards behind it. Follow Portugal St, cross the railway line, then a path alongside a stone wall (all rather Yorkshire). On the hilltop beyond Park St is 7 **Old Ross Burial Ground** (1835). Several British Redcoats are among the subterranean, plus Daniel Herbert the Ross Bridge convict stonemason (died 1868, aged 67).

Backtrack through the rambling 8 **Anglican Pioneer Cemetery** and 9 **Ross Catholic Cemetery**. Head north along Park St, turn left onto Bridge St, right onto Bond St, then left again onto Badajos St. The noble 10 **St John's Anglican Church** dates from 1869.

Follow Church St to the 1847 11 **schoolhouse**, and admire the beautiful 1889 12 **post office** across the street, with its elegant wrought-iron portico. Finally, succumb to 'Temptation' with a cold pint at the 1835 13 **Ross Hotel**.

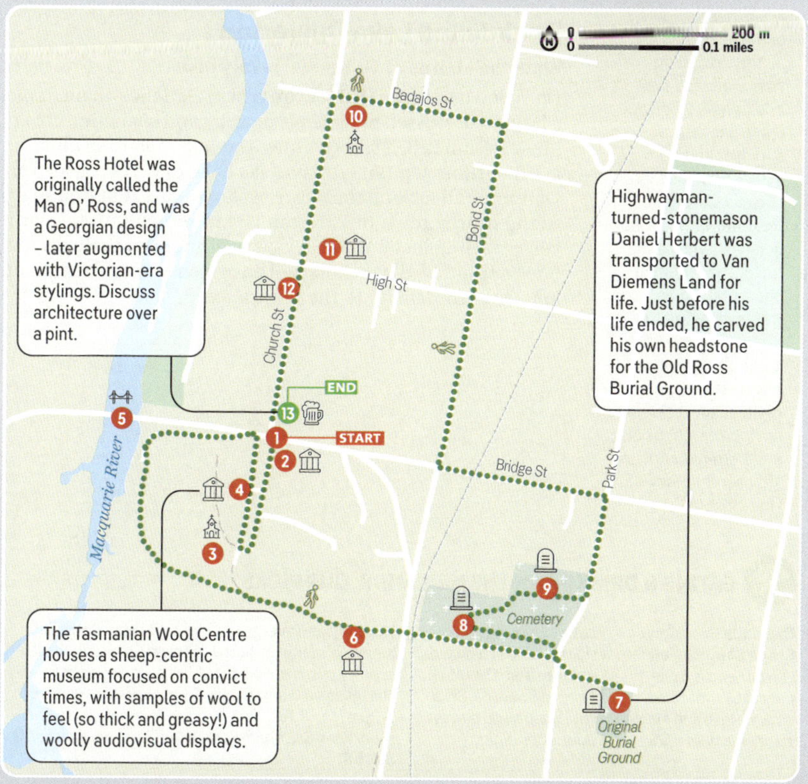

SHADOWS OF THE PAST

The Midland Hwy between Hobart and Launceston is Tasmania's main north–south link road – and a route that comes with a rich history. The next time you're driving this way, keep an eye out (no, not you, driver) for the 16 large silhouette sculptures adorning the hills and roadside verges between Tunbridge and Kempton. The project, by artists Folko Kooper and Maureen Craig, illustrates snippets of the highway's history, including stagecoaches and bushrangers, convict chain gangs, a surveyor and even a pack of thylacines (Tasmanian tigers). However, the quirkiest two are the travelling hangman and a policeman wheeling a drunk in a wheelbarrow. For some background on the artists and loads of detail on each of the sculptures, check out southernmidlands.tas.gov.au/shadows-of-the-past.

Bridge because it was built from more than 1.5 million red bricks, baked on site. The red-brick theme continues along the town's main street, where the **Convict Brick Trail** *(northernmidlands.tas.gov.au)* is set into the footpath. Each brick details the crimes, sentences and arrival dates of convicts such as Ephram Brain and English Corney, sent here for sins as various as stealing potatoes, bigamy, murder and being an 'indefatigable burglar'.

Oatlands Architectural

Time-travel along Oatlands' main street

Bypassed by the Midland Hwy since 1985, Oatlands contains Australia's largest single collection of Georgian architecture. The stately (and now rather quiet) main street feels like a film set, with its 87 historic sandstone buildings. The site for the town was chosen in 1821 and 80km of streets planned for this grand Midlands capital, but things never really took off. Today you can time-travel up and down the main street and check out the old town jail, former supreme court and defunct military precinct. The **Oatlands History Room** *(southernmidlands.tas.gov.au/museums; adult/child $3/1)* is also worth a look – an old garage full of old photos, bootmaking equipment, radios, lamps, farm gear and sundry historical knick-knacks.

Duck-Filled Lake Dulverton

Walk the shores of Oatlands' lovely lake

Duck down to **Lake Dulverton** east of Oatlands' main drag – a large lake crossed by a couple of weirs and encircling craggy Mary's Island. If it's been rainy the lake fills to brimming; at other times (eg 1993 to 2010) it's bone dry. There's a lovely walking trail around the western shoreline, extending south to the nearby town of Parattah (14km return in total); or if you're feeling lucky you can cast a fly into the shallows and hook a trout. Bird-watchers will have plenty to squawk about, and frogs contribute to the natural cacophony.

EATING & DRINKING IN THE MIDLANDS: OUR PICKS

Oatlands Pancake & Crepe Shop: Sometimes all you need is a pile of pancakes with some strawberries and maple syrup. *10am-2pm* $$

Lake Leake Inn: Old shingle-clad fishing pub en route from Campbell Town to Swansea. Sip a cold Boag's and discuss trout. *noon-8pm*

Huntington Tavern: Kempton's straight-laced country pub is the place to shovel down lamb shanks. *3-8pm Mon & Tue, 11am-10pm Wed-Sat, noon-8pm Sun* $$

JJ's Bakery Campbell Town: Shiny doughnuts, lemon tarts and hot pies and pasties for passing road warriors. *7am-5pm Mon-Sat, from 8am Sun* $

Highland Lakes

TROUT FISHING | LAKESIDE CAMPING | WILDERNESS TRAILS

Tasmania's wild and windswept Central Plateau sits above the clouds (and trees) at around 1050m – a stark, rocky expanse pockmarked by small tarns and large freshwater lakes brimming with trout. Arthurs Lake, Lake August and Bronte Lagoon all have their fly-fishing fans (trout were introduced to Tasmania in 1864), but mammoth 114-sq-metre Yingina/Great Lake reigns supreme as the Australia's largest freshwater lake.

Fishing shacks, lodges and basic campgrounds cluster like barnacles around the larger lakes, though services are scant. Miena, the main township (population 120-something), has fuel, beds, two pubs and a general store.

But it's the great outdoors that visitors seek: casting a fly, waking up in a campervan next to gently lapping water, cycling or hiking remote trails, or just taking a (rather wild) Sunday drive. This is popular terrain during summer; spring and autumn are more relaxed. Winters here are downright savage – expect plenty of snow (all part of the appeal).

GETTING AROUND

You will need your own vehicle here. You can get to gateway towns like Deloraine, Bothwell and Ouse via limited public transport, but there are no services to the Central Plateau beyond these. The main Highland Lakes Road (A5) between Deloraine and Bothwell and on to Melton Mowbray is sealed, but most of the smaller roads are unsealed – so if you've got access to a 4WD, even better.

Fly-Fishing Nirvana

Wade into a misty lake and hook a trout

Catching brown and rainbow trout in the Highland Lakes should be as easy as getting your feet wet – but you still need timing and skill! There are also sustainability-informed restrictions on fish size, daily catch allocations and the types of tackle permitted in various areas in different seasons: the **Inland Fisheries Service** *(ifs.tas.gov.au)* sells licences and offers priceless advice. Live bait (a grasshopper, grub or worm) is tried and true, but bait fishing is banned in most inland Tasmanian waters – it's too effective to give the fish a sporting chance. Artificial lures and flies are more acceptable, coming in myriad shapes, sizes, weights and colours: 'Cobra' wobbler might work for you in lakes, or a 'Celta' in streams.

TOP TIP

Short on time? From Launceston, spin a loop around Yingina/Great Lake via the switchbacks beside Quamby Bluff to Pine Lake. Truck through Liawenee and Miena (grab picnic supplies at Great Lake General Store) before completing the loop via Poatina – a three-hour, 220km circuit.

SIGHTS
1 Australasian Golf Museum
2 Pine Lake
3 Tarraleah

ACTIVITIES
4 Miena Village Guiding
5 Ratho Farm
6 Tasmanian Trail

EATING
7 Bronte Park General Store
see 6 Central Highlands Lodge
see 4 Great Lake General Store
see 4 Great Lake Hotel
see 3 Highlander Arms
see 1 Sealy's Store

DRINKING & NIGHTLIFE
see 1 Castle Hotel
8 Lawrenny Estate

SHOPPING
see 4 Great Lake General Store

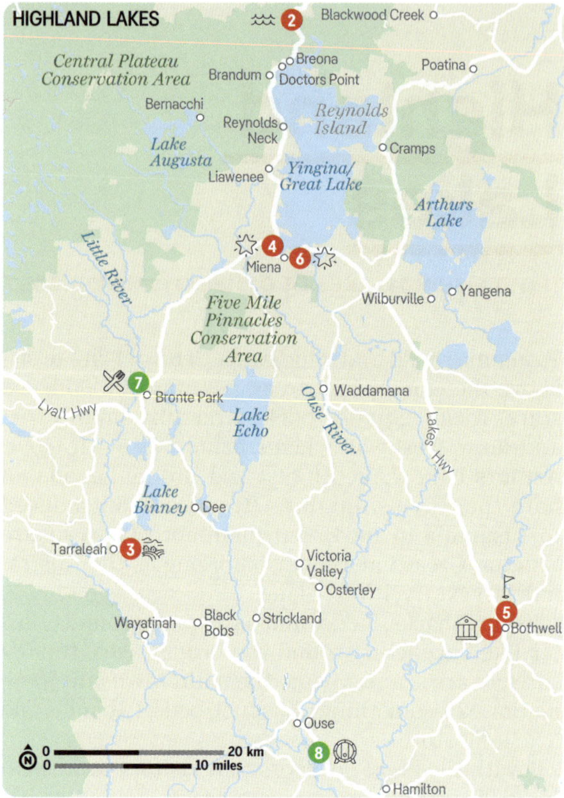

Engaging a professional fly-fishing guide for lessons or a guided trip is a stellar idea: try **Rod & Fly Tasmania** *(rodandfly.com.au)*, **Miena Village Guiding** *(mienaguidingtasmania.com.au)* or **Trout Guides and Lodges Tasmania** *(www.troutguidestasmania.com.au)*. Prices range from $600 to $900 per person per day. And don't forget your licence!

Ancient Trees & Alpine Tarns

Accessible Gondwanaland

Edging 1200m above sea level about halfway between Deloraine and Liawenee, the short nature trail to picturesque **Pine Lake** is a wonderful meet-and-greet with Highlands flora. A level boardwalk, suitable for wheelchairs, runs 400m to the lake from the car park on Highland Lakes Rd (A5). En route you'll pass an ancient copse of pencil pines *(Athrotaxis cupressoides)*. These tapering trees aren't actually pines at all, and are found nowhere else beyond Tasmania's high and wild Central Plateau. Pencil pines are super-slow growing, reproducing via cloning themselves, and can reach 1200 years old. They're also highly susceptible to bushfires and are at risk on a warming planet.

STEVE LOVEGROVE/SHUTTERSTOCK

Ratho Farm

Tee-Off in Bothwell

The oldest golf course outside of Scotland

At Bothwell on the eastern edge of the Highlands, Scottish heritage runs deep: the town has adopted tartan street signs and is obsessed with golf. Next to the visitor centre, the **Australasian Golf Museum** *(ausgolfmuseum.com; $5)* has a putting green where you can test old-style clubs, and a stupendous selection of golf-themed Jim Beam bourbon decanters (sadly, empty). The oldest golf course outside of Scotland is in Bothwell too, rolled out of the dust at **Ratho Farm** *(rathofarm.com/golf; 9/18 holes $35/50)* in 1822 by Scottish settlers. It's an eccentric 18-hole prospect: watch out for sheep, hedges, hay bales and fences (local rules: if you hit a fence, you can replay the shot without penalty). There's convict-built accommodation here too.

Cycle the Tasmanian Trail

Bike across Tasmania, coast to coast

Rambling between Devonport and Dover for 480km, the multi-use **Tasmanian Trail** *(tasmaniantrail.com.au; membership $70)* follows back roads, forestry tracks and private paths

THE GENTLE ART OF FLY-FISHING

Brad Harris, ex-editor of *FlyLife* magazine, shares some insider tips.

Tasmania has three distinct seasons for trout fly-fishing.

In spring, when lakes are flooded and fish feed around the edges, dawn and dusk are optimal casting times. Summer brings hatching mayflies and beetles – match your fly colour to the insect. Try a dark brown Parachute Emerger or yellow/green Foam Beetle.

In autumn on the lakes, try Beetle or small Mayfly dry flies or Woolly Bugger and Stick Caddis wets. During drizzly weather, look for water with mayflies, and on sunny days sight-fish in shallow clear lakes and rivers. Don't mix the two.

Pack a 9ft 5-weight rod with floating line and learn to cast in the wind.

Polarising sunglasses are essential!

EATING & DRINKING IN THE HIGHLANDS: OUR PICKS

Great Lake General Store: Hot coffee, pies and toasties complement picnic supplies and fishing flies. At Miena. *8am-6pm* $

Bronte Park General Store: Trout flies outnumber toasted sandwiches, but the latter won't break the bank. *7.30am-5pm, from 8am Sat & Sun* $

Great Lake Hotel: Ace pub fare (pizzas, steaks, schnitzels, wallaby burgers), with serves as big as the 4WDs in the car park. In Miena. *11am-9pm Wed-Sat, to 3pm Sun* $$

Central Highlands Lodge: Cold beers, hearty food, friendly locals and a roaring fire welcome weary fisher-folk. *11am-9pm* $$

THE FAMILY THAT BOUGHT A TOWN

About 30km northwest of Ouse, Tarraleah is an isolated Highlands village built in the 1920s and '30s for hydroelectric workers. It was a busy town with shops, a church, a golf course and 100 homes, but Tarraleah declined when the hydro work dried up. Most of the houses were removed in the 1990s, and in 2002 a Queensland family bought the whole town. They poured buckets of cash into the place, then sold it to private developers who've spent millions more. Today, **Tarraleah** *(tarraleahlodge.com.au)* offers accommodation (a caravan park, cabins, houses and an Art Deco lodge) and makes a great base for bushwalking and fly-fishing adventures. Even in the mists of July it's a curiously engaging place.

ANDREW BAIN/ALAMY

Tasmanian Trail (p135)

across farmland, river valleys, forests and the stark Central Plateau. Riders of all skill levels can tackle it, but there are a few tough sections and several (possibly dodgy) river crossings – not to mention some serious altitude gain. The trail sidesteps national parks and major towns, but it's never far from a cosy bed. Most riders take 10 to 14 days to complete the route, but if you don't have that kind of time, Miena in the middle of the Highland Lakes is a handy staging post. Pick up supplies at the **Great Lake General Store**, and get riding. The trail is managed by volunteers who sell a guidebook via membership, and supply keys to locked gates and amenities. You don't need to book, and the trail is navigable in either direction. Hot tip: the southwesterly wind is better behind you than in your face (ride north).

Gin tasting flights from $10; whisky from $45.

EATING & DRINKING IN THE HIGHLANDS: OUR PICKS

Sealy's Store: A warming wood heater, proper coffee and interesting pies and soups in an 1850 corner shop in Bothwell. *9am-3pm* $

Highlander Arms: At Tarraleah, this pub-style restaurant does hearty evening meals (lasagne, schnitzels, steaks, burgers). Reduced winter hours. *5.30-7.30pm Mon-Sat* $$

Castle Hotel: Bothwell's National Trust–listed pub was first licensed in 1829, making it one of the oldest pubs in Australia. Cold beers, hot dinners, loyal locals. *11am-9pm*

Lawrenny Estate: At Ouse, a Highlands' southern access town, this gorgeous, early-1800s estate bottles up limited-release single malts and crystal-clear gins. *10am-4pm*

Wild Rivers

WHITE-WATER RAFTING | BUSHWALKING | REMOTE WILDERNESS

West of the Highland Lakes and lush Derwent Valley, Australia's deepest lake lies waiting at the southern end of Cradle Mountain-Lake St Clair National Park. Leeawuleena/Lake St Clair is the finishing line for the legendary Overland Track (lots of hungry hikers), but you don't have to hike that far to experience this sublime place – there are lovely short walks here too.

Further west again, the majestic Franklin-Gordon Wild Rivers National Park covers over 4000 sq km of the Tasmanian Wilderness World Heritage Area and is as wild as the name suggests. Raging, convoluted rivers, mist-shrouded peaks and impenetrable southwest Tasmanian bush – a visit here is to time travel, catching a glimpse of Gondwanaland, the forest closing in on all sides. Rafting the Franklin River is undoubtedly Tasmania's most exciting, once-in-a-lifetime adventure, while the three- to five-day return trek to the sheer summit of 1446m Frenchmans Cap is a less-peopled hike than the busy Overland Track.

TOP TIP

For a quick glimpse of the fabled Franklin River, take the eponymous Nature Trail (1km) from a picnic area on the Lyell Hwy about 25km west of Derwent Bridge. The easy, accessible loop track passes through lush forest before following the fern-lined mossy riverbank back to the road.

Rafting the Franklin River

White-knuckle, white-water adventure

White-water rafting trips on the Franklin River within **Franklin-Gordon Wild Rivers National Park** *(parks.tas.gov.au)* depart from **Collingwood Bridge** on the Lyell Hwy,

GETTING AROUND

Derwent Bridge and Leeawuleena/Lake St Clair are 2½ hours from both Hobart and Launceston by car (the latter via the Central Plateau). The Hobart–Queenstown coach service trucks along the Lyell Hwy through Derwent Bridge and past Frenchmans Cap car park on Tuesday and Friday in both directions. Private bushwalker shuttles connect Leeawuleena/Lake St Clair with Hobart, Launceston and Cradle Mountain. They're expensive, but handy for the Overland Track (park your car at Leeawuleena/Lake St Clair, shuttle to Cradle Mountain, then walk back to your wheels). Most roads beyond the Lyell Hwy are unsealed.

HIGHLIGHTS
1 Cradle Mountain-Lake St Clair National Park
2 Franklin-Gordon Wild Rivers National Park

SIGHTS
3 Collingwood Bridge
4 Frenchmans Cap
5 Leeawuleena/Lake St Clair

ACTIVITIES
6 Donaghys Hill
see 3 Franklin River Rafting
see 5 Larmairremener Tabelti
see 3 Tasmanian Expeditions
see 3 Water By Nature

SLEEPING
7 Narcissus Hut
8 Pumphouse Point

EATING
9 Derwent Bridge Wilderness Hotel
10 Hungry Wombat Cafe
see 5 Lake St Clair Lodge

INFORMATION
see 5 Leeawuleena/ Lake St Clair Visitor Information Centre

TRANSPORT
see 5 Lake St Clair Ferry

40km west of Derwent Bridge, and take eight to 10 days end to end. Be prepared for wet, cold, adrenalin-packed days, riverside camps, sublime scenery and quite a few portages. It's an unforgettable journey (at $4K-plus, you won't be forgetting anything in a hurry) – passing the narrow **Irenabyss**, the scary **Great Ravine**, and famed **Rock Island Bend**, pin-up for the 'No Dams' campaign. The paddling usually ends at Sir John Falls, where the yacht *Stormbreaker* shunts you across Macquarie Harbour to Strahan. No experience is required, but this is one trip you should do with experienced professionals: try **Franklin River Rafting**, **Tasmanian Expeditions** or **Water By Nature**.

Australia's Deepest Lake

Walk the shores of Leeawuleena/Lake St Clair

More sightseer than mountaineer? Within **Cradle Mountain-Lake St Clair National Park**, many walks around the 215m-deep, shimmering **Leeawuleena/Lake St Clair** *(parks.tas.gov.au; day pass per person/vehicle $24/48)* don't require an Overland Track Permit or a week in the mountains – just some decent shoes and a national parks pass. From the

SHORELINE SCENES: LEEAWULEENA/LAKE ST CLAIR

Overland Track too long? Tackle the final day of the 'OT' as a day walk, skirting shimmering Leeawuleena/Lake St Clair.

START	END	LENGTH
Leeawuleena/Lake St Clair Visitor Information Centre	Leeawuleena/Lake St Clair Visitor Information Centre	17.5km; 5–6hr

At the southern end of the lake at Cynthia Bay, check in for your pre-booked ferry ride at ❶ **Leeawuleena/Lake St Clair Visitor Information Centre** (p140). Chugging north across the misty lake, the 25-minute ride to ❷ **Narcissus Bay** is a super-scenic meet-and-greet with Australia's deepest lake.

The trail begins behind ❸ **Narcissus Hut**, heading across a marshy plain below towering Mt Olympus (1472m). Beyond the marsh, the trail enters an ancient rainforest – a damp realm of gnarled roots, colossal trunks and chuckling creeks.

Around two hours into the walk, the track descends to the shore at ❹ **Echo Point**, where a rustic cabin and jetty are evidence of human habitation. Behind the cabin, the trail passes a series of gargantuan swamp gums standing in splendid solitude. When one of these giants succumbs to gravity and falls towards the lake, it squashes the undergrowth and opens up a view across the water.

At ❺ **Watersmeet**, where the fast-flowing Cuvier River meets the Hugel River, the forest dries itself out and becomes open woodland.

Beyond the bridge, wide gravel fire trails suddenly fill with cheery couples and snack-munching families, exploring the short trails around the visitor centre. The cafe's chilly drinks fridge beckons.

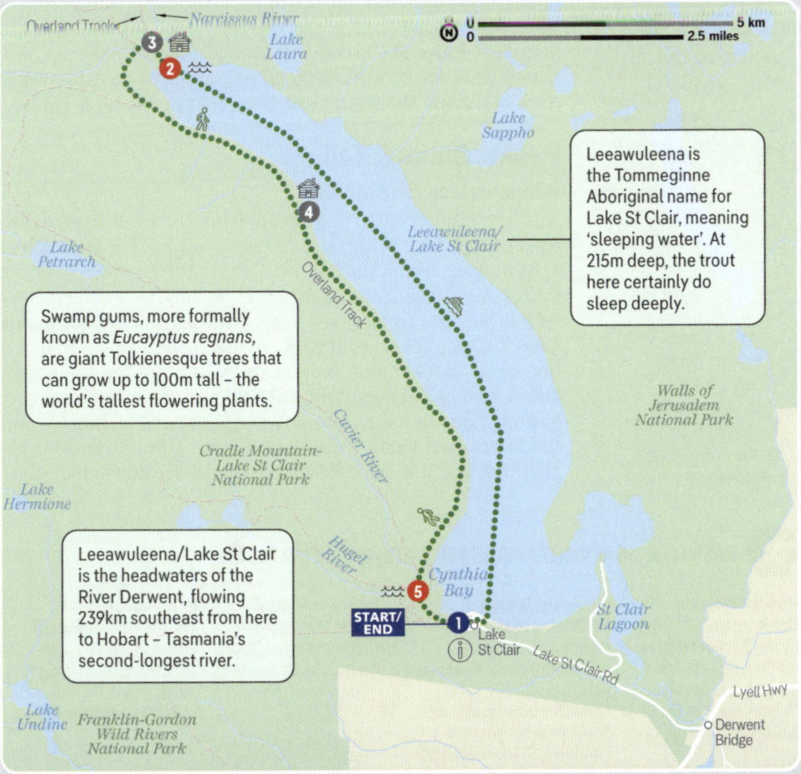

SAVING THE FRANKLIN

Franklin-Gordon Wild Rivers National Park was the site of Australia's biggest environmental battle – the Franklin River Blockade of the early 1980s. Despite national park and World Heritage status, Tasmania's Hydro Electric Commission (HEC) pushed plans to dam the Franklin, sparking mass protests. In 1981, 46% of Tasmanians scribbled 'No Dams' across their ballot papers in a referendum. In 1982, dam construction began, prompting hundreds of protesters to blockade the Franklin. Over 1400 people were arrested in protests that gained global attention. The issue became central to the 1983 federal election, won by the Labor Party on a 'No Dams' platform. The new government halted the dam, enshrining World Heritage protection for the Franklin and Gordon Rivers.

FILEDIMAGE/SHUTTERSTOCK

Pumphouse Point, Leeawuleena/Lake St Clair

Leeawuleena/Lake St Clair Visitor Information Centre at Cynthia Bay (5km from Derwent Bridge), the excellent cultural **Larmairremener Tabelti** trail runs through myrtle beech forest to the confluence of the Cuvier and Huegel Rivers (aka 'Watersmeet'; 3.5km return). Or get out onto the lake onboard the **Lake St Clair Ferry** *(lakestclairlodge.com.au; one way $55; 9am, 12.30pm & 3pm)* to Narcissus Bay then walk back along the shore – an excellent 17.5km day walk (p139).

Peaks, Small & Tall

Windows into the Southwest

An easy 2.2km return boardwalk from the Lyell Hwy, 34km west of Derwent Bridge, leads to the impressive **Donaghys Hill** lookout. From the top, high above the confluence of the Collingwood and Franklin Rivers, excellent fine-weather views roll across the treetops to lofty, hat-looking **Frenchmans Cap**. To scale this 1446m white quartzite dome is a challenging three- to five-day, 46km return walk from the Lyell Hwy, 29km west of Derwent Bridge. There's a river crossing, soggy plains, bald rock escarpments and plenty of altitude – and the Southwest views from the top are astounding. BYO everything (including experience doing this kind of epic walk).

EATING & DRINKING APRÈS WILDERNESS: OUR PICKS

Hungry Wombat Cafe: On the highway by the Derwent Bridge roadhouse: satisfying burgers, bacon rolls, toasties and hot chips. *8.30am-4.30pm* $

Derwent Bridge Wilderness Hotel: Favourite for a post-Overland feast, the steaks are everything you've been fantasising about over your dehydrated noodles. *11.30am-8pm* $$

Lake St Clair Lodge: Fresh off the boat from Narcissus, burgers, beers and hot chips have never looked so good. *8am-8pm* $$

Pumphouse Point: The best meals west of Hobart, in spectacular accommodation that you'll never forget. No kids; very LGBTIQ+-friendly! $$$

Places We Love to Stay

$ Budget $$ Midrange $$$ Top end

Oatlands

Oatlands Free Camping FREE Down by Lake Dulverton with the ducks; you're allowed a stay of 72 hours. There's toilets and a shower nearby (and Callington Mill Distillery).

Lodgings $$ This two-bedroom historic wooden cottage on the main street sleeps up to six; lovely two- and four-berth suites also available.

Elm Cottage Barn $$$ Gorgeous 1837 sandstone converted barn, opening on to a private garden. A secluded retreat for couples.

Ross

Ross Caravan Park $ Peaceful grassy sites and a few cabins by the Macquarie River. Adjacent to Ross Bridge and an easy walk to all the sights.

Riverview at Ross $$ Quiet, clean faux-colonial motel-style units off the main drag by the river, a short stroll from the bridge.

White Croft Cottage $$ Timber-lined, one-bed self-catering cabin with peaceful agrarian views, just a block from the pub. The outdoor bath is a winner!

Four Winds B&B $$ Contemporary house on the hill near the Old Ross Burial Ground (spooky!), with two double bedrooms and a shared lounge. No kids.

Campbell Town

Ivy on Glenelg $$$ Two tastefully furnished self-contained apartments and one lavish B&B room cater for two to six guests on a quiet backstreet.

Bothwell

Bothwell Hotel $$ A 1836 inn run by the Ratho Farm crew with comfortable en suite rooms and communal spaces, right in the village.

Ratho Farm $$$ Mixture of convict-built buildings/barns renovated into rooms and cabins of various capacities on a beautiful, historic farm/golf course just outside Bothwell.

Miena

Pumphouse Bay Camping Area $ Camping in the trees alongside Arthurs Lake near the pumphouse with decent amenities. A solid family choice.

Central Highlands Lodge $$ On the southern outskirts of town, this jaunty, rough-sawn timber lodge offers clean, comfortable cabins.

Great Lake Hotel $$$ On the crossroads, the Great Lake has a selection of spacious self-contained rooms or cheaper 'fishing cabins' with shared facilities.

Lyell Hwy Lakes

Bronte Lagoon $ Peaceful bush camp sites in among the trees, right by the water's edge. Toilets are near the boat ramp.

Bradys Lake $ Breezy camp sites by the boat ramp, popular with larger groups and travellers in vehicles (there's not a whole lot of shelter).

Tungatinah Lagoon $ Pretty bush camp sites inside the treeline on the edge of the lagoon. Well-sheltered; toilets on site.

Tarraleah $$ Old hydro town revamped as a resort (p136), with cottages, lodges, a restaurant and campgrounds to suit every price range. Quiet over winter.

Leeawuleena/ Lake St Clair

Fergy's Paddock $ For the hard-core, this walk-in bush camping area is a short stroll from the visitor centre on the lakeshore. National park fees apply.

Lake St Clair Tourist Park $ Bunkhouse accommodation behind the Lake St Clair visitor centre, with shared amenities and random camp sites. National park fees apply.

Derwent Bridge Chalets & Studios $$ These self-contained, self-catering cabins on the highway near the roadhouse are the best choice in Derwent Bridge, 5km from the lake.

Pumphouse Point $$$ Exclusive and exquisite; the place to contemplate the wilderness through floor-to-ceiling windows by a raging fire with a glass of Moët. World class.

For places to stay in the east coast, see p185

AMELIE B/SHUTTERSTOCK

Above: Bay of Fires (p171); Right: Little penguin (p162), Bicheno

THE MAIN AREAS

MARIA ISLAND NATIONAL PARK
Wildlife, bushwalking and island history.
p148

SWANSEA & FREYCINET NATIONAL PARK
Vineyard-hops, granite peaks and Tasmania's most famous beach.
p152

BICHENO
Penguins, surf beaches and premium whisky.
p162

ST HELENS
Mountain biking, sand dunes and beaches.
p167

Researched by
Andrew Bain

The East Coast

BEACHES, WILDLIFE, WHISKY AND WINE

Tasmania's spectacular east coast is a cavalcade of stellar beaches, wildlife-rich islands and relaxed spots for seafood and wine.

A land of quiet bays, horizon-illuminating sunsets and arcing sandy shores, Tasmania's east coast is sea-salted, sparkling and rejuvenating. A world away from the dense rainforests, ragged coastlines and craggy alpine areas elsewhere in the island state, its shimmering white sands and gin-clear waters could easily be mistaken for a tropical screensaver, but water temperatures here stay stubbornly cool throughout the year, even in summer. Regardless, this is Tasmania's sunny side, gleefully taking advantage of its rain-shadowed position to grow delectable wines, turn on sun-bright colours – be it sand, water or the orange lichen that flares across its granite headlands – and generate some of the state's most user-friendly surf. These elements have all combined to make this coast a popular holiday destination for Tasmanians and mainland Australians. Add into this the relatively new arrival of world-class mountain biking in Derby and St Helens, far-from-the-madding-crowd hiking on the peaks and beaches of Flinders Island, one of Australia's pin-up beaches at Wineglass Bay, and oysters and myriad other seafood straight from the sea and you have all the makings for what could be one of the world's great seaside holiday destinations, were it another 10°C or so warmer. Find an empty beach or three, however, and you might well decide that's for the best, anyway.

KIM MCKEAY/SHUTTERSTOCK

BAY OF FIRES
Fiery in name, fiery in colour.
p171

DERBY
World-class mountain biking among mining relics.
p175

FLINDERS ISLAND
Tasmanian mountains and beaches in microcosm.
p180

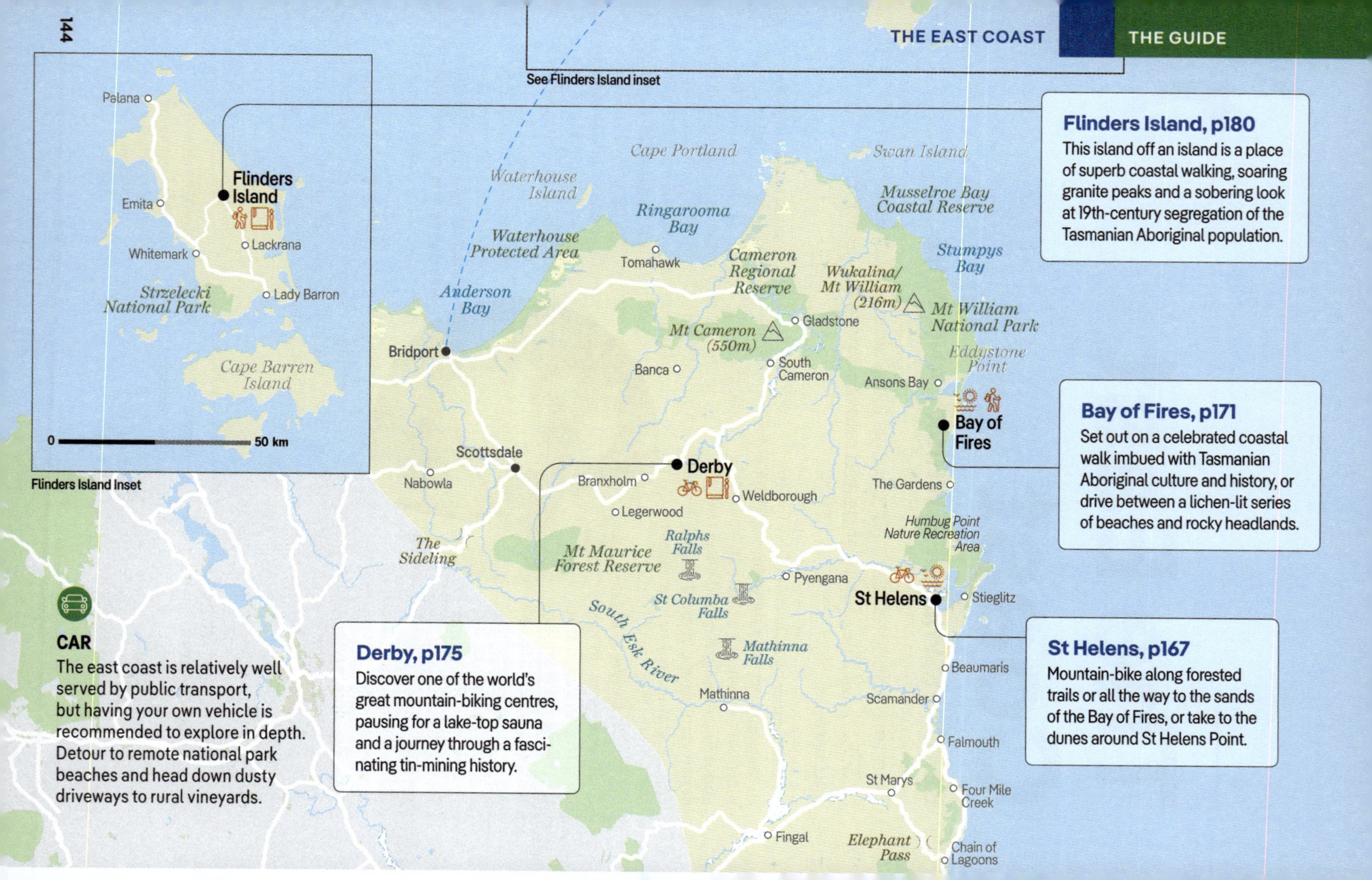

Flinders Island, p180

This island off an island is a place of superb coastal walking, soaring granite peaks and a sobering look at 19th-century segregation of the Tasmanian Aboriginal population.

Bay of Fires, p171

Set out on a celebrated coastal walk imbued with Tasmanian Aboriginal culture and history, or drive between a lichen-lit series of beaches and rocky headlands.

St Helens, p167

Mountain-bike along forested trails or all the way to the sands of the Bay of Fires, or take to the dunes around St Helens Point.

Derby, p175

Discover one of the world's great mountain-biking centres, pausing for a lake-top sauna and a journey through a fascinating tin-mining history.

CAR

The east coast is relatively well served by public transport, but having your own vehicle is recommended to explore in depth. Detour to remote national park beaches and head down dusty driveways to rural vineyards.

Find Your Way

Centrally located, Freycinet National Park is the east coast's must-visit place, but the entire coast is lined with beaches, good food, wine and whisky.

BIKE

Tasmania's east coast is one of Australia's most popular cycle-touring routes. The Tasman Hwy along it is narrow and requires care, and is best avoided during summer school holidays.

BOAT

Board a ferry to explore Maria Island National Park and take a cruise to Wineglass Bay. Flinders Island can be reached aboard a car ferry, but it's a long and often tempestuous trip across Bass Strait.

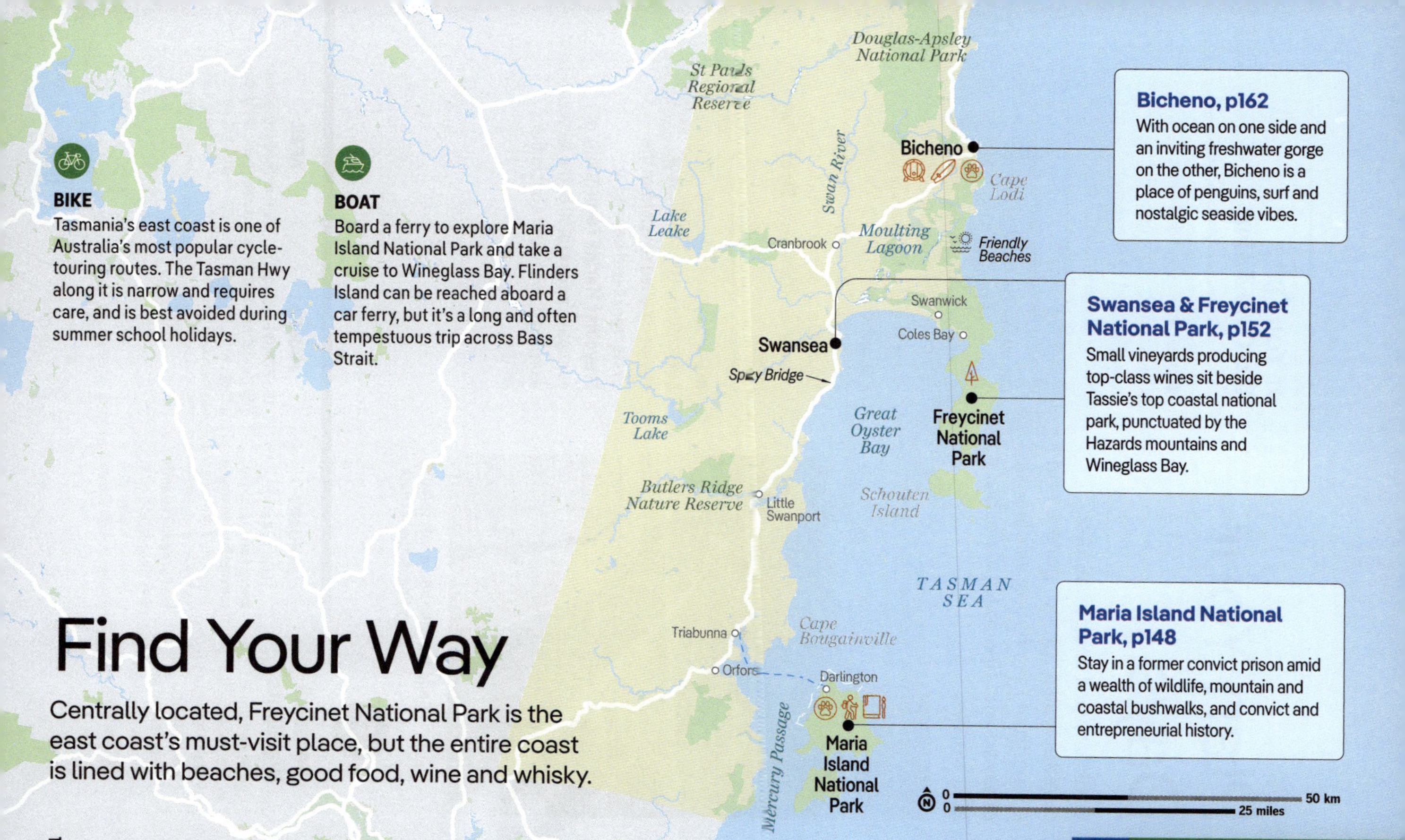

Bicheno, p162

With ocean on one side and an inviting freshwater gorge on the other, Bicheno is a place of penguins, surf and nostalgic seaside vibes.

Swansea & Freycinet National Park, p152

Small vineyards producing top-class wines sit beside Tassie's top coastal national park, punctuated by the Hazards mountains and Wineglass Bay.

Maria Island National Park, p148

Stay in a former convict prison amid a wealth of wildlife, mountain and coastal bushwalks, and convict and entrepreneurial history.

Plan Your Days

Look forward to spectacular coastal walks, interior gorges and a wealth of fascinating wildlife, all enjoyed with fine food, wine, beer and whisky.

DAVID STEELE/SHUTTERSTOCK

Cape Tourville boardwalk (p160), Freycinet National Park

If You Only Do One Thing

- Base yourself in Bicheno or Coles Bay to experience the absolute best of **Freycinet National Park** (p158). Set off in search of the perfect curve of Wineglass Bay, Tasmania's pin-up beach, whether on foot or on a boat trip, and find more water views on a **kayak trip** (p161), paddling across the base of the Hazards and into dreamily named Honeymoon Bay. More great views await on the boardwalk at **Cape Tourville** (p160), or down to the granite-lined shores of **Sleepy Bay** (p160).

- Pause your park explorations briefly to find the freshest of seafood pulled direct from the oyster racks and beyond at **Freycinet Marine Farm** (p160), or even take a **tour** (p161) of the farm, slurping down oysters out in the water.

Seasonal Highlights

Eat and drink exceedingly well at festivals throughout the year, and be immersed in spectacular winter light shows.

JANUARY

Head to **Kate's Berry Farm** (p155) for summertime treats, or skip across the water to Flinders Island for the **Furneaux Islands Festival**, held over a January weekend.

MARCH

The **ECHO Festival** (p154) celebrates local food, wine, art and music around Swansea.

APRIL

Autumn has settled into its calm best, the ocean retains a hint of warmth, and the holiday crowds have thinned, so dive in.

Three Days to Travel Around

- Begin in Hobart, crossing to the east coast for a first stop at **Maria Island National Park** (p148), where an intersecting world of natural and human history awaits, from the greatest concentrations of wombats you'll ever see to the World Heritage–listed convict settlement at Darlington and cliffs patterned like artistic masterpieces. Continue north into the low-key vineyards that make up the **East Coast Wine Trail** (p156) and make your way to Bicheno in time to watch the **little penguins** (p162) march ashore, or to experience Devils in the Dark at **East Coast Natureworld** (p163).

- When the next day breaks, head out for a dawn stroll along the **Foreshore Footway** (p165) and stick around for a tasting at **Waubs Harbour Distillery** (p165) and lobster rolls at the **Lobster Shack** (p165).

A Weeklong Stay

- Replete with coastal views and fine seafood, **St Helens** (p167) is a natural base for a longer stay on the east coast. World-class mountain biking is on offer at both St Helens and nearby **Derby** (p175) and, if you've got the time, two iconic guided multiday walks along the **Bay of Fires** (p171) are highly recommended. At the very least, take a drive to the **Gardens** (p174), building in time for stops along the bay's constellation of lichen-spattered beaches.

- If you're still in the market for more walks, make the short hop by plane across Bass Strait to **Flinders Island** (p180), where empty beaches beckon and mountain climbs call.

JULY

Mid-winter in Bicheno. The penguins waddle home earlier and the annual **Bicheno Beams** (p154) festival lights up the evening sky.

SEPTEMBER

Runners gravitate to Flinders Island for its **Running Festival** (p154), while whales are starting their coastal journey back to southern waters.

OCTOBER

Four days of all things grapes at the **Great Eastern Wine Week** (p154), with events sprinkled among the vineyards of the East Coast Wine Trail.

NOVEMBER

It's Bicheno's turn to celebrate east-coast gourmet highlights with the **Bicheno Food & Wine Festival** (p154).

Maria Island National Park

WILDLIFE | WALKS | HISTORY

Captivating Maria (pronounced Muh-*rye*-uh) Island is a carefree, car-free haven – a top spot for walking, wildlife watching, cycling, camping and delving into the island's fascinating convict and entrepreneurial history.

The island towers 711m out of the sea and is wrapped in a curious collection of cliffs – one composed of ancient marine fossils, another naturally decorated like an artwork in sandstone. In the 1960s the island was chosen as a Noah's Ark of sorts to preserve native animal species, and today there's no surer spot in Tasmania – nay, Australia – to see wombats, Forester kangaroos, wallabies and grey-plumed Cape Barren geese as they together nibble the Darlington lawns. There's also an insurance population of Tasmanian devils (they're beset with disease across most of Tasmania) that was released here in 2012 and is thriving.

In 1972 Maria Island was gazetted as a national park, as much for its history as for its natural assets, and Darlington Probation Station is UNESCO World Heritage listed. In Tasmania's Aboriginal palawa kani language, Maria Island is known as wukaluwikiwayna.

GETTING AROUND

From the wharf in Triabunna, **Encounter Maria Island** *(encountermaria.com.au)* runs four ferries daily (three daily, other than Tuesday and Thursday, from May to August) to Maria Island. Walking suffices for exploring Darlington, but to head further afield, a mountain bike is handy. Bring your bike or book a hire one with Encounter Maria Island. **Maria Island Cruises** *(eastcoastcruises.com.au)* operates full-day cruises from Triabunna, including a two-hour guided walk around Darlington.

Discover Darlington

Convict history and Italian industriousness

Step off the ferry at Darlington's pier and almost immediately you pass the island's oldest building, the 1825 **Commissariat Store**, now housing displays and information on the island. Maps detailing recommended walking and biking routes are also available.

Above the bay is **Darlington**, officially the World Heritage-listed Darlington Probation Station. Built in 1830, the **penitentiary** is one of the few buildings remaining from the island's first convict period (1825–32), before it was abandoned

TOP TIP

Prepare ahead – you can't buy food or drink on the island. Self-catering overnight visitors can stock up at Triabunna's **Spring Bay IGA**.

SIGHTS
1 Bishop and Clerk
see 3 Coffee Palace
2 Commissariat Store
3 Darlington
4 Fossil Cliffs
5 Mt Maria
6 Oast House
7 Painted Cliffs
see 3 Penitentiary
8 Ruby Hunt's Cottage

SLEEPING
see 3 Darlington Camp Site
9 Encampment Cove Camp Site
10 Frenchs Farm Camp Site

in favour of Port Arthur. During the island's second convict era from 1842 to 1850, more than 00 prisoners were crammed into each room. Things are a little cosier these days with the penitentiary serving as rustic **accommodation** *(parks.tas.gov.au; up to 2 people $44)*, with six-bunk rooms (with wood heaters), shared bathrooms and coin-operated showers. BYO bedding, lighting (there's no electricity), food, cooking gear and ghost stories. It's often full of school groups, so plan ahead (the wombats outside the front door come free). There's also camping at the base of **Darlington's lawns** *(parks.tas.gov.au; camping for 2 people $13)* – regularly visited by Tasmanian devils – as well as further-flung **Frenchs Farm** *(free)* and **Encampment Cove** *(free)*.

Allow half a day to wander among the historic buildings scattered around Darlington, including one of Australia's oldest (1844) **oast houses**, used for drying hops, and the **Coffee Palace**, built by Italian entrepreneur Diego Bernacchi (p150) in 1888. Originally more a restaurant than a cafe, it's now a monument unto itself, with past menus hinting at Maria Island's heyday, but minus the food. It's free to enter anytime.

Wander Among Wildlife

Wombats aplenty

Forget spending binocular-wielding hours stalking wildlife. Simply step out onto the lawns that run down to the shores from Darlington and you'll be all but stepping over wombats (we counted 132 one day), Forester kangaroos and Cape Barren geese. One of the surest places to observe the locals is around **Ruby Hunt's Cottage**, a rustic heritage bungalow where Maria Island's long-term radio operator lived until 1968.

MEET THE BERNACCHIS

Nobody ever accused Diego Bernacchi of lacking ambition. Born in northern Italy in 1853, Bernacchi emigrated to Australia in 1884, quickly acquiring a lease on Maria Island, where he planted grapevines, spun together a silk industry and built a cement works – the silos and remains of a factory beside the Darlington pier provide reminders of that enterprise. Hoping to encourage tourism, Bernacchi spruiked the island as the 'Riviera of Australia' and rather immodestly renamed Darlington as San Diego. By 1882, the businesses had gone bust, though Bernacchi returned in 1918 for one more attempt at creating a cement works on the island.

In 1899 Diego's son Louis became the first Australian to overwinter in Antarctica as part of the Norwegian Egeberg Borchgrevink's *Southern Cross* expedition.

Tasmanian devils have made a habit of hanging out around the Darlington campground, and the grasslands around the airstrip north of Darlington are good for roo and wallaby sightings. Bird-watchers will be happy to know that 11 of Tasmania's 12 endemic bird species have been sighted on the island.

Island Rambles

From Painted Cliffs to island peaks

You're spoiled for choice – coast or mountains – when walking on Maria Island, and all of the following trails begin in Darlington.

At the southern end of Hopground Beach, the naturally patterned, sandstone **Painted Cliffs** (one hour's walk from Darlington) are the island's signature scene. From Darlington, walk along the road past Ruby Hunt's Cottage (p149) and then descend to Hopground Beach – the short trail into the cliffs begins at the far end of the sand. Aim to be here within two hours either side of low tide (if it coincides with late afternoon when the sun paints the cliffs a fiery orange, all the

EATING BEFORE & AFTER VISITING MARIA ISLAND: OUR PICKS

Fish Van: Fresh seafood so close to the Triabunna fishing fleet that the van is almost afloat. *11am-6.30pm* $

Elly's Tasting Table: Orford's best cafe serves up all-day breakfasts; be sure to try Elly's own salted caramel popcorn. *8am-2pm* $$

Darlington Vineyard: Cheese platters team with local wines in Orford at the east coast's southernmost vineyard. *11am-4pm Thu-Sun* $$

Aquila Art Lounge: Savoury pancakes and Thai dishes prepared with garden ingredients inside a Triabunna home. *9am-2.30pm Tue-Thu, 9am-2pm & 5-8pm Fri & Sat, 9am-1pm Sun* $$

TOM JASTRAM/SHUTTERSTOCK

Painted Cliffs

better), when it's possible to walk along the shelf of rock at the base of the cliffs – it's the only way to actually view the cliffs.

Other walks include a two-hour loop to the **Fossil Cliffs**, and then up Skipping Ridge to climb the rugged peak of **Bishop and Clerk** (599m; around four hours return from Darlington) for bird's-eye views over Darlington and Tasmania's east coast. Be sure to descend to the platform at the base of Fossil Cliffs to get a perspective on the millions of marine fossils embedded into the cliffs. The island's most challenging hike is to its highest point, 711m **Mt Maria**. The seven-hour return hike follows the Painted Cliffs walk towards Hopground Beach, turning onto the Inland Track before reaching the cliffs. Around 2km on, the Mt Maria path turns away up the mountain, the summit of which delivers brilliant views over the island's narrow isthmus and far beyond.

To see the island from toe to tip – Haunted Bay to the Fossil Cliffs – join the luxury guided four-day **Maria Island Walk** *(mariaislandwalk.com; from $3050)*.

Underwater Sights

Marine wildlife viewing

The seas around Maria's north coast are a designated marine reserve, with fishing banned along and around the Darlington coast. The reserve protects giant kelp forests and caves around Fossil Bay, which are excellent for diving and snorkelling (bring all your own gear). Other snorkelling spots include the ferry pier and Painted Cliffs. Wear a wetsuit if you want to stay submerged for more than five minutes.

DEVIL ISLAND

In the 1960s, Maria Island was chosen as a sanctuary in an attempt to save threatened species such as Forester kangaroos and the Bass Strait subspecies of wombat from extinction. There was an irony of sorts to the project – this island once used to imprison convicts now being employed to release animals – but it was an unbounded success.

History repeated itself in 2012, when 20 Tasmanian devils – all free of the dreaded devil facial tumour disease (DFTD) – were released on the island to serve as a geographically isolated insurance policy in the hope of saving the fast-declining population. Numbers on the island have since increased to more than 100 animals. These days, you're unlikely to encounter any wild devils on Tasmania's mainland, but chances are excellent on Maria.

Swansea & Freycinet National Park

WINE | FOOD | COASTAL SCENERY

TOP TIP

Swansea makes a feasible alternative base for Freycinet National Park, with cheaper accommodation than Coles Bay. From Swansea, it's a 50-minute drive into the park.

Founded in 1820 as 'Great Swanport', Swansea stakes out a beautiful spot along Jubilee Beach, peering across Great Oyster Bay to Freycinet Peninsula and lumpy Schouten Island, and yet somehow it retains a low-key, undeveloped vibe. With its mild climate and maritimes breezes, the town also sits on the fringe of one of Tasmania's premier wine-growing regions, creating a fine base for sipping trips along the East Coast Wine Trail, the centrepiece of which is clustered just to the town's north. Complementing the wine is gourmet produce such as super-fresh oysters served from a retro caravan, seasonal berries and salt drawn from some of the world's cleanest water.

Across the bay is the long, thin figure of Freycinet National Park, headlined by Wineglass Bay but with so much more on offer – peaks with grandstand views, wildlife, walks both short and long, and complementary beaches that are smaller and quieter.

Strands & Spikes

A curious bridge and a string of empty beaches

About 7km south of Swansea, right beside the Tasman Hwy, **Spiky Bridge** was built by convicts in the early 1840s using thousands of local fieldstones, and crowned with jagged shards of stone (the 'spiky' of the name). Nearby beaches worthy of investigation include **Cressy Beach**, with a tiny rock arch

GETTING AROUND

Tassielink buses connect Swansea to Hobart, Bicheno and Coles Bay. To head out on the East Coast Wine Trail, having a private vehicle is recommended. See winetasmania.com.au for detailed touring info. Wineries are largely grouped around Cranbrook, north of Swansea.

Guided tours are offered by the **Long Lunch Tour Co** *(longlunchtourco.com.au)* and **Ageing Barrel Tours** *(ageingbarrel.com.au)*. **Swansea Cycle Tours** *(swanseacycletours.com.au)* runs guided bike trips between the vineyards.

SWANSEA & FREYCINET NATIONAL PARK

HIGHLIGHTS

1 Freycinet National Park

SIGHTS

2 Cape Tourville
3 Cressy Beach
4 East Coast Heritage Museum
5 Friendly Beaches
6 Kelvedon Beach
7 Mt Amos
8 Sleepy Bay
9 Spiky Bridge
10 Tasman Sea Salt
11 Wineglass Bay Lookout

ACTIVITIES

12 ALL4 All Terrain Tours
see 12 Freycinet Adventures
13 Freycinet Air
see 4 loontitetermairrelehoiner
14 Oyster Bay Tours
15 Wineglass Bay Cruises

SLEEPING

16 Freycinet Lodge
17 Piermont
18 Swansea Beach Chalets
19 Wagners Cottages

EATING

see 4 Alimento
see 14 Freycinet Marine Farm
see 15 Géographe
see 12 Granite
see 17 Homestead
20 Kate's Berry Farm
21 Melshell Oyster Shack

TRANSPORT

see 15 Freycinet Aqua Express

EAST COAST FESTIVALS

ECHO Festival: Local food, wine and art, but this autumn festival in Swansea, organised by internationally renowned country singer (and local resident) Ange Boxall, is headlined by music. March.

Bicheno Beams: A free and family-friendly celebration of light, with nightly light shows playing across the Bicheno sky. June and July.

Flinders Island Running Festival: Lace up for the 3km evening Glow Run along a lit course, or bang out a full marathon. September.

Great Eastern Wine Week: This October toast to local wine sees tastings, dinners and other immersive vineyard events scheduled across four days at all 14 east-coast wineries.

Bicheno Food & Wine Festival: A festival with an ocean view held on Bicheno's foreshore amid plentiful food, wine and music. November.

FILEDIMAGE/SHUTTERSTOCK

in its far headland, and **Kelvedon Beach**, decorated with arguably Tasmania's most evocative boat shed.

A Coastal Trail around Town

Ocean views on the loontitetermairrelehoiner walk

Named after the Tasmanian Aboriginal people that lived in the area, the 2.3km **loontitetermairrelehoiner** rounds the headland between Swansea's Waterloo Beach and the Esplanade, wrapping around the town golf course as it goes. One of Tasmania's 60 Great Short Walks, it passes a muttonbird (short-tailed shearwater) rookery en route and has lovely views across Great Oyster Bay to Freycinet Peninsula. During the summer breeding season, the adult muttonbirds return at dusk after feeding at sea. The trail begins from the large car park by the town jetty and is especially good in the early morning as the sun rises over Freycinet Peninsula.

Get Salty

Meet a salt sommelier at Tasman Sea Salt

Change up the flavours along the East Coast Wine Trail with a tour and tasting at **Tasman Sea Salt** *(tasmanseasalt.com.au)*. The 45-minute Saltworks Tour ($35) guides you through the unique and simple production process, from the pumping of sea water from directly in front of the small plant to the evaporation tanks and the crystallisation plates. The 1½-hour Salt Sommelier ($95) tour then heads to the nearby Mayfield Estate cellar door, where the salts – some infused with Tasmanian ingredients such as mountain pepperberry – are paired with food (and any wine you purchase) in a tasting

loontitetermairrelehoiner track

session. The setting, looking out onto Freycinet Peninsula and Schouten Island, is a briny bonus.

The saltworks is at the end of Mayfield Jetty Rd, 17km south of Swansea.

History & Heritage

Step into the East Coast Heritage Museum

Inside Swansea's original schoolhouse, in the middle of the main street, this **museum** *(eastcoastheritage.org.au; entry by donation)* covers Aboriginal artefacts, colonial and convict history, whaling and the plight of the thylacine (including a tiger trap from the late 19th century). Among the most engaging of the items on display are eggs from the now-extinct Tasmanian emu and an 1860s diorama of Swansea.

ON THE TRAIL OF TASTE

Too many tastings not enough? Set out on the northwest's **Tasting Trail** (p228) to find more than 40 producers concocting gourmet goodness.

The retro caravan is as appealing as the oysters.

EATING AROUND SWANSEA: OUR PICKS

Kate's Berry Farm: Head 3km out of town for berry-inspired bites: scones, waffles, fruit pies and ice cream. *9am-3pm Sat-Tue* $

Alimento: Restaurant and providore with a Spanish-accented *pintxos* menu, welcoming vibe and well-stocked bar of local tipples. *7am-8pm Tue-Sat, to 3pm Sun & Mon* $$

Melshell Oyster Shack: Fresh bivalves that you can enjoy while overlooking the oyster racks of this working Dolphin Sands farm, 15km east of town. *10am-4pm Mon-Fri* $

Homestead: Mediterranean-style dining with fresh ocean views in Piermont's heritage farmhouse; Thursday is pasta night. *12.30-3pm & 6-9pm Tue-Sat* $$$

ROAD TRIP

Drive the East Coast Wine Trail

The East Coast Wine Trail stretches almost the length of the coast, encompassing 14 vineyards, many of them family owned and distinctive in their cellar-door experiences. The greatest concentration of wineries is around Swansea, where cellar doors are suitably bunched like grapes around Cranbrook, just to the town's north, and sprinkled down the Tasman Hwy south of town. Throw in a dash of salt and some convict relics, and it makes for a fine east-coast cruise.

1 Boomer Creek Vineyard

Near the wine trail's southern end, **Boomer Creek** is a small, family-owned vineyard that also features an olive grove and a working sheep and cattle farm. Platters and craft beer (and local tea and juices) partner with cellar-door tastings and views over Schouten Island and Freycinet Peninsula.

The Drive: Head 8km north on the Tasman Hwy, turning right onto Mayfield Jetty Rd and following it to its costal end.

2 Tasman Sea Salt

Swap wine for salt at **Tasman Sea Salt** (p154), where sea water is evaporated and crystallised in a remarkably simple yet unique process. If you're here purely for wine, never fear – the premium Salt Sommelier tour concludes with tastings in the cellar door of neighbouring Mayfield Estate vineyard.

The Drive: Return to the highway, but prepare to stop almost immediately – Mayfield Bay is just 2km up the road.

3 Mayfield Bay Conservation Area

From the picnic/camping area beside the highway, take the five-minute walk to **Three Arch Bridge**, one of Tasmania's lesser known convict-built bridges. Constructed in 1845, it has three narrow stone

STEVE WATERS/LONELY PLANET

Boomer Creek Vineyard

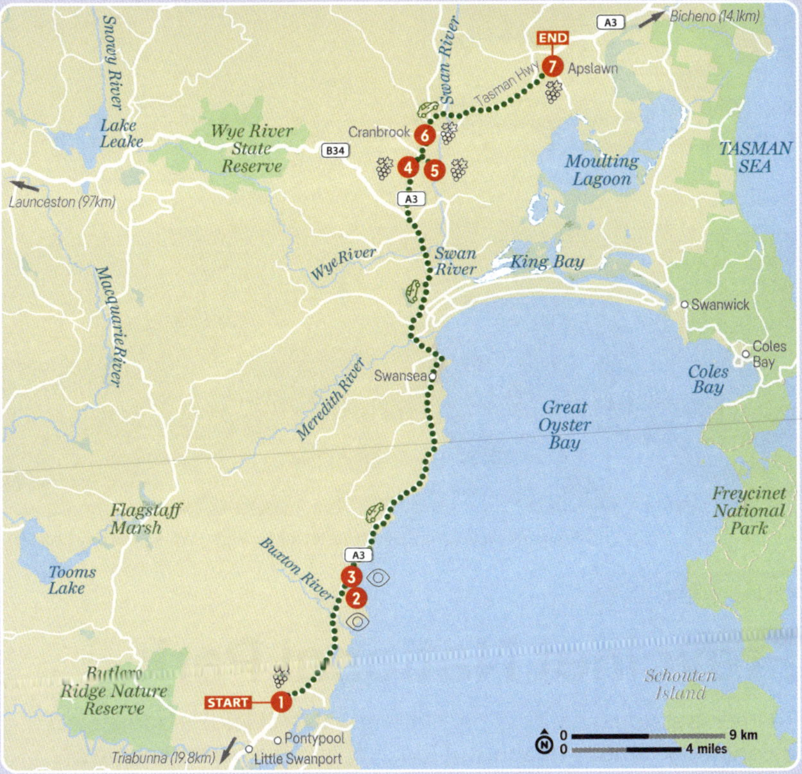

and brick arches, with the Tasman Hwy still hurtling over it high above.

The Drive: Pass on through Swansea and 13km out its other side to the first of Cranbrook's collection of cellar doors.

4 Milton Vineyard

This 22-hectare **vineyard** offers tastings in an elegant weatherboard cottage, with views over a small lake. The cellar-door restaurant, A Tale Among the Vines, uses produce from the winery's own farm.

The Drive: Continue north for 1.5km, turning right into Spring Vale Vineyard's long driveway.

5 Spring Vale Vineyard

Tastings at **Spring Vale** take place in a convict-built 1842 stable. Apéro Bistro, a French-Australian restaurant looking over the vines, opened on site in late 2025.

The Drive: Continue around 3km to Gala Estate's eclectic cellar door, beside the highway.

6 Gala Estate

Billed as the second-oldest family business in Tasmania (Mt Amos in Freycinet National Park is named after one of the owner's ancestors), the cellar door of farm-based **Gala Estate** is inside Cranbrook's old timber post office, with plenty of rustic touches. It was awarded Tasmania's 'Pinot Producer of the Year' in 2023, 2024 and 2025, making your choice of drop obvious.

The Drive: Climb over Cherry Tree Hill, taking note of the native cherry trees, and wind down the slopes to Devil's Corner, 10km from Gala Estate.

7 Devil's Corner

Wine tastings at **Devil's Corner** can be combined with wood-fired pizza and local seafood from on-site food vendors. Be sure to climb the lookout tower for the classic view over Moulting Lagoon to the Hazards mountains in Freycinet National Park.

TOM JASTRAM/SHUTTERSTOCK

Above: Wineglass Bay view from Mt Amos; Right: Wineglass Bay Cruises

TOP EXPERIENCE

Freycinet National Park

Tasmania's oldest national park (along with Mt Field) is dominated by one very famous beach, but look beyond the perfect curve of Wineglass Bay and you'll find equally beautiful, less-crowd-drawing bays and beaches, excellent coastal bushwalking and the pink-tinged slopes of the granite Hazards mountains, which might provide the finest views of all.

DON'T MISS

- Wineglass Bay
- Cape Tourville
- Evening kayak tour
- Sleepy Bay
- Friendly Beaches
- Wineglass Bay Cruises
- Mt Amos

Cheers to Wineglass Bay

With its curvaceous arc of talc-white sand fringed with clear waters, Wineglass Bay is unquestionably Tasmania's most famous beach and one of the very symbols of the state. Just don't come expecting a lazy day at the beach. Getting onto its celebrated sands requires a 6km return walk, crossing through a low pass in the Hazards. The majority of visitors pull up short, at the **Wineglass Bay Lookout** (2.6km return) clipped onto the slopes of the Hazards, giving a wide view over the bay.

If you want to reduce your step count, jump aboard the **Freycinet Aqua Express** *(freycinetaquaexpress.com.au;*

PRACTICALITIES

- parks.tas.gov.au/explore-our-parks/freycinet-national-park
- national parks day pass per vehicle/person (not in a vehicle) $48/24

PHILIP GAME/ALAMY

adult/child one way $75/60, return $120/100) water taxi, which heads to Hazards Beach five times daily. From here, you can walk across the isthmus to Wineglass Bay in less than 30 minutes.

If even that sort of exertion sounds a step too far, there are less-energetic ways to see the bay. **Wineglass Bay Cruises** *(wineglassbaycruises.com.au; adult/child from $200/125)* runs daily five-hour boat trips from Coles Bay around the southern point of Freycinet Peninsula and into Wineglass Bay. Boats stop in the bay for lunch afloat, but you'll also see the rest of the park's rugged coastline along with possible dolphins, sea eagles, seals and perhaps even migrating whales. If weather conditions make the seas too rough for the boat to enter Wineglass Bay, an alternative route explores the coastline of little-visited Schouten Island. Full refunds are given to passengers who decide not to travel on this alternative route, but even without a visit to Wineglass Bay, it's still an interesting and worthwhile experience. Booking ahead is essential.

Locally based **Freycinet Air** *(freycinetair.com.au; per person $325)* operates 25-minute scenic helicopter flights, providing the upstairs look at the bay.

Other Walks around Wineglass Bay

Freycinet is laced with walking trails, taking in sections of coastline and the mountains that furnish the peninsula. For an even wider perspective on Wineglass Bay (and far beyond), the summit of **Mt Amos** is unrivalled. This steep climb scales the granite slopes of the Hazards peak to a boulder-dotted summit that seems to hover above the bay, with Mt Graham and Mt Freycinet forming a high wall behind it. Note that this is the most challenging short walk in the park – it's largely on bare, sloping granite (and did we mention steep?) – and

CAMPING IN FREYCINET

One of Freycinet's treasured delights is its camping. Wildly popular are the camp sites strung along Richardsons Beach and Ranger Creek – both beside the visitor centre – and ever-so-romantic Honeymoon Bay. Away from the hum of activity, there are two free beachside campgrounds at the Friendly Beaches. For those prepared to work for their tent-sized piece of paradise, there are walk-in camp sites at Hazards Beach (two to three hours' walk from the car park), Cooks Beach (4½ hours) and, to add a famous site to your camping CV, at the southern end of Wineglass Bay (two hours). The park is a fuel-stove-only area, so campfires are not permitted. Limited water may be available, but it's best to bring your own.

EATING AROUND FREYCINET

All of Freycinet's eating options are outside the park, whether in and around Coles Bay or at Freycinet Lodge. Start your day with a haloumi brioche or *huevos rancheros* at **Granite** (or return on Friday or Saturday night for pizza), or grab breakfast with a Hazards view at **Géographe**. Oysters and mussels come fresh from the farm racks at **Freycinet Marine Farm**, served alongside scallops, salmon and fish and chips in a convivial outdoor setting. At Freycinet Lodge (p185), dine on the deck for views along Richardsons Beach and across the water to Coles Bay at Richardson's Bistro. The lodge's Bay Restaurant puts a more refined spin on things, with an emphasis on local seafood.

the slopes get treacherously slippery when wet, so don't attempt the 3.6km return climb after rain. The walk begins at the Wineglass Bay trailhead, deviating just a few minutes down the track.

The **Wineglass Bay and Hazards Beach Circuit**, one of the state's 60 Great Short Walks, follows the main walking route to Wineglass Bay, but instead of retracing your steps back over The Hazards, take the trail that crosses the isthmus to parallel Hazards Beach. From here, the 11km circuit rounds the western base of the Hazards to return to the Wineglass Bay car park.

Beyond Wineglass

The 20-minute wheelchair-accessible circuit around **Cape Tourville** is one of the national park's most popular short walks. There are glimpses into the mouth of Wineglass Bay, and it's a good spot to see migrating whales. Look for tell-tale spouts on the near horizon. Markers set into the boardwalk emphasise the size of these marine giants, and there are good views north along the Friendly Beaches and beyond towards Bicheno. The cape is topped by the whitewashed Cape Tourville Lighthouse, built in 1971.

Down the slopes from the Cape Tourville car park, a smaller car park marks the start of the 500m return walk to **Sleepy Bay**. A well-formed track firstly leads through the forest – keep an eye out for the occasional echidna – before a stepped trail continues down to a compact and rocky bay with lichen-encrusted rocks and turquoise waters. Completing the trail only takes around 20 minutes, but it's the kind of place you'll want to enjoy for a couple of hours and it's a magical place to watch a sunrise.

In the park's north, stretching in a long sandy line, are the **Friendly Beaches**, which offer a long stretch of unbroken

TASSIEKARIN/GETTY IMAGES

Kayaking in Freycinet National Park

beach walking. Simply step out onto the sand from along Friendly Beaches Rd and keep walking till you've had enough.

The Big Loop

Freycinet's grandest adventure on foot is the **Freycinet Peninsula Circuit**, a two- to three-day, 27km loop of the park. Setting out from the Wineglass Bay car park, it can be walked in either direction (anticlockwise is our pick), taking in Hazards and Cooks beaches on the Great Oyster Bay coastline, crossing Mt Graham for an elevated view over the peninsula and striding the length of Wineglass Bay. There are camp sites at Hazards Beach, Cooks Beach and at the southern end of Wineglass Bay. Water supply at the camps can sometimes be an issue, so check ahead at the park visitor centre.

Adventures on the Water

Local tour operators offer a range of guided experiences in and around the park. **Freycinet Adventures** *(freycinetadventures.com.au; adult/child $145/115)* runs three-hour guided kayaking trips, crossing Coles Bay to the granite toes of the Hazards, passing a former granite quarry and stopping in at quixotic Honeymoon Bay. There are morning and twilight trips, with the latter catching the Hazards at their colourful best in the day's last light. No prior kayaking experience is necessary, and it's a safe and achievable adventure for families (suitable for kids aged seven and above).

For more water play, hire a SUP from **Freycinet Paddle Boards** *(freycinetpaddleboards.com.au; half/full day $50/70)* and go exploring on Coles Bay's (usually) sheltered waters. It also rents out sit-on-top kayaks as well as gear for snorkelling, fishing, camping and surfing.

Outside the park, **Oyster Bay Tours** *(oysterbaytours.com; $170)* offers two-hour guided experiences at the Freycinet Marine Farm, where you'll don waders and head out into the shallow waters to harvest and shuck oysters straight from the rack.

Guided Land Adventures

ALL4 All Terrain Tours *(all4.com.au; 2hr/half-day $269/369)* runs two-hour and half-day ATV spins through the park forest to the sea cliffs of Cape Tourville and the sandy southern end of the Friendly Beaches. Hire a hardtail or dual-suspension e-bike from **Freycinet Lodge** (p185; *half/full day hardtail $79/99, dual suspension $99/139*) and you can pedal the 4km bike path running from the park visitor centre to the Wineglass Bay car park, or set out on dirt roads across the peninsula to the southern end of the Friendly Beaches.

THE BLOODY GLASS

See Wineglass Bay from above and it seems obvious that it was named for its curvaceous shape, but it was in fact named for the presence of a whaling station at the bay's southern end in the early 19th century. When whales were butchered, the bay's water ran red with blood.

TOP TIPS

- The national park visitor centre is one of the best informed in the state, so be sure to drop in when you arrive at the park.
- If you fancy camping at Richardsons Beach or Honeymoon Bay for the summer season (18 December to 10 February), plan ahead. Sites are so prized that they're allocated by a ballot, which is drawn in early August. Ballot applications can be made through the park website.
- Avoid parking issues at the Wineglass Bay car park by walking or cycling to the trailhead along a 4km shared-use path from the visitor centre.

Bicheno

WILDLIFE | WAVES | WHISKY

Bicheno is a fishing port that's all but put its feet up and become a seaside holiday town – one of the most likeable in Tasmania. The town's workaday fishing fleet still comes home to harbour in the Gulch with pots of lobsters and scaly loot, but it's the beaches, the surf and the marine life that draw most to the town now. Bicheno remains surprisingly low key given its appeal and its proximity to Freycinet, but what has changed is its palate. From lobster rolls beside the gin-clear Gulch to a maritime whisky distillery and a pumping new craft brewery, Bicheno has sloughed off its fish-and-chip ways and gone gastronomic.

Nightlife here means penguins or pub, but quiet nights are an excuse to rise early, hit the surf, join the locals (including Olympic gold medallist Shane Gould) for a dawn swim, or wander the Foreshore Footway amid the first beams of the day.

GETTING AROUND

Tassielink buses run daily from Hobart to Bicheno. These buses also link Bicheno to Coles Bay (excluding Sunday) for visiting Freycinet National Park. Calow's Coaches operates east-coast services between Bicheno and Hobart, as well as a service between Coles Bay and St Helens that stops in Bicheno. Getting north from Bicheno to Douglas-Apsley National Park requires a private vehicle.

Bicheno's Penguin Power

Witness the nightly march

Bicheno's wildlife stars are the little penguins that waddle onto local beaches around dusk. They're often seen around the Blowhole (p165) and at Redbill Beach (p164) and Waubs Beach (p164), but the only sure sightings come on a guided experience with **Bicheno Penguin Tours** *(bichenopenguintours.com.au; $55)*. The one-hour tours visit a private area behind a beach with a rookery that's home to around 350 of the world's smallest penguins. It's reached along an accessible pathway with penguin-friendly solar lighting. Departure times vary across the year, depending on the hour of dusk. Photos (no flash!) are allowed, but free photos are also available through a QR code on the bus. Penguin numbers peak from November to January. Bookings are essential and shuttle-bus transfers to the viewing site from central Bicheno are included. Closed-toe shoes and a warm jacket are recommended, even during a Tasmanian summer.

TOP TIP

Join the Bicheno Wild Ocean Swimmers (aka the Coffee Club) for a dawn swim at Waubs Beach; they meet each morning at 7.30am by the Surf Lifesaving Club, with its design inspired by cray pots, and visitors are welcome.

HIGHLIGHTS
1 Blowhole
2 Foreshore Footway

SIGHTS
3 Diamond Island
4 Redbill Beach
5 Rice Pebble Beach
6 The Gulch
7 Waubs Beach
8 Waubs Harbour Distillery
9 Whalers Hill

ACTIVITIES
10 Bicheno Penguin Tours
see 8 Bicheno's Glass Bottom Boat
11 Governor Island Marine Reserve

SLEEPING
12 Bicheno by the Bay
13 Diamond Island Resort

EATING
14 Le Coq
15 Lobster Shack

DRINKING & NIGHTLIFE
16 Bicheno Beer Co
see 14 Farm Shed

SHOPPING
17 Long Point Surf

A World of Wildlife

Meet devils, wombats and more

Wildlife interactions continue at **East Coast Natureworld** *(natureworld.com.au; adult/child $32/19)*, about 7km north of town. This wildlife park is packed with native and non-native animals, including Tasmanian devils, wallabies, quolls, tiger snakes, wombats and enormous kangaroos. Special encounters (additional to the admission cost) include the opportunity to get up close with wombats, echidnas and baby devils, as well as sugar gliders, a palm-sized species of possum specially adapted to 'fly' between tree branches. The Ultimate

ATOSAN/SHUTTERSTOCK

Blowhole

Tour ($275) is a private 1½-hour guided experience with all four animal encounters, as well as time in the keeper kitchen helping to prepare the animal meals for the day. Special Devils in the Dark night encounters combine munching on cheese and drinking local wine – that's you, not the devils – with front row seats from which you can watch the stars of the show devouring an entire carcass.

Many of the animals at Natureworld have been rehabilitated after being found injured or abandoned in the wild, but other truly wild birds and animals also hang out on the 60 hectares of coastal bushland and lagoons.

Water World

Surf, dive or find a window into the sea

Bicheno's heartbeat is the surf, and some of Tasmania's best and most user-friendly waves are found along its coastline. The 1km-long curve of sand at **Redbill Beach** is the spot of choice, with a good shore break, while it's a short cruise up the coast to a break at the mouth of the **Scamander River**. Occasionally, especially after a storm, a powerful wave on the outside of **Governor Island** attracts hard-core tow-in surfers.

The diving and snorkelling is equally good. **Governor Island Marine Reserve** is considered one of the world's best temperate-water dive locations, and winter brings the best visibility – brrrrr! Divers also take the plunge at the likes of Hairy Wall (a 35m underwater cliff covered in seawhips) and Golden Bommies (a pair of 10m granite pinnacles aglow with yellow zoanthids). Snorkellers will find their happy underwater place by the pier at the southern end of Waubs Bay and at Rice Pebble Beach. Bicheno has no dive shops or operators,

BEACHES & ISLANDS

Waubs Beach: Nearest to Bicheno town centre, this relatively safe ocean beach is good for swimming on calm days.

Redbill Beach: Bicheno's main surf beach is one hop north of Waubs Beach, with a 1km-long stripe of sand.

Diamond Island: Off Redbill Beach's northern end, this granite outcrop, connected to the mainland by a sandy isthmus, becomes accessible by foot at low tide.

Rice Pebble Beach: Tucked-away beach, accessed from the Blowhole car park. Compact and sheltered cove with coarse sand.

Denison Beach: Stretching for almost 10km north of Bicheno, and more rugged and exposed than the beaches near town. Often impressively deserted.

so come prepared. Surfers can source information and gear at **Long Point Surf**.

A drier ocean experience comes aboard **Bicheno's Glass Bottom Boat** *(bichenoglassbottomboat.com; tours $40),* the only glass-bottom boat operating in Tasmania. Departing three times a day from near the Gulch, guided experiences last around 40 minutes. Booking ahead is recommended around Christmas/New Year, Easter and on holiday weekends.

Walks Around Town

Blowholes and boulders

Beginning by Redbill Beach (at the end of Gordon St) at Bicheno's northwestern edge, the **Foreshore Footway** is a 3km (one way) stroll along beaches and rock platforms, finishing at the Blowhole on the southeastern side of town. Highlights include Waubs Beach and the **Gulch**, a deep and clear ocean ravine separating Governor Island from the Bicheno shoreline. At the **Blowhole**, swells squeeze into cracks in the shore, surging skyward as geysers of white water. Don't get too close or you'll get unexpectedly drenched. Once you reach the Blowhole, it's worth continuing along the coast for a few hundred metres to Rice Pebble Beach, hidden away within the folds of the coastline. Rice Pebble is reached along a track that heads south from the Blowhole car park.

Bicheno is punctuated by a couple of granite-studded hills, including **Whalers Hill**, from where 19th-century whalers watched for the telltale blows of whales. Today it's an easy 10-minute climb from a signed pullout on Foster St to a pair of lookouts: one over the Gulch and Governor Island; the other across the town and northern coastline. Do as the name suggests and scan the sea for migrating whales in spring.

Hatch a Whisky at Waubs Harbour

Spirits infused with a taste of the ocean

Located in a former oyster hatchery with views of the Gulch – you might spot dolphins in summer and, further out, whales in spring – **Waubs Harbour Distillery** *(waubsharbourwhisky.com; tastings/tours $40/70)* produces single-malt whiskies that are influenced by the consistency of the maritime climate, with a briny edge that comes from the sea air. All but the growing of the grain is done on site. Book ahead online for a one-hour guided tasting of three core whiskies and a

COAL TOWN

Bicheno's raison d'être seems blatantly apparent – the ocean, right? – with whaling and fishing long propelling the local economy, but there was a time when coal was king. The black fuel was discovered north of the town in the mid-19th century. A 5km-long tramway was built into Bicheno, the town's harbour was expanded, and ships sailed to and from with their holds full of coal. Today, there's little sign of Bicheno's 'coal-den' days, but there is **Old Mines Lagoon**, the original mine site, 7km north of town, abutting East Coast Natureworld (p163). Elements of the mine's infrastructure are still lying about in the area, and the wildlife park has a display about the mine and its workings.

Bicheno Brewing Beers are made on site.

EATING & DRINKING IN BICHENO: OUR PICKS

Le Coq: Bicheno's finest restaurant, Francophoning the town one pork rillette and cannellini bean stew at a time. Date-night material. *5-9pm Tue-Sat* **$$$**

Lobster Shack: Crack open half a cray and enjoy the elevated views of the Gulch, Governor Island and the fishing fleet. *11am-7pm* **$$**

Farm Shed: Offers a full suite of east-coast wines combined with cheese and charcuterie platters. *10am-5pm*

Bicheno Beer Co: Buried behind Blue Edge bakery, with fire-warmed beer garden, brewing shed and regular boiler-maker BBQs. *2-9pm Fri & Sat, 1-5pm Sun*

THE STORY OF WAUBA DEBAR

European settlement began in Bicheno when whalers and sealers came to the Gulch in 1803. The town became known as Waubs Bay Harbour in 1832 to honour a Paredarerme woman. The woman, Wauba Debar, rescued two drowning men when their boat was wrecked offshore. At the heart of the town, Waubs Beach is now one of Bicheno's most popular strands, with a memorial to Wauba Debar set behind the beach's eastern end – her grave is empty because the body was exhumed by a museum in 1893. After Wauba's death in 1832, the settlement bore her name until the 1840s, for it was renamed after James Ebenezer Bicheno, a colonial secretary of Van Diemen's Land.

SOPHIE COSTELLO/SHUTTERSTOCK

Douglas-Apsley National Park

limited-release whisky in the restored ocean-view tasting room, or incorporate a tour of the distillery and bond rooms. Tours and tastings run Tuesday to Saturday.

Dig Deep into Douglas-Apsley

Bushwalks to gorges and waterholes

The east coast's big-name, big-drawing national parks might all be coastal, but you don't have to look far behind Bicheno's back to find the interior delights of **Douglas-Apsley National Park**. From its car park, 12km west of town at the end of Rosedale Rd, it's a short stroll (15 minutes return) to a freshwater swim at **Apsley Waterhole**, while one of Tasmania's 60 Great Short Walks loops out from the waterhole, crossing a ridge to make a rock-hopping return through **Apsley Gorge** (four to five hours) with swim options aplenty. Walking through the gorge requires some dexterity and it should only be attempted in dry conditions.

One of the state's least-known multiday hikes, the **Leeaberra Track** traverses the park from north to south, mixing deep gorges with dry sclerophyll forest and patches of rainforest. The three-day, 28km track can only be walked north to south (to limit the spread of phytophthora), so you'll need to somehow arrange a car shuttle. Track finding can be difficult, so it's suited only to experienced hikers with good navigational skills.

St Helens

MOUNTAIN BIKING | BEACHES | WALKING

The salty scent of St Helens' origins as a fishing and whaling settlement linger, but these days this holiday town on the broad, protected sweep of Georges Bay is more interested in mountain biking, beach bumming and pouring craft beer. Suitably named after a ship, St Helens has been transformed in recent years by mountain biking, a spillover of the success of nearby Derby. And while it's the tiniest skip from town to the beaches of the celebrated Bay of Fires, what many visitors fail to notice is that the beaches on St Helens Point, south of town, are just as bright and bold. With a palpable history that takes in fishing, whaling, swanning (harvesting the bay's black swans for their downy underfeathers), farming and tin mining, St Helens feels alive and lived in – no tourism fakery here – adding to its seaside charms.

GETTING AROUND

Calow's Coaches runs buses from St Helens to Bicheno and Coles Bay (for Freycinet National Park), stopping at Beaumaris, Scamander and St Marys en route. Another Calow's route heads west to Launceston. Having your own vehicle is essential to visit Pyengana and make your way north to Binalong Bay and the Bay of Fires.

Mountain Biking Around St Helens

Stacked loops and a marathon-length classic

Following in the well-rutted trails of nearby Derby, St Helens has quickly developed into one of Australia's best mountain-biking towns. The network's main hub, on Flagstaff Rd, 6km south of town, is framed around a stacked loop of trails – largely green (easy) loops that whirl through the forest before returning to the busy trailhead area (which has a cafe). Dropping into these loops from higher up the slopes at Loila Tier are bombing descents such as **Send Helens**, **Old Salty Dog** and **Seeya Later**.

St Helens' hero trails are the 27km **Dreaming Pools** and, primarily, the isolated **Bay of Fires** trail. Around five hours is needed to complete this 42km trail, beginning at a trailhead atop the Blue Tier mountains, which is served by shuttles from both St Helens and Derby – the networks bleed into each other at this high point. As the name suggests, the Bay of Fires trail ends by the sands of Swimcart Beach (p174) on the Bay of Fires. Be prepared with snacks, water and the right gear to patch up both yourself and your bike if necessary.

TOP TIP

St Helens is regarded as Tasmania's ocean-fishing capital, and charter boats offer fishing trips in the sheltered waters of Georges Bay, or further out to where the big game fish play.

SIGHTS
1 St Helens History Room

ACTIVITIES
2 Gravity Isle
3 Vertigo MTB

SLEEPING
4 Panorama Hotel

EATING
5 Lifebuoy Cafe
6 Skippers

DRINKING & NIGHTLIFE
7 Easy Tiger
8 The Social

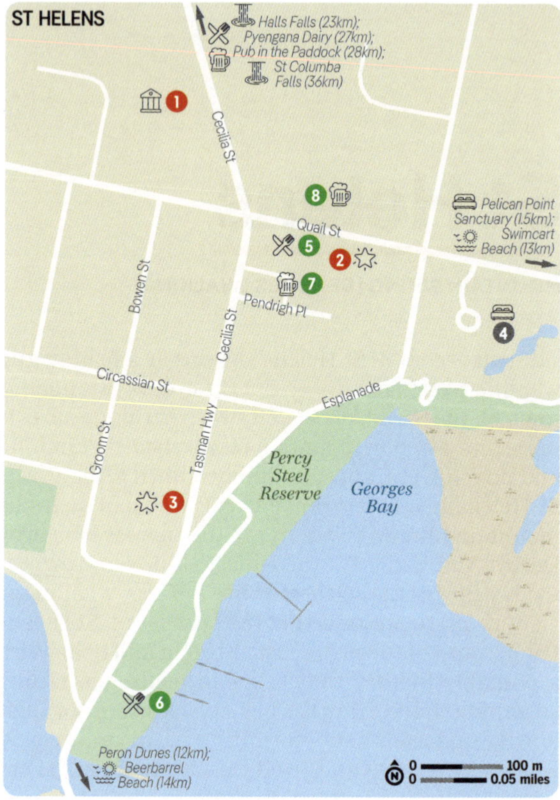

The trail network offers everything from family-friendly experiences to trails suitable for seasoned riders. Bike hire and shuttles, which typically cost $10 per run or $50 for unlimited uplifts in a day, can be arranged through **Gravity Isle** or **Vertigo MTB**.

Take a Local History Lesson

Amble among artefacts at the St Helens History Room

The **St Helens History Room** *(sthelenshistoryroom.com; adult/child $5/3)* is an interesting regional museum, with more than 1000 artefacts squeezed into a large room behind the visitor centre, cataloguing the town's social and natural history. Collections include Tasmanian Aboriginal stone tools, maireener shell necklaces and a kelp water carrier; the trade tools of early whalers and swanners (swan hunters); relics from the local tin mine, which was the world's largest open-cut mine in the late 1800s. Don't miss the amazing old horse-drawn hearse, and an eight-minute film introducing the Trail of the Tin Dragon (p178) tourist route, which focuses on Chinese tin mining in Tasmania's northeast.

ANDREW BAIN/LONELY PLANET

Beerbarrel Beach

Get to the Point

Sand aplenty at St Helens Point

St Helens Point Conservation Area covers much of a long spit just to the south of St Helens. It's stitched with beaches, the best (and best named) of which is **Beerbarrel Beach**, its white sands studded with bleached granite boulders. Close by are the **Peron Dunes**, where short walking trails ascend the soft slopes to an open, desert-like expanse of sand. Bring boogie boards or similar to slide down the dunes if you have kids in tow.

The conservation area also offers the best walking around the St Helens area, which was appropriately known to the Tasmanian Aboriginal people as Kunnara Kunna, meaning 'easy walking place'. From Beerbarrel Beach, it's a one-hour return walk to **Burns Bay**, rounding Tasmania's easternmost point, while you can also cross through the Peron Dunes to **Maurouard Beach** (around one hour return). Pick up the 'Walking In and Around Break O'Day' printout from the St Helens visitor centre for full details of walks in the conservation area.

Detour to Pyengana

Waterfalls, a watering hole and cheese

About 26km west of St Helens, tiny **Pyengana** ('Pie-en-gah-na' – an Aboriginal word describing the meeting of two rivers) slumbers in an impossibly emerald-green valley with some interesting diversions.

In the 1890s European pioneers noted the area's high rainfall and brought in dairy cattle, which thrived on the lush grass. Exporting milk from this isolated valley was impractical, but once converted into cheese and butter the produce could survive the slow journey to market. They've been making cheese in the valley since 1895, a tradition now upheld by **Pyengana**

EAST COAST WHALE TRAIL

With around 40 cetacean (whales and dolphins) species frequenting Tasmanian waters, the east coast is often a grandstand for whale activity, with humpback and southern right whales, in particular, regularly sighted during their annual migrations. Between May and July they head north from Antarctica to give birth in warmer South Pacific waters, returning south from September to December.

The **East Coast Whale Trail** is a series of 14 recommended viewing locations along the coast. Stops feature information boards about the whales. Around St Helens, there are stops at Beerbarrel Beach, Burns Bay and the Gardens, while Shelly Point, 15km south of town, has binoculars to assist with your whale viewing. Find more information at the Break O'Day Council website *(bodc.tas.gov.au)*.

THE MYSTERY OF BRENDA HEAN

In 1972, Tasmanian environmental activists were protesting the impending damming of Lake Pedder in the state's southwest. As part of the campaign, pilot Max Price and activist Brenda Hean flew out of Hobart on 8 September in a Tiger Moth on a mission to reach Canberra to take up the fight. The pair radioed into St Helens, but were never heard from again and didn't make it to Flinders Island for a planned refuelling stop. No wreckage or bodies were ever found. A few days before the flight, Hean had received a threatening phone call and the plane's hangar was alleged to have been broken into the night before they flew.

Accident or foul play? The debate continues.

DALE LORNA JACOBSEN/SHUTTERSTOCK

Cheese platter, Pyengana Dairy (p169)

Dairy *(pyenganadairy.com.au)*. Watch cheese being made through a pair of large windows and then settle into a free tasting – the cloth-matured cheddar is its signature – or a cheese platter or other dairy-driven offerings at the farmhouse cafe. Head out the back to watch the cows let themselves in and out of Australia's oldest robotic milking shed.

Nearby, the well-named **Pub in the Paddock** is most famous for Priscilla, its beer-drinking pig. Grab a meal, a drink or shout Priscilla a (very watered down) beer. The area has some beautiful waterfalls, including **St Columba Falls** (30 minutes return), one of Tasmania's highest, and **Halls Falls** (one hour return), set below a weir built by Chinese tin miners in the 1880s. There's a lovely set of rock pools between the weir and the falls. St Columba Falls are 10km further up the valley road from Pyengana. To reach Halls Falls, return to the Tasman Hwy, turn right and look for the sign 2km down the road; the trailhead is 1km off the highway.

Movies screen daily at Easy Tiger's cinema.

EATING & DRINKING IN ST HELENS: OUR PICKS

The Social: Choose between the retro lounge and the fire-warmed beer garden for craft beer and the likes of Balkan arancini. *3-8pm Wed & Thu, to 10pm Fri* $$

Lifebuoy Cafe: Nautically themed setting for breakfast and lunch in a space shared with a homewares shop. *7am-2pm Mon-Fri, to 1pm Sat* $$

Skippers: The freshest of seafood, served from a floating restaurant moored beside the fishing fleet. *11.30am-2.30pm Wed, Thu & Sun, to 7pm Fri & Sat* $$

Easy Tiger: What do you get when you combine a craft brewery, cinema, burger joint and bar? Ever-eventful Easy Tiger. *8am-10pm*

Bay of Fires

BEACHES | COASTAL WALKING | INDIGENOUS CULTURE

With its orange lichens looking as fiery as its name, Larapuna/Bay of Fires is the most compelling natural feature of Tasmania's northeast. Here, white beaches are broken up by jumbled granite boulders coloured like orange rind. Binalong Bay, the only town along the bay, sits at its southern tip and has brilliantly white beaches and artistic sprawls of granite, but this is just a prelude to the coastal landscape beyond. Climb into your car and head out along the Gardens road, stopping at the many beaches beside the road. Pause at each one to clamber onto rocky, lichen-covered headlands, stroll along white-sand beaches, or simply laze on the sand. There's little to do here beyond marvel at the colours, which can occupy hours, but it's all best seen on one of the coast's multiday guided walks, including a four-day, three-night guided walk run by the Tasmanian Aboriginal community, adding insight into their connection to the area.

GETTING AROUND

To explore Larapuna/Bay of Fires, you'll need your own wheels. St Helens-based Vertigo MTB (p168) and Gravity Isle (p168) both hire out bikes (including e-bikes). They're ostensibly for mountain-biking the trails, but could be used to explore the Bay of Fires.

Experiencing the Wukalina Walk

Indigenous culture, history and beauty

Hike the coastline from Wukalina/Mt William to Eddystone Point on the four-day guided **Wukalina Walk** *(wukalinawalk.com.au; $3295)*, run by the Tasmanian Aboriginal community. The walk delves into bush tucker, middens, Aboriginal culture and the history and striking beauty of this fabled coastline. Two nights are spent at krakani lumi, a standing camp with sleeping pods inspired by ancient Aboriginal shelters, with the final night in lighthouse keeper cottages at Eddystone Point. Expect cultural activities, including weaving and kelp-basket making, and learning about the history and language of the Tasmanian Aboriginal community. The walk runs from September to May and covers around 35km in total.

TOP TIP

The bay looks small, but allow plenty of time. The road to the Gardens doesn't continue north to Ansons Bay and Mt William National Park, so you'll need to backtrack, and many of the roads around the northern sections are unsealed.

SIGHTS
1 Eddystone Point Lighthouse
2 Mt William National Park
3 Priory Ridge Wines

SLEEPING
4 Arthouse Bay of Fires
5 Bay of Fires Bush Retreat
6 Deep Creek Campground
7 SABI
8 Stumpys Bay
9 Top Camp

EATING
10 Gladstone Hotel
11 Lease 65
see 7 The Hub – Seaside

Walking the Bay of Fires

A multiday beach hop

The vibrant Larapuna/Bay of Fires coastline springs to intimate, colourful life on the five-day, four-night **Bay of Fires Signature Walk** *(taswalkingco.com.au; from $2995)*. Setting out from Boulder Point in Mt William National Park, and concluding at the walk's luxurious Bay of Fires Lodge near Ansons Bay, highlights include a night at a secluded beach camp, lunching in the dunes behind the Eddystone Point Lighthouse and kayaking on Ansons River. The final two nights are spent at the lodge, with views over the beaches, open fire and even spa treatments. Fine food and wine are all included. A more concise Bay of Fires Long Weekend three-day, two-night experience, walking from Deep Creek to the lodge, is also available.

The Lowest Mountain & the Highest Wildlife

Wildlife, beaches and bush camping in Mt William National Park

Reaching almost to Tasmania's northeast tip, isolated **Mt William National Park** *(parks.tas.gov.au)* features long sandy

KEIICHIHIKI/GETTY IMAGES

Wallaby, Mt William National Park

beaches, prolific wildlife and the eponymous Wukalina/Mt William. Standing 216m above sea level, it's more a glorified hill, but it still affords views over the stunning coastline and the southern Furneaux Islands. A one-hour return trail to the summit departs from the Wukalina/Mt William car park. It includes a short, steep section near the top.

A primary reason for the park's creation in 1973 was to protect Tasmania's remaining Forester (eastern grey) kangaroos, which faced extinction in the 1950s and '60s. They're now thriving and best seen at dawn or dusk along the **Forester Kangaroo Drive**, an unsealed 12km loop road in the park's north. Wallabies, wombats and echidnas are also on the car-window sighting list.

In the park's south is tall **Eddystone Point Lighthouse**. You can't enter the lighthouse, but you can wander around the point for great coastal views along the beach-lined Bay of Fires coastline. Eddystone Point is 50km from St Helens, along mostly gravel road.

There's beachside camping under the sheoaks in four separate campgrounds at **Stumpys Bay**, as well as at **Top Camp** near Musselroe Bay and beside tannin-stained **Deep Creek** in the park's south.

DUAL PLACE NAMES

The Bay of Fires could easily have taken its name from the fiery orange lichen that lights up the granite headlands along this 29km-long sweep of white sand and crystal-clear seas. But it was, in fact, named for the fires of Aboriginal people sighted by Tobias Furneaux when the HMS *Adventure* sailed past in 1773. To the Tasmanian Aboriginal people, however, the Bay of Fires area was known as Larapuna.

In 2013, Larapuna/Bay of Fires was among a group of six spots in Tasmania to be officially recognised as places with Aboriginal or dual names – English and Aboriginal. They were the first of a growing list of places with dual names. At the time of writing, 44 places around Tasmania have officially adopted dual names, including Wukalina/Mt William.

EATING & DRINKING AROUND THE BAY OF FIRES: OUR PICKS

Lease 65: Grab your oysters from the waterside farm shed and head for your favourite Bay of Fires beach. Cash only. *11am-3pm Mon-Fri* $

The Hub – Seaside: Great deck views as far as Eddystone Point and a large roster of wood-fired pizzas and local craft beers. *noon-8pm* $$

Gladstone Hotel: Classic pub grub (hello rissoles and mixed grill) by the edge of Mt William National Park. *noon-2pm Wed-Sun, 5.30-8pm daily* $$

Priory Ridge Wines: Generous tastings of seven wines ($15) from the east coast's northernmost vineyard inside a rustic wooden shearing shed turned cellar door. *11am-4pm Fri-Sun*

DRIVE THE GARDENS ROAD

Take the road from Binalong Bay to the Gardens and find yourself driving through Bay of Fires beach royalty.

START	END	LENGTH
Binalong Bay	The Gardens	19km; 25min

This drive reveals the centrepiece beaches of the Bay of Fires, turning onto the Gardens road (C848) 2km west of Binalong Bay. Get acquainted with the beach beauty to come at 1 **Jeanneret Beach**, a small curl of white sand pinched between granite outcrops. Its ends are often protected from wind and waves, making it a good swim or snorkel stop. There's a fair chance you'll share 2 **Swimcart Beach** with a mountain biker or three as it's the gleaming finish line for the Bay of Fires trail (p167). 3 **Cosy Corner North** is arguably the most beautiful beach spot along the bay. Wander to the beach's northern end to explore the granite outcrops and rock platforms covered in the Bay of Fires' signature orange lichens.

From the 4 **Sloop Reef** day-use area, a faint walking trail heads for about five minutes to the end of the point, looking over the reef with its largest rock looking strangely like someone flipping the bird. After crossing stout-coloured Big Lagoon, the road ends past the little cluster of homes known as 5 **The Gardens**, where a short walking track heads to a lookout platform and a small beach at the foot of a lone home. A scramble over the coastal boulders will reveal other views along the coast. It's lichen heaven.

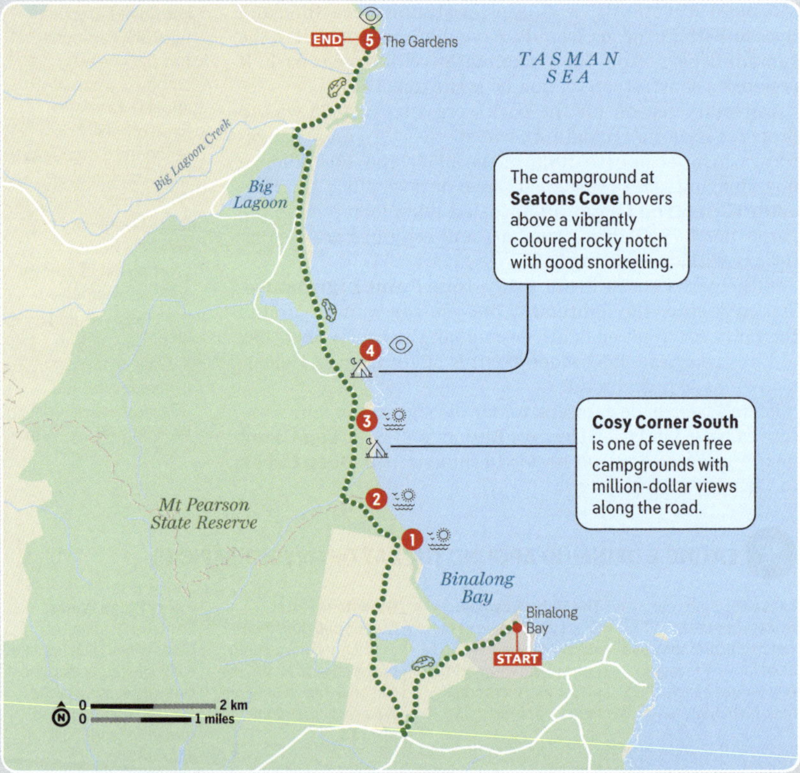

Derby

MOUNTAIN BIKING | MINING HISTORY | CRAFT BEER

There's no mistaking Derby's modern raison d'être. Bikes hang from buildings, the main street is a long strip of bike shops, and accommodation rentals jostle to provide the best bike facilities. Once a forlorn former tin-mining town, Derby was transformed in 2015 when it opened its Blue Derby network of mountain-bike trails to instant, mass popularity. Today it's not unusual to see more bikes than cars trundling through town and it is, without question, the doyen of Australian mountain-biking towns. It's no stretch to say that this is the town that kickstarted Australia's love affair with mountain biking. With popularity has come other changes: a glut of accommodation, craft-beer and wood-fired-pizza joints, and even a floating sauna that attracts weary bikers and wellness seekers alike. Yet under all this there remains a hint of Derby's original calling as a tin-mining town, a time that spanned seven decades from the 1870s.

TOP TIP

So many of Derby's once-abandoned cottages have been repurposed for visiting mountain bikers, and prices can be eye-watering. Consider Branxholm, 8km to the west, as an alternative. The two towns are connected by the green (easy) Valley Ponds mountain-bike trail.

Get Riding

Discover some of the world's best mountain biking

The hub of Derby's mountain-biking scene is the **Blue Derby trail network** *(ridebluederby.com.au)*, named for the town's proximity to the Blue Tier mountain range and offering more than 125km of trails. Trails range from easy to extremely difficult, and from 1km tootles to combined 40km all-day epics. A proportion of trails are accessed by shuttle, but there are

GETTING AROUND

MTB Express *(mtbexpress.com.au)* runs transfers to Derby from Launceston airport, often combined with shuttle packages on the trails. The more laborious option is bus 777, which has daily afternoon departures from Launceston to Derby, stopping at Branxholm en route. From Launceston, it's a drive of around 1½ hours to Derby. The fastest route from Hobart to Derby is via Campbell Town, a drive of around four hours. From St Helens, it's a drive of around one hour along winding, forested roads.

SIGHTS
1 Derby Schoolhouse Museum
2 Little Blue Lake
3 Mt Paris Dam
4 Tasty Trout Falls

ACTIVITIES
5 Air-Ya-Garn
6 Atlas Trail
7 Axehead Trail
8 Bark Off Biking
9 Blue Tier Trail
10 Derby Tunnel Trail
11 Evolution Biking
12 Flickity Sticks Upper
13 Floating Sauna Lake Derby
14 Lake Derby Trail
15 North East Rail Trail
16 Relics Trail
17 Return to Sender Trail
18 Sawtooth Trail
see 11 Vertigo MTB

SLEEPING
19 Tin Dragon Cottages
see 1 Tin Mountain

EATING
see 8 The Hub
20 Tin Timbers Cafe
21 Weldborough Hotel

DRINKING & NIGHTLIFE
see 1 LOT 40

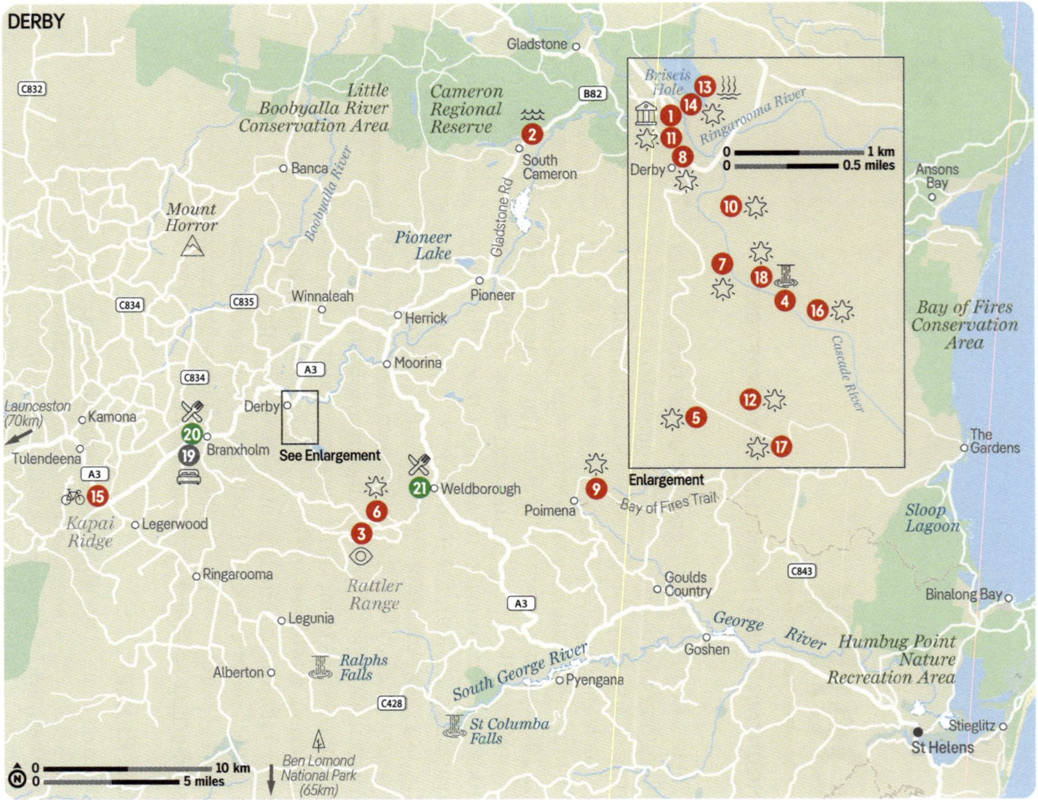

also plenty of trails you can access directly from town. At the bottom of Christopher St, a signboard at the main trailhead has maps and ride suggestions.

A favourite short loop is a combination of the green (easy) **Axehead**, **Relics** and **Sawtooth** trails, climbing through a tight (but simple) set of switchbacks known as Twisties and passing **Tasty Trout Falls**. A fun deviation on the return section of the loop is to dive down the **Derby Tunnel** trail, which heads through a low tunnel dug by one miner to transport his tailings beneath the lease of another miner – the ceiling is so low that you have to crouch as you roll through on your bike. Another easy loop out of town is **Lake Derby**, a 2km lap of Briseis Hole, a flooded former mine.

Shuttle runs close to town include Black Stump, from where you can access flowing downhill runs such as **Flickity Sticks Upper** (and the connecting Flickity Sticks) and **Return to Sender** (both blue, or intermediate). For the more skilled and airborne, the black (difficult) **Air-Ya-Garn** branches off Return to Sender for a faster, jump-filled return to Derby. Further afield, standout trails include **Blue Tier** and **Atlas** (both blue). Sometimes described as one of the world's great rides, the former sets out from atop of the Blue Tier range, plunging through deep rainforest to end just down the road from the Weldborough Hotel. Atlas starts 6km out the other side of the hotel, completing the descent back to Derby. A great day out is to take a shuttle to Blue Tier, ride to Weldborough and then catch another shuttle from the pub to the Atlas trailhead. Shuttle operators offer this combo as a package.

Shuttle services are run by **Vertigo MTB** *(vertigomtb.com.au)*, **Bark Off Biking** *(barkoffbiking.com.au)* and **MAD-MTB** *(madmtb.com.au)*. To rent bikes, including e-bikes, contact Vertigo MTB, Bark Off Biking and **Evolution Biking** *(ebiketasmania.com.au)*.

Lake-Top Sauna

Taking it easy Derby-style

Balanced on a pontoon atop forest-framed Briseis Hole – aka Lake Derby – the **Floating Sauna Lake Derby** *(floatingsauna.com.au; $55)* is a wood-fired surprise that can ease the fatigues of mountain biking or simply be enjoyed as an indulgent pleasure. Walk or ride the 800m from town along the Lake Derby trail to the pontoon, where sauna sessions last for one hour. It's customary to spend about 10 minutes in the baking heat before leaping into the chilly lake. Rinse and repeat for an hour. It's mentally challenging and physically invigorating at the same time. Book ahead.

Rail-Trail Cycling

Pedal the North East Rail Trail

A gentle counterpoint to the bravado of Derby's mountain-bike trails, the **North East Rail Trail** stretches for 26km from Billycock Hill, 15km west of

DERBY'S MTB HISTORY

Derby first shone as a tin-mining centre, but today it's the town that mountain biking reinvented. After the mines closed in the 1940s, Derby virtually slipped from the map – the highway passed through it, but few people found a reason to even stop – but with 2015's opening of the Blue Derby trail network, the air was pumped back into the town's tyres. Derby quickly became one of the world's most revered mountain-bike destinations, and in 2017 and 2019 it hosted rounds of the Enduro World Series. In an island state that's quickly become Australia's standout mountain-biking destination, the breadth and variety of Derby's trail network can be challenging but remains unparalleled. It's all about the flow.

THE RISE & RISE OF MOUNTAIN BIKING

Derby's mountain-biking success has spawned trail networks across the state. Find yet more flow in **Queenstown** (p273), **Maydena** (p118) and **St Helens** (p167).

Derby, to Scottsdale. Setting out from beside the Tasman Hwy just beyond Legerwood, it follows the course of the Launceston to Branxholm railway, which ceased service in 1976. The trail, which has only gentle gradients, runs through a combination of fern-covered slopes, plantation pine and farmland, with its finest moment coming as it burrows into an old railway cutting, where the cliff-like walls rise up to 10m overhead. You'll need a car shuttle to ride the rail trail one way; otherwise, plan on a 52km ride.

TRAIL TALES

Buck Gibson, owner of Vertigo MTB, outlines his favourite Derby rides. *@vertigomtb*

Blue Tier: This 23km point-to-point ride has engaging flow and a real Gondwana feel about it. Finish at the Weldborough Hotel for lunch in the beer garden.

Lake Derby & Wotcha Upta: A great chill-out ride for the day's end, with a chance to spot a platypus. The climb up the old mine face brings impressive views over Briseis Hole and town.

Triple 3: A new hand-built black-diamond trail with granite and slab features that stretch my abilities and require 100% focus.

Axehead/Long Shadows to Hazy Days: Great e-bike loop that I do more than any other ride. Twisties and Tasty Trout Falls never get old and the Hazy Days descent has everyone grinning, regardless of skill level.

A Tin-Inspired Heritage

Explore Derby's history of tin-mining

One hundred years ago, Derby was a thriving mining centre, springing up when tin was discovered here in 1874. The rush in search of the grey gold attracted thousands of fortune seekers, and several mines operated in and around Derby. At the height of its boom, the town's population numbered 3000.

Many of the miners attracted to Derby in the 1870s came from the goldfields of Victoria, and a large number of them were Chinese. At its peak, there were 1000 Chinese miners in and around Derby, Weldborough and nearby Moorina, outnumbering Europeans. Documenting this Chinese mining heritage throughout the region is a tourist route called the **Trail of the Tin Dragon**. The trail runs between Launceston and St Helens, and key sites with interpretation panels crop up along the route. At **Moorina**, 12km west of Derby, a panel tells of the days when this speck of a settlement, then called Krushka's Bridge, was the largest in the area. The cemetery immediately behind contains a Chinese memorial and funeral oven. Another panel in **Branxholm** tells of Tasmania's first race riot, when angry European settlers tried to stop 12 Chinese miners from crossing the bridge en route to the tin mines. In **Weldborough**, Tasmania's first casino was in one of the old wooden buildings opposite the hotel. For a grounder on the Trail of the Tin Dragon, call in also at the St Helens History Room (p168).

Derby's centrally located **Derby Schoolhouse Museum** has a particular focus on the area's mining days, especially the disaster of 1929 when, after five days of heavy rain, a mining dam burst near Derby and 14 people died in the resulting flood.

Out & About in Derby

Ditch the bike for a historic dam and a brilliantly blue lake

Take a day off the bike and tour a couple of vivid sights in easy reach of town. Tasmania's brightest, bluest lake, **Little Blue Lake**, lies pooled along the base of Poonerluttener/Mt Cameron, 20 minutes' drive northeast of Derby on the B82. The narrow lake fills the hollow of an old mine, glowing aqua. Random unsigned walking trails head around the lake, and while its colour is pretty and inviting, it's a sneaky siren – don't enter the water, which contains high aluminium levels and other minerals. To walk around the lake takes less than an hour.

ANDREW BAIN/LONELY PLANET

Mt Paris Dam

Returning towards Derby, turn away onto Mt Paris Dam Rd (C425) from the eastern edge of Branxholm, or from opposite the Weldborough Hotel, to find **Mt Paris Dam**, an atmospheric concrete relic in a beautiful pocket of ferny forest. Built in 1935 to serve the Mt Paris tin mine, it's 250m long and 16m high, but when it was decreed in 1985 that the dam was at risk of collapse in event of flood, slots were cutting into the wall. The Cascade River now pours through the slots, like a win for nature over industry.

LEGERWOOD'S CARVED MEMORIAL TREES

Located 15km southwest of Derby (look for the sign on the left after passing through Branxholm on the way to Scottsdale) is the rural hamlet of **Legerwood**. When the small town was forced to lop the gigantic trees along its main street – planted to commemorate its WWI soldiers – it came up with a novel idea to harness what was left of those trees deemed unsafe. In 2004 Legerwood commissioned chainsaw sculptor Eddie Freeman to carve dramatically posed figures of the soldiers (and other significant local people) from the tree stumps that remained. There are 25 different arboreal sculptures commemorating the contribution of local soldiers, many of whom served as ANZACs in the Gallipoli campaign of 1915.

EATING & DRINKING AROUND DERBY: OUR PICKS

Tin Timbers Cafe: Licensed cafe luring bike riders down the Valley Ponds trail to Branxholm for its home-baked gourmet pies. *9am-2pm Mon, Tue, Thu & Fri, to 3pm Sat & Sun* $

The Hub: A mountain biker's two best friends – craft beer and wood-fired pizza – in a warm cottage setting. *noon-8pm* $$

LOT 40: Cafe out the front and party – bar, brewery, distillery – out the back at this cavernous venue at the town's heart. *cafe 8.30am-2.30pm, bar 2pm-late Thu-Sun, from 4pm Mon-Wed*

Weldborough Hotel: Isolated 1876 country pub by the end of the Blue Tier mountain-bike trail. A good selection of craft beers. *11am-late* $$

Flinders Island

WALKING | HISTORY | SCENERY

TOP TIP
Kate Mooney has been caring for orphaned wombats for more than 25 years, and is happy for visitors to drop into her home to ooh and aah over the animals. Find her on Instagram at @flindersislandwombat.

Take greater Tasmania's mountains, beaches and farmland and distil them into an even smaller island and you have Flinders Island, the largest of the 52 Furneaux Group islands on the eastern edge of Bass Strait. Once part of a land bridge that connected Tasmania to mainland Australia, the island's lichen-tinged coastline and soaring mountains resemble a spectacular geological mashup of the Bay of Fires and Freycinet Peninsula.

With a population of just 900, Flinders is an easy-going rural community living mostly from fishing and agriculture, but tourism is also developing, with a considered focus on regenerative activities and practices of benefit to both travellers and the local community. Flinders offers great coastal bushwalking, copious wildlife, fishing in deep and clear waters, and snorkelling, diving and safe swimming in the island's arcing bays. Factor in brilliant seafood, grass-fed lamb and island-crafted wine and whisky, and there's plenty to look forward to after a day's adventures.

Wybalenna's Troubled History

Evocative site of Aboriginal segregation

Few historic sites are as powerful as windswept **Wybalenna** *(free)*. A restored chapel and an overgrown cemetery are all that

GETTING AROUND

Sharp Airlines flies to Flinders Island from Launceston and Melbourne's Essendon airfield. The more brutal way here (though it allows you to bring your own car) is aboard an eight-hour car ferry (Tuesday only) from Bridport with **Bass Strait Freight** *(bassstraitfreight.com.au)*. Book in advance to rent a car with **Flinders Island Car Rentals** *(ficr.com.au)*. Some island roads, especially in the north, are unsealed, and are busy with wildlife around dawn and dusk – try to limit your evening driving.

SIGHTS
1 Castle Rock
2 Dock
3 Fotheringate Beach
4 Furneaux Distillery
5 Furneaux Museum
6 Killiecrankie Bay
7 Mt Killiecrankie
8 Strzelecki Peaks
9 Unavale Vineyard
10 Wybalenna

ACTIVITIES
see 5 Flinders Island Dive
11 Killiecrankie Enterprises
12 Trousers Point

SLEEPING
see 11 Crayshack
13 Island Quarters

EATING
see 13 Flinders Island Bakery
14 Furneaux Tavern
see 13 Interstate Hotel
see 13 Missing Goose

TRANSPORT
15 Flinders Island Car Rentals

remain of this misguided settlement, where 134 Tasmanian Aboriginal people were relocated from mainland Tasmania in 1834 to be 'civilised and Christianised'. By the time Wybalenna was closed down in 1847, only 47 Aboriginal people had survived and they were transported to Oyster Cove, south of Hobart. It was a tragic conclusion to a failed plan devised by George Augustus Robinson, an English schoolteacher and colonial administrator.

Head into the chapel for displays on the settlement, while there's a gated cemetery just behind, where the headstone of Mannalargenna, chief of the Trawlwoolway tribe, can be seen. Other gravestones remember settlers who lived and died on Flinders Island, but the graves of other Aboriginal people who died here are unmarked. This is sacred Aboriginal ground: be respectful. A nearby timber shearing shed is being restored as a community and cultural space.

Exploring Flinders Island History

A museum of island memories

Graced with an elevated location above Emita Beach on Flinders' west coast, the volunteer-run **Furneaux Museum**

WINDY WAYS

Drive north from Sawyers Bay, near Emita, and you'll soon pass a roadside sign marking the line of the 40th parallel south. Welcome to the Roaring Forties. This latitudinal band across the southern hemisphere is notorious for its winds, and on Flinders Island (and King Island) it can the bane of campers, kayakers and boaties (and seemed to pin me to the spot for hours when I once set out to cycle around the island). Spring and early summer (September to December) are typically when the winds are at their wiliest on Flinders Island, with average 3pm speeds of around 27km/h – for comparison, that's about 9km/h faster than in Hobart across the same months.

ALEX CIMBAL/SHUTTERSTOCK

Castle Rock

(furneauxmuseum.org.au; $10) records the history of the Furneaux Islands. The museum building is modern, but heritage structures scattered about the property include cells from the Whitemark police station dating from 1916 and a 1920s muttonbird-processing shed. Around the grounds are whalebones, blubber pots and rusty ship propellers, evidence of Flinders' whaling history. The interior focuses on local flora and fauna, muttonbirding and the stories of long-standing island families. The museum's Aboriginal section includes beautiful shell necklaces and a display about nearby Wybalenna (p180). The museum is closed on Mondays.

Sandy Strolls

Walks along a colourful coastline

With three of the state's 60 Great Short Walks, Flinders Island punches above its weight as a bushwalking destination. Foremost among the trio is the 1½-hour circuit around **Trousers Point**. Beginning near **Trousers Point Beach**, a mountain-backed cove lined with eroded and lichen-covered

EATING & DRINKING ON FLINDERS ISLAND: OUR PICKS

Flinders Island Bakery: Try curried scallop pies and savoury sausage rolls at this friendly spot favoured by locals. *8am-4pm Mon-Fri* $

Missing Goose: A rotating roster of dishes, cocktails and its takeaway Pizza Qube next door. *9am-8pm Thu-Sun* $$

Furneaux Tavern: Focused on local produce and seafood. Dine in or grab takeaway fish and chips. *noon-1.30pm Thu-Sun & 5.30-8pm daily* $$

Interstate Hotel: Whitemark's historic pub. Coffee and cake in the morning; pub standards at night. Book for dinner. *7.30am-1.30pm & 5-7.30pm Mon-Sat* $$

boulders, the walk negotiates a granite headland overlaid with layered Quaternary-period sands to incorporate a diverse landscape of beaches and dunes. Two beautiful beaches with surging tidal pools compete for attention, while conical Mt Chappell Island, said to be home to the world's largest tiger snakes, sits just offshore. Return to the Trousers Point Beach car park inland along a gravel road from equally beautiful **Fotheringate Beach**, or stick around to explore this beach and its low cliffs.

Castle Rock is the destination for the second Great Short Walk. From Allports Beach, it takes around 1½ hours to reach the hulking boulder plugged in the sands of Marshall Beach, following a series of beaches along the way. An unsealed road running west from Palana Rd provides a quicker look.

Arguably better than both walks is a coastal path from **Killiecrankie Bay** to the **Dock**. At the bay's northern end, the walk passes a small beach and large limestone arch in protected **Stacky's Bight**, then heads beneath Mt Killiecrankie's high cliffs – popular with rock climbers – to the paradisiacal scatter of rocks and islands at the Dock.

Diamond Fever

Fossick for treasure

The gorgeous arc of Killiecrankie Bay is home to a literal island treasure: Killiecrankie diamonds. Technically they're a topaz, but it's a great treasure hunt to go fossicking, typically around so-called Diamond Gully at the northern end of the beach. Hire a shovel and a sieve from **Killiecrankie Enterprises** *(0428 592 130; open by appointment)* and you'll also be given a couple of small stones (to help identify diamonds as you fossick) and instructions on where best to search. Margaret at Killiecrankie Enterprises also sells loose stones and set jewellery, available directly or at Bowman's Store in Whitemark.

Take to the Mountains

Climb to epic coastal views

Flinders Island's third Great Short Walk is also its most challenging – the four- to five-hour return hike to its highest point, the 756m **Strzelecki Peaks**. It's a steep and strenuous walk, though there's nothing overly technical about the route, and the views over Trousers Point and well beyond are definitely worth the effort. The weather can be changeable on the summit, so be prepared for all conditions.

Flinders' second peak of walking choice is 316m **Mt Killiecrankie**, rising from the northern end of Killiecrankie Bay. It can be ascended on trails that leave from the end of the beach on Killiecrankie Bay (look for the wooden signs as you continue along the coast from the beach), or from a signed trailhead on the road to the Dock. Ascend and return on the same route, or continue on to combine the peak with the coastal walk from Killiecrankie Bay to the Dock for a rewarding half-day hike.

EXPLORING FLINDERS ISLAND

Flinders Island Adventures: Book a fishing charter with this local outfit, which also runs walking tours, including a seven-day all-inclusive guided walk. Also half- and full-day 4WD and luxury van tours.

Flinders Island Dive: There's great diving and snorkelling in the clear waters around the island, especially amid the sea caves, shoals and reefs. Fishing tours also offered.

Flinders Island Aviation: Offers scenic flights over the craggy peaks of Flinders and the surrounding isles. Options range from 30-minute highlight flights to longer customised air tours.

Tasmanian Expeditions: Guided multiday walking adventures on Flinders Island. Accommodation is in a very comfortable coastal eco-camps.

Roaring 40s Kayaking: Seven-day paddling trips along Flinders Island's shores and outlying islands.

WHY I LOVE FLINDERS ISLAND

Andrew Bain, Lonely Planet writer

Islands are among my favourite places on earth, especially those blessed with hiking trails, and Flinders is incontestably my favourite island in Australia. By morning I can be on the wind-whipped summit of the Strzelecki Peaks and by afternoon cooling off among the orange lichens and blue seas of Trousers Point. Locals have a bit of a beach rule here – if you get to a beach and there's someone there, head to another, because there's always going to be an empty strip of sand somewhere nearby. It's a chance to have a Robinson Crusoe moment, brave a frigid Bass Strait swim and ponder island delights. And it's all the better if you have a few hours of Strzelecki sweat to wash away.

ADAM GIBSON

Furneaux Distillery

Flinders' Whisky & Wine

An island of local provenance

The architect-designed tasting room at **Furneaux Distillery** *(furneauxdistillery.com.au)*, opened on coastal Furneaux Farm in 2024, is a spectacular location to sip contentedly on a single malt. The jagged Strzelecki Peaks rise to the south, the distillery's own barley fields sway in maritime breezes, and it's an easy walk to the sheltered rock pools of Sawyers Bay. Distiller Tom Ambroz strives to harness local ingredients: smoky Flinders Island peat transforms rainwater collected from the stillhouse's roof, and ocean breezes drift through the bond store as the whisky matures. For his award-winning Untamed gin, Tom incorporates island botanicals such as kunzea (a flowering wild shrub), native rosemary and fragrant, aniseedy wild fennel. The tasting room is open from noon to 3pm Monday to Friday, offering tasting flights, bar snacks and **tours** *(2pm; $40)*.

At the southern end of the island, **Unavale Vineyard** *(unavale.com.au)* produces wines that are equally dependent on local conditions. Postage-stamp-sized plantings of pinot noir, riesling, cabernet sauvignon and chardonnay thrive in eroded granite soils, while the Strzelecki Peaks offer protection from maritime winds. Drop in for a one-on-one tasting with winemakers Barry and Cassie between 11am and 4pm, and book ahead for a grazing platter or a vineyard tour. On the way to Unavale along Coast Rd, look out for Cape Barren geese grazing in the paddocks.

Places We Love to Stay

$ Budget $$ Midrange $$$ Top End

Near Maria Island p149

Twamley Farm $$ Options include a cosy Farm Pod, a converted stable and a renovated shearers' hut. Around 26km southwest of Triabunna.

Triabunna Barracks $$$ Four luxury B&B suites in a restored 1840s barracks and stables just a couple of hundred metres from the ferry wharf.

Spring Bay Mill $$$ From beach shacks to old workers' quarters and glamping tents around what was once the world's largest woodchip mill at Triabunna's edge.

Swansea MAP p163

Swansea Beach Chalets $$ Oceanfront self-contained chalets at the northern end of Jubilee Beach – the front line of chalets all but overhang the beach.

Wagners Cottages $$$ Four stone cottages, including a heritage-listed 1860 cottage, garlanded by rose-filled gardens at Swansea's southern edge.

Piermont $$$ Stylish one-, two- and three-bedroom stone cabins fan out from an 1830s farmhouse with views across Great Oyster Bay. Amenities include a pool, a tennis court and the excellent Homestead restaurant (p155).

Freycinet National Park MAP p153

Freycinet Lodge $$$ Cradled within the park, with wooden cabins discreetly dotted along the coast and through the bush. Direct access to Richardsons Beach and Honeymoon Bay.

Edge of the Bay $$$ Relaxed resort with waterside digs with views of the Hazards. Facilities include an on-site restaurant and access to bikes, kayaks and stand-up paddleboards. Located 4km northwest of Coles Bay.

Freycinet Holiday Houses $$$ More than 70 rental holiday homes in Coles Bay, ranging from couples-friendly cottages to sprawling homes accommodating up to 10 people.

Bicheno MAP p163

Diamond Island Resort $$ Motel-style rooms, but with direct beach access, penguins walking past the door and free penguin-viewing tours for guests.

Bicheno by the Bay $$ Self-contained motel units, flash new waterfront units and cosy A-frame chalets in a bushy oceanside setting. Shared facilities include a pool, a tennis court and a lake with kiddie kayaks.

St Helens MAP p168

Panorama Hotel $$ The restaurant deck at this wide-winged seafront hotel has just about the best water view in town, and Ocean View rooms (worth the splurge) look over a bird-filled lagoon.

Pelican Point Sanctuary $$$ Bird is the word at this 35-hectare coastal sanctuary, with rooms each containing a bird guide and binoculars and floor-to-ceiling windows overlooking a small lake. Almost 50 bird species have been spotted on the property.

Bay of Fires MAP p172

Bay of Fires Bush Retreat $$$ Boutique glamping enlivened by birdsong in a forested setting a few minutes' drive from Binalong Bay.

SABI $$$ Even in the full scrum of summer beach season, this bush-fringed stone cottage is a pocket of Japanese-styled calm, right down to the wine-barrel onsen.

Arthouse Bay of Fires $$$ Splash out on this architecturally designed beach house with contemporary decor and classic Bay of Fires vistas. Sleeps up to four.

Derby MAP 176

Tin Dragon Cottages $$ Five eco farmstay cottages at Branxholm's edge. Fon Hock cottage has a cute outdoor spa, while Settlers Hut, set in native bush, sleeps four and is geared to mountain bikers.

Tin Mountain $$$ A trio of stylishly elevated units sleeping up to eight and peering down onto the Ringarooma River. A trail rolls right by the doors.

Flinders Island MAP p181

Island Quarters $$ Modern and spacious self-contained, one-bedroom apartments conveniently located in Whitemark.

Crayshack $$$ Killiecrankie beach shack turned luxe hideaway, with views across the bay, three bedrooms, outdoor bath and a quaint old outhouse.

Researched by
Andrew Bain

Launceston & Around

GOURMET LIFE IN A GORGE-SPLIT CITY

After Launceston's gracious blend of culture, art, architecture, nature and gastronomy, explore the historic hinterland, national parks and Tasmania's premier wine-growing valley.

Launceston, Tasmania's second city, is Australia's third-oldest city and holds a special place in the history of the island state, and in the nation itself. Arrayed at the point where the North and South Esk Rivers merge to form Kanamaluka/Tamar River, it's a compact city that adroitly combines urban and natural pleasures. Cool craft-beer bars energise 19th-century spaces and former mercantile warehouses, and whisky distilleries sit like satellites outside the city. However, it's Cataract Gorge – a chasm just 20 minutes' walk from the city centre – that gives the city of 90,000 people its natural stripes, as well as holding much Tasmanian Aboriginal connection and history.

NESS VANDERBURGH/LONELY PLANET

Framing Kanamaluka/Tamar River as it flows north into Bass Strait, the banks of the Tamar Valley feature world-class wineries, while Beaconsfield's mining past, which encompassed both boom times and tragedy, is featured at the poignant Beaconsfield Mine and Heritage Centre. Near the point where the river pours into Bass Strait, there's more colonial history at George Town and Low Head, and wildlife is strangely predominant, from the nibbled lawns of Narawntapu National Park to a nightly penguin march in Low Head and the curious cuteness of platypuses, echidnas and seahorses in a pair of Beauty Point wildlife centres. To the east, Ben Lomond National Park, reached through an exacting series of hairpin bends, provides Tasmania's best skiing in winter and the easiest chance to stand atop one of Tasmania's highest peaks in summer.

THE MAIN AREAS

LAUNCESTON
Food and heritage in Tasmania's northern gem.
p190

TAMAR VALLEY
History, wine, wildlife and a surprising national park.
p204

For places to stay in Launceston and around, see p213

TRABANTOS/SHUTTERSTOCK

Left: Savoury pastry, Launceston (p190); Above: Tamar River, Launceston (p190)

Find Your Way

Anchored by Launceston's gourmet and heritage charms, this compact but diverse region straddles the wide Kanamaluka/Tamar River as it flows north to Bass Strait. Further afield, there are two national parks – coastal and mountain – to explore.

Tamar Valley, p204

Come for the wine, but stay for the wildlife and beaches, the seafaring history and perhaps a spot of wetland bird-watching.

Launceston, p190

Graze your way through this UNESCO City of Gastronomy then find the deep gorge that reaches almost to the city centre.

CAR

Having your own vehicle is highly recommended, as it's the most interesting and efficient way to explore this area, especially when venturing out to vineyards and the natural bookends of Ben Lomond and Narawntapu national parks.

BUS

Buses motor up both sides of the Tamar Valley from Launceston, stopping in George Town, Low Head, Beaconsfield and Beauty Point. Cressy-bound buses pass through Evandale and Longford. You'll have to plan carefully to make timetables accommodate sightseeing visits.

ANDREW BAIN/LONELY PLANET

Woolmers estate (p201), Longford

Plan Your Time

Check out the charm and character of Tasmania's second city, but also visit a world-class wine region and the creatures and crags of a pair of national parks.

An Urban Weekend

- It'd be a culinary sin to miss a cafe breakfast in this City of Gastronomy, even if only to fuel up for a morning on the trails through **Cataract Gorge** (p194). Visit **QVMAG**'s (p191) brace of museums and galleries and discover one of the world's best collections of Salvador Dalí sketches at **dAda mUse** (p198). The next day, find the stories behind the facades on a **Wallaby Walkabout Tours** (p190) walk through the city centre.

A Few Days Beyond the City

- Spend a day around **Pipers Brook** (p204), imbibing sparkling wine, before heading west to watch **little penguins** (p209) shuffle ashore in Low Head in the evening. Cross the river to mingle with native animals at **Narawntapu National Park** (p212), then swing through **Longford** (p201) and **Evandale** (p201) for a history fix before making the dizzying drive up Jacob's Ladder to **Ben Lomond National Park** (p202).

Seasonal Highlights

SPRING

Launceston welcomes spring with the eclectic **Junction Arts Festival** (p198), while there are alpine wildflowers in Ben Lomond National Park.

SUMMER

Launcestonians head to their beach of choice in **Bridport** (p202), while **Festivale** (p196) brings a sunny glow to the city food scene.

AUTUMN

Tour through the **Tamar Valley** (p204) to see the colourful grapevines, while March is the time to grab a final swim in **First Basin Pool** (p194).

WINTER

Skiers cross their fingers for snow on **Ben Lomond** (p202), while it's a good time to frequent cocktail bars and distilleries in and around Launceston.

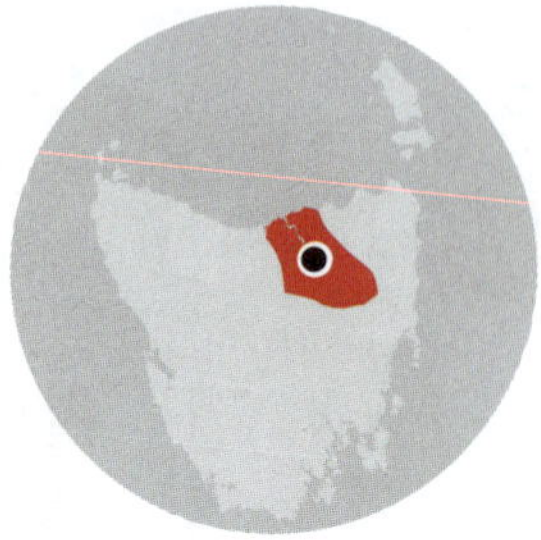

Launceston

HISTORY | FOOD | FESTIVALS

It's hard to imagine a city more likeable than Launceston. 'Lonnie', as the locals call it, is large enough for a bit of urban buzz, but small enough for country congeniality to be the rule rather than the exception. Tasmania's second-largest city revels in its standing as a UNESCO City of Gastronomy – one of only two in Australia – while the city is a mosaic of architectural styles, making every street a strip of discovery.

Few cities have Launceston's natural edge, with deep and powerful Cataract Gorge slicing through the hills improbably close to the city centre. Museums and galleries showcase everything from thylacine tales to Port Arthur prison doors and Salvador Dalí sketches, while the global gastronomic badge means the restaurant, cafe and bar life is top notch, with produce as fresh as the Tassie air. Lonnie loves a good festival, so keep an eye out for food, beer or art celebrations as you journey.

GETTING AROUND

Central Launceston is compact and walkable. The city's free Tiger Bus service was discontinued in 2025, but Metro buses operate through the city and suburbs. Options for transport to and from Launceston Airport include a shuttle-bus service operated by **Wild Island Adventures** *(wildislandadventure.com; $27)*. A taxi to or from the airport will cost around $40.

TOP TIP

In 2021, Launceston was awarded City of Gastronomy status by UNESCO. Discover the region's bountiful produce at Harvest, a weekly Saturday morning market held in a city car park (71 Cimitiere St). Expect craft beer, cider, honey, salmon and more. Many of the producers and suppliers are organic and sustainable.

Go Walkabout

Exploring Aboriginal and colonial history

Spending a couple of hours with Geoff McLean from **Wallaby Walkabout Tours** *(launcestonwalkingtours.com.au; tours $45)* is a brilliant way to learn about Launceston history, both colonial and from a Tasmanian Aboriginal perspective.

Geoff leads two tours – one on city architecture and history and another with an Aboriginal focus through Cataract Gorge (p194). The city tour is a pleasantly rambling journey past Gothic churches and down hidden laneways and is peppered with tales of the various larrikins, rascals and reprobates that lived in Launceston in earlier times. You'll soon known your Launceston Gothic from your Launceston brutalism, and a whole lot between.

Tasmanian Grand Designs

The best of Tassie timber at Design Tasmania

Tasmania has some beautiful and rare timbers and nowhere will you see them in more beautiful form than in the wood

HAIREENA/SHUTTERSTOCK

Queen Victoria Museum

gallery at **Design Tasmania** *(designtasmania.com.au; free)*. These are exquisite pieces – chairs, cabinets, desks, stools – shaped from Huon pine, blackwood, sassafras and King Billy pine by some of Tasmania's best timber artisans, including Kevin Perkins and Peter Adams. Additional galleries showcase other designs and materials from Tasmanian creators, all just as finely crafted.

Launceston's Cabinet of Curiosities

See thylacines, shipwrecks and art at QVMAG

Australia's largest regional museum, the **Queen Victoria Museum** *(QVMAG; qvmag.tas.gov.au; free)* is a real treasury of Tasmanian time. There are the requisite dinosaurs and megafauna, but pride of place goes to an exhibition on the cherished thylacine – learn the various Aboriginal names for the animal, see their fragile, almost-bird-thin bones and stuffed skins, and find displays about the sad tale of their loss (it turns out that the biggest trader in live thylacines was Launceston's City Park Zoo).

Don't miss the original cell doors from Port Arthur and the gallery on the *Sydney Cove*, Australia's oldest-known shipwreck,

continued on p196

BEST TASMANIAN-MADE SHOPPING

Glass Manifesto: Venture out to riverside Kings Wharf for high-quality glass art from Anne Clifton and Peter Bowles, whose creations feature in galleries across the world.

Stockton & Co: A lovely collection of design, homewares and artworks from the likes of Tassie-favourite Tom Samek.

Spotted Quoll: A treasure trove of unique Tasmanian-made items, from clothing to gin kits to glassware cut with Tasmanian scenes.

Design Tasmania: Design Tasmania's shop is effectively a gallery within a gallery, with works of wood, fine jewellery, ceramics and glass.

Alps & Amici: Launceston's top gourmet stop, from its house-made granola to ready-made meals from the chef owner.

In 1956, Stelo fired up Australia's first commercial espresso machine.

EATING IN LAUNCESTON: OUR PICKS

Stillwater: Fine dining harnessing local ingredients in a restored 1830s flour mill by the mouth of Cataract Gorge. *10am-10pm Mon-Sat* $$$

Black Cow Bistro: Classy steakhouse offering the best of Tasmania's beef and Wagyu in an Art Deco former butchery. *5.30-10pm Mon-Sat* $$$

Stelo @ Pierre's: Smooth-as-velvet Italian dining to go with the velvet-covered ceiling. The house-made pasta is the hero. *11am-3pm Tue-Fri & 5.30-11pm Tue-Sat* $$$

Cataract on Paterson: Local favourite with the chance to cook your own steak and seafood on a 400°C volcanic stone. *5pm-late* $$$

HIGHLIGHTS
1 Queen Victoria Art Gallery

SIGHTS
2 dAda mUse
3 Design Tasmania
4 Henty House
5 Launceston Synagogue
6 Majestic Theatre
7 Milton Hall
8 St Johns

ACTIVITIES
9 Cataract Walk
10 Tamar River Cruises
11 Zig Zag Track

SLEEPING
12 Change Overnight
13 Hotel Verge
14 Peppers Silo
15 The Florance

EATING
16 Black Cow Bistro
17 Cataract on Paterson
18 LeKoh
19 Mad Apple
20 Stelo @ Pierre's
21 Stillwater

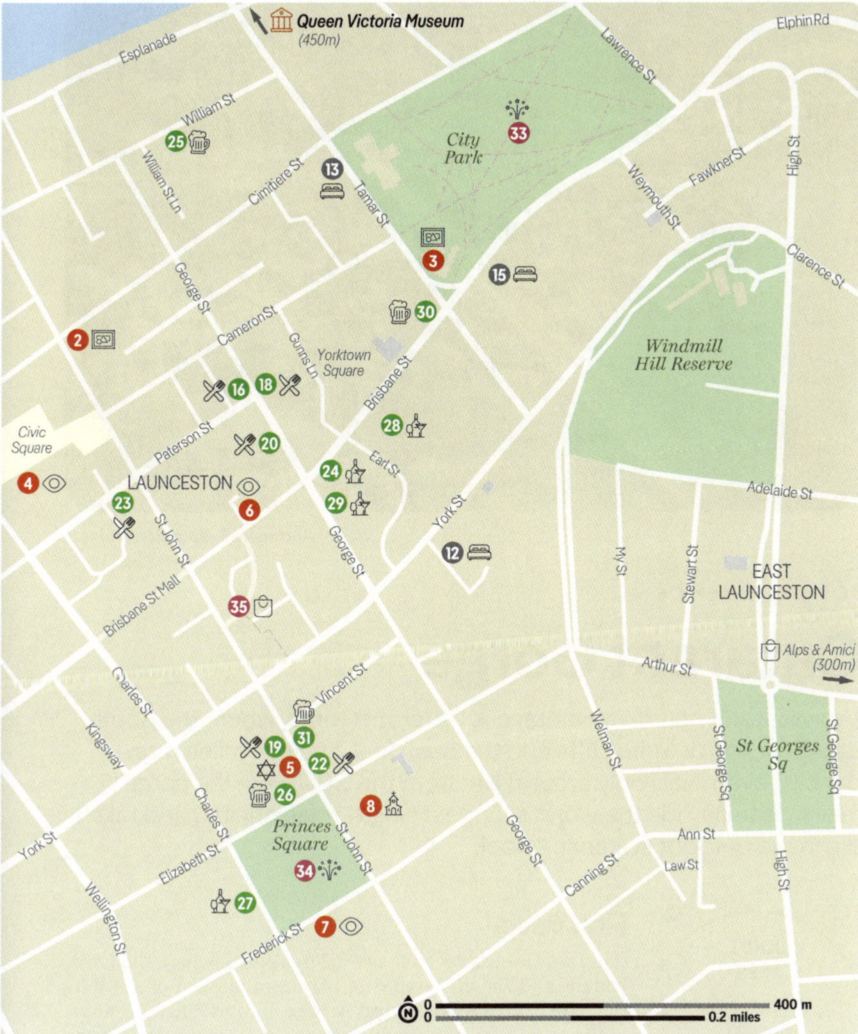

22 Tinka Coffee Brewers
23 Valley Coffee

DRINKING & NIGHTLIFE
24 Barrel Collective
25 Boag's Brewery
26 Du Cane Brewery & Dining Hall
27 Havilah
28 Midnight Rambler
29 Nomy
30 Royal Oak Hotel
31 Saint John
32 Urbane

ENTERTAINMENT
33 Festivale
34 Junction Arts Festival

SHOPPING
see 3 Design Tasmania Shop
35 Spotted Quoll
see 19 Stockton & Co

LKONYA/SHUTTERSTOCK

Alexandra Suspension Bridge

TOP EXPERIENCE

Cataract Gorge

Launceston's natural advantage is Cataract Gorge, where the South Esk River, the dolerite cliffs and the bush feel a million miles from the city, even if it is only around 1km from the CBD. Hike the gorge's riverside trails, ride the world's longest single-span chairlift and take a dip in the outdoor swimming pool.

DON'T MISS

- Gorge Scenic Chairlift
- Duck Reach Power Station
- Wallaby Walkabout guided tour
- Tamar River Cruises boat trip
- Alexandra Suspension Bridge

First Basin

Cataract Gorge's green heart is First Basin, where the gorge widens and the city comes to play. Straddled at one end by the **Alexandra Suspension Bridge**, built in 1904, it's home to the world's longest single-span chairlift (457m), the **Gorge Scenic Chairlift** *(gorgechairlift.com.au; adult/child one way $15/10)*, which crosses the South Esk River – Tasmania's longest river – from the lawned southern banks to the Victorian-style garden on the northern banks. Take some time to wander through this lush, rotunda-graced garden, where peacocks and wallabies roam.

Set within the grassed southern bank is **First Basin Pool**, a public swimming pool that's typically filled with water and

PRACTICALITIES

● launceston.tas.gov.au/Parks-Gardens-Active-Recreation/Parks-and-Gardens/Cataract-Gorge-Reserve-First-Basin ● free ● 24hr open from November to March. Just above the pool is the **First Basin Cafe Bistro**.

Gorge Walks

First Basin is connected to Kings Bridge, and ultimately the city centre, by the Cataract Walk and Zig Zag Track. Both are around 1km in length, but are very different in nature. The **Cataract Walk** is the flatter, gentler option, running along the cliffs on the northern bank, providing good views of the river and the gorge's dolerite columns. The **Zig Zag Track** takes a more venturesome approach, with some steep pinches as it burrows into the gorge along the southern bank.

At First Basin, the 900m **First Basin Loop** does exactly what the name on the tin suggests, lapping the basin's lagoon-like widening of the river as the chairlift whirrs past overhead. Arguably the best walk inside the gorge is the **Duck Reach Trail** (4km return), which sets out from First Basin and heads upstream along the southern bank, passing Sentinel Lookout to reach the historic **Duck Reach Power Station**. It was one of the world's first publicly owned hydroelectric power stations, electrifying Launceston for six decades from 1895.

For a cultural (and natural) perspective on the gorge, join a guided walk with Wallaby Walkabout Tours (p190). Guide Geoff McLean is proud of his First Nations heritage and also has experience in lecturing in Aboriginal history and culture at the University of Tasmania, and these gentle walks, which head into little-known parts of the gorge, include insights into Aboriginal culture, spirituality and tribal histories.

From the Water

Cataract Gorge was formed by water, so it makes sense to see it from the water, joining a 50-minute Cataract Gorge Adventure Cruise aboard the gracious 1890s-style *Lady Launceston* with **Tamar River Cruises** *(tamarrivercruises.com.au; adult/child $45/20)*. Boats depart from Home Point at the city centre's edge and touch on three rivers – Kanamaluka/Tamar, North Esk and South Esk – which all converge here. Heading under Kings Bridge, the boat cruises a few hundred metres upstream beneath the gorge's dolerite walls. In summer, seals are sometimes spotted on the rocks, and there's even an occasional platypus sighting.

The most frenzied water sight comes when water is released from Trevallyn Dam, just upstream from the gorge, and Tassie's white-water paddlers get busy in the big and steep rapids that pour through the narrow chasm.

ABORIGINAL CONNECTION

Delve into the Tasmanian Aboriginal connection to Cataract Gorge at the **Orb** *(theorb.tas.gov.au/connection-to-country/cataractgorge)*, a website of learning resources put together by the Tasmanian Aboriginal community. The excellent Cataract Gorge page features stories and information, including a walk through the gorge, from three prominent community members: Aunty Patsy Cameron, Dean Greeno and Cecilia Wheatley.

TOP TIPS

- If driving to the gorge, the main car park is on the southern bank of First Basin, at the end of Basin Rd.
- Lifeguards are on duty at First Basin Pool daily through summer school holidays (around Christmas to the end of January) and on weekends (11am to 4pm) outside of that time.
- There's access to First Basin for people in wheelchairs or requiring mobility assistance on the First Basin Inclinator, which runs between the car park and the picnic grounds.
- Want to watch the white-water paddlers brave the rapids? Find water-release dates and times for Cataract Gorge at hydro.com.au/water/water-releases/upcoming-releases.

continued from p191

which ran aground on Preservation Island in Bass Strait in 1797. The museum displays the ship's rudder, a cannon and beer bottles from the wreck – yeast from this beer is believed to be the world's oldest brewing yeast (and has been used to brew beer in recent years).

The museum's artistic sibling, the **Queen Victoria Art Gallery** *(qvmag.tas.gov.au; free)*, is on a separate site and is home to the First Tasmanians Gallery, showcasing shelters, tools and bush foods for Tasmanian Aboriginal people, including kelp water carriers and beautiful rice shell and maireener shell necklaces, as well as a small-scale bark canoe built by the late Rex Greeno.

Colonial paintings, including works by John Glover, are the pride of the rest of the collection in a meticulously restored 19th-century building on the edge of Royal Park.

Check the website for interactive QVMAG Arts on Site workshops.

Raise a Glass to Boag's

Visit Launceston's historic brewery

James Boag's beer has been brewed on William St since 1881. Visit the heritage **Boag's Brewery** *(jamesboag.com.au; tours $37)* on a guided 1½-hour tour packed with history and anecdotes about northern Tasmania's most famous beer. Tours begin in the newly renovated and expanded 1830s Tamar Hotel (now the brewery visitor centre) across the road from the brewery, where windowless attic rooms were installed to allow drunk brewers to sleep things off – it was permitted to drink on the job until a few decades ago.

The tour is a walk through the brewhouse and the brewing process, now largely automated other than the taste testers (dream job alert!) before finishing with – likely the reason you're here – a tasting session of three beers. Book online for daily departures at 11am, 1pm and 3pm.

Festival City

Celebrate with food, wine, music and art

Tasmanians love a festival and the good people of Launceston are no exception. Time a visit to experience one of the city's two major annual festivals. Be sure to book accommodation well ahead.

Held in February, **Festivale** *(festivale.com.au)* is Launceston's foodie highlight, with three event-packed days in City

HISTORIC ARCHITECTURE

Geoff McLean is the authoritative history buff and walking guide behind Wallaby Walkabout Tours. These are some of his favourite Launceston buildings. *@wallaby_walkabout_tours*

St Johns: This 1824 Colonial Gothic-style Anglican Church was the first brick building in Launceston.

Milton Hall: An 1842 Greek Revival-style building that was once a church. Also the birthplace of the Australian flag.

Launceston Synagogue: One of Australia's longest-operating synagogues. Wonderful heritage and distinctive Egyptian-style architecture.

Majestic Theatre: Completed in 1917, Launceston's first purpose-built cinema features a wonderfully distinctive Grecian architectural style.

Henty House: A prime example of post-modern brutalist architecture. A great future-classic building to view and experience.

EATING IN LAUNCESTON: BEST CAFES

Tinka Coffee Brewers: Scandi style, serious coffee nous and good breakfast dishes. *8am-1pm* $$

Valley Coffee: This glass-sided virtual hole in the wall is one of the city's earliest risers, with good coffee and toasties. *6am-1pm Mon-Fri, to noon Sat* $

Mad Apple: Behind an apple-coloured paint job, it serves veg- and vegan-friendly feeds such as banoffee crepes and carrot porridge. *8am-4pm* $$

LeKoh: The new cafe kid in town, with inventive charcoal-grilled toasties to fire up the day. *6am-2.30pm Tue-Fri, from 9am Sat* $$

A PATCHWORK OF ARCHITECTURE WALK

Launceston has arguably the most architectural variety of any Australian city. Discover its most curious designs and quirks on foot.

START	END	LENGTH
Launceston Synagogue	River's Edge	2km; 1hr

Start by the 1 **Launceston Synagogue**. Built in 1846, it's Australia's second-oldest synagogue and a rare example of Egyptian Revival architecture. Head into the curving Quadrant Mall to find the 2 **former Wills building** – you'll know it by the 2nd-level window that looks like a TV screen. The window was installed in the then electronics shop in 1962 to mark the arrival of TV in Launceston.

It's a few steps on to 3 **Launceston's smallest building**, squeezed next to the old Majestic Theatre. If the laneway beneath the hanging building is open, head in to see a tin-pressed ceiling, making it clear that the lane was once part of the building. One corner up, 4 **Holyman House**, built as the headquarters for a shipping and airline company, is shaped like the bow of a cruise liner. Pop inside, sit on the wooden seat and look up – the floors overhead resemble the decks of the liner.

Anchoring City Park's western edge, 5 **Albert Hall** was built in 1891 in classical Victorian style (and redeveloped with a funky new wing out the back in 2025) and contains Australia's largest pre-1860 organ, complete with bellows uniquely made of kangaroo skin. Cross the North Esk River, passing QVMAG, to end the walk beside the furrowed steel facade of 6 **River's Edge**, the University of Tasmania's new showpiece construction. The peaceful Raiwunna Garden out the back contains native plantings and artworks from two Tasmanian Aboriginal artists.

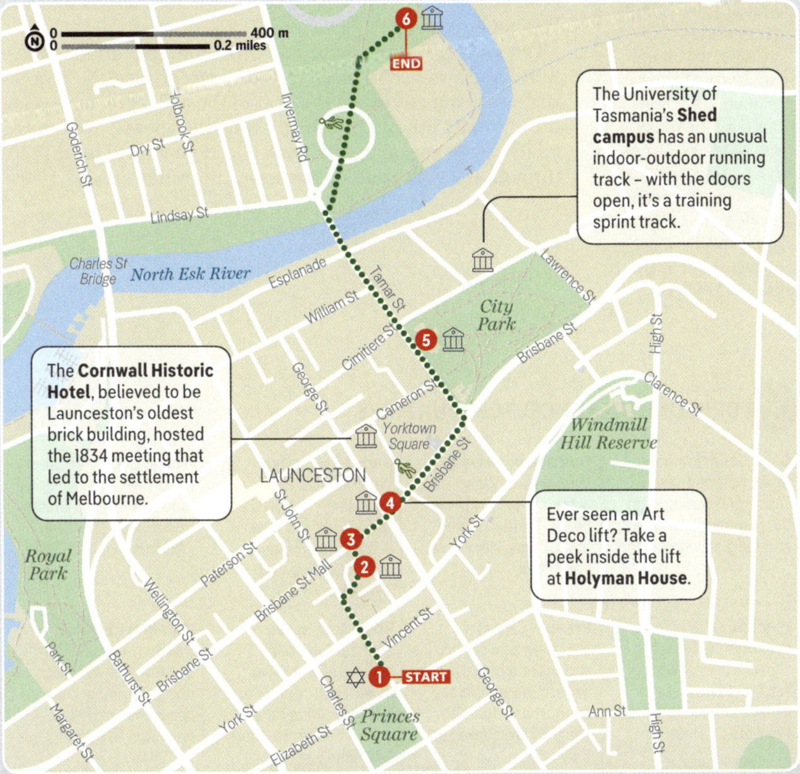

LORD SCABAR

Strolling Launceston's streets can become a bit of a street-art treasure hunt once you begin to notice stencils of black cats on walls, along with tiny houses, doors and windows installed in random locations. These are the work of Lord Scabar, Launceston's version of the anonymous street artist Banksy. The first black cats appeared in the city in 2022, though the doors, windows and houses had been appearing for the previous decade. They pop up in arbitrary places, but generally look low on buildings for the cats and up higher (placed to prevent theft) for the doors and windows. To get you started, seek out the cat and a window on the walls of Mad Apple (p196). Check out also Lord Scabar's Facebook page.

Park featuring plenty of eating, drinking, arts and live music. Tasmanian food, beer, wine and spirits are all showcased, and regular masterclasses could include sparkling-wine appreciation, or just why Tasmanian whisky is so damn good. It's a great opportunity for Launceston to flaunt its 2021 UNESCO City of Gastronomy recognition.

First held in 2011, the **Junction Arts Festival** *(junctionartsfestival.com.au)* was envisioned as a one-off event, but has been held annually since then. Based around Princes Sq, the centre of Launceston is transformed across two weekends to celebrate to arrival of spring in September. Events and attractions include one-off performances, food trucks and pop-up bars, and gigs often take place in unconventional buildings and surprising public spaces.

A Surreal Collection of Art

Australia's largest Salvador Dalí collection

Launceston is probably not the place where you expect to find one of the world's largest collections of Salvador Dalí drawings, but that's the delight of **dAda mUse** *(dadamuse.com.au; ground floor/2nd level free/$10)*. Acquired over 35 years by a Launceston eye surgeon, the world-class collection now totals around 1500 artworks, a small portion of which is on display across the two levels of the 1842 Johnstone and Wilmot building.

The sketches (and occasional oil) show the unmistakably weird and wonderful mind of Dalí, and for the $10 extra investment, you get to see the best of the collection on level 2, including 25 lithographs inspired by the opera *Carmen*. Exhibitions change quarterly. Book ahead for guided tours ($25) through the collection on Saturday mornings.

DRINKING IN LAUNCESTON: OUR PICKS

Saint John: Eighteen taps of predominantly Tassie craft beers, with thirst-generating tacos and burgers. *noon-late*

Du Cane Brewery & Dining Hall: Wood-fired pizza and locally brewed beers. Try the Turning of the Fagus Hazy Pale. *noon-9pm*

Barrel Collective: Welcoming bar serving exclusively Tasmanian whisky, gin and wine. *4-10pm Sun & Mon, to 11.30pm Tue-Thu, 2-11.30pm Fri & Sat*

Nomy: Bright and breezy retro-style bar with good moods and good whisky prices. *3pm-late Mon-Thu, from noon Fri-Sun*

Havilah: Cosy up to the concrete bar for a short but sweet wine list, including three of its own labels. *4pm-late Wed-Mon*

Urbane: Expect a cocktail menu of classics and Urbane twists at this welcoming waterfront Seaport bar. *3pm-late Thu & Fri, from 1pm Sat & Sun*

Royal Oak Hotel: Launceston's best traditional pub. Live music from country and folk through to local noise merchants. *3pm-late Wed-Sat*

Midnight Rambler: Bourbon 'n' blues in a suitably well-hidden, unsigned and grungy speakeasy-style bar. *5pm-2am Fri & Sat*

Beyond Launceston

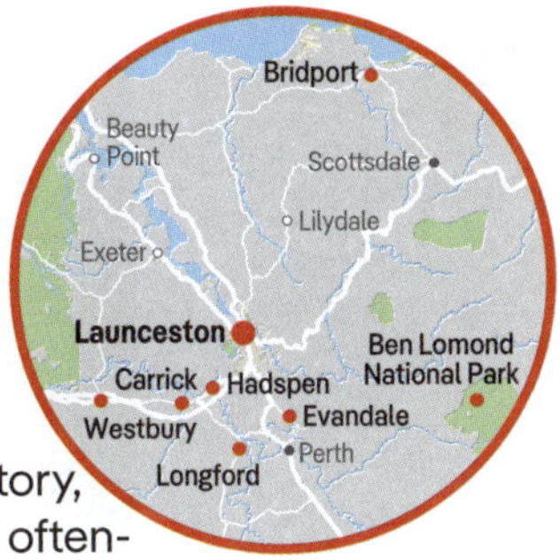

An intersection of convict and colonial history, and the contrast of sunny beaches and an often-overlooked alpine area.

As Australia's third-oldest city after Sydney and Hobart, Launceston is ringed by reminders of a significant colonial heritage. South of the city, a trio of towns – Westbury, Carrick and Hadspen – could have stepped straight from the set of *Bridgerton,* while the 19th-century lifestyles of the rich and famous also feature at Clarendon Estate south of Evandale. Longford's contribution to Tasmania's storied past are the convict-built, World Heritage–listed farms of Woolmers Estate and Brickendon.

Beaches and bunkers vie for your attention at Bridport, now firmly established as one of Australia's top golfing destinations, though locals just love it for the beaches. Look up and there's the surprise sight of Tasmania's second-highest peak looming in Ben Lomond National Park, isolated from the main cluster of mountains in the Central Highlands.

Places

Hadspen, Carrick & Westbury

TIME FROM LAUNCESTON: **15MIN**

Ye olde Tasmania

A trio of hamlets southwest of Launceston forms a historic string of settlements worth a visit. In Hadspen, **Entally House** *(entallyestate.com.au; adult/student $15/12, grounds only $7)* was built in 1819 by shipping entrepreneur Thomas Haydock Reibey. The estate is one of Tasmania's loveliest country homesteads and paints a vivid picture of affluent rural life back in the day. Wander around the sparsely furnished house before rolling out a picnic rug in the meticulously tended garden. There's also a boutique winery with tastings. Interesting fact: Mary Reibey, Thomas' mother, is on the Australian $20 note.

From Hadspen, it's 7km west to **Carrick** where the handsome four-storey **Carrick Mill** (1846) is now a popular antiques shop. Head around the corner, into Church St, to find **Archer's Folly**, the ruins of a massive home built by settler John Archer in 1847 and destroyed by fire in 1978.

Further west, **Westbury's** contribution to the region's heritage vibe includes a feast of historic buildings, a lovely village green that adds to its distinctly English air, and a 6m-high set of **cricket stumps** commemorating local lad Jackie Badcock, the first Tasmanian to score a Test cricket century for Australia.

GETTING AROUND

Having your own transport is recommended for exploring outside of Launceston. The city's Metro bus service connects Hadspen to central Launceston, while Kinetic's intercity service between Launceston and Devonport stops in Westbury. Tassielink's Launceston to Cressy bus, which runs up to nine times a day, stops in Evandale and Longford. A winter shuttle bus runs from Ben Lomond National Park's lower car park up the mountain.

POPPY FEVER

Nearly half of the world's legal poppy crop is grown in the fields of Tasmania, creating an industry worth up to $90 million a year. The opiate alkaloids used in painkillers and other medicines are extracted at the sprawling Extractas Bioscience plant near Westbury.

The growing and harvesting of poppies in Tasmania is strictly controlled by the state government and the Poppy Advisory and Control Board. When flowering, they create a beautifully colourful rural scene, but never try to jump the fence into a poppy field – access is illegal and most are protected by electric fences. Believe the warning signs on fences, too: the unrefined sap from opium poppies is toxic and will more likely send you to the afterlife than get you high.

ANDREW BAIN/LONELY PLANET

Bob Brown's cottage, Oura Oura

An environmental pilgrimage to Oura Oura

The Tasmanian Wilderness World Heritage Area protects almost 25% of Tasmania, but it's a small reserve at its northern edge that might be considered the spiritual home of Australia's conservation movement. **Oura Oura** ('yellow-tailed black cockatoo') was the home of Bob Brown, leader of the Franklin River blockade in the early 1980s and future Australian Greens leader, for almost 40 years. Many of the blockade's meetings were held here, and in 2011, Brown gifted the 28-hectare property to Bush Heritage.

It's a beautiful (and beautifully quiet) setting beside the Liffey River, with the cliffs of Drys Bluff towering overhead. From the car park, it's a 400m walk to Brown's cottage, crossing a footbridge over the river. Wait quietly here and there's always a chance of spotting a platypus. The long and tough trail to 1299m **Drys Bluff** (seven hours return) begins on the property.

Access to Oura Oura is from the C513, 26km south of Westbury.

EATING & DRINKING AROUND WESTBURY & CARRICK: OUR PICKS

Love Lucy Boots: Westbury cafe making coffee and toasties by morning and pouring wine during Sunday sessions. Mesmerising vintage decor. *7.30-11am Thu-Mon, 2pm-late Sun* $$

Western Tiers Distillery: Whisky, gin and *poitín* (Irish moonshine) as well as grazing boards and pizza in Westbury. Tours and tastings available. *10am-4pm*

Carrick Inn: Approaching 200 years of age, and serving up meals since 1883, with lunch and dinner, and cafe fare in between. *11am-11pm Tue-Sun* $$

No 10: Westbury corner cafe-restaurant with gourmet pies and the likes of scallop and bacon skewers and stuffed crumbed mushrooms. *10am-3pm Fri-Sun & 6-9pm Fri & Sat* $$$

Evandale

TIME FROM LAUNCESTON: **20MIN**

Tasmania's grandest colonial home

Heading down the elm-lined driveway of **Clarendon Estate** *(nationaltrust.org.au/places/clarendon-estate; adult/child $25/10)* is like stepping onto the set of *Gone With the Wind*. With its imposing columns, the 1838 mansion built for wool grower and merchant James Cox is furnished in period style and open for self-guided visits.

Take time to wander the expansive gardens, which fill with daffodils in spring. The coach house out the back is particularly beautiful, built with convict-made bricks and imported tiles. The estate is also home to the **Australian Fly Fishing Museum**.

An airport distillery

As notable for its location as its libations, **Launceston Distillery** *(launcestondistillery.com.au; tasting/tour $15/20)* fills Tasmania's oldest aviation building, Hangar 17 at Launceston airport (4km from Evandale) – check out the photo of Queen Elizabeth II walking past the hangar in 1954. Tastings and one-hour distillery tours (Monday to Saturday) put new meaning into the phrase 'tasting flight'.

Longford

TIME FROM LAUNCESTON: **20MIN**

World heritage-listed estates

By the confluence of the South Esk and Macquarie Rivers, Longford was founded in 1807 when free landholding farmers were moved to Van Diemen's Land from Norfolk Island. It's one of the few Tasmanian towns not established by convicts. Two colonial farms on its outskirts, Woolmers Estate and Brickendon, form part of UNESCO's Australian Convict Sites World Heritage listing.

Woolmers *(woolmers.com.au; adult/child $25/4)*, a pastoral estate built by Thomas Archer in 1817, remained in the ownership of the Archer family until 1994, and its lovely grounds include a rose garden featuring thousands of roses and the oldest shearing shed – a rare if not unique example of a two-storey shearing shed – still in use in Australia. Guided 45-minute tours meander through the homestead, still furnished with the family's possessions, or explore the property's convict buildings. Thomas' brother William established nearby **Brickendon** *(brickendon.com.au; adult/child $20/8)* in 1824. Wander through its convict-built farm village and heritage gardens,

HAWTHORN HEDGES

Spend any time in Hadspen, Carrick and Westbury and you'll quickly detect that their early English settlers suffered from architectural homesickness, recreating the towns in the image of home. This extended into the roads and lanes beyond, which are lined with hawthorn hedges, giving them the feeling of country lanes meandering through an English landscape. Originally planted by convicts as fencing for newly established farms, there's now said to be an estimated 3000km of hawthorn hedges around Tasmania. Many are now unmaintained and scraggly, though some farmers have taken to reviving the ancient art of hedge laying. Take a country drive and you might just find yourself wondering if you've crossed generations and continents, and hankering for a Devonshire tea.

EATING & DRINKING AROUND EVANDALE & LONGFORD: OUR PICKS

Clarendon Arms: Classic 1847 Evandale pub with a lovely beer garden and warming British-pub-style food. *9am-4pm Wed, to 5pm Thu, Fri & Sun, to late Sat*

Ingleside Cafe: Spacious cafe inside Evandale's 1867 municipal offices, with a sunny side courtyard. *7am-5pm Mon-Fri, 8am-4pm Sat & Sun* $

Woolmers Restaurant: Take a light lunch in Woolmers' elegant dining room, wrapped around a 1927 Wolseley vintage car and peering on to the rose garden. *10am-3.30pm Wed-Sun* $$

Ernest & Ernesto: Enjoy the Cuban-themed clutter (and excellent coffee) of this Longford espresso and dessert bar. *7.30am-2pm Tue-Fri, from 9am Sat*

NORTHERN TASMANIA'S BEST CRAFT BEERS

Northern Tasmania's craft-beer scene is thriving. Check out the fridge at Saint John (p198) in Launceston for lots of local surprises, or plot a course along the **Tasmanian Beer Trail** *(tasbeertrail.com)*.

Hut to Hut Walk Pale Ale: Crammed with Tasmanian Cascade and Galaxy hops and one of Launceston-based Du Cane's (p198) most refreshing beers.

Fog on the Tamar: On-trend hazy pale ale from Ocho at Beaconsfield's Miners Gold Brewery (p209).

Tasmanian IPA: Hoppy West Coast-style IPA crafted by Launceston's Morrison Brewery.

23 Stitches Pale Ale: Mountain-biked Derby's 23 Stitches trail? Now try the citrusy pale from Little Rivers named in its honour.

Old Mate: Porter meets coffee in this rich, dark blend from Burnie's Communion Brewing.

meeting the farm animals as you do. The 2.8km **Convict Trail Walk**, crossing the Macquarie River on a suspension bridge, links the two properties, if you fancy a walk.

Bridport

TIME FROM LAUNCESTON: **1HR**

Tee up at Barnbougle

Launcestonians tend to think of Bridport as a distant beach suburb and they flock here over summer. The attractive town on the sparkling shores of Anderson Bay has the nostalgic feel of a '70s seaside town and is lined with great beaches, but it's most revered among golfers. Sitting 5km east of town, **Barnbougle** *(barnbougle.com.au)* is a trio of links-style golf courses that almost singlehandedly put Tasmania on the world golf map. The Dunes is a challenging par-71 links course in rolling coastal sand dunes, while Lost Farm is a 20-hole links challenge 4km down the road. Bougle Run is a 14-hole short course. In 2024, *Australian Golf Digest* rated Dunes as Australia's fourth best golf course, while Lost Farm was ranked seventh. They're popular courses, so book well ahead.

Bridport Walking Track

Stretching for 11km, the **Bridport Walking Track** *(bridportwalkingtrack.com.au)* effectively laps the town, following its coast and then disappearing among the forest and flowers behind. It's a leisurely three-hour walk, but it's also divided into three sections – River-Forest (4.6km), History Foreshore (4.1km) and the Wildflower Reserve (2.3km) – if you fancy something shorter.

The latter two sections are the track's highlights. Along the coast, seek out Mermaids Pool, looking like a piece of the Bay of Fires dropped into Bridport, and the long lines of pylons from the namesake pier at adjoining Old Pier Beach. On the **Wildflower Reserve** stretch, look out for native orchids in bloom from September to December.

Ben Lomond National Park

TIME FROM LAUNCESTON: **1HR**

Tasmania's top ski field

Around 50km east of Launceston, **Ben Lomond National Park** encompasses the entirety of the Ben Lomond massif, an elevated plateau whose loftiest point, Legges Tor (1572m), is Tasmania's second-highest peak (after 1617m Mt Ossa). You'll notice Ben Lomond's leviathan profile from much of the

EATING & DRINKING AROUND BRIDPORT: OUR PICKS

Bridport Cafe: Good coffee, breakfast specials and views at this long-standing licensed cafe along the main strip. *8am-3pm* **$$**

St Mark's Bridport: Restaurant and cocktail bar in the former St Mark's church. Eat in with the congregation or outside. *9am-3pm Mon, to 9pm Wed-Sat, to 5pm Sun* **$$**

Lost Farm: Refined all-day dining with dune-top views at Barnbougle. Also a post-golf sports bar. *6.30am-9pm* **$$$**

Little Rivers Brewing Co: Scottsdale craft brewery with a taproom serving pizza and its mountain-bike-inspired beer series. *noon-4pm Wed, Thu, Sat & Sun, to 8pm Fri*

LIAM PREECE/SHUTTERSTOCK

Jacob's Ladder, Ben Lomond National Park

northern Midlands, and the cliff-rimmed massif offers bushwalking, rock climbing and the best equipped of Tasmania's ski fields (Mt Mawson in Mt Field National Park is the other). The unsealed road to Ben Lomond, coiling through a section of hairpin bends known as **Jacob's Ladder**, is arguably the most spectacular stretch of road in the state.

In winter, Ben Lomond is Tasmania's only alpine resort, offering its most reliable (albeit not very reliable) skiing. **Ben Lomond Snow Sports** *(tasmania.ski)*, at the foot of the ski slopes, has lodge accommodation and offers lessons and equipment hire. Snow coverage can be patchy, but the ski season generally runs from early July to late September. Three 'snow guns' top up the natural snow. Downhill skiing, snowboarding, cross-country skiing and tobogganing are all available when the conditions are right. See benlomond.org.au for snow reports and webcams.

The easiest and safest way onto the mountain in winter is on Ben Lomond Snow Sports' shuttle bus from the bottom car park; it operates from 8.30am to 4.30pm. If driving, all vehicles are required to carry correctly fitted snow chains from June to September. Hire these from ARB in Launceston or Hobart. The Parks & Wildlife Service has a pre-recorded phone message (0429 646 557) to advise visitors of road conditions on the mountain. Note that rental-car companies may refuse to honour insurance if their vehicle is in an accident or damaged on the unsealed road. National park entrance fees apply.

Summer on the slopes

From spring to autumn, Ben Lomond is magnificent, with great, and yet largely unheralded, bushwalking. Walks accessing the alpine landscape include the 10km, three-hour return **Carr Villa to Alpine Village Track**, ascending through boulder fields to Ben Lomond's open plateau and the summit of Legges Tor before continuing to Alpine Village. A shorter, easier way onto Legges Tor is along the easy-to-moderate **Summit Link Track** (1km return) from the Alpine Village.

WHY NO SNOW?

Tasmania is Australia's southernmost state – next stop, Antarctica – and thus the coldest. So it should by rights have the country's best snow conditions, right? Wrong. Snowfall on Ben Lomond (and even more so at the more southerly Mt Mawson) are flukey and snow is never guaranteed, even in the cold depths of winter.

There are two main reasons for this unreliability of snow. Wrapped in mild seas, Tasmania has a temperate maritime climate, keeping conditions on the island warmer than you might expect. It's also a relatively low-lying island – Ben Lomond's ski slopes top out below 1600m (and Mt Mawson's at little more than 1300m), while mainland ski resorts such as Falls Creek and Thredbo have higher ski runs at 1800m to 2000m.

Tamar Valley

WINE | WILDLIFE | MARITIME HISTORY

TOP TIP
Need a designated driver for those cellar-door stops? **Tamar Valley Wine Tours** *(tamarvalleywinetours.com.au)* operates tours among the wineries, including a Saturday hop-on, hop-off service between 10 vineyards. Or you can even drop into a trio of cellar doors by helicopter with **Unique Charters** *(uniquecharters.com.au)*.

A terrain of rolling vineyards, orchards and stands of native forest, the Tamar Valley is intersected by the wide Kanamaluka/Tamar River, a tidal waterway running 64km north from Launceston to Bass Strait. Along both sides of the river, more than 30 vineyards are gathered together into the Tamar Valley Wine Route. The western bank is definitely prettier, but the eastern bank hosts bigger-name sparkling vineyards around Pipers Brook.

The Batman Bridge (named for John Batman, who sailed from Kanamaluka/Tamar to found Melbourne, rather than the superhero) unites the two shores near Deviot. Historic highlights of the East Tamar include George Town, Australia's third-oldest settlement, and the nearby Low Head Pilot Station, while on the West Tamar the former gold-mining town of Beaconsfield stands in contrast to nearby Beauty Point's twin opportunities to see some of nature's quirkiest creations. Behind Beauty Point's back, there's excellent beach walking and wildlife aplenty at Narawntapu National Park.

The Tamar's Bubbly Side

Taste world-class sparkling wines around Pipers Brook and Lebrina

Sparkling wines thrive around Pipers Brook and Lebrina, along the Tamar Valley's eastern edge, with the bubbly stuff

GETTING AROUND

Visiting much of the Tamar Valley, especially vineyards, by public transport is impractical, so having your own car is best. Public transport does exist, but you'll need to double back to Launceston to reach different parts of the region. Manions' Coaches runs regular bus services from Launceston to Beauty Point via Legana, Rosevears and Beaconsfield. Kinetic's East Tamar service runs from Launceston to George Town and Low Head.

MARCIN MADRY/SHUTTERSTOCK

Tamar Valley vineyard

here among the finest in the world. In 2024, **House of Arras** *(houseofarras.com.au)* winemaker Ed Carr was named Sparkling Winemaker of the Year at the International Wine Challenge, adding to a long list of global gongs won by this Pipers Brook winery. Book ahead at its cellar door, where options range from tastings ($35) to a Wine and Wildlife Tour ($195) that wanders through the vineyards in search of grapes and native critters. Seek out also sparkling-only **Jansz** *(jansz.com.au)*, where tastings take place in the large, light-filled Jansz Wine Room. Choose from introductory ($15) and estate ($20) tastings of four wines, or the ultimate tasting ($30) of all six Jansz sparklings.

Further south in Lebrina, **Clover Hill Wines**' *(cloverhillwines.com.au; tastings $25)* beautiful rammed-earth and rusted-steel cellar door looks out over the winery's natural amphitheatre of vines. Tastings range across eight sparkling wines, including six exclusive to the cellar door. Little more than a flying champagne cork away is appointment-only **Apogee** *(apogeetasmania.com; tastings $20)*, a small vineyard from the doyen of Tasmanian winemaking, Dr Andrew Pirie, who planted one of the state's first vineyards nearby in 1974.

TASMANIAN WINE VARIETALS

Tasmania is a cool-climate wine region, a place where you're more likely to encounter the gentility of pinot noir than big, bolshy syrahs and cab savs. In 2025, 48% of the grapes planted around Tasmania were pinot noir, making this by far the most common grape grown around the state. Next in the queue was chardonnay, representing 29% of the Tasmanian plantings. In a sign of the changing wine times, pinot gris slipped past sauvignon blanc in 2023 to become the third most prolific grape, now accounting for 8% of the Tassie vines (to sauvignon blanc's 6%).

In the wider scheme, the Tasmanian industry remains boutique, with the state's estimated crush in 2025 being less than 19,000 tonnes, or just 1.2% of Australia's total crush.

EATING AROUND THE EAST TAMAR: OUR PICKS

Lock Shop Cafe: Lock in a stop at this unusual Lilydale cafe, a retro-furnished former petrol station attached to a safe-making business. *7am-2pm Mon, Thu & Fri, from 9am Sat & Sun* $$

Clover Hill Wines: Pair a wine tasting with a multi-course, Japanese-style *omakase* (chef's choice) dining experience. *noon-2pm Sat & Sun* $$$

Delamere Vineyards: Pick your own lunch picnic items (and the blanket to go with them) from the open pantry at this Pipers Brook cellar door. *10.30am-4.30pm Thu-Mon* $$$

Hillwood Farmgate: Grab breakfast, scones or muffins on a working berry farm, with pick-your-own berries in summer. *9am-5pm* $$

TAMAR VALLEY

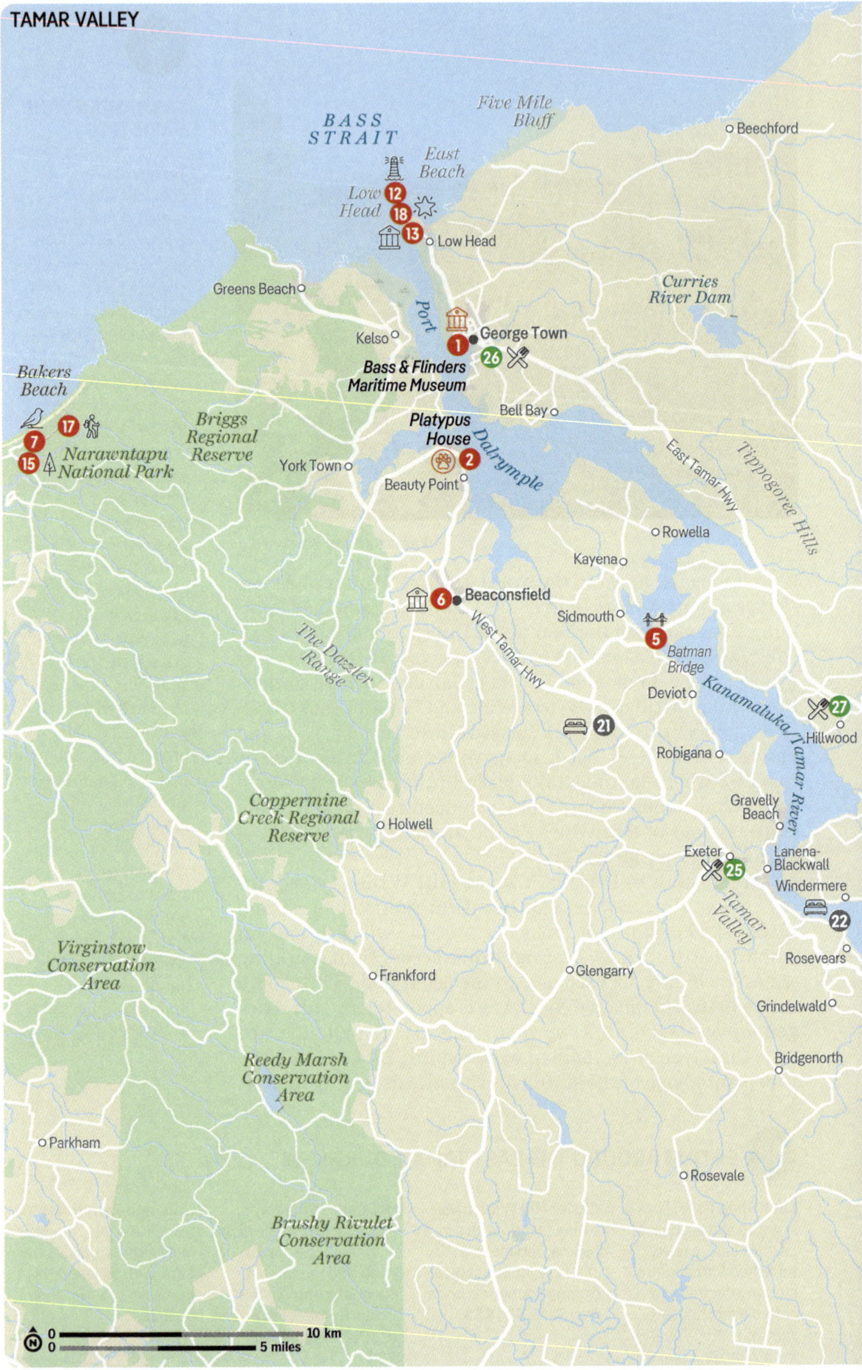

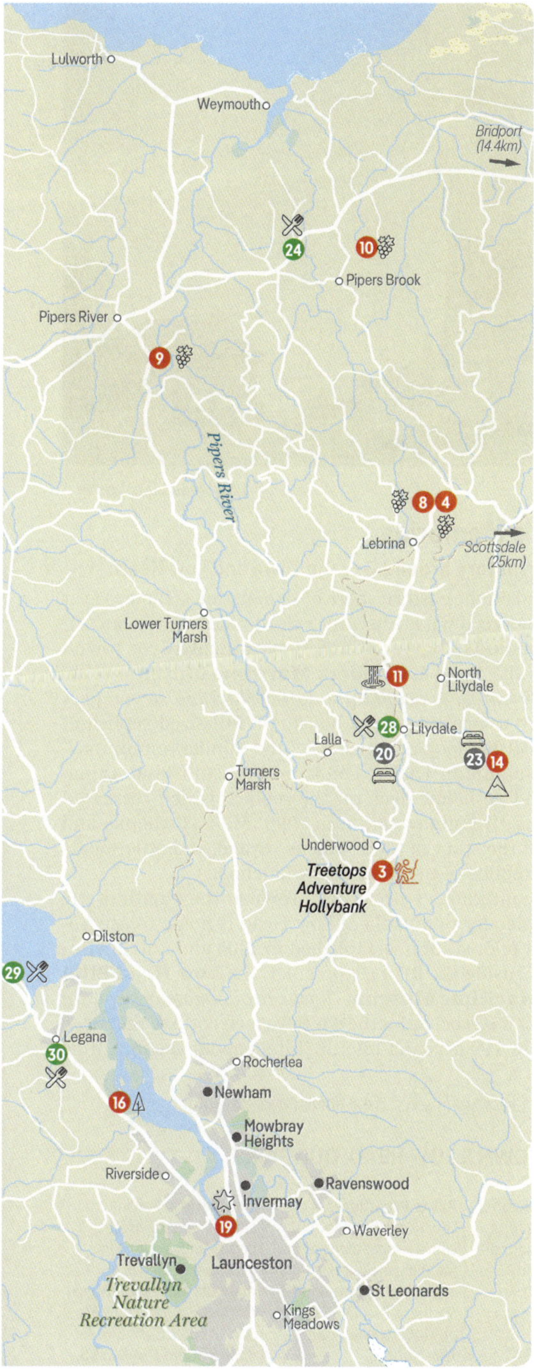

HIGHLIGHTS
1 Bass & Flinders Maritime Museum
2 Platypus House
3 Treetops Adventure Hollybank

SIGHTS
4 Apogee
5 Batman Bridge
6 Beaconsfield Mine & Heritage Centre
7 Bird hide
8 Clover Hill Wines
9 House of Arras
10 Jansz
11 Lilydale Falls
12 Low Head Lighthouse
13 Low Head Pilot Station Maritime Museum
14 Mt Arthur
15 Narawntapu National Park
16 Tamar Island Wetlands

ACTIVITIES
17 Archers Knob
18 Low Head Penguin Tours
see 2 Seahorse World
19 Tamar River Cruises

SLEEPING
20 Cherry Top Farmstay
21 Domescapes in the Vines
22 Rosevears Hotel
23 Trig

EATING
see 8 Clover Hill Wines
24 Delamere Vineyards
see 1 Don Mario's
25 Exeter Bakery
26 George Town Seafoods
27 Hillwood Farmgate
28 Lock Shop Cafe
see 13 Pilots Providore
see 2 River Cafe
see 22 Rosevears Hotel
29 The Ducks
see 1 The Pier
30 Timbre Kitchen

DRINKING & NIGHTLIFE
see 6 Miners Gold Brewery
see 25 Tamar Valley Wine Centre
see 25 The Cabin

BATMAN BRIDGE

As Kanamaluka/Tamar River winds its way north from Launceston to Low Head for more than 60km, there's only one place to cross the river by road. Spanning the river near Deviot, the **Batman Bridge** is named in honour of John Batman, the 19th-century grazier and entrepreneur who's best known for his role in the founding of Melbourne in 1835, sailing out from Kanamaluka/Tamar River and crossing Bass Strait into Port Phillip.

Opened in 1968, the 432m-long Batman Bridge was the first cable-stayed bridge in Australia, and one of the first of this innovative design in the world. To see the bridge from the river, book a Batman Bridge Luncheon Cruise with Tamar River Cruises (p195). If travelling by car, there's a picnic area (Batman Bridge Reserve) on the eastern bank beside the bridge.

FLUKETH/SHUTTERSTOCK

Low Head Lighthouse

Maritime Memories

Seafaring history around George Town and Low Head

Established on the eastern shore of Kanamaluka/Tamar River in 1804, George Town is Australia's third-oldest European settlement, behind only Sydney and Hobart. Explore the town's history at the **Bass & Flinders Maritime Museum** *(bassandflindersmuseum.com.au; adult/child $13/5)*, a compact museum in a former cinema housing a full-sized replica of the *Norfolk*, the sloop in which Bass and Flinders circumnavigated Tasmania in 1798 to confirm it was an island. Climb aboard and go below deck on the replica, which recreated the famous circumnavigation in 1998. Maps, logbooks and diaries tell the story of their famous voyage, and other boats include a replica of the *Elizabeth* whaleboat.

Almost contiguous with George Town at the mouth of the river, the slender peninsula of Low Head is home to Australia's oldest pilot station, established in 1805 and still operating today. Inside the historic precinct, the **Low Head Pilot Station Maritime Museum** *(lowheadpilotstation.com.au; adult/child $5/3)* occupies the whitewashed cottage that once housed Low Head's chief pilot. Exhibits about the maritime

Opened in 1960 as George Town's first licensed restaurant.

EATING AROUND GEORGE TOWN & LOW HEAD: OUR PICKS

The Pier: Tuck into Cape Grim beef and locally caught seafood on an al fresco deck watching a Tamar sunset. *noon-late* $$

George Town Seafoods: Fish and chips, scallops and other seafood done well. Also BBQ-ready takeaway fresh fish and shellfish. *9am-5pm Mon-Fri* $

Pilots Providore: At the Low Head Pilot Station, with a simple menu of toasties packed with ingredients from some of northern Tasmania's best producers. *10am-3pm Thu-Mon* $

Don Mario's: Italian staples – pasta, risotto, pizza – with a strong line in seafood, often to a dramatic tenor soundtrack. *11.30am-2.30pm Thu & Fri, 8am-2.30pm Sat & Sun & 4.30-8.30pm Thu-Sun* $$

history of northern Tasmania include a deep-sea diving suit weighing more than 70kg and items salvaged from shipwrecks, while kids will love sending messages in morse code and discovering the locally made wooden surfboard that looks more like an ironing board. At the peninsula's northern end, the red-and-white **Low Head Lighthouse** stands sentinel with sweeping views across Bass Strait and the river mouth. You can't enter the lighthouse but you can wander the grounds. Its foghorn – which apparently used to confuse local cows – rumbles into action at noon on Sundays for its weekly test-honk.

Penguin Time at Low Head

Waddle in for a perfect twilight tour

Each night, the beach below Low Head Lighthouse gets busy with little penguins returning to their coastal burrows after spending the day feeding at sea. **Low Head Penguin Tours** *(penguintourstasmania.com.au; adult/child $50/25)* runs environmentally focused, wheelchair-friendly tours that leave nightly at sunset from a signposted spot just before the lighthouse. Book ahead for the one-hour tours and wrap up warmly, even in spring and summer. Cameras are allowed, but no flash photography – bright light spooks the penguins.

Forest Fun in Lilydale

Waterfalls and sky-high forest thrills

Take to the trees with a fun day out at **Treetops Adventure Hollybank** *(treetopsadventure.com.au/location/tas-hollybank)* near the town of Lilydale, south of the Pipers Brook wine region. Exciting adventures include tree-top ropes courses, mountain biking, Segway tours and a 400m-long zip line – all in a shaded blue-gum forest. North of town, a short walking trail heads along the riverbank to the twin tumbles of **Lilydale Falls**. It's a five-minute walk to the first falls, and an additional five minutes to the second. Energetic types can propel themselves up to the challenging summit of **Mt Arthur** (1188m; five to seven hours return), which looms above the town.

Tamar Island Wetlands

Bird-watching and Kanamaluka/Tamar River views

Just 10km north of central Launceston, the **Tamar Island Wetlands** are accessed by a 2km accessible boardwalk,

PIPERS BROOK'S ORIGIN STORY

Half a century after pioneering Tasmanian winemaker Dr Andrew Pirie took a calculated risk on a river valley northeast of Launceston, the Pipers Brook region is one of the world's best spots to produce sparkling wine. Other cool-climate varietals, including chardonnay and pinot noir, are now also Pipers Brook stars. Pirie was honoured to have had Queen Elizabeth II enjoy his wine on two separate occasions, and his win in 1994's International Wine Challenge in London put Tasmanian wine on the global wine map. He's still making wine around Lebrina, now on a vineyard informed by the winemaking practices of Champagne, but he's joined by vineyards both big and small in a historic subregion at the heart of the Tasmanian viticultural story.

DRINKING IN THE TAMAR VALLEY: IT'S NOT ALL CELLAR DOORS

Miners Gold Brewery: Sneak past the brewing tanks to the rustic lounge of this Beaconsfield craft brewer. *4-9pm Thu, 11am-9pm Fri & Sat, 11am-4pm Sun*

Rosevears Hotel: Pick from a half-dozen Tassie craft beers or a neat list of local wines and head for the outdoor deck, the width of the road from the river. *noon-late*

Tamar Valley Wine Centre: Save the cellar-door hop by stopping in at this wine-lined Exeter bar with vino from all the Tamar vineyards. *9am-3pm Sun-Tue, to 7pm Wed & Thu, to 9pm Fri & Sat*

The Cabin: Find arguably the valley's best caffeine hit at this Exeter cafe, where farmhouse rustic meets industrial chic. *6am-1.30pm Mon-Fri, from 7am Sat & Sun*

BEACONSFIELD MINE DISASTER

Gold was discovered in Beaconsfield, a small town set in apple-growing country, in 1877, but the gold lost its shine in 2006 when the mine collapsed. There were 17 miners underground at the time. Fourteen scrambled to safety, but the collapse killed one miner and trapped two others in a cage 1km underground for two weeks before they were rescued. After an exhaustive rescue operation that made global headlines, especially when one of Australia's best-known TV journalists died of a heart attack on the scene, miners Todd Russell and Brant Webb emerged to the intense glare and attention of both Australian and international media. The mine reopened in November 2006, seven months after collapse, but closed again in 2012.

passing the disc-shaped visitor centre and crossing channels of the river to reach Tamar Island, strangely covered in exotic oaks and conifers. From the boardwalk that joins the second islet to Tamar Island, look north to see the skeletal remains of the *Platypus,* one of 14 vessels intentionally sunk between the 1920s and 1970s. Now it's a popular resting place for cormorants and egrets. Exploring the reserve in the late afternoon is recommended, when many species are more active (around 200 bird species have been recorded at this end of Kanamaluka/Tamar River).

Exploring Golden Beaconsfield

A history both golden and dark in a former mine

Beaconsfield's fortune was founded on gold, and the **Beaconsfield Mine & Heritage Centre** *(beaconsfieldheritage.com.au; adult/child $24/9)* includes displays on the town's golden past, as well as a compelling exhibition devoted to the 2006 mine rescue. Interactive displays include the opportunity to crawl into a recreation of the claustrophobic steel cage in which the two miners were trapped. You can also climb partway up the head frame of the gold mine. Download the *Beaconsfield Walk of Gold* map from the centre's website for a 1.8km walking tour through the town and its history.

A Wharf Full of Wildlife

Beauty Point's quirky critters

Side-by-side atop the wharf in Beauty Point, 6km north of Beaconsfield, are two distinctive wildlife attractions. The focus at **Platypus House** *(platypushouse.com.au; adult/child $30/15)* is on the world's only two monotremes, the platypus and the echidna. Platypuses, including Big Jupiter, the largest platypus in captivity, swim about in glass-sided tanks, while in the 'echidna garden', the spiky critters wander around your feet as guides dish out feed. Guided tours depart on the hour.

At adjacent **Seahorse World** *(seahorseworld.com.au; adult/child $28/13),* the namesake marine creatures are hatched and raised to supply aquariums worldwide. Compulsory 50-minute guided tours take you through the farm where up to 90,000 seahorses drift about. There's also a room devoted to the critically endangered red handfish and spotted handfish, some of the strangest creatures you'll ever see, found only in the waters of southeastern Tasmania.

EATING AROUND THE WEST TAMAR: BEST FEEDS

River Cafe: With the Tamar lapping near to its doors, this licensed Beauty Point cafe has a seafood-strong lunch menu. *8.45am-4pm Fri-Mon, to 3pm Tue-Thu* $$

The Ducks: Head to the deck for Tamar views and dishes such as prawn and cheese linguini or crumbed scallops. *noon-3pm Tue-Sun & 5.30-8.30pm Fri & Sat* $$$

Timbre Kitchen: Menus at this excellent vineyard restaurant change daily according to what local backyard growers deliver. *11am-4pm Thu & Sun, to 10pm Fri & Sat* $$$

Exeter Bakery: A Tamar staple, with pies that range from wallaby to curried scallop and even Jack Daniel's whisky. *7am-3pm Mon-Sat* $

DRIVE THE WEST TAMAR

Dip into wineries but discover a lot more beside on this drive along the Kanamaluka/Tamar River's vineyard-rich western bank.

START	END	LENGTH
Launceston	Beauty Point	75km; 1½hr

The West Tamar Hwy sets out from Launceston beside Kanamaluka/Tamar River, making ❶ **Tamar Island Wetlands** (p209) an appropriate first stop. Wander the boardwalks to Tamar Island, keeping a watch for birdlife. The major reason to veer into ❷ **Rosevears** is the road itself, with Rosevears Dr clinging to the river's edge – it's the river's most beautiful stretch of road. Back on the highway, double back momentarily to ❸ **Brady's Lookout**. Bushranger Matthew Brady, known as the 'Gentleman Bushranger' for his impeccable mid-theft manners, used this rocky outcrop to spy prospective victims on the road below. The lookout has a wide view along the Tamar and as far afield as Ben Lomond.

In Exeter, detour west on the B71 to ❹ **Notley Fern Gorge**, where a 45-minute loop trail descends into a fern-filled fantasy. Return to the highway and continue north. At ❺ **Swinging Gate Vineyard**, the farmhouse-rustic cellar door offers traditional Tassie varietals as well as a solid sideline in pet nats. You can even stay among the vines in a Domescapes (p213) glamping tent. If the best wines are dependent on sun, it's doubly so at ❻ **Moores Hill Estate**, a solar-powered vineyard – Tasmania's first off-grid winery – beside the highway. In Beauty Point, trade wine for wildlife, choosing your creature of choice between the swimmers at ❼ **Seahorse World** and the monotremes at neighbouring ❽ **Platypus House**.

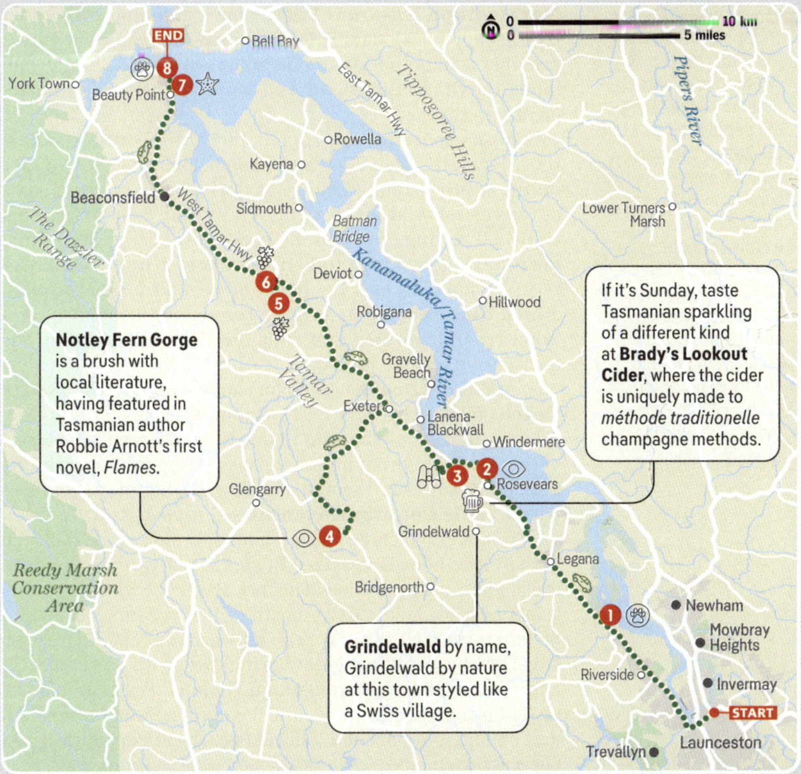

WHERE ARE THE WOMBATS?

Narawntapu National Park has long been dubbed 'Tasmania's Serengeti', in reference to the wealth of wildlife that roams the marsupial lawns of Springlawn. See it at dawn and dusk and it can look almost like a sporting crowd of Forester kangaroos and wallabies, but not so many years ago it also teemed with wombats, cute nuggets of fur that blithely strolled the heavily nibbled lawns. Today it's rare to spot a wombat here, with a sarcoptic mange outbreak decimating the population in the 2010s. The good news? Camera surveys in 2025 revealed that wombats might be returning – the cameras captured 35 wombat visits into the observed areas, compared to just three recorded visits in 2022. Perhaps there's hope on these Serengeti plains?

CAPE COCONUT/SHUTTERSTOCK

Kangaroos, Narawntapu National Park

Wildlife by the Waves

Coastal walks and marsupial mobs at Narawntapu National Park

Narawntapu National Park – once moonlighting under the less appealing name of Asbestos Range National Park – presents a combination of open plains, wetlands and woodlands in which almost the full suite of Tasmanian native creatures thrives.

At dusk especially, marsupials including Forester kangaroos, Bennett's wallabies and pademelons emerge to graze on the neatly trimmed lawns at Springlawn, offering some of the easiest wildlife viewing in the state. Popular walking trails, all setting out from the park visitor centre at Springlawn, include a climb to 114m **Archers Knob** (two hours return) for a view over the park and beyond, a short stroll to a **bird hide** peeping across the lagoon at Springlawn, or a 21km coastal traverse that runs the shoreline length of the park (seven to nine hours).

Long **Bakers Beach** is good for sandy strolls, while **Badger Beach** offers perhaps the best swimming, but at all times careful attention should be paid to tide times. Narawntapu is one of the few Tasmanian national parks set up for horse riding, with horse yards and set horseback trails. Equine adventures with **Cradle Country Adventures** *(cradleadventures.com.au; from $399)* include a three-hour ride along Bakers Beach and a three-hour Grass Tree Bush Ride. It can also arrange overnight accommodation at historic Bakers Beach Homestead.

Just over an hour's drive north of Launceston, Narawntapu can be visited as a day trip, but there are also four camp sites. The best equipped is at Springlawn, with powered sites and a shower block. Narawntapu National Park can also be visited from Devonport (around 35 minutes), and there's B&B and holiday-park accommodation nearby at Port Sorrell and Greens Beach.

Places We Love to Stay

$ Budget $$ Midrange $$$ Top End

Launceston

MAP p192

Change Overnight $$ Dark and Mona-esque, this funky hotel in a converted warehouse has a big heart – a portion of your payment goes to your choice of one of nine causes.

Hotel Verge $$ Sophisticated style with a hint of industrial design combines with the on-site Diverge restaurant at this hotel opposite Albert Hall.

Peppers Silo $$$ Check into a 1950s grain silo. To get the full rounded-silo effect, book a Gorge River room, facing the city and gorge. And be sure to say hi to Archie, the hotel dog, at check-in.

The Florance $$$ Charm and elegance await behind the striking stained-glass entrance to this stylish B&B elevated above leafy City Park. Breakfast is enjoyed in a sunlit conservatory.

Hadspen, Carrick & Westbury

Stable Lofts $$$ Dubbed Mare, Pony, Foal and Filly, this quartet of two-storey self-contained cottages set within a formal garden is a wonderfully relaxing place to stay in Carrick.

Red Feather Inn $$$ Hadspen's gorgeous 1844 Red Feather Inn offers French Provincial-style boutique accommodation. Options range from attic doubles to a cottage sleeping eight.

Quamby Estate $$$ Classy country-house hotel in an 1828 homestead outside of Westbury. Also a nine-hole golf course and dinners in Quamby's formal dining room.

Longford

Woolmers Estate $$ Sleep in World Heritage–listed lodgings in Woolmers' six self-contained farm cottages, giving you out-of-hours freedom to wander.

Brickendon $$ Another World Heritage sleep, whether in 1830s cottages built by convicts, or three newer self-contained farm cottages.

Bridport

Barnbougle $$$ You don't have to be a golfer to fancy a stay in one of Barnbougle's dune-top Ocean Villas, looking out over Bass Strait, or its cluster of course-side wooden villas.

Tamar Valley

MAP p206

Rosevears Hotel $$ Two lines of glass-fronted apartments on the slope above the pub with long river views. A cut above the standard hotel accommodation.

Cherry Top Farmstay $$ On a hill above Lilydale with views of Mt Arthur and self-contained accommodation. Join in a range of farm activities, helping out in the veggie patch, sharing breakfast or dinner with the farm owners (book ahead) and letting the kids sow seeds.

Trig $$$ Perched on the lower slopes of Mt Arthur near Lilydale, these two well-spaced eco-cabins (one a converted shipping container) are a perfect romantic retreat.

Domescapes in the Vines $$$ Glamping domes with stargazing windows among the vines at Swinging Gate Vineyard on the western side of the Tamar Valley.

George Town & Low Head

Low Head Pilot Station $$ Low Head's historic pilot station precinct and lighthouse offer 10 self-contained cottages sleeping between two and 10. Good option for families.

The Pier $$ Motel-style rooms aligned beside and behind the 1840s double-storey wooden hotel, all overlooking Kanamaluka/Tamar River.

Beaconsfield

Goldfields Studio Apartment $$ Sleeping up to four, this central Beaconsfield apartment is set up with a full kitchen, within walking distance to the Beaconsfield Mine and Heritage Centre and handily located for exploring the Tamar Valley.

Exchange Hotel $$ Very comfortable double rooms with private bathrooms, high ceilings and period furniture in a lovingly restored 1879 pub.

Beauty Point

Beauty Point Cottages $$ Two glass-fronted, self-contained cottages at the top of a gorgeous garden, with home baking and a private path down to the riverbank.

Wingtons Glamping $$$ Around 14km north of Beauty Point at Clarence Point are these three glamping tents decorated to reflect the gracious golden days of travel. There's a wood-fired sauna and seawater plunge pool.

For places to stay in the northwest and Cradle Country, see p247

STEVE WATERS/LONELY PLANET

Above: Dove Lake (p242) and Cradle Mountain (p240); Right: Lifeguards, Boat Harbour Beach (p235)

Researched by Andrew Bain

The Northwest & Cradle Country

GOURMET GOODNESS, WILD COASTLINES AND ALPINE ADVENTURES

Explore a diverse region of great local produce, fuelling mountain adventures in Tasmania's alpine heart and coastal exploration.

The northwest is both Tasmania's food bowl, with the fertile red soil to prove it, and its most compelling mountain region, dominated by the bowed figure of Cradle Mountain. Large parts of the region are routinely overlooked by travellers in the dash elsewhere after arriving in Devonport on the *Spirit of Tasmania* ferry, but the haste should be tempered by time in the hinterland of the diverse northwest. Influenced by a tasting trail that stretches the length of the region, Devonport's cafe, bar and restaurant scene is the best in the northwest, and cheese, ice cream, truffles, whisky, wine and beer are all highlights of an area made for relaxed road tripping. The nearby towns of Sheffield and Mole Creek provide arty and subterranean distractions, while west of Devonport, Burnie is the urban hub of a coastal area stretching from penguin-obsessed Penguin to rugged and spectacular Table Cape and Rocky Cape National Park.

Easily reached from Burnie airport, King Island is a surprising destination parcelled into perfect pasture that produces prime beef and dairy products, but also ringed with unexpected pockets of wild coastline.

In the northwest you'll find there are definitely enough distractions to fuel a week of discovery before you (eventually and inevitably) make it down to Cradle Mountain.

THE MAIN AREAS

Find Your Way

From welcoming small cities and towns dotted along a spectacular coastline, this region extends southwards to a rural hinterland of food producers, eventually linking to the alpine spectacle of Cradle Mountain.

CAR

Many visitors arrive with their own vehicle in Devonport aboard the *Spirit of Tasmania* ferry, and having a car is essential to getting to the best of the gastronomic and natural offerings across the region.

King Island, p236

A foodie's fantasy, wrapped inside shipwrecks, lighthouses, cliffs, a world-class surf beach and a pair of Australia's best (and most windswept) golf courses.

BASS STRAIT

BUS

Public transport links Devonport and Burnie to Launceston and Hobart, while bus is a good way to explore east along the coast to Penguin and Ulverstone and west to Wynyard. Buses also run from Launceston, Devonport and Hobart for hikers accessing Cradle Mountain's Overland Track.

Burnie, p229

See penguins along Burnie's redeveloped oceanfront and find Australia's largest distillery peering down from the slopes behind.

Devonport, p220

The car-ferry gateway to Tasmania. Explore Devonport's food scene, maritime heritage and beaches before taking a road trip into the hinterland for its caves, canyons and more gourmet treats.

PLANE

The northwest has two primary airports, Devonport and Burnie, with flights to and from Melbourne operated by Qantas and Rex Airlines. Sharp Airlines flies from Burnie to King Island and Launceston. Note that Burnie's airport is in nearby Wynyard.

Cradle Mountain, p240
The mountain figure as familiar as Tasmania itself – hike beneath it, onto it and past it on the Overland Track, or get distracted instead by a menagerie of marsupials.

Plan Your Days

Ease into a road trip teeming with gourmet producers and river, land and subterranean adventures. Take time to enjoy the northwest coast with its volcanic shores and relaxed beachside towns. And then savour the spectacle of Cradle Mountain.

ANDREW BAIN/LONELY PLANET

Boat Harbour Beach (p235)

If You Only Do One Thing

- Experience the best of Cradle Mountain, circumnavigating the popular trail around **Dove Lake** (p242) or, for the scramblers in the room, climbing **Cradle Mountain** (p242), even though it'll eat up a day in itself. Schedule an after-dark visit to **Devils@Cradle** (p240) to check out Tasmanian devils' and quolls' nocturnal mischief-making, and dine on local produce at **Hellyers Restaurant** (p241).

- Time still to fill? Plunge deep into **Dove Canyon** (p243) on a canyoning trip, go kayaking on Dove Lake with **Cradle Mountain Canyons** (p243), take to the skies on a chopper flight over the peaks with **Cradle Mountain Helicopters** (p243), or simply wind down and do nothing at **Waldheim Alpine Spa** (p242) or **Cradle Mountain Sauna** (p242).

Seasonal Highlights

Expect significant seasonal diversity across the northwest. Locals take it in their stride with a busy annual programme of festivals and events.

JANUARY

The peak of summer and a good time for hiking on (usually) drier trails. Seek out quiet hikes (and cooling swims at the likes of Anniversary Bay) in **Rocky Cape National Park** (p235).

FEBRUARY

The region's mild summer rolls on while Australian music acts with a blues, country and Americana focus enliven **FOKI** (Festival of King Island).

APRIL

More than 30 producers along the **Tasting Trail** (p228) open the gates to a weekend of food festivities for TrailGraze.

Three Days to Travel Around

- Embark on a meandering road trip south towards Cradle Mountain, taking in the region's food scene and a mouth-watering tasting trail. Options include sustainably farmed salmon, truffles, and world-beating cheese, chocolate and ice cream.

- Balance all this feasting with subterranean tours in the caves around **Mole Creek** (p227), a hike into **Liffey Falls** (p226) or a **float** (p226) – at times wild, other times mild – through the bubbling rapids of the Meander River. There's more Tassie devil action at Mole Creek's **Trowunna Wildlife Sanctuary** (p227) and you can teeter on the edge at **Leven Canyon**'s (p227) Cruikshanks Lookout.

- This relatively compact area is linked by rural backroads, and **Deloraine** (p224), Mole Creek and **Sheffield** (p225) are recommended options for overnight stays.

A Week-Long Stay

- Before heading south to Cradle Mountain, Tasmania's northern coast beckons. If you've just arrived on the *Spirit of Tasmania* ferry, linger to learn about **Devonport**'s (p220) maritime heritage, its hidden-in-plain-sight petroglyphs and eat and drink well in its craft-beer bars and casual cafes.

- To the west, **Penguin** (p232) will make you smile just as much as its name does, while the real penguins prefer to come ashore right by the city centre in **Burnie** (p229), or on long **Lillico Beach** (p222).

- Slip out Burnie's western side to rise onto the leviathan spectacle of **Table Cape** (p234), especially if spring has sprung and it's tulip time, and back down onto the sandy beauty that is **Boat Harbour Beach** (p235).

SEPTEMBER

For the winter warriors, it's the final wintry month on the **Overland Track** (p244) before the permit season begins in October.

OCTOBER

Things are getting colourful atop Table Cape as the bulbs at **Table Cape Tulip Farm** (p234) bloom into being. Wynyard even has the one-day Tulip Festival to help celebrate things.

NOVEMBER

In spring there's an arty focus, with Sheffield's annual **International Mural Fest** (p225) and Deloraine's **Tasmanian Craft Fair** (p224).

DECEMBER

It's berry season. Pick-your-own berries are a Tassie summer tradition, and in the northwest there are berry farms in the likes of Christmas Hills and Turners Beach.

Devonport

MARITIME HISTORY | EATING & DRINKING | RIVER & OCEAN VIEWS

Tasmania's third-largest city is the port for the red-and-white *Spirit of Tasmania* ferries that connect the island state with the Australian mainland. Most ferry passengers typically scatter immediately to other destinations around the state, but it's worth spending some time in town before disappearing. Market Square Pavilion has a craft brewery and a distillery eyeballing each other across the entrance, or head to the riverfront to take in the city's newest addition, an elevated walkway that protrudes over the Mersey River as it flows to its finish in Bass Strait. Fuel up in Devonport's cafes, explore beaches and delve into a wealth of history, from the home of an Australian prime minister to ancient petroglyphs carved into the stone of lighthouse-topped Mersey Bluff. The city gets jumping and jiving in multiple venues in late July for the annual Devonport Jazz Festival.

GETTING AROUND

If you've arrived on the *Spirit of Tasmania*, it's a drive of around 5km to central Devonport. Taxis usually meet the ferry. Uber rideshare services are also available. From Devonport, Kinetic runs bus services to Launceston, Burnie, Ulverstone, Latrobe and Sheffield.

Light & Culture on Mersey Bluff

Find petroglyphs around the base of a lighthouse

Standing atop Mersey Bluff, Devonport's red-and-white-striped **lighthouse** illuminates the entrance to the Mersey River, where there are sometimes decent enough waves to draw surfers. From the base of the lighthouse, there are good coastal views, but the real treasures here are a scattering of petroglyphs scratched into the rock around the bluff. Begin a visit with a self-guided tour through the **Tiagarra Cultural Centre** *(tiagarra.com.au; adult/child $10/5)*, one of the oldest Aboriginal keeping places in Australia, telling the story of Tasmanian Aboriginal life and survival. Displays include recreations of Tasmanian Aboriginal shelters as well as stone tools, information about food sources and plenty of historical photos. Afterwards, set out on the 10-minute **Tiagarra walking track**, which begins from beside the centre and loops around the bluff. White marker posts along the track denote the locations of the petroglyphs.

TOP TIP

Check the ferry times and head to Devonport's new elevated walkway as the *Spirit of Tasmania* is departing or arriving. The ships pass within metres of the walkway's end – it feels almost as if you can reach out and touch them.

HIGHLIGHTS
1 Bass Strait Maritime Museum
2 Julie Burgess

SIGHTS
3 Back Beach
4 Coles Beach
5 Devonport Regional Gallery
6 East Devonport Beach
7 Home Hill
8 Mersey Bluff Beach
9 Mersey Bluff Lighthouse
10 Tiagarra Cultural Centre

SLEEPING
11 Grand on Macfie

EATING
12 Drift
13 Elegance Lounge Seafood Bar & Grill
14 Laneway
15 Mrs Jones

DRINKING & NIGHTLIFE
16 Empress Craft Beer
see 5 Frankie J's
17 Pam's Bottles & Cups

SHOPPING
see 14 General Store

DEVONPORT'S BEST BEACHES

Mersey Bluff Beach: Devonport's main beach is patrolled during summer. Public toilets, changing rooms, electric BBQs and an excellent children's playground are close by.

Back Beach: Accessed via Coles Beach Rd, this quiet unpatrolled beach is tucked into the western foot of Mersey Bluff.

Coles Beach: Popular – though unpatrolled – swimming beach framed with rock. There are public toilets, picnic shelters and an outdoor shower.

East Devonport Beach: A quieter option on the eastern side of the Mersey River.

Lillico Beach: Around 7km west of Devonport with no sand, but lots of penguins coming ashore over its stones every evening.

PICTURESQUE JAPAN/SHUTTERSTOCK

Don River Railway

Maritime Memories

Learn about Devonport's seafaring history

Housed in the former harbour master's residence (c 1920), the **Bass Strait Maritime Museum** *(bassstrait.museum; adult/child $12/5)* is a small but worthwhile museum displaying the maritime history of Bass Strait and Devonport. Among its large collection of ship and ferry models is the Our First Mariners Sea Country People display, looking at Tasmania's Aboriginal seafarers and canoe-building traditions. The knockout exhibit is an interactive simulator that allows museum-goers to sail the SS *Woniora* in or out of the Mersey River mouth – choose between a clear day and a stormy night.

Enter the Lyons' Den

Visit the home of the only Australian prime minister from Tasmania

A whitewashed weatherboard home set in a pretty, hedge-lined garden on a rise above town, **Home Hill** *(nationaltrust*

EATING & DRINKING IN DEVONPORT: THE CITY'S BEST

Laneway: This hip cafe offers stellar all-day breakfasts and the sense of being one of Devonport's cool kids. *6am-3pm* $$

Drift: Beachside brunch at the surf lifesaving club, with excellent coffee and the expected eggy/avo offerings under a plant-strung ceiling. *6.30am-4pm* $$

Elegance Lounge Seafood Bar & Grill: Locally caught seafood accented with Sri Lankan spices. *noon-2pm & 5-9pm* $$

Mrs Jones: Long lounge space upstairs at the surf lifesaving club, with great views matched by the food. *noon-3pm Fri-Sun & 5.30-9.30pm Wed-Mon* $$$

Ghost Rock Wines: Seasonally changing cellar-door menu loyal to local produce, with views over the vines to Bass Strait, 17km east of town. *11am-5pm Wed-Sun* $$$

Pam's Bottles & Cups: Dinner in this pink-walled, mirror-balled laneway cocktail bar feels like an intimate house party. *5pm-midnight Fri & Sat, noon-4pm Sun*

Empress Craft Beer: Friendly craft-beer bar with 14 taps and hoppy surprises from Australia and around the world. *2-9pm Tue-Thu, noon-midnight Fri & Sat, noon-8pm Sun*

Frankie J's: Teaming pizza with beer, wine and cocktails, this bar gets crazy on weekends. *5-9pm Wed, to 10pm Thu, 3pm-midnight Fri, 5pm-midnight Sat*

.org.au/places/home-hill-2; adult/child $20/10)* was the residence of Joseph Lyons, Australia's 10th prime minister (and the only Tasmanian to be prime minister), and his wife Dame Enid Lyons, the first woman elected to Federal Parliament in 1943 and the first woman to serve in Federal Cabinet. Built in 1916, the house was extended in stages to accommodate the power couple and their 12 children. There are plenty of political and family mementos on show on the compulsory guided tour (10am, 11am, 1pm and 2pm Wednesday to Friday and 12.30pm and 2pm Saturday), plus original furnishings. It's just off the Bass Hwy, a five-minute drive from town.

An Artistic Heart

Catch an exhibition at one of Tasmania's best regional galleries

Spread over two levels in the Paranaple Arts Centre, the **Devonport Regional Gallery** *(paranapleartscentre.com.au; free)* houses changing exhibitions of local work as well as the excellent biennial (odd-numbered years) City of Devonport Tasmanian Art Award (aka Tidal), which attracts entries from prominent Australian visual artists.

Explore by Rail

Board a historic railway

Take a 30-minute railway ride into history aboard the **Don River Railway** *(donriverrailway.com.au; adult/child $20/15)*. The diesel locomotive runs along the historic Melrose Line beside the Don River (on the hour from 10am to 2pm, Thursday to Sunday), cruising past well-preserved signal boxes and other heritage railway buildings. From Monday to Wednesday you can still visit the interesting museum with its locomotives and brightly painted rolling stock – you don't have to be a trainspotter to enjoy what is the largest collection of rail history in Tasmania. Check the website for occasional special events such as after-dark Halloween departures and Murder Mystery journeys.

Boating on Bass Strait

Sail on a restored fishing ketch

Built in 1936 to work Tasmania's rich crayfish waters, and capable of holding 4000 crayfish in its working days, the **Julie Burgess** *(julieburgess.org; adult/child $80/40)* is a meticulously restored ketch – the last of almost 150 ketches that were operated by five generations of the Burgess family – offering public sailings from October to June. The 2½-hour trips into Bass Strait towards Don Heads take place on Sunday afternoons. Note that tours only operate in favourable weather conditions. See the website for special sailings such as weekend wind-down cruises and day trips to the likes of Port Sorell.

THE PERFECT TASSIE PICNIC

Devonport's **General Store** is a brilliant destination to stock up on gourmet fixings for on-the-road picnics. Here's what to buy before hitting the road.

- Rum-soaked Tom al Ron cheese from **La Cantara Cheeses** and **Homestead** duck pâté.
- Bill's savoury marmalades from the **Tasmanian Gourmet Kitchen** in Cambridge. Ideal with a chunky roast pork sandwich.
- Lavosh crispbread made with east-coast Tasman Sea Salt. Perfect with a cheese board.
- Whisky-barrel-aged maple syrup from **Wild Mother Tasmania**, perfect with goat's cheese such as the **Tasmania's Westhaven** cheese in the fridge.
- A few cans of Imperial Oyster Stout from Burnie's Communion Brewing Co (p231).

On Friday nights from 4pm to 8pm, the General Store is transformed into a cosy bar serving platters of local cheese, charcuterie and salmon.

Beyond Devonport

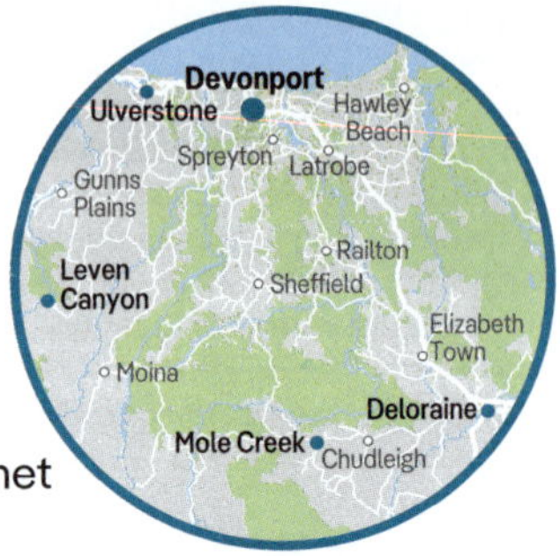

Explore rural backroads to discover gourmet producers, get active on forested trails or escape into a subterranean karst underworld.

Stretching south of Devonport is a traditional rural area being energised by a range of new, and often handcrafted, artisanal produce. Craft beer, ice cream, sustainably farmed salmon, cheese, chocolate and honey all turn a drive here into a virtual motorised gourmet market. Counterbalancing that, it's also a region brimming with active opportunities. Peer deep into a canyon, bob through the gentle rapids of the Meander River, or head underground into Mole Creek's network of elaborate caves. Local wildlife may be noticing your every move while you're hiking, but a wildlife park is still your best chance of seeing a wombat or Tasmanian devil. The region can be visited on day trips from Devonport, but Deloraine, Sheffield and Mole Creek all have good accommodation options.

GETTING AROUND

Kinetic's northwest bus services can get you from Devonport to Ulverstone and Sheffield, while its intercity Burnie to Hobart service has stops in Ulverstone, Mole Creek and Deloraine. To get the best of the area, however, requires a private vehicle, especially if you're heading out in search of the region's food producers.

Ulverstone

TIME FROM DEVONPORT: **15MIN**

Boating with birds

Arranged around the mouth of the Leven River, Ulverstone has a decent local history **museum**, and the centre of town is anchored by the quirky Shrine of Remembrance Clock Tower, but most visitors are here to head out on the river with **Leven River Cruises** *(levenrivercruises.com.au; adult/child from $83/37)*. From the water you might see endangered azure kingfishers, soaring white-bellied sea eagles and possibly a platypus on the two- to four-hour cruises. Also popular are the Forest Nature Trail Cruise (BYO lunch) and the Twilight River Cruise. Booking ahead is essential.

Deloraine

TIME FROM DEVONPORT: **40MIN**

Stroll the Sculpture Trail

Framed around the languid curves of the Meander River, Deloraine has an arty inclination, headlined by November's annual **Tasmanian Craft Fair**, attracting creative types from all around Australia, but you can follow the **Great Western Tiers Sculpture Trail** *(greatwesterntiers.net.au/sculpture-trail)* at any time. The trail spreads as far as Mole Creek, Meander and Liffey, but the greatest concentration is in Deloraine, with almost half of the 16 sculptures clustered along

ANDREW BAIN/LONELY PLANET

Great Western Tiers Sculpture Trail, Deloraine

the banks of the river in town. A 1km loop walk between the road bridge and the footbridge upstream by the caravan park reveals seven major sculptures. Keep an eye out also for the tiny native-animal sculptures dotted among them.

Part of the loop incorporates the **Kooparoona Niara Cultural Trail** *(greatwesterntiers.net.au)*, a short, accessible section of the riverside path highlighting Tasmanian Aboriginal culture. It has sections of native plantings and artworks inspired by Tasmanian Aboriginal culture. Beginning under the railway bridge beside the train park, it finishes at a yarning healing circle 300m downstream.

Hunt out a truffle

In winter, Tasmanian thoughts inevitably turn to open fires, whisky...and truffles. Australia's first black truffles were harvested at the **Truffle Farm** *(thetrufflefarmtasmania.com.au; tours from $125)* in 1999 by Tim Terry, and today the property is run by Tim's daughter, Anna. Scratch out a visit to the farm and you can join the truffle dogs on a hunt for the black gold. The farm has the traditional winter truffles but also summer truffles, meaning the hunt goes on almost year-round (December to September). Tours conclude with the likes of truffle pizzas and truffle toasted sandwiches. The Winter Warmer Hunt ($170) ends around a fire pit, tasting the range of truffle

TASMANIA'S TOWN OF MURALS

In the 1980s, Sheffield was a typical small Tasmanian country town experiencing rural decline, but astute townsfolk decided to paint large murals on walls around town. A few decades later, Sheffield has become a veritable outdoor art gallery. More than 160 large-scale murals enliven Sheffield's townscape, many depicting scenes from the district's pioneer days. Courtesy of the town's annual **International Mural Fest**, held in early November, the number and diversity of colourful outdoor artworks increases every year. The very first mural, and still one of the most striking, is on the wall of the Masonic Lodge on High St, depicting Gustav Weindorfer (p246) in ponderous mode in a hut filled filled with native animals.

EATING & DRINKING AROUND DELORAINE: OUR PICKS

Frank & Lotti: Salads, top coffee and whatever has been freshly baked that day – quiches, cakes, or perhaps pork chipotle pistachio sausage rolls. *8am-2pm Mon-Sat* $$

T's: Paddock-to-plate Chinese dining in Sheffield, with heritage-breed lamb and pork from the owner's own farm. Say hi to Bella the robot waiter. *11.30am-2pm & 5-8pm Thu-Sun* $$

Sailors Nook: Deloraine's newest cafe has grown from food-truck origins into a casually cool corner cafe, complete with 'Naughty Corner'. *8am-2pm Thu-Sat, from 9am Sun* $$

Bush Inn Brewhouse: Try a Turbo Red IPA with one of the house sourdough pizzas at this craft brewery inside an 1848 former pub. *noon-9pm Wed-Sat*

AUSTRALIA'S MOST VERSATILE RACEHORSE

A large statue in front of Deloraine's visitor centre makes it clear that the town's most famous resident wasn't a person. It was a horse. The statue is of Malua, a horse that won a string of Australia's top races in 1884, from 1100m sprints to Australia's most famous race, the 3200m Melbourne Cup. Later, as a nine-year-old, Malua won the 4800m Australian Grand National Hurdle, earning the stallion the unofficial title as Australia's most versatile racehorse.

Malua was trained at **Calstock Estate**, a manor-like property just beyond Deloraine's southern edge, passed en route to Liffey Falls and Quamby Bluff. Malua was inducted into the Australian Racing Museum's Hall of Fame in 2007.

ARTHERNG/GETTY IMAGES

Liffey Falls, Deloraine

products. Nearby **Truffles of Tasmania** *(trufflesoftasmania.com.au; tour $120)* also has winter truffle-hunt tours (June to September) that include tastings of fresh truffles and other truffle products.

Deloraine adventures

Backed by the high peaks of the Great Western Tiers, Deloraine makes a fine base for some excellent walks and adventures. The shortest and most popular of the walking routes to **Liffey Falls** (45 minutes return), a four-tiered cascade that's one of Tasmania's most classically beautiful waterfalls, begins from a picnic area on the C513, 30 minutes' drive southeast of town. The walk follows Liffey River downstream, past a chain of cascades, to the base of the falls.

On the drive to Liffey Falls, you pass the trailhead to **Quamby Bluff** (four to five hours return), one of the region's most prominent peaks. The northernmost mountain in the Tasmanian Wilderness World Heritage Area, it offers balcony views over northern Tasmania. The trail starts from a small roadside car park on the A5, around 20km south of town. Shorter but sharper is the 2km return climb to **Projection Bluff**, along the rim of the Great Western Tiers. The ascent, which begins from a pullout on the A5, 8km past the turning into Liffey falls, passes through a fairy-tale section of rainforest before

EATING & DRINKING AROUND MOLE CREEK: OUR PICKS

Wandering Trout: Off-grid craft brewer with convivial 'host's table' dinners and accommodation upstairs. *4-10pm Wed-Sun*

Mole Creek Hotel: Bar meals with a small list of German specials, weekend dinner pizzas and a fascination with the Tassie tiger. *noon-2pm & 6-8pm* $$

Mole Creek Takeaway: Burgers and other fried nibbles (and the only coffee in town) behind the curved glass wall of the visitor centre. *8.30am-5pm Sun-Thu, to 6pm Fri & Sat* $

Hearth of Chudleigh: Cafe-cum-antique emporium looking like a cross between a 1950s shop and your grandpa's farmhouse. *11.30am-5pm Wed-Sat, noon-7pm Sun* $

rising into subalpine scrub and a view over the northern end of the Central Highlands.

Meandering down the Meander

Take to the cold waters with a river sledding float down the Meander River with **Meander Wilderness Experiences** *(meanderwildernessexperiences.com; adult/child $150/130).* Piloting a glorified li-lo, these trips bump through small rapids and drift across the calm stretches between, providing a fun look at the river and its encasing forest. Children need to be at least 130cm in height, and tours depart from the Meander Memorial Hall, 17km south of Deloraine.

Mole Creek

TIME FROM DEVONPORT: **50MIN**

Adventures under and above ground

Tasmania has Australia's deepest and some of its longest cave systems, and the most extensive and accessible networks are in fittingly named Mole Creek. Among the 500-plus caves in **Mole Creek Karst National Park** *(parks.tas.gov.au; cave tours adult/child $19/10),* two can be visited on tours operated by rangers. **Marakoopa Cave** is the larger cave, with glowworms, while the subterranean formations in compact **King Solomons Cave** are more densely clustered.

The diminutive town of Mole Creek also makes a good base for hiking trips into **Walls of Jerusalem National Park**, an isolated Central Plateau park with glacial lakes and a ring of peaks ('the walls') with biblical names. The walls are hard to reach in a day-long return walk, but make for excellent overnight hikes. To hike here requires advance registration – head to the park website to check available dates.

Wander among wildlife

At the western edge of town, the privately owned **Trowunna Wildlife Sanctuary** *(trowunna.com.au; adult/child $35/20)* has a strong focus on conservation. Wildlife includes Tasmanian devils, wombats, quolls and raptors, and you can also wander among wallabies. Informative 45-minute tours (11am, 1pm and 3pm) get you up close to devils and wombats, and you'll also see devils being fed in a no-holds-barred display of bared teeth and bones being crunched. You can even take part in day-long workshops ($500) on devil or wombat care.

THE WORLD BENEATH OUR FEET

Deb Hunter, recently retired owner of Wild Cave Tours, has been caving around Mole Creek for 50 years.

Of all the densely cavernous karsts in Australia, Mole Creek has become probably the most desired destination, because it's so convenient. You can stay somewhere in comfortable accommodation and there's not going to be a five-hour bushwalk to get to a cave. Mole Creek Caves are famous for the beauty and abundance of their mineral formations, and you won't see better than in the two show caves. The style of those caves and the passion of the guides is enough for 99% of people. If you want to explore further, there are four caving clubs in Tasmania and they welcome newcomers.

Leven Canyon

TIME FROM DEVONPORT: **50MIN**

Peer into a deep and rugged canyon

Cutting a 12km-long gash through the northwest's hinterland, **Leven Canyon** provides one of Tasmania's most rugged views. Take the 20-minute return walk to Cruikshanks Lookout and you'll be staring 275m down onto the Leven River, typically a torrent of water as it fights through the canyon, and out onto craggy Black Bluff, the headwaters of the river. Other walks include a 45-minute loop that takes in Cruikshanks plus the lower Edge Lookout as well as the Fern Walk, and a 1½-hour scramble along the canyon floor.

A CAVE CRAWL

Head underground again in Tasmania's far south at **Hastings Caves** (p116), also home to a thermally heated swimming pool.

TASTING TRAIL ROAD TRIP

Tasmania's Tasting Trail stretches from Launceston to Smithton, with more than 40 tasty stops along its course. Consider this shorter drive an appetiser.

START	END	LENGTH
Devonport	Mole Creek	80km; 1½hr

From Devonport, drive 9km southeast to ❶ **Anvers Tasmania**, a wonderland of Belgian-style artisanal chocolate and the only chocolatier in Australia with access to Fortunato No. 4, a Peruvian cacao bean thought to be extinct until its rediscovery in 2009. What's chocolate without cheese? The next stop, 29km south, is ❷ **Ashgrove Cheese**, where the 'dairy door' gives you a windowed peek into the making and maturation process. There are tastings and an interpretation room telling the story of the farming Bennett family and their 2400 cows. An 8km hop down the road is ❸ **Van Diemen's Land Creamery**, with more than 20 flavours of gelato, sorbet and ice cream on offer. The pepperberry and leatherwood ice cream is as Tasmanian as a black down jacket.

Turn off the highway at Deloraine and make your way to ❹ **Meander Valley Vineyard**, the only Australian winery producing baco noir. Just 3km down the road, ❺ **41° South Tasmania** is an inland salmon and ginseng farm, drawing the water for its salmon tanks from Western Creek and filtering it back through a cleansing wetland. Take a self-guided walk around the farm and wetland before driving 7km to the ❻ **Truffle Farm** (p225) to join the dogs on a hunt for black truffles, before rolling on to ❼ **Mole Creek** (p227), where you can choose between honey tastings and caves.

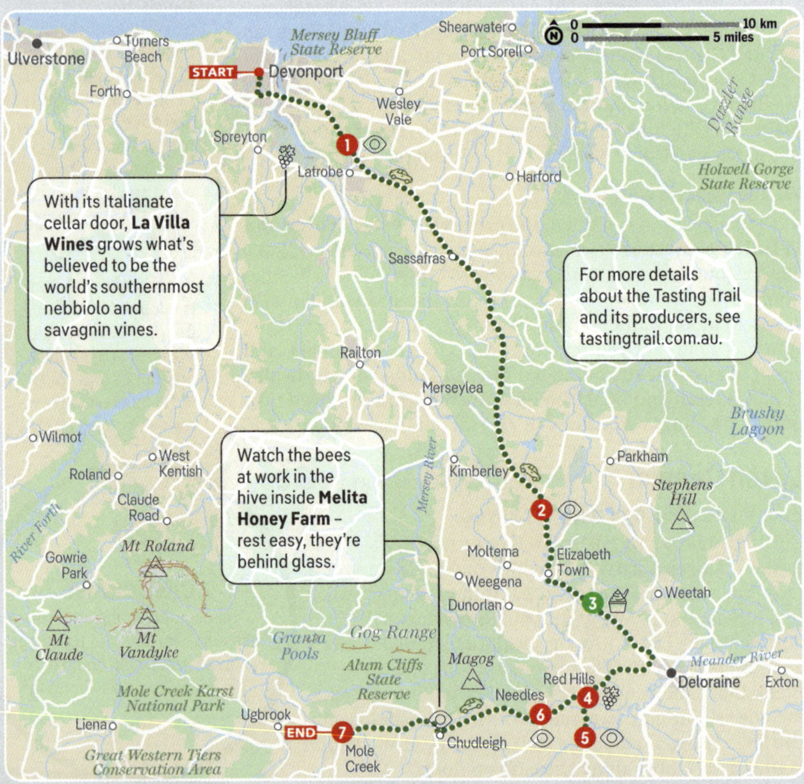

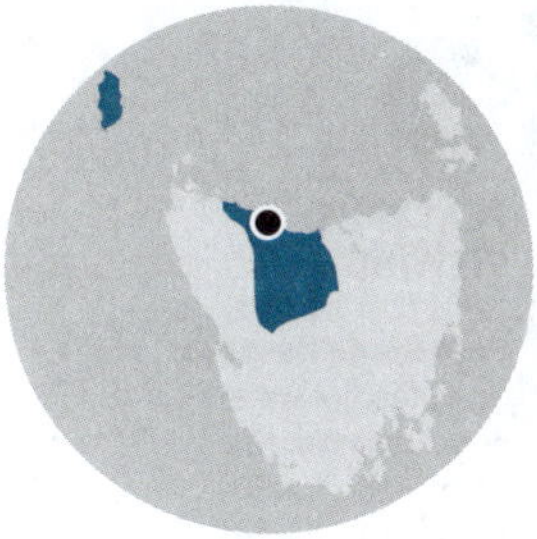

Burnie

PENGUINS | WHISKY TOUR | BLOOMS

Few cities have had to reinvent themselves quite like Burnie. When industry ruled the city – Burnie's huge pulp and paper mill closed in 2010 – the sea at times ran orange with effluent. The Australian activist band Midnight Oil even wrote a song about the city's polluting ways. But today, behind its gritty industrial veneer, Burnie is a place transformed. Symbolic of the change are the little penguins that march to within metres of the city centre, the platypus that swim in its streams and the blooms of a rhododendron garden that brighten the city's edges. The city-centre buildings end by a beach, and cafes, a craft brewery and Australia's largest whisky distillery – the brainchild of local dairy farmers – bring life to the city. Too often visitors break ranks in their hurry to see Stanley or Cradle Mountain, but it's worth sticking around for a bit to get to know Burnie.

GETTING AROUND

Burnie can be reached directly from Melbourne, with Qantas and Rex Airlines operating services across Bass Strait to Burnie airport, 19km out of town in Wynyard. Kinetic buses connect Burnie to Devonport, Launceston, Hobart, Stanley and Smithton, while local Metro buses run along the coast to Wynyard and Penguin. Once here, Burnie's attractions are scattered, making a car the best way to take them in.

Burnie's Penguin Parade

Urban birds on dusk

Burnie is one of the best places to see penguins along the north coast, especially as the **Little Penguin Observation Centre** is reached by a short walk along a waterfront esplanade. From October to March, volunteers from **Friends of Burnie Penguins** *(burniepenguins.com)* are on hand to provide information and guide viewing of the birds as they surf ashore remarkably close to the city centre. The volunteers provide a free informative talk about the little penguins and then the birds begin appearing from the sea, heading for their burrows beside the foreshore walkway, with the lights of the port and the city twinkling across the beach.

Check the website for the best viewing times across the year.

TOP TIP

If you're confining yourself to Burnie's coastal strip, the newly extended Burnie Coastal Pathway, a shared-use path that currently reaches from Wynyard to the Emu River in South Burnie, has it covered.

Whisky, Burnie-Style

Stroll through the angel's share

Australia's largest distillery, **Hellyers Road** *(hellyersroaddistillery.com.au; standard/premium tour $25/35)*, was started

PLATYPUS VIEWING

Fern Glade Reserve: Scan the flat waters as you wander the Fern Glade track (500m one way) in this Burnie reserve primarily established for its platypus population.

Tasmanian Arboretum: Founders Lake is described by the Australian Platypus Monitoring Network as 'the most productive single site (in Australia) to see a platypus' – we saw four in the space of five minutes. It's 15 minutes' drive south of Devonport.

Warrawee Forest Reserve: Outside of Latrobe, Platypus Pool, around 1.3km upstream of the Shale Rd car park, is an obvious starting point.

Mole Creek Hotel: Want a platypus with that beer? Step out the back of the pub (p227), where the clear, shallow stream gets regular monotreme sightings.

Oura Oura: Pause by the bridge over the Liffey River (p200).

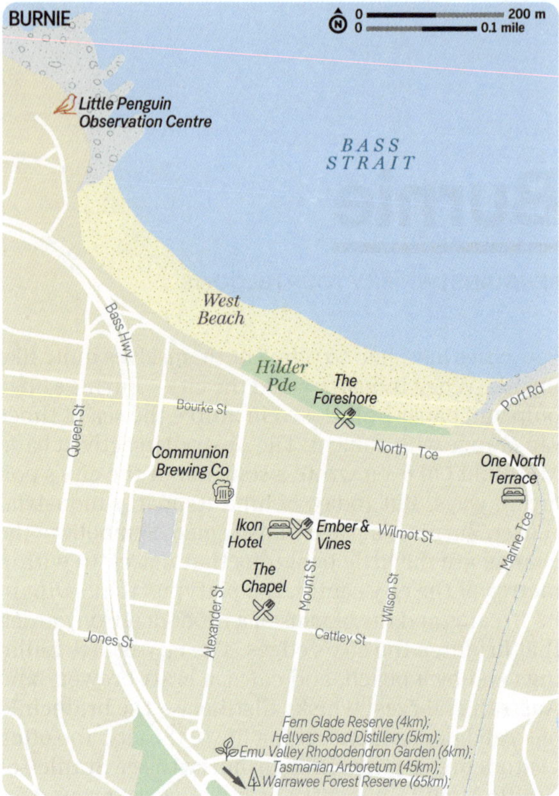

by local dairy farmers on the slopes above Burnie, and today turns out a range of single malts and creamy whisky liqueurs. Informative 30-minute Whisky Walk tours depart at 10.30am, 11.30am and 3pm, and are a glimpse into the bond store (with barrels up to seven deep), and the distillery itself, but put aside romantic notions of copper stills – this is the stainless-steel world of a large distillery. The tour includes a tasting of one whisky – pay for the premium tour and your nip is upgraded to a 21-year-old drop – and the chance to pour and purchase your own bottle at the finish. You can also just stop in for a tasting flight of three or four whiskies, or a single nip.

Burnie's Floral Edge

Stroll through Emu Valley Rhododendron Garden

Burnie's brightest scenes are found at **Emu Valley Rhododendron Garden** *(emuvalleyrhodo.com.au; adult/concession $15/13)*, a brilliantly colourful 11-hectare garden with more than 24,000 plants at Burnie's southern edge. There's plentiful ferns, three lakes (with possible platypus sightings) and

ANDREW BAIN/LONELY PLANET

Emu Valley Rhododendron Garden

cherry blossoms, but it's predominantly about rhododendrons. Peak flowering is from September to November, while autumn colours are just as showy from April to June. There are four suggested walks around the garden, ranging from five minutes to one hour – pick up the walk brochure when you arrive.

There's a cafe on site, looking over the garden and the main lake, and visitors needing mobility assistance can hop aboard a buggy to tour the garden.

Donates 100L of water to communities in need for every beer sold.

EATING & DRINKING IN BURNIE: OUR PICKS

The Chapel: Everything from apple crumble rolled oats through to cocktails, the new form of spirits in this former Wesleyan church. *7am-2.30pm Mon-Fri, 8am-2pm Sat & Sun* **$$**

Ember & Vines: Old pub, new restaurant, with a well-thought-out menu – think maple-glazed port cutlet or gnocchi with pumpkin and asparagus. *10.30am-10pm* **$$$**

The Foreshore: Fish and chips and other ocean treats – chowder, scallop stir fries – delivered with Bass Strait views. *8am-8pm* **$$**

Communion Brewing Co: Craft beers and beery food – burgers, wings, parmis – inside one of Burnie's first car-yard warehouses. *noon-9pm Sun-Thu, to 10.30pm Fri & Sat*

Beyond Burnie

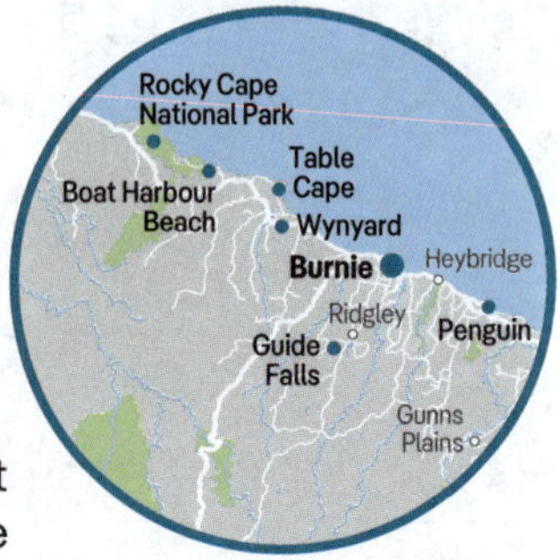

Set out in search of one of Tasmania's best beaches, its smallest national park and the springtime glow of tulips.

Places

Step beyond Burnie's bounds and nature quickly reasserts itself. Rising as round as a full stop to the city's immediate west is Table Cape, the flat-topped remains of a volcano that helped create northwest Tasmania's fabulously rich red soils, but it gets even more colourful in spring when Table Cape's signature tulips bloom. Further west still, the coastlines of parcel-sized Rocky Cape National Park are serrated with rock and punctured with cliffs of immense cultural value to the Tasmanian Aboriginal community. Penguin is as cute as the town's name suggests, and if you thought Wineglass Bay was Tasmania's best beach, spare an hour or a day for Boat Harbour Beach and you might just change your mind.

Penguin

TIME FROM BURNIE: **15MIN**

Everything but penguins

The seaside town of Penguin knows how to work a theme. The 3m-high **Big Penguin** takes pride of place along the main street, and images and logos of penguins grace bins, bollards and shop logos. The only things missing are actual penguins – though you need only go to Burnie or Lillico Beach (p222), 25km east of Penguin, to find the birds. Penguin is a likeable town, strung along a caramel-coloured beach with a vibrant cafe culture. It's also backed by the rugged Dial Range, which has a good selection of walks, including a steep one-hour return climb to Mt Gnomon Lookout and a four- to five-hour return climb of Mt Dial. Also on the slopes of the Dial Range, just 2km from town, is the **Penguin Mountain Bike Park**, with around 6km of trails, connecting into another network of mountain-biking trails across the range. For an informed stroll through town, find two self-guided town walks at penguinheritagetrail.com.au.

If you're continuing on to Ulverstone (p224), 12km to the east, consider taking the coastal Penguin Rd instead of the highway. Wriggling along the volcanic-black shoreline, it's among the most beautiful sections of coastal road in the state.

Guide Falls

TIME FROM BURNIE: **20MIN**

Do go chasing waterfalls

One of the northwest's most impressive and easily accessed waterfalls is just 16km south of Burnie, off the Ridgely Hwy

GETTING AROUND

Suburban Metro buses connect Burnie to Penguin and Wynyard, but to venture anywhere beyond – even out to Table Cape at Wynyard's edge – you're going to need your own set of wheels. Kinetic's Burnie–Smithton bus stops in Boat Harbour, but around 4km from the beach.

PAWAN KAWAN/SHUTTERSTOCK

Big Penguin statue, Penguin

near West Ridgley. From grassy picnic grounds beside Guide River, a sealed and accessible path goes around 100m to a lookout platform beside **Guide Falls**, a three-step waterfall that begins as a cascade before taking its largest leap of around 20m. A set of stairs continues down to the most impressive of the viewpoints by the base of the falls. Tracks run along the river's edge here, providing different perspectives.

If this stop whets your appetite for waterfalls, continue heading south on the highway for another 60km. Outside the tiny town of Waratah (with its own high waterfall pouring through the centre of town), off Butlers Road, the 3km return walk to **Philosopher Falls** explores an intersection of nature and industry. The trail, which at times is lined with colourful fungi, heads through moss-cushioned rainforest, crosses the nascent Arthur River and follows a large water race built by silver and lead miners in the 1920s – at one point, the water race even becomes the trail. Viewed from a lookout platform at the base of a long set of steps, the falls form a skinny line of water seemingly pouring directly from the forest. The whimsical name of the waterfall owes nothing to philosophy; it was named for John 'Philosopher' Smith, the miner who 'discovered' the falls in 1871.

TOP NORTHWEST MARKETS

Penguin Market: Tasmania's largest undercover market is held inside Penguin's former primary school every Sunday from 9am to 3pm with 60 stalls of arts, crafts and other goods.

Wynyard Foreshore Markets: Hunt out bric-a-bric and browse-worthy stalls crammed with books and vintage vinyl on the first and third Sunday of the month (8am to 2pm).

Devonport Farmers Market: Meet the farmers at the showgrounds and stock up on local produce on the second and fourth Saturday of the month.

Devonport Twilight Markets: Monthly Friday night market (4pm to 8pm) with food trucks aplenty and art and crafts in the Market Square Pavilion.

Latrobe Village Market: Held on Sunday mornings in Latrobe's main street with around 40 stalls selling an array of items.

EATING & DRINKING IN PENGUIN: OUR PICKS

Penguin Beer Co: Burgers, quesadillas and tacos, with a good range of craft brews, at Penguin's only genuine waterfront hangout. *noon-8pm Sun, Mon, Wed & Thu, to 9pm Tue, Fri & Sat* $$

Penguin Pantry: Proudly local providore with a corner cafe serving coffee and toasties. *7.30am-4pm Mon-Fri, to 3pm Sat & Sun* $

Seasons by the Sea: Tapas menu and pizzas plus a large deck that's a front-row seat to the trains that infrequently roll through town. *noon-2.30pm Thu-Sun & 5-8pm Wed-Sat* $$$

Thai Tonic Cafe: Cosy cafe that blossoms into a Thai restaurant in the evening. The little chandelier-lit sitting room is hard to resist. *hours vary* $$

BLOOMIN' AMAZING

As you continue travelling across northern Tasmania, check out these floral wonders.

Emu Valley Rhododendron Garden: Rhododendrons, ferns, lakes and platypuses on Burnie's back doorstep (p230).

Bridestowe Lavender Estate: Near Nabowla, 20km south of Bridport, Bridestowe is the southern hemisphere's largest lavender farm. Visit in the flowering season from mid-December to late January.

Bridport Wildflower Reserve: From September to December, delicate native orchids appear in this wildflower reserve, part of the town's coastal walking track.

Westbury poppy farms: Northern Tasmania's agricultural heartlands are enlivened by fields of purple poppies (p200), used for the opiate alkaloids industry.

Ben Lomond National Park: During spring and summer, head to Ben Lomond to find walking trails shimmering with colourful alpine wildflowers.

FILEDIMAGE/SHUTTERSTOCK

Table Cape Tulip Farm and lighthouse

Wynyard & Table Cape

TIME FROM BURNIE: **20MIN**

Tulip time

Less than 20km west of Burnie, Wynyard is virtually a satellite town nestled at the foot of Table Cape, a volcanic remnant shaped by time and tide into a flat-topped promontory. Named by Matthew Flinders in 1798 during his circumnavigation of Tasmania with George Bass, it's topped by a **lighthouse** and a nearby coastal **lookout**. The pair are connected by 30-minute return walking trail running along the cape's edge; tours of the lighthouse had temporarily ceased at the time of our visit, so check ahead with the Wynyard visitor centre.

The cape is best known for the springtime tulip displays at **Table Cape Tulip Farm**, when even the cape's bright-red soils are eclipsed by the bright blooms. In October, when the bulbs flower, there's a mesmerising display of colours ranging from bright yellow to iridescent purple. Blooming dates are never certain, but the best time is most likely around the second week in October.

Fossil finds

At the foot of the cape, by Wynyard's edge, **Fossil Bluff** (and adjoining Fossil Bluff Beach) is the point where a huge glacier flowed from East Antarctica across Tasmania and entered the sea, leaving a mass of sediment that is now the bluff. Head to the base of the bluff at low tide and you'll find marine fossils embedded in the rocks. A 30-minute return walk ascends from the car park to the top of the bluff for views over Wynyard and east to the Dial Range, while at low tide you can walk along the rock platforms that line the base of the bluff. It's a return walk of an hour to the breakwater at the mouth of the Inglis River in Wynyard.

Boat Harbour Beach

TIME FROM BURNIE: **30MIN**

Sandy perfection

At the western foot of Table Cape, Boat Harbour Beach is a brilliant contrast of white sand pincered by black rock. With zhooshed-up shacks rising almost directly from its sands, and the cliffs of Table Cape slipping away in the distance, it has worthy claims on being the most beautiful beach in Tasmania. The usually calm seas are patrolled in summer and perfect for kids and families, so settle in, stroll the sands and consider making it a beach base outside of Burnie. At the time of writing, a new community hub with surf lifesaving club, cafe and BBQ and picnic areas was under construction, so watch this space.

Rocky Cape National Park

TIME FROM BURNIE: **45MIN**

Tasmania's smallest national park

Stretching west of Boat Harbour for a rugged 12km along Bass Strait, **Rocky Cape National Park** protects a broad cape known to Tasmanian Aboriginal people (who made their homes in seaside caves here thousands of years before European occupation) as Pinmatik. Drive out to the squat lighthouse on the cape's tip for excellent Bass Strait views, and set out on nearby short walks to large **North Cave** (15 minutes return) and smaller **South Cave** (10 minutes return). Interpretive signs explain the cultural significance of the caves. Out of respect for the Tasmanian Aboriginal community, do not enter the caves.

From the Sisters Beach park entrance, at the eastern end of the park, the best walk is to **Anniversary Bay** (three-hour circuit), where the crystalline waters invite a swim.

WHY I LOVE ROCKY CAPE NATIONAL PARK

Andrew Bain, Lonely Planet writer

Rocky Cape might well be considered the forgotten cape of Tasmania's northwest, pinched between the attention-stealing Table Cape and The Nut, and yet it's wilder and arguably more culturally rich than both. Everything about this national park is raw, from its stout lighthouse to the frayed outcrops of rock that frame its edges, coloured in the orange lichen that the east coast likes to believe it's trademarked, but hasn't. I love the quietness of its trails – no Cradle crowds here – and when I stand on the viewing platform outside the entrance of North Cave (the first cave ever mapped by European settlers in Australia), it's so easy to imagine this shelter in use by many generations of Tasmanian Aboriginal people.

EATING IN WYNYARD & BOAT HARBOUR: OUR PICKS

Wynyard Seafoods: Fish and chips the traditional way – from the fishing wharf, with picnic tables beside. *11.30am-2pm Tue-Sat & 4.30-7pm Thu-Sat* **$$**

The Vault: Cafe by day, bar by night inside a former bank with Tassie's coolest wall of books. *7am-9pm Tue-Sat, to 3pm Sun & Mon* **$$**

Bruce's Cafe: On Wynyard's beachside outskirts, with good coffee and equally good seaside vibes. *8am-3pm Tue-Sun* **$$**

Seekers: A beach outlook and a bright beachy vibe for breakfast, fish and chips or scallop rolls right on the sands of Boat Harbour Beach. *8am-4pm* **$$**

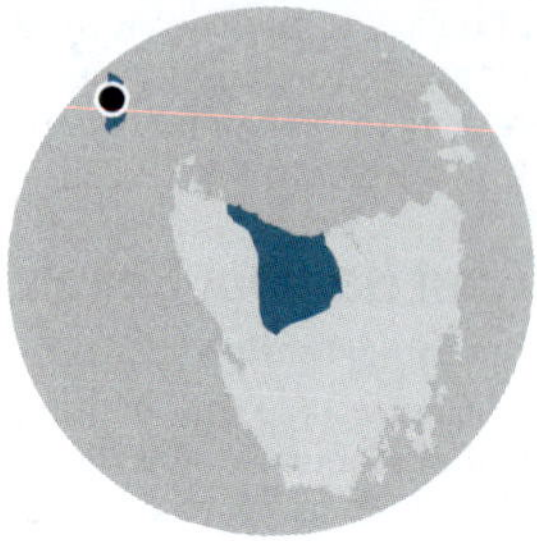

King Island

FOOD | RUGGED COASTLINES | GOLF

GETTING AROUND

Sharp Airlines flies to King Island from Burnie, Launceston and Melbourne (Essendon), while Rex Airlines services the island from Burnie and Melbourne (Tullamarine). Book ahead for car hire with **King Island Car Rental** *(kingislandcarrental.com.au)*. If you want to be shown around the island, contact **King Island Tours** *(kingislandtours.com)*, which runs one- and four-day island tours as well as thematic tours.

TOP TIP

Pick up a copy of the 'What's happening on King Island this week' printout from the visitor centre in Currie to get a rundown on island events during your stay, from tours to restaurant opening times, yoga sessions and run club.

Tasmania's second-largest offshore island, known to locals as 'KI', is a place of superlatives: the southern hemisphere's tallest lighthouse, the world's smallest suspended lake (Penny's Lagoon), two golf courses ranked among Australia's top 25 and one of the world's best surfing waves. It's quite a list for a relaxed island just 64km long and 26km wide.

Long before Tasmania earned its spurs as a gourmet destination, King Island (population 1600) was already forging its own distinct reputation for fine cheese, beef and seafood. And little has changed. The island is parcelled into paddocks by wind-breaking stands of melaleuca trees, with more than 100,000 beef cattle roaming those pastures, and a cheese factory turns out some of Australia's best-known fromages. Visit and you'll find an island peppered with shipwrecks, lighthouses, wild coastlines and the local flavours for which KI is celebrated. The island loves a good festival, too – your luck is in if your visit coincides with FOKI (Festival of King Island; February) and November's classical-music celebration, Moondance.

Local Tastes

King Island cheese, beer and whisky

If King Island is known for any one thing, it's food. **King Island Dairy** *(kingislanddairy.com.au)* is one of Australia's most revered names in cheese and, after almost closing in 2024, it was purchased by new owners and continues to produce its award-winning cheeses. Visit its Cheese Shop, attached to the dairy, 8km north of Currie, for free tastings of six cheeses, from lush bries to chunky cheddars and pungent blues, enjoyed with Tassie beers, ciders and wine.

Occupying a tin shed in the paddocks midway between Currie and Grassy, the **King Island Brewhouse** is co-owned by Corey and Sarah Brazendale. After meeting on a slow boat to

SIGHTS
1 Calcified Forest
2 Cape Wickham Lighthouse
3 Cataraqui Memorial
4 Currie Lighthouse
5 King Island Dairy
6 King Island Distillery
7 King Island Historical Museum
8 Martha Lavinia Beach
9 Seal Rocks Lookout
10 Shannon Wreck

ACTIVITIES
11 Cape Wickham Golf Links
12 King Island Golf Club
13 Ocean Dunes

SLEEPING
see 6 Island Breeze Motel
14 Kittawa Lodge
15 Lunarsea

EATING
16 Chefanie's at View
17 FoodWorks
18 Island Larder
19 Oleada
20 The Boathouse
see 15 Wild Harvest

DRINKING & NIGHTLIFE
21 King Island Brewhouse
22 King Island Distillery Bass Strait

TRANSPORT
see 22 King Island Car Rental

Antarctica, they opened the brewery in 2021. The taproom has six beers, from session ales to a stout and an alcoholic ginger beer. Friday night is wood-fired-pizza night.

The island is home to two distilleries. Contact Heidi Weitjens at the **King Island Distillery** to tour her original spirits shed by Currie's racecourse, while the island's coolest bar, owned and operated by the similarly named **King Island Distillery Bass Strait**, is curiously inside the tiny airport. Try the local moonshine, limoncello or gin (or a tasting paddle of the range), along with coffee, gourmet toasties and even King Island Dairy platters, while cosied up to the padded bar with its brass shelving.

A Seabound History

Lighthouses and shipwrecks

On arrival at the airport, pick up the *King Island Maritime Trail* brochure detailing more than a dozen lighthouse and shipwreck sites around the island's perimeter. The most evocative of the wreck stops include a memorial to the **Cataraqui**, which ran onto a reef south of Currie in 1845 and remains

THE RESTAURANT WITH NO FOOD

By the water in Currie Harbour, **The Boathouse** is a dining venue like no other. Known locally as 'the restaurant with no food', the brightly coloured boatshed with a sunny dining room and rustic outdoor tables is the best place to enjoy King Island's excellent local produce. It has a BBQ, compact kitchen, plates, cutlery and seriously eclectic decor – think chandeliers hanging among fishing nets. **FoodWorks** in Currie puts together picnic and BBQ hampers perfect for the occasion (24-hour notice required) – pick one up, pop an LP on the Boathouse's 1970s turntable (complete with a rag-tag collection of old vinyl records) and enjoy perhaps the finest island picnic of your life. Just don't forget to do the dishes.

ANDREW BAIN/LONELY PLANET

Calcified Forest

Australia's worst peacetime maritime disaster, with the death of 400 aboard, and the remains of the **Shannon**, a Murray River paddle steamer that wrecked while being delivered across Bass Strait, sitting among the waves on Yellow Rock Beach.

Crowning the island's northern tip is 48m-high **Cape Wickham Lighthouse**, the southern hemisphere's tallest lighthouse, built in 1861 in response to the *Cataraqui* disaster. With ships often mistaking its beam for Cape Otway Lighthouse in Victoria and continuing to slam into the side of King Island, **Currie Lighthouse** followed 18 years later. **King Island Walks** *(kingislandwalks.com.au; adult/child $50/30)* runs tours of this lighthouse on Wednesday and Sunday, ascending its 93 spiralling steps and viewing the massive original lens of Cape Wickham Lighthouse in a cottage at its base.

Alongside Currie Lighthouse, the **King Island Historical Museum** *(kingisland.net.au; adult/child $10/2)* has a room devoted to the *Cataraqui,* with salvaged artefacts such as a cannon and fragments of its hull. Look also for the display on the extinct King Island emu.

EATING ON KING ISLAND: OUR PICKS

Island Larder: KI's best coffee, great cakes and the likes of chilli scrambled eggs and breakfast burritos. *7am-2pm Mon-Wed & Fri, 8am-1pm Sat & Sun* $

Oleada: Italian-accented dining in a tiny, map-covered Currie restaurant, with local island produce right down to the gins and beers. *6-10pm Wed-Sat* $$$

Wild Harvest: Five-course degustation dining in shearing-shed-chic surrounds at this restaurant poised high above Grassy Harbour. *6-10pm Sat* $$$

Chefanie's at View: Salt-and-pepper squid, karage chicken and roast specials overlooking Currie's golf course. *3-6.30pm Thu & Fri, 10am-4pm Sat* $$

Wild Island

Discover KI's natural edges

King Island can feel more naturally tame than Flinders Island, but King too has its wild sides. Along its southwestern edge, on Seal Rocks Rd, a 30-minute return walk leads to a lookout platform at **Calcified Forest**, a desert-like patch of sand in the bush – the 'forest' of the name is the remnants of sand that cemented itself around tree roots 7000 years ago. Seal Rocks Rd then continues to the **Seal Rocks Lookout**, peering over the island's most dramatic slice of coast. The 1½-hour return **Copperhead** walk runs north from the lookout along the top of wave-beaten cliffs. Be sure to go all the way to the trail's end to find a moment of island humour.

In the island's far north, the waves at long, dune-backed **Martha Lavinia Beach** were once named among the world's 10 best surfing spots and have attracted the celebrity likes of Kelly Slater and Pearl Jam frontman Eddie Vedder.

For guided exploration on foot, King Island Walks offers a pair of hiking tours (from $355), as well as a tour to view platypus and penguins ($350) – the latter waltz ashore on the Grassy breakwater each dusk.

Play Australia's Best Golf Course

Take a drive of a different kind

With a little imagination, it's not hard to picture King Island as a golf green in the middle of a very large water hazard. Fittingly, **Cape Wickham Golf Links** *(capewickham.com.au; 9/18 holes from $108/180)*, almost wrapped around the toes of its namesake lighthouse, was named Australia's best golf course by *Australian Golf Digest* in 2024. The best bit? Anyone can play it. Close behind on the list of top golf courses, at No 13, was **Ocean Dunes** *(oceandunes.com.au; 9/18 holes from $100/160)*, just to Currie's north. Book ahead at either, or both, and prepare for a challenging day out – with King Island straddling the 40th parallel, aka the Roaring Forties, windy games are all but guaranteed.

If those two testing layouts seem too challenging, there's always Currie's little **King Island Golf Club** *(golfkingisland.com; $40)*.

THREE HUMMOCK ISLAND

The third of Tasmania's Bass Strait islands with visitor facilities is little-known **Three Hummock Island** *(threehummockisland.com.au)* to King Island's south. Once a summer hunting ground for Tasmanian Aboriginal people, it was named by Matthew Flinders in 1798 for its three low hills. Run as a farm in the mid-20th century, its old homestead is now used as visitor accommodation, sleeping up to eight people. There's little to do on the island, but that's the reason you come – to walk empty beaches, hike to its highest point (237m South Hummock), spy some of its 90 recorded bird species, fish or simply watch kangaroos and Cape Barren geese grazing the field in front of the homestead. Access is by charter flight or boat – see the website for the various options.

Cradle Mountain

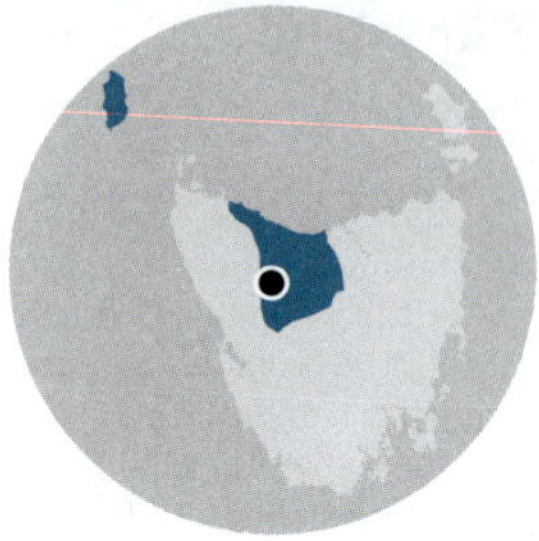

HIKING | ALPINE VIEWS | WILDLIFE

TOP TIP
Never bank on the last shuttle bus of the day. Aim for a slightly earlier one back from Dove Lake or Ronny Creek, in case everyone else has the same idea about catching the final service back.

Part of the Tasmanian Wilderness World Heritage Area, Cradle Mountain-Lake St Clair National Park is a rugged 1262-sq-km agglomeration of glacier-sculpted mountains, gorges, lakes, tarns and alpine moorland. For hikers, it's best experienced on the 65km Overland Track, traversing exposed alpine plateaus and rainforest and passing craggy bluffs on its journey from Cradle Mountain to Lake St Clair. The park's centrepiece is the distinctive Cradle Mountain, where, by the park edge north of the mountain, a well-set-up travellers' village in Cradle Valley has emerged as the gateway to the peak and its surrounding alpine splendour. Hiking trails range through the landscape, looping lakes and rising to lookouts and summits, and a convenient shuttle-bus service makes the logistics of access easy. At the end of the day, Cradle Valley offers plenty of soothing rewards, from spas and a sauna to good restaurants and bars – heck, you can even dine with a Tasmanian devil.

Devils in the Dark

Meet Tasmania's cutest carnivores

Located among the visitor facilities in Cradle Valley, **Devils @Cradle** *(devilsatcradle.com; adult/child $27.50/15)* is a conservation-focused centre for Tasmanian devils, spotted-tail quolls and eastern quolls. Housing up to 50 devils, the sanctuary is open all day for self-guided visits, keeper tours (10.30am

GETTING AROUND

From the **Cradle Mountain visitor centre**, shuttle buses run to Dove Lake, stopping at the ranger station, Snake Hill and Ronny Creek en route. Private vehicle access along the Dove Lake road is only allowed outside of the buses' operating hours. The bus timetable changes across the months and seasons (though never earlier than 8.10am or later than 7pm) so check the park website *(parks.tas.gov.au/explore-our-parks/cradle-mountain)* for details. Limited parking for cars (no campervans) at Dove Lake is on a first-come, first-served basis.

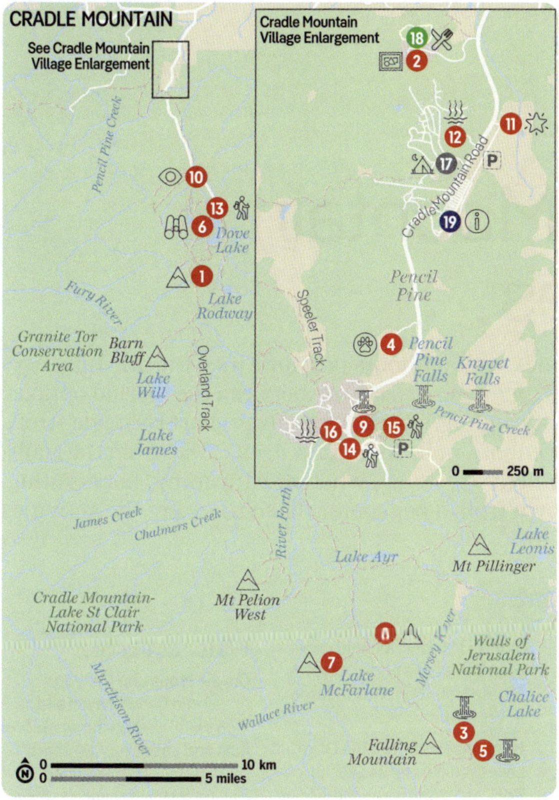

SIGHTS
1 Cradle Mountain
2 Cradle Mountain Wilderness Gallery
3 D'Alton Falls
4 Devils@Cradle
see 3 Fergusson Falls
5 Hartnett Falls
6 Marions Lookout
7 Mt Ossa
8 Mt Pelion East
9 Pencil Pine Falls
10 Ronny Creek

ACTIVITIES
see 19 Cradle Mountain Canyons
11 Cradle Mountain Helicopters
12 Cradle Mountain Sauna
13 Dove Lake Circuit
14 Enchanted Walk
15 Rainforest Walk
16 Waldheim Alpine Spa

SLEEPING
see 16 Cradle Mountain Lodge
see 12 Cradle Mountain Wilderness Village
17 Discovery Parks Cradle Mountain

EATING
18 Altitude
see 19 Elements
see 12 Hellyers Restaurant
see 16 Tavern Bar & Bistro

INFORMATION
19 Cradle Mountain Visitor Centre

TRANSPORT
see 19 McDermotts

and 3pm) and feeding tours (1pm), but try to schedule an evening visit when the animals are most active and the bush resounds with their banshee screams. After Dark Feeding Tours (adult/child $37.50/20) start at 5.30pm, with 8.30pm tours also running on demand in peak season. Sunset Experience ($99/75) tours have you meeting the devils and quolls, and conclude with a feeding – sweet treats for you and sweet meats for the devils. Joey Encounters ($75/50) at 4pm (and noon from October to April) are an opportunity to see Tassie's cutest juvenile marsupials. Book ahead for tours.

Its more refined counterpart, Highland Restaurant, is in the same building.

EATING AROUND CRADLE MOUNTAIN: OUR PICKS

Elements: Simple breakfasts and lunches – bacon and egg muffins, burgers, croissants – at the park visitor centre. *8.30am-4.30pm* $

Altitude: The house restaurant at Cradle Mountain Hotel has Tassie tastes such as Cape Grim beef and Huon Valley trout. Or perhaps a sweet-potato steak? *5-9pm* $$$

Hellyers Restaurant: Refined fireside dining focused on ingredients from more than a dozen Tassie producers at Cradle Mountain Wilderness Village. *noon-3pm & 5-7.30pm* $$$

Tavern Bar & Bistro: Popular three-tiered tavern with pub classics, a pool table and two open fires adding warmth and mood. *noon-late* $$$

HELP ME PICK:

Cradle Mountain Activities

Cradle Mountain abounds with outdoors possibilities – the dilemma here is not in how to get busy, but in how to choose between the myriad options. Hiking is the hero activity and the offerings run from short riverside strolls to an agile, day-long ascent of Cradle Mountain itself. Away from the trails, there's a range of other active pursuits, whether canyoning, horse riding, kayaking or peering down from a helicopter. Then there are the activities designed purely to soothe.

What to do if you want...

The classic scene

Dove Lake Circuit Hiking the 6km circumnavigation of Dove Lake, pooled at the foot of Cradle Mountain, is the classic half-day out in the park. The circuit is best walked in a clockwise direction and follows a well-formed track. The loop passes Glacier Rock, still bearing the scratch marks from the glacier that ground against it, and passes through the Ballroom Forest, a beguiling stand of rainforest worthy of a fantasy novel, but it's the boat shed near the circuit's end, standing as foreground to Cradle Mountain, that forms Tasmania's most famous mountain scene. Two to three hours.

Elevated views

Marions Lookout Get a taste of the Overland Track, and an eyeball on Cradle Mountain, by following the track's opening steps along Ronny Creek (keep an eye out for wombats) and ascending past Crater Lake to the chain-assisted final climb to lofty Marions, looking down onto Dove Lake and across to Cradle Mountain. Two to three hours return.

Hansons Peak Take the Dove Lake Circuit as far as Glacier Rock and then rise up the slopes (partly assisted by chains) to this ridgetop peak standing almost nose to nose with Cradle Mountain's Little Horn summit. Three to four hours return.

Mountain kudos

Cradle Summit Climbing Cradle Mountain is a big step up from most other trails here. It's a full-day affair and, beyond Kitchen Hut, transforms into a rock hop and a scramble – if you didn't know you had groin muscles before, you will by the end of this day. The reward? Sublime views over equally impressive Barn Bluff all the way to Mt Ossa (Tasmania's highest mountain) and beyond. Check the weather forecast carefully and don't overestimate your capabilities. Eight hours return.

Water activities

Cradle Mountain Canyons Abseil into Dove Canyon and then swim, wade, jump, walk, float and abseil your way past six waterfalls on this guided canyoning trip through the cracks of the Earth. There's an easier, family-friendly trip (suitable for children eight years and above) upstream in Lost World Canyon.

Dove Lake Kayak Paddle across Dove Lake in a hand-built King Billy pine kayak, viewing Cradle Mountain from a water-top perspective. Run by Cradle Mountain Canyons.

To rest and recuperate

Cradle Mountain Sauna This sauna in a shipping container, with a floor-to-ceiling window into the bush, has an open-air Huon-pine cold shower. Located at Cradle Mountain Wilderness Village.

Waldheim Alpine Spa A full roster of wellness treatments – massage, facials, hot stones – at Cradle Mountain Lodge.

POSNOV/GETTY IMAGES

Dove Lake and Cradle Mountain

HOW TO

When to go Snow can fall anytime around Cradle Mountain, but the best and warmest conditions are most likely from October to April.

Getting there Cars can't be driven into the park during the day; hop aboard a park shuttle bus, departing from the park visitor centre, instead.

Top tip The visitor centre has staff on hand to help you with decisions and advice for your day's outings; call in before you set out into the park.

Prepare ahead It rains seven out of 10 days around Cradle Mountain (and snows more than 50 days a year), so carry warm clothing and wet-weather gear regardless of the sky's appearance.

Tour Operators

Cradle Mountain Canyons *(cradlemountaincanyons.com.au)* Canyoning trips through a trio of gorges, kayaking on Dove Lake and, further afield, packrafting trips through the Alum Cliffs gorge near Mole Creek.

Cradle Country Adventures *(cradleadventures.com.au)* Explore the wider Cradle Mountain area on horseback with guided trail rides along rivers and through forests.

Cradle Mountain Helicopters *(cradlemountainhelicopters.com.au)* Spectacular flights over Tasmania's mountainous heart depart from near the Cradle Mountain visitor centre car park. Options range from a 20-minute Cradle Mountain and Fury Gorge Adventure, which flies over Dove Lake and past Cradle Mountain to Australia's deepest gorge, to an hour-long Overland Adventure, seeing the course of the Overland Track from the heady comfort of a helicopter seat and returning over the Walls of Jerusalem.

McDermotts *(mcdermotts.com.au)* This coach company runs a range of guided trips inside the park. Hikers wanting a guide can sign up for walking trips to Marions Lookout, the Dove Lake Circuit and Cradle summit. A night-spotting tour heads into the park after dark, with a short boardwalk stroll to spot wombats, wallabies and other native creatures.

Cradle Mountain Lodge *(cradlemountainlodge.com.au)* This Cradle Valley hotel runs day tours for both guests and nonguests, ranging from guided walks to a spotlighting safari, a fly-fishing tutorial and an Aboriginal Heritage and Bush Tucker tour.

FILEDIMAGE/SHUTTERSTOCK

TOP EXPERIENCE

The Overland Track

From Ronny Creek near Cradle Mountain south to the shores of Lake St Clair, Tasmania's alpine Overland Track is Australia's premier multiday walk. On a six-day, 65km journey past five of Tasmania's 10 highest peaks, look forward to diverse terrain, including rainforest, gorges and alpine moors, on trails that weave through the most spectacular mountain scenery Tasmania can deliver.

DON'T MISS

- Marions Lookout
- Pelion Hut views
- Mt Ossa ascent
- Mersey River Waterfalls
- Du Cane Hut

Starting at Ronny Creek

During the hiking season (October to May), the Overland Track can only be walked north–south, setting out from **Ronny Creek**, 7km from the Cradle Mountain visitor centre. Walking to Ronny Creek along the Cradle Valley boardwalk is an option, but few hikers want to add to the load ahead, so catch the shuttle bus to Ronny Creek.

Best Time to Go

The best time to walk the track is during Tasmania's summer and early autumn (December to April), when the weather is warmer, days are longer and alpine plants are in flower. A permit system operates during the hiking season and the number of people setting out each day from Ronny Creek is capped. If your preferred day is already booked out, you can always check with guided-walk operators for vacancies on departures. During the winter off-season (June to September), walkers numbers are naturally reduced, but this period of snow and ice is only recommended for more experienced bushwalkers.

PRACTICALITIES

● parks.tas.gov.au/explore-our-parks/cradle-mountain/overland-track ● adult/child $300/260

How Difficult Is the Walk?

The Overland Track is classified as Grade 4 ('bushwalking experience recommended. Tracks may be long, rough and steep. Directional signage may be limited'), though it's not as challenging as other Tasmanian trails such as the South Coast Track and Frenchmans Cap. The Overland Track largely threads through the mountains, rather than grinding over them, reducing the amount of ascent and descent, though there's still plenty of walking at altitudes above 1000m on exposed plateaus. If you have experience with multiday hikes and a solid fitness base, it's an achievable independent adventure. Inexperienced hikers should join a guided walking group. The track is not recommended for children under eight years.

What to Pack

Year-round the weather can be very changeable – it's not uncommon to encounter snow in December – and hikers need to be thoroughly prepared. Be equipped with footwear and technical apparel covering all four seasons, potentially all occurring on the same day. If you're hiking independently, you'll also need to carry all your food, and you're required to carry a tent in case of emergency.

Where You'll Sleep

There are six public huts for independent hikers dotted along the track, each with camping nearby. Huts are typically rustic affairs with wooden bunks, composting toilets and space for cooking and eating, though a couple have had upgrades in recent years.

Recommended Detours

The track is stitched with detours to mountain summits, waterfalls and lakes. Cradle Mountain (p242) is an obvious goal for many, and it's passed on the first day out from Ronny Creek, a short distance beyond Marions Lookout (p242). From Kitchen Hut, the side track to Cradle's summit crosses scree fields and requires some scrambling. From Pelion Gap, just beyond Pelion Hut (night three, normally), side trails veer off to **Mt Pelion East** and **Mt Ossa**. As Tasmania's highest peak (1617m), Ossa is a siren for many hikers, but be aware that it's a four- to six-hour side trip from the gap. The easiest side trips are to a trio of waterfalls – **Hartnett Falls** (one hour) and the twinned **D'Alton Falls** and **Fergusson Falls** (one hour) – on the section between Kia Ora Hut and Windy Ridge (typically the penultimate day).

Ending at Narcissus & Lake St Clair

If you're a stickler for go to whoa, the final stretch of the Overland Track is from Narcissus to Cynthia Bay, 17.5km along the shores of Lake St Clair, but most hikers jump on the ferry from Narcissus across the lake to end at the Lake St Clair visitor centre. Book the ferry online with lakestclairlodge.com.au.

GUIDED WALKS

Several well-regarded operators offer guided hikes along the Overland Track. The plushest option is the Cradle Mountain Signature Walk with **Tasmanian Walking Company** *(taswalkingco.com.au; from $4495)*, staying in its private huts. It also offers an eight-day winter crossing. **Tasmanian Expeditions** *(tasmanianexpeditions.com.au; from $3395)* runs camping-based hikes as well as special family and winter trips, along with self-guided walks that include all transfers, food and logistics.

TOP TIPS

- A fee-based permit system is in place from 1 October to 31 May, with departures limited to a maximum of 34 independent hikers a day.
- Bookings for each season open in early July and places fill fast, so try to book early.
- A valid national parks pass is needed for walking year-round.
- Campfires are banned on the track. Carry a fuel stove for cooking.
- Cradle Mountain Coaches and eGuide run transfers from Devonport, Launceston, Deloraine, Sheffield and Hobart to Cradle Mountain, with returns to the same cities and towns (or back to Cradle Mountain) from Lake St Clair.

THE WEINDORFERS' LEGACY

Gustav Weindorfer was an Austrian immigrant fundamental to the preservation of the Cradle Mountain area. In 1910, he built Waldheim, a wooden cabin and, with his wife Kate, lobbied successive governments to preserve the area. Despite the challenging access to the remote region, the Weindorfers consistently promoted Cradle Mountain to visitors, and Kate's botanical expertise and knowledge of the local flora and fauna deepened their appreciation of the landscape. Following her death in 1916, Gustav moved permanently to Waldheim and dedicated his life to conservation. Cradle Mountain became a scenic reserve in 1922 and, 40 years after Gustav's death, was declared a national park in 1971. The original Waldheim was replaced in 1976, but remains a poignant tribute to the Weindorfers' enduring legacy.

CATHERINE SUTHERLAND/LONELY PLANET

Enchanted Walk track

Shuttle-Free Walks

Strolls at the park edge

Not all the walks at Cradle Mountain require hopping aboard the park shuttle and heading in to Dove Lake or Ronny Creek. The park border runs along the edge of Cradle Mountain Lodge, with a selection of walks departing from near the lodge's entrance. The short **Pencil Pine Falls** track (10 minutes return) descends through a mossy bank of rainforest to a lookout platform overhanging Pencil Pine Creek. Head another 10 minutes downstream and you'll find **Knyvet Falls**. Pencil Pine Falls can also be seen from the accessible **Rainforest Walk** (10-minute circuit) on the opposite bank, which departs from the ranger station. Continuing downstream, the **Dove Canyon Circuit** (two to three hours) follows an unmaintained track to the edge of the impressive canyon.

Heading in the opposite direction from Cradle Mountain Lodge, the **Enchanted Walk** (20-minute circuit) heads along both banks of Pencil Pine Creek, crossing below Pencil Pine Cascades and again below a narrow, moss-covered gorge. Painted crawl-tunnels along the way make this a fun one for kids. It's also a good walk for spotting wombats among the buttongrass tussocks.

Art in Nature

See nature-inspired art

Put aside Cradle Mountain's natural artistry for an hour inside the **Cradle Mountain Wilderness Gallery** *(cradlemountainhotel.com.au; free)*, attached to Cradle Mountain Hotel. Spread across nine rooms, it features works celebrating Tasmania's environment by Tasmanian photographers (including the revered Peter Dombrovskis, whose sublime 'Morning Mist, Rock Island Bend' photo helped turn national sentiment in the Franklin River anti-dam campaign in the early 1980s) and other artists. All works or prints are for sale.

Places We Love to Stay

$** Budget **$$** Midrange **$$$ Top End

Devonport

MAP p221

Compass Hut $$ Three-self-contained, off-grid tiny homes set on the grassy slope of a farm – sheep will likely be your nearest neighbours – 10 minutes' drive inland from Devonport.

Grand on Macfie $$ Six elegant bedrooms and views over the city are highlights of this B&B in a mansion dating from 1899. High tea each weekend.

The Cove $$ Two lines of adult-only clifftop chalets, 6km west of Devonport, that wrap around the cove of the name with wild Bass Strait views and penguin visitors in the evening.

Deloraine

Blake's Manor $$ Self-contained heritage accommodation in a row of 1838 cottages, plus a well-priced family suite with views of Quamby Bluff.

Arcoona Manor $$$ Country-like grandeur in the heart of town. Pick from five B&B suites in the 1892 mansion – the Cedar Suite peers into century-old cedars, while the Meander Suite has river views.

Sheffield

Silver Ridge Retreat $$ Nestled under the rugged face of Mt Roland, 12km southwest of Sheffield, these self-contained studios and cottages have stunning mountain views.

Eagle's Nest Retreat $$$ Brilliant Mt Roland views at three spectacular holiday houses with picture windows and mountain-view spas, 7km southwest of Sheffield.

Mole Creek

Blackwood Park Cottages $$ Six comfortable self-contained cottages, including a 19th-century sandstone cottage, feature on a working sheep farm with curious alpacas.

Mole Creek Cabins $$ Self-contained cabins and larger houses suitable for families, conveniently by the entrance to Trowunna Wildlife Sanctuary.

Burnie

MAP p230

Ikon Hotel $$ Spacious, high-ceilinged apartments enlivened with vintage French advertising feature in a former heritage pub at the city's heart.

One North Terrace $$ Burnie's newest hotel, propped atop a low line of basalt column cliffs, with views over Bass Strait and the port.

Penguin

The Madsen $$ This well-managed boutique hotel is housed in a grand former bank building on the waterfront.

Mt Gnomon Farm $$$ Five glamping domes circle around this heritage-breed farm's sundial-inspired veggie garden, 9km south of town. Each dome has a different perspective – sunset, ocean or mountain.

Wynyard

Alexandria B&B $ Striking 1905 Federation House on the banks of the Inglis River, with three guest rooms – the Tulip Room has a garden deck.

Coastal Pods Wynyard $$$ A wonderful design of shipping containers puzzled together into stylish accommodation by the river mouth with great little reading rooms.

Boat Harbour Beach

Tidal Whispers $$$ Classic 1940s shack, sleeping up to four, that steps straight onto the sand at Boat Harbour Beach.

King Island

MAP p237

Lunarsea $$ Super-cosy cottage accommodation with a retro vibe in Grassy village. It has a coffee pod machine and complimentary KI cheese in the fridge.

Island Breeze Motel $$ Modern rooms and self-contained A-frame chalets at the northern end of Currie.

Kittawa Lodge $$$ Kittawa's two stand-alone one-bedroom lodges with rugged coastal views are King Island's most luxurious place to stay. Rates include provisions for all meals.

Cradle Mountain National Park

MAP p241

Discovery Parks Cradle Mountain $ Campground etched into the bush, with options running from tent sites and dorm beds to newly installed premium mountain cabins with heated floors, bathtubs and floor-to-ceiling windows.

Cradle Mountain Wilderness Village $$$ Timber chalets grouped in native bush, with a warming lounge bar, complete with board games, for mellow après-hike wind-downs.

Cradle Mountain Lodge $$$ Reclined against the park border, with cabins dotted through the bush, easy access to the park shuttle, a spa complex and its own fly-fishing lake (p243).

Researched by
Andrew Bain

Takayna/Tarkine & the West Coast

RUGGED, REMOTE AND (ALMOST) OFF THE MAP

From ragged coastlines to one of the world's largest temperate rainforests, the west coast is both raw and remarkable.

Nowhere is the phrase 'wild west' more appropriate than along Tasmania's roughest edge. Here the world's second-largest temperate rainforest sits side by side with one of Australia's most inaccessible national parks. Mirror-finish rivers split World Heritage–listed rainforest, and mountains hold the weather that hurries across the Southern Ocean, dumping its rain and feeding the rainforests. The west coast is a land of endless ocean beaches energised by ocean winds, ancient forests slathered in moss and tannin-tinted rivers infused with the hardworking heritage of settler enterprise. Framing the rugged northwest corner is the mystical Takayna/Tarkine, one of the planet's greatest wilderness areas and a region with deep historical and cultural significance to Tasmania's Aboriginal community. Travellers wishing to combine relaxation and remoteness will gravitate to isolated Corinna on the Pieman River, connected to the world by unsealed road and a quirky river ferry. Stanley draws the oohs and aahs for its curious The Nut and its cute penguins, while Strahan and Queenstown form an uneasy neighbourly truce – the former green and pristine, with river trips as idyllic as any in the world, and the latter brutalised by mining and yet still strangely beautiful.

JAX10289/SHUTTERSTOCK

Pack a sense of adventure and good walking shoes. That way, you can smoothly detour from one of Tasmania's great one-day road trips to an array of bushwalks, river rambles and coastal strolls.

THE MAIN AREAS

STANLEY
Views, penguins and a colourful townscape.
p254

TARKINE WILDERNESS
Rainforest, raw coastline and Tasmanian Aboriginal heritage. p258

CORINNA
A golden spot among the greenery.
p264

STRAHAN
Boat trips into natural and convict history.
p267

QUEENSTOWN
A scarred mining past amid the mountains.
p271

For places to stay in Takayna/ Tarkine and the west coast, see p277

KAZUKI YAMAKAWA/SHUTTERSTOCK

Left: Empire Hotel (p273), Queenstown; Above: Tarkine Wilderness (p258)

Find Your Way

Get behind the wheel for remote exploration, detouring off main roads to lakes, lookouts, walks and waterfalls, before boarding boats for fascinating river trips through rainforest.

CAR

Having a car is the best way to explore this region. Unsealed roads thread through Takayna/Tarkine, but 2WD is sufficient if you're travelling the main routes, including the gravel Western Explorer Road.

BUS

Buses link west-coast towns to Burnie and, in the case of Queenstown, to Hobart. Kinetic bus services radiate from Burnie to Stanley, Smithton, Rosebery, Zeehan, Strahan and Queenstown.

BOAT

If you're heading to Corinna and into Takayna/Tarkine from the south, you'll cross the Pieman River on the wonderfully nostalgic Fatman Barge ferry. Boat cruises from Strahan and Corinna are the best ways to view the Gordon and Pieman rivers.

Stanley, p254
Ascend The Nut for coastal views, explore early settler history at Highfield and silently cheer on the penguins as they pop ashore each evening.

Tarkine Wilderness, p258
Ramble through rainforest and feel the fury of the Southern Ocean as its slams into the coast near Arthur River, then set out on one of Tasmania's great short road trips.

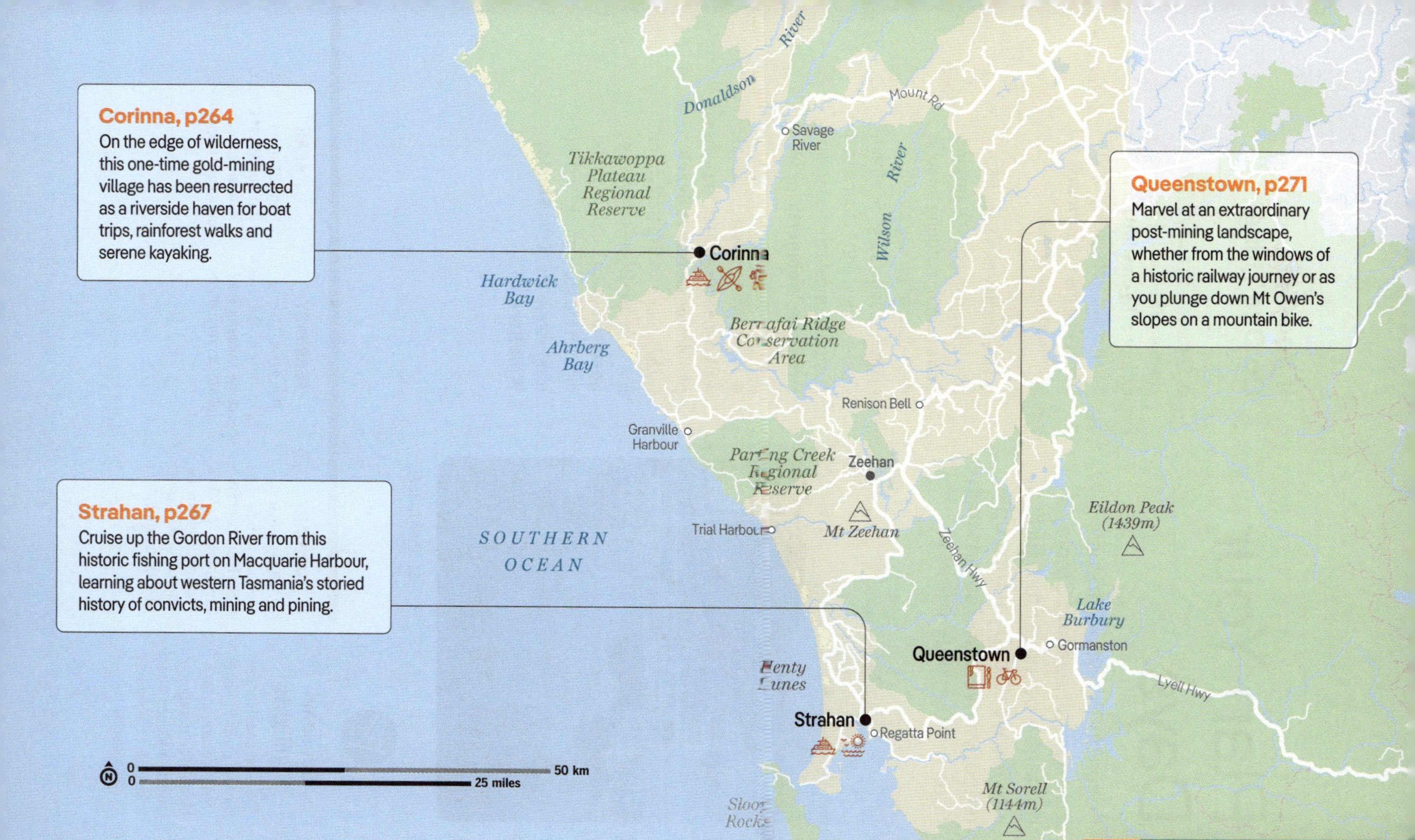
Corinna, p264
On the edge of wilderness, this one-time gold-mining village has been resurrected as a riverside haven for boat trips, rainforest walks and serene kayaking.
Queenstown, p271
Marvel at an extraordinary post-mining landscape, whether from the windows of a historic railway journey or as you plunge down Mt Owen's slopes on a mountain bike.
Strahan, p267
Cruise up the Gordon River from this historic fishing port on Macquarie Harbour, learning about western Tasmania's storied history of convicts, mining and pining.
Donaldson River
Mount Rd
Savage River
Wilson River
Tikkawoppa Plateau Regional Reserve
Corinna
Hardwick Bay
Ahrberg Bay
Renison Bell
Granville Harbour
Zeehan
Mt Zeehan
Trial Harbour
Zeehan Hwy
Eildon Peak (1439m)
Lake Burbury
Gormanston
Queenstown
Lyell Hwy
Strahan
Regatta Point
Mt Sorell (1144m)
SOUTHERN OCEAN
0 50 km
0 25 miles

Plan Your Days

Focus on Takayna/Tarkine's green greatness and Stanley's heritage vibe, or venture further into the west for boat trips up reflective rivers and steam-train rides through the rainforest.

A PERIAM PHOTOGRAPHY/SHUTTERSTOCK

Strahan (p267)

If You Only Do One Thing

- Settle into **Stanley** (p254), climbing **The Nut** (p254; whether on foot or by chairlift) for a perspective from on high and wandering the fishing town's charming main street.
- Use Stanley as a base from which to set out on the **Tarkine Drive** (p260), motoring through the Takayna/Tarkine's vast rainforest and its wild Southern Ocean edges, and to tour one of Australia's most storied farming properties, **Woolnorth** (p259).
- In the evening, watch penguins walk beneath you from the viewing platform on **Godfreys Beach** (p257), tuck into fish fresh from Hursey's own boats at **Hursey Seafoods** (p257) and finish the night in the steampunk (and much else) surrounds of the **Stanley Wine Bar** (p257).

Seasonal Highlights

The west coast largely hunkers down in winter, arising in spring for a biennial celebration of the arts in Queenstown to kickstart the sunnier seasons.

JANUARY

With summer in full swing, head for the heights of **Mt Murchison** (p276) on foot, or roll down the slopes of **Mt Owen** (p273) on a mountain bike.

FEBRUARY

Run 22km, 37km or 62km through the forest at the **Takayna Trail** (p263) ultramarathon.

APRIL

Hang 10 at the surfing **Rip Curl West Coast Classic** (p262) in the big waves of Marrawah.

Three Days to Travel

- After exploring Stanley and its surrounds, drive south to **Strahan** (p267). Devote a day to a cruise on the **Gordon River** (p267) for reflections and rainforest almost without equal. After all that classic beauty, rough things up with a visit to **Ocean Beach** (p269), where thousands of kilometres of Southern Ocean comes to an abrupt and thunderous end.

- Continue to **Queenstown** (p271) for the rude shock of its moonscape slopes and to pay homage to the generations of skin lost on the **Gravel** (p274), its infamous football oval. Steam through the rainforest on the **West Coast Wilderness Railway** (p271), go **mountain biking** (p273) on the slopes of Mt Owen, or settle into an afternoon screening at the **Paragon Theatre** (p274) to learn about the campaign to save the Franklin River from damming.

A Week-Long Stay

- Incorporate a stay in an old miner's cottage at **Corinna Wilderness Village** (p277), either travelling down the isolated Western Explorer Road from Stanley or approaching from the south via Zeehan, where you can break up the drive with a stop at keyhole-shaped, glow-worm-inhabited **Spray Tunnel** (p275).

- Corinna sits on the southern fringe of the Takayna/Tarkine rainforest, so take a couple of days to absorb this global treasure. Hire a kayak at dawn and paddle down the Pieman River to **Lovers Falls** (p266) and the wreck of the **SS Croydon** (p265), and cruise the river aboard the **MV Arcadia II** (p265) to experience nature at its most placid (on the river) and its most furious (at Pieman Heads) at once.

MAY
Sample northwest seafood, beef, cheese and beer at the **Stanley & Tarkine Forage Festival**.

JUNE
Winter is here, meaning the rains are filling the waterfalls, which begin to pour powerfully all across the region.

SEPTEMBER
Penguin breeding season begins around September, so penguin numbers are at their highest in Stanley from around now until March,

OCTOBER
The Unconformity (p273), a dark and fun Queenstown arts festival, is held on even-numbered years at venues across town.

Stanley

HISTORY | COASTAL VIEWS | PENGUINS

GETTING AROUND

Kinetic buses on the daily service between Burnie and Smithton stop in Stanley. The town's historic main street is compact and walkable, and it's a short stroll to the chairlift and the start of the walking track onto The Nut. You'll need your own transport to reach Highfield Historic Site, which is 2km north of town.

People go nuts about Stanley, the tourism jewel of this corner of Tasmania. It's the combination of The Nut, a volcanic plug rearing out of the sea, and the cute-as-the-Cotswolds cottages that dot the few streets of the town below. It's the penguins that shuffle ashore each night, often wandering past their own habitat into the habitat of the town's streets. And it's the readiness of views from along the ridge that rises above town like a low green wave, whether from manorial Highfield Historic Site, a lookout tower, or the bathtub of your own hotel room.

Stanley is unquestionably one of Tasmania's great beauty spots. You can almost fall over backwards on the steep concrete path up to the summit of The Nut, or swing in the breeze on its trapped-in-time chairlift, then descend to find shops more interested in whisky tastings than fashion, and a wine bar where steampunk and shiraz happily intersect.

Ascending The Nut

Climb an iconic landmark

Known to the area's Aboriginal people as Moo-Nut-Re-Ker and labelled 'Circular Head' by explorer Matthew Flinders, **The Nut** is the 12-million-year-old plug of an extinct volcano. At 143m in height it can be seen for many kilometres around Stanley, which sprawls across its base. One local story (apocryphal or otherwise) tells that early settlers tried to blast away part of the plug and found it 'a hard nut to crack', hence the name.

To reach the summit of The Nut, either hike up the short, sharp and steep 20-minute **Zig Zag Track** or climb aboard the old-school **chairlift** *(thenutchairlift.com.au; adult/child one way $14/9, return $21/14)*. It's particularly worth catching the chairlift down, when it provides the best views. Stanley is spread out before you, Highfield Historic Site is framed by farmland on the near horizon and there are brilliant views of Godfreys and Tatlows beaches. There's a reading room at

TOP TIP

Time your visit for Stanley's tastiest time, the **Stanley & Tarkine Forage Festival**, held in May and featuring its signature Degustation Dinner.

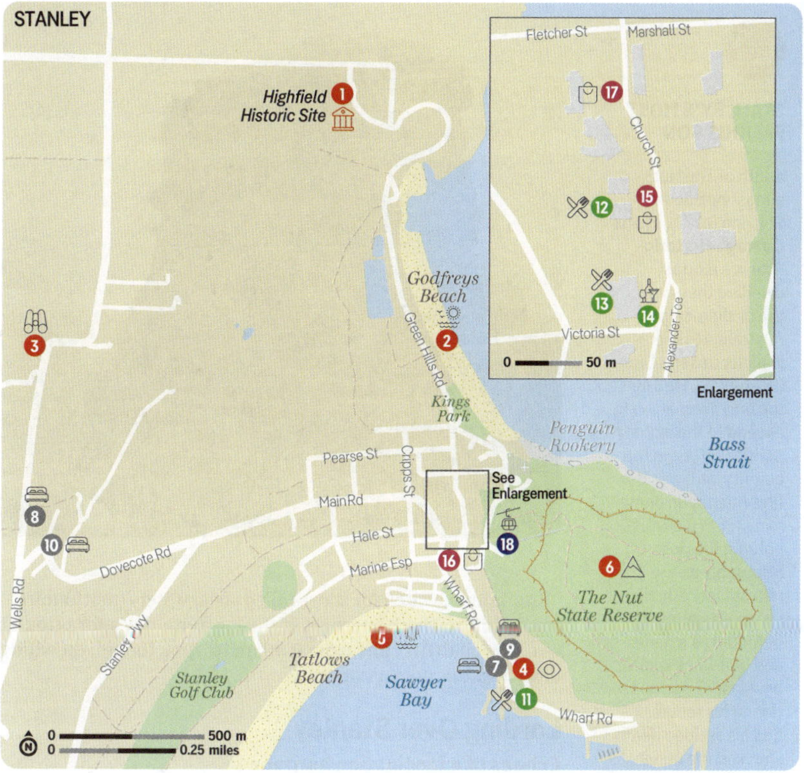

HIGHLIGHTS
1 Highfield Historic Site

SIGHTS
2 Godfreys Beach
3 Lookout Tower
4 Lyons Cottage Historic Site
5 Tatlows Beach
6 The Nut

SLEEPING
7 Ark
8 Horizon Deluxe Apartments
9 Ship Inn
10 Stanley Seaview Inn

EATING
11 Hursey Seafoods
12 Marleys
13 Stanley Hotel

DRINKING & NIGHTLIFE
14 Stanley Wine Bar

SHOPPING
15 Angel's Share
16 Cow & Calf Gallery
17 Providore 24
see 12 Sticks & Stones Shells & Bones

TRANSPORT
18 Chairlift

the back of the top chairlift station if you want to browse up (or just escape the winds).

Once you're atop The Nut, with its windswept and wind-pruned plateau (with one conspicuous stand of trees), a 2km walking track circles the summit. Dotted along it are four lookout points. **Highfield Lookout** (the first of the viewpoints if you walk anticlockwise around the plateau) looks down onto Stanley, while nearby **Tatlows Lookout** stares along its namesake beach. **Fisherman's Wharf Lookout** does indeed stare down onto the fishing wharf, while the oceanside **Pinmatik/Rocky Cape Lookout** can see as far east as Pinmatik/Rocky Cape and distant Table Cape. The Nut's highest point is passed just before the return to the top chairlift station.

STANLEY'S MOST FAMOUS SON

South of The Nut, almost beside the Ship Inn (p277), **Lyons Cottage Historic Site** is a modest dwelling that was the birthplace of Australian Prime Minister Joseph Lyons (1879–1939). He's still the only Tasmanian to ascend to the highest political office in the country, and was the first Australian prime minister to die while holding the post. Reputedly a very relaxed individual, Lyons was often depicted as a genial and laid-back koala in newspaper cartoons during his tenure, and his sudden death shocked the nation during Easter in 1939. In 1943 his widow Enid Lyons was the first woman to be elected to Australia's House of Representatives and also the first woman appointed to the Federal Cabinet.

In summer, watch for short-tailed shearwaters (muttonbirds) returning to their burrows at dusk after a day's foraging at sea. The chairlift runs from 9.30am to 4pm, though on windy days, it often doesn't operate.

Lording Over Stanley

Echoes of a fascinating heritage

It doesn't take much imagination to picture **Highfield Historic Site** *(parks.tas.gov.au; adult/child $15/5)*, built in 1835 for the chief agent of the Van Diemen's Land Company, as the grandest address in town. Looking down on Stanley from the ridge above, it's an exceptional example of Regency-period architecture in Tasmania. Self-guided tours cover the house, the pretty garden and the outbuildings, including stables, grain stores, workers' cottages and the chapel. The pattern from one of Highfield's original wallpapers now graces street signs around Stanley. With views of The Nut and the shallow, sandy arc of Godfreys Beach, the outlook from beside the ruins of the **convict barracks** 100m north of Highfield is the classic Stanley photo opportunity.

Continue driving south around the ridge-top road and you'll come to a small **lookout tower** gazing over the fields to Stanley and The Nut. A sculpture across the road commemorates Arthur Long, the first person to fly a plane across Bass Strait. Long took off from Stanley on 17 December 1919. On making it to Torquay, Victoria, almost four hours later he concluded that an air service between Hobart and Melbourne would never be feasible.

A PRIME MINISTERIAL HOME

To see where Joseph Lyons spent his adult life, along with his equally esteemed wife Enid, drop into **Home Hill** (p222) in Devonport.

SLOVEGROVE/GETTY IMAGES

Highfield Historic Site's convict barracks ruins and The Nut (p254)

Beaches & Birds

A nightly penguin parade

The southern end of **Godfreys Beach** is the centrepiece of Stanley nightlife, at least as far as its little penguins are concerned. At dusk from September to March, penguins wander ashore, climbing through the rocks to pass directly beneath the penguin-viewing boardwalk (and often far into the town's streets). The boardwalk is handily lit with the red lights commonly used to assist with penguin viewing. Please don't use a flash when taking photos. Note that the surf and tides at Godfreys Beach can sometimes be capricious, and it's not recommended for swimming. At low tide, the far (northern) end of the beach provides particularly good views along the length of the sand to the hulking figure of The Nut.

More sheltered on the southwestern edge of The Nut, **Tatlows Beach** is a safer option. At more than 4km in length, it's also perfect for that long morning or evening beach walk.

SHOPPING IN STANLEY

Providore 24: One-stop shop for gourmet Tassie produce, from bread to cheese, wine, beer, chocolate and Stanley-processed pickled octopus. There's even a share plot of herbs out the front.

Angel's Share: Tastings and sales of whiskies from more than two dozen Tassie distilleries, as well as unexpected tipples such as chilli vodka and absinthe. Also sells knitwear, handbags and jewellery.

Cow & Calf Gallery: Photographic gallery of David Murphy's Tasmanian images, with a sprinkling of work by other local artists and photographers.

Sticks & Stones Shells & Bones: How many chances do you get to buy 500-million-year-old items? All things stone, shells and fossils, along with local artwork. Attached to Marleys.

EATING & DRINKING IN STANLEY: OUR PICKS

Hursey Seafoods: Takeaway fish and chips downstairs, bistro dining upstairs, with seafood fresh off its own fleet of boats. Takeaway all day. *noon-2.30pm & 5.30-8pm* $$

Stanley Hotel: Steak and seafood both come with low food miles at this popular pub that dominates Stanley's streetscape. *noon-8pm* $$$

Marleys: Popular cafe with views out to Tatlows Beach as you tuck into spicy abalone or a salad of beef, haloumi, nuts and fruit. *7am-4pm Fri-Tue* $$

Stanley Wine Bar: Settle into an antique armchair and enjoy the cabinet-of-curiosities surrounds, from steampunk to uranium glass. *5-9pm Thu-Sat*

Tarkine Wilderness

WILDERNESS | RAINFOREST | INDIGENOUS HISTORY

GETTING AROUND

Smithton-based Tall Timbers (p277) offers 4WD tours of the Tarkine, but to explore this remote region, your own vehicle is best. A 2WD will be fine for the sealed Tarkine Drive and the largely unsealed Western Explorer Road that runs through Takayna/Tarkine to Corinna, but consider a 4WD if exploring beyond.

Known as Takayna to the Tasmanian Aboriginal people, the Tarkine Wilderness is a 4470-sq-km stretch of temperate rainforest between the Arthur River in the north, the Pieman River in the south, the Murchison Hwy to the east and the Southern Ocean to the west. It's a globally significant ecosystem, claimed as the world's second-largest expanse of temperate rainforest, that encompasses a vast rainforest, tracts of buttongrass plains, savage ocean beaches, sand dunes and extensive coastal heathlands. Because of its remoteness, ferocious weather and isolation, Takayna/Tarkine survived almost untouched by modernity well into the 20th century, and the region still offers a frontier-style experience for those keen to explore it. From either Stanley or Smithton, embark on the Tarkine Drive, a fascinating road trip stretching from the rugged coastline around Arthur River to dense forest and a fern-shrouded sinkhole.

A Gateway for Exploring

Tours discovering nature and history

Stretching along the Duck River, 22km west of Stanley, **Smithton** is a gritty but friendly agricultural service centre for beef production, dairy farming and cropping (especially potatoes). When you're in town, be sure to breathe in deeply. Smithton is buffeted by the Roaring Forties winds, which blow east unimpeded across the Southern Ocean all the way from South America, and the Baseline Air Pollution Station at nearby Cape Grim declares the air around these parts to be the world's cleanest.

To experience this pristine environment, visit **Woolnorth**, 25km from Smithton. Once Australia's largest dairy operation, the 220-sq-km property was the only property in the country established by royal charter. Started by the Van Diemen's Land Company in 1827, it has farm buildings that predate the establishment of Melbourne, and today it's home to enormous wind turbines harnessing the power of the Roaring

TOP TIP

Delve deeper on a guided walk through Takayna/Tarkine. Operators include **Tarkine Trails** *(tarkinetrails.com.au)* and **Tasmanian Expeditions** *(tasmanianexpeditions.com.au)*. The latter's six-day trips include a smoking ceremony and cultural discussion with a member of the Tasmanian Aboriginal community at Sundown Point State Reserve (p262).

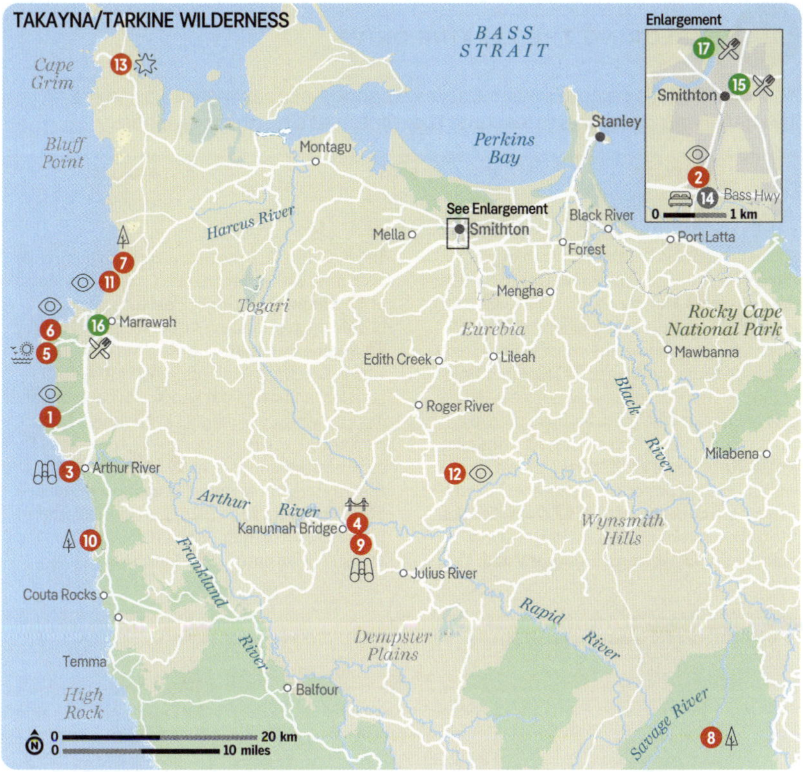

SIGHTS
- 1 Bluff Hill Point
- see 1 Bluff Hill Point Lighthouse
- 2 Duck River Meadows Dairy
- 3 Gardiner Point
- 4 Kanunnah Bridge
- 5 Lighthouse Beach
- 6 Nettley Bay
- 7 Preminghana Indigenous Protected Area
- 8 Savage River National Park
- 9 Sumac Lookout
- 10 Sundown Point State Reserve
- 11 Taypalaka/Green Point
- 12 Trowutta Arch

ACTIVITIES
- see 3 Arthur River Canoe & Boat Hire
- see 3 Arthur River Cruises
- 13 Woolnorth Tours

SLEEPING
- 14 Tall Timbers

EATING
- 15 Hugo's Brew & Chew
- see 14 Kauri Bistro
- 16 Marrawah Inn
- 17 Tarkine Fresh Oysters

INFORMATION
- see 2 Smithton Visitor Centre

Forties. **Woolnorth Tours** *(woolnorthtours.com.au; adult/child $90/50)* offers 2½-hour tours of the property, visiting the wind farm and Cape Grim and also taking in the region's Aboriginal history – company owner Laura Dabner is a proud Tasmanian Aboriginal descendant. The tours offer the only public access to Woolnorth, which was officially renamed Temdudheker/Woolnorth in 2021 as part of Tasmania's dual-naming changes (p173).

From September to mid-July, Smithton's **Tall Timbers hotel** (p277; *talltimbershotel.com.au*) offers full-day 4WD tours into the Takayna/Tarkine wilderness. Other tours on offer include visiting the ghostly ruins of the Balfour Mine, Aboriginal

EXPLORING THE TARKINE DRIVE

This wonderfully remote drive explores a section of coast as wild as any in Tasmania and disappears deep into the rainforest's northern reaches.

START	END	LENGTH
Marrawah	Smithton	180km; 4hr

Fill up on petrol in Smithton or Stanley, as there's no petrol available along this fully sealed drive. From ❶ **Marrawah**, it's 15km to ❷ **Bluff Hill Point Lighthouse**, an excellent vantage point for a first taste of the coast's wild energy. Continue south for 10km to ❸ **Gardiner Point** (p263), a natural frontier so wild it's earned the title of Edge of the World. Further south, by the shack village of Nelson Bay, ❹ **Sundown Point State Reserve** (p262) features a 2km walk to ancient petroglyphs. Approaching the fishing-shack community of ❺ **Couta Rocks**, the drive turns inland to pass the northern entry to the ❻ **Western Explorer Road**. The Tarkine Drive now meanders through temperate rainforest with recommended stops 17km ahead at ❼ **Kanunnah Bridge**, ideal for a picnic beside the fast-flowing Arthur River, and nearby ❽ **Sumac Lookout**, with elevated Arthur River views. Two short rainforest walks (30 and 40 minutes) and overnight parking for caravans and campervans are highlights at ❾ **Julius River**, 6km ahead, while platypuses are sometimes seen on the 30-minute walk at ❿ **Lake Chisholm**. The drive's standout feature, the collapsed sinkhole at ⓫ **Trowutta Arch** (p263), is reached after a further 50km of forest-framed driving. From the arch, it's 31km north to ⓬ **Smithton**.

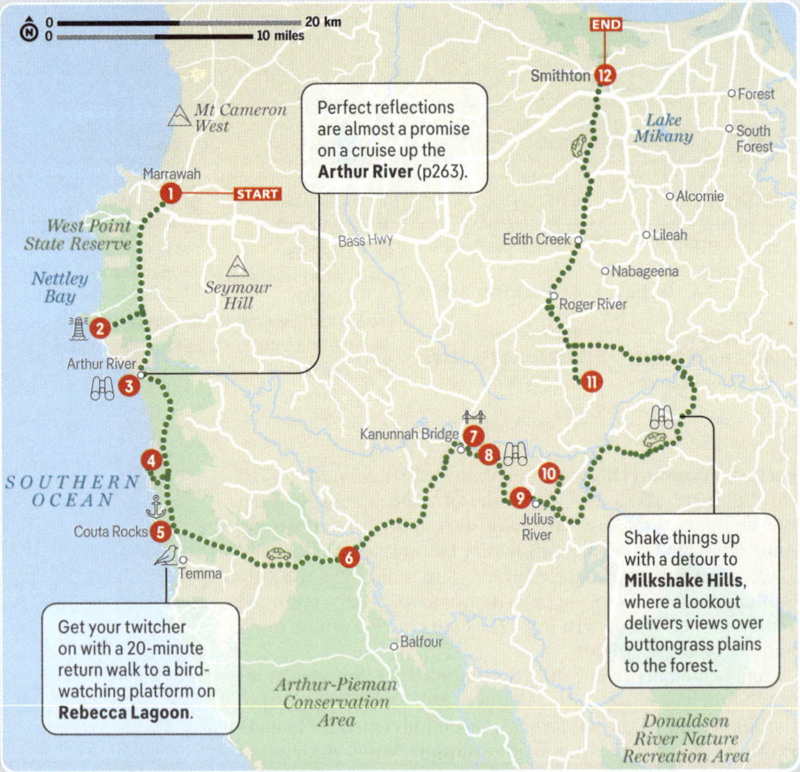

PAWAN KAWAN/SHUTTERSTOCK

Smithton visitor centre

heritage tours, and a Tasmanian tiger tour that visits the last known places inhabited by thylacines.

Meet the Cheesy Cows

Robotic milking and cheese tastings

When Venezuelan veterinarians Genaro and Rosselyn Velasquez emigrated to Tasmania, they began working as share farmers in Tasmania's northwest before leasing the robotic **Duck River Meadows Dairy** *(duckrivermeadowsdairy.com.au; tours adult/child $30/15)* farm in 2019 and deciding, almost on a whim, to make cheese. Today, under the label La Cantara, they produce a range of Venezuelan-style cheeses, including their signature Queso Blanco and cheeses washed in both rum and red wine. Guided tastings of nine cheeses ($5, refundable with any cheese purchase) are available at the **Smithton visitor centre**, but you can also delve deeper with a tour of the dairy and the attached cheese-making operation, which is behind the visitor centre. You'll get to watch the cows stroll in and out of the automated milking shed as they choose, and get a glimpse into the cheese-making process.

SAVAGE RIVER NATIONAL PARK

Welcome to the wilderness. Though sitting close to civilisation (Burnie is about 40km away as the currawong flies), the remote 180-sq-km **Savage River National Park** is inaccessible. The park protects part of the largest contiguous region of cool temperate rainforest surviving in Australia, as well as pristine blanket bogs, undisturbed river catchments and rare wildlife.

There are no roads and no facilities for visitors. Only the very hardiest of bushwalkers make it in here. Limited access into the adjacent Savage River Regional Reserve is possible by 4WD from the east via the Murchison Hwy and from the south via the Waratah–Corinna Rd, though even some of these roads have become overgrown.

EATING AROUND THE TARKINE: OUR PICKS

Hugo's Brew & Chew: Licensed cafe with Smithton's best breakfasts – there's even a Breaky Board, combining everything, if you can't choose. *6am-3.30pm Mon-Fri, 7.30am-1pm Sat* $$

Tarkine Fresh Oysters: Oysters straight out of the baskets at this onshore Smithton oyster farm with cafe seating. *10am-3pm Tue-Sat* $

Kauri Bistro: Inside Tall Timbers (p277), this grill restaurant in Smithton, the town closest to Cape Grim, suitably specialises in Cape Grim beef. *7-9am & 6-9pm* $$$

Marrawah Inn: Grills up local meats such as Cape Grim beef and Robbins Island Wagyu. Takeaway coffee from 9am. *11.30am-2pm & 5.30-8pm* $$

MARRAWAH SURF BREAKS

Marrawah's **Rip Curl West Coast Classic**, held each April, is Australia's second-longest-running surfing competition, having celebrated its 50th anniversary in 2025. The region has a number of excellent surfing spots and, even if you're not a board-rider, it's worth checking out the power and spectacle of these waves.

Taypalaka/Green Point, about 2km from Marrawah, has a break that's impressive in southerly conditions. Nearby **Nettley Bay** is a reliable point break that's at its best in winter.

Lighthouse Beach at West Point, south of Marrawah, is best in easterly conditions and can be flat in summer. **Bluff Hill Point** has great reef surfing and is also best in easterly conditions. The surf beach is to the right of the lighthouse off Bluff Hill Point Rd.

ANDREW BAIN/LONELY PLANET

Petroglyphs, Sundown Point State Reserve

Takayna's Aborginal Heritage

Petroglyphs and Aboriginal connection

The far northwest of Tasmania has been home to the Tasmanian Aboriginal Tarkininer people for more than 35,000 years. Evidence of their habitation is clearly visible along much of the Takayna/Tarkine coast, and experts call this one of the most important archaeological regions in the world.

Arguably the most significant Aboriginal site on the west coast is 7km north of Marrawah at the **Preminghana Indigenous Protected Area**. Returned to Aboriginal ownership in 1995, it's home to low-lying slabs of rock with petroglyphs dating back two millennia, tool quarries and living sites. The petroglyphs have been covered over to protect them, but you can drive in to a **lookout platform** with views to Cape Grim and interpretive signs detailing the Tasmanian Aboriginal connection to the land. Just below the lookout, a walking track heads for 1km to the long, wave-beaten beach at the foot of Mt Cameron West, with Woolnorth's wind turbines cartwheeling at its northern end.

According to the Parks & Wildlife Service, around 25% of Tasmania's recorded ceremonial stone arrangements are found around the **Sundown Point State Reserve** area (known as laraturunawn to Tasmanian Aboriginal people), along with one of the many known Tasmanian petroglyph sites. Drive to the end of Nelson Bay Rd, turning right by the shack settlement of Nelson Bay, 13km south of Arthur River, and an unsignposted 2km return walk heads north along the coast to the mouth of a stream, where the circular petroglyphs can be seen.

A Rugged & Windswept Coastline

Head to the Edge of the World

There are only a few hardy souls who call **Arthur River** their full-time home – the rest of the population is made up of 'shackies' and fisherfolk who love the wild remoteness of the country around here. Seemingly teetering on the very edge of the planet, Arthur River is a highlight of the Tarkine Drive (p260) and also near the starting point for an adventure down the Western Explorer Road to Corinna and further on to Zeehan and Strahan.

Signposted off the main road on the southern side of Arthur River, **Gardiner Point** is Tasmania's self-proclaimed 'Edge of the World' – the sea here stretches uninterrupted to Argentina, 15,000km away over wild seas. There's a plaque at the point and the jagged coastline is smothered in logs washed in by the Southern Ocean. Walk out on a well-formed track to a viewing platform offering coastal views. It's a great place to take those leaning-into-the-wind, world's-end photos.

From September to April, **Arthur River Cruises** *(arthurrivercruises.com.au; adult/child from $180/100)* runs two boats up the Arthur River, both taking in spectacular forest reflections on the shimmering backwaters. Its historic red boat, the MV *George Robinson,* has been plying the remote waterway for almost 40 years. Look forward to a five-hour trip into the rainforest and a gentle stroll along the bank of the Frankland River. Lunch is amid the trees at Turks Landing at the junction of the two rivers. Cruises on the MV *Reflections* include a gourmet BBQ lunch of Cape Grim beef at Warra Landing. This more modern boat features an upper-level deck for 360-degree views. Another option to explore the river is to canoe upstream to a picnic spot or waterfall (or even a two- or four-day self-guided paddle down the river), with canoes available to rent at **Arthur River Canoe & Boat Hire**. It also hires out motorised dinghies.

An Arch in the Forest

Swap trees for a vivid sinkhole

The sinkhole known as **Trowutta Arch** is passed along the Tarkine Drive (p260), but it's also just a short skip out of Smithton (well, a 30-minute drive) and well worth a visit in its own right. Set outside the tiny town of Trowutta, the arch is reached along a 1km return track, beginning off Gun Rd. The walk is through a lush patch of rainforest to the fern-guarded arch. Set within is the sinkhole – a collapsed cave – filled with water that's almost unearthly green in colour.

TAKAYNA TRAIL

Since 2014, Takayna/Tarkine has been the setting for the annual **Takayna Trail** *(bobbrown.org.au/event/takayna-trai)* ultramarathon. Run each February by the Bob Brown Foundation, an environmental activist body, the event features three courses – 22km, 37km and 62km – running through rainforest and across buttongrass plains on challenging and sometimes steep terrain. The event aims to bring awareness to the threats to this mighty forest (mostly mining) and raise money for the fight to protect it. Places fill up fast – in 2025, there were 167 runners across the three courses – and even if you don't want to run, you can volunteer to work at the event, which is a good chance to see the forest from a different perspective. Register through the website.

Corinna

RIVER CRUISING | WALKING | GOLDEN HISTORY

As a former gold-mining town inside the rainforest of Takayna/Tarkine, Corinna is the green and gold of Australia made literal. In the late 1800s, when it was at its mining peak, Corinna had two hotels, a post office and a population of 2500. Now it's a tranquil place with only one business, Corinna Wilderness Village, providing accommodation in cottages and camp sites, pub/restaurant meals and rainforest-encased cruises down the Pieman River to one of Australia's wildest beaches. Switch off your phone – there's no mobile service or wi-fi – and focus on kayaking atop the tannin-coloured river, or embarking on walks through the rainforest. Getting here is quite the experience, involving a sometimes bone-shaking journey on unsealed roads and a river crossing on a two-vehicle barge from yesteryear, but one of Tassie's finest wilderness destinations is an Aussie classic. It's like an outback in green.

GETTING AROUND

There are three routes to Corinna: down the Western Explorer Road (C249) from Smithton, via 80km of unsealed roads; southwest from Waratah along the C247, with the last 26km unsealed; and north from Zeehan. The latter is best for rental cars (but check your insurance). It includes crossing the Pieman River on the **Fatman Vehicle Barge** *(per vehicle $30)* right before Corinna. The barge runs 9am to 7pm in summer, and to 5pm in winter.

Corinna's Rainforest Rambles

Riverside hikes through history and nature

Corinna *(corinna.com.au)* is the trailhead for some fabulous walks, ranging from short riverside strolls to an elevated mountain view.

Beginning in the village, the **Whyte River Track** is a one-hour loop that sets out through undulating rainforest before following the Whyte River to its confluence with the Pieman River. Birds, wallabies and pademelons are often seen, and platypuses may be sighted around dawn and dusk. Featuring beautiful reflections, the river is also a good spot for photography.

One of Tasmania's 60 Great Short Walks, the **Huon Pine Walk** (20 minutes return) begins at the Corinna car park and follows the shaded banks of the tannin-laced Pieman River through an open section of moss-covered rainforest. Signs along the accessible boardwalk identify various rainforest tree species, but the star tree is at its end: an ancient Huon pine, angling out over the river.

☑ TOP TIP

Corinna's Tannin restaurant is open for lunch and dinner, September to May, so bring breakfast supplies with you. Accommodation includes self-contained kitchenettes or on-site BBQs.

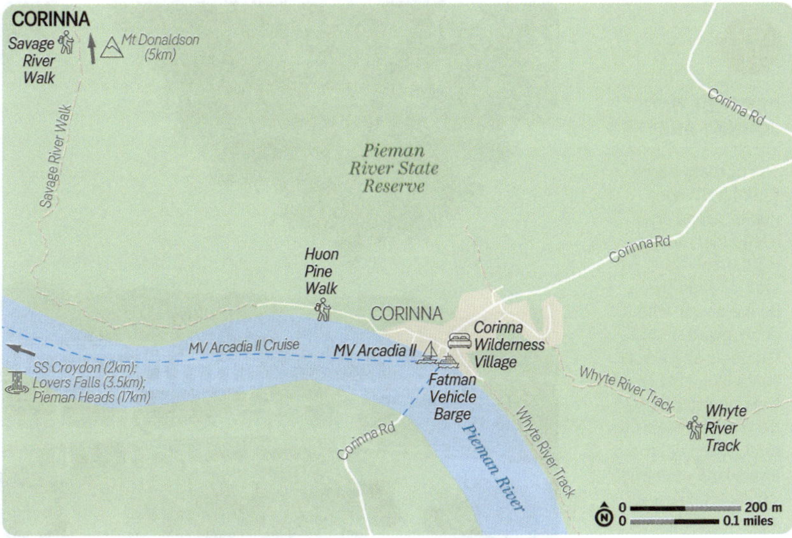

From the end of the Huon Pine boardwalk, the **Savage River Walk** continues along the bank, beginning a 3km (one way) journey through a lovely stretch of rainforest. Gnarled myrtle beeches are a highlight of the climb over Ahrberg Hill, before the trail descends to a pontoon beside the wreck of the **SS Croydon**. Parts of the largely intact wreck still rise above the river surface. A return hike from Corinna takes around three hours.

Away from the rivers, starting around 9km north of Corinna, another recommended walk (8km return) ascends 438m **Mt Donaldson**, with brilliant views of the rainforest, Southern Ocean and south as far as Mt Murchison.

Cruising & Paddling the Pieman River

Waterways to falls, ocean and a shipwreck

Wilderness cruises to **Pieman Heads** are on the **MV Arcadia II** *(corinna.com.au/river-cruises; adult/child $132/69),* the only Huon-pine-built river cruiser still operating in the world.

Departing Corinna around 10am, often on a river shrugging off morning mist, the boat takes around 1½ hours to reach Pieman Heads. It's a journey on dark, mirror-flat waters that's infused with commentary from knowledgeable skippers. The Pieman's history of 'mining and pining' is covered, along with local legends such as river ferryman Johnny Ahrberg (p266). At the heads, it's an easy walk past a sprinkling of fishing shacks to the wild and windswept ocean beach, covered in logs and buffeted by the Southern Ocean and the winds of the Roaring Forties. After 1½ hours at Pieman Heads (an opportunity to eat your supplied lunch), the boat departs around 1pm to cruise back to Corinna village by 2.30pm.

REMEMBERING JOHNNY AHRBERG

The Ahrberg Bar at Corinna's Tarkine Pub is named after a legendary former resident of the area, a tough-living Scandinavian who once rowed single-handedly all the way south along the coast to Strahan (and back). Born in Stockholm in 1859, Johnny Ahrberg arrived in Corinna as a miner in 1896 after more than 20 years working on boats around the world. After the gold rush petered out in 1899, he decided to stay in the remote area he'd grown to love, and was the ferryman at remote Pieman Heads – and the settlement's sole occupant – until his death in 1937. The wide bay on the southern side of Pieman Heads is now known as Ahrberg Bay, and Ahrberg Hill is crossed on the Savage River Walk (p265).

POSNOV/GETTY IMAGES

Pieman River ferries (p265)

A second cruise option is on the *Sweetwater,* a smaller eight-person craft that heads to Savage River and the wreck of the SS *Croydon* (p265). The one-hour **cruise** *(adult/child $69/32)* also visits **Lovers Falls**. Some guests choose to walk back to Corinna from the pontoon at Savage River along the Savage River Walk (p265). This cruise typically departs at 3pm, after the return of the MV *Arcadia II,* but dates and times change, so check Corinna's website for departures.

Corinna Wilderness Village also has a collection of around a dozen sit-on-top kayaks, which can be hired (half-/full day $50/75) to paddle downstream to Lovers Falls and the SS *Croydon,* or upstream and into Whyte River. Book kayaks online – follow the 'Unique Experiences' link on Corinna's website – or at reception on arrival.

Strahan

RIVER CRUISES | WILD BEACH | HUON PINE

Wonderfully remote and tucked behind Tasmania's longest (and arguably wildest) beach, Strahan is based on Macquarie Harbour, a huge body of water six times the size of Sydney Harbour. It's an excellent place to overnight and hear heritage tales of the hardworking miners and piners who forged a tough and resilient living in this rugged area.

Superb Macquarie Harbour boat trips, featuring plenty of historic and natural insight, venture through the World Heritage–listed rainforest that blankets the Gordon River, while attractions in town after a day on the water include a historic Huon pine sawmill and a thoroughly entertaining theatrical institution relating a rousing convict tale. Most travellers come to Strahan for the boat cruise, but you can also experience the wave-beaten stripe of Ocean Beach and the sandy expanses of the soaring Henty Dunes, along with the rainforest-wrapped beauty of Hogarth Falls in this isolated slice of Tasmania's west coast.

GETTING AROUND

Strahan can be reached from Cradle Mountain via Tullah and Zeehan, or on the Lyell Hwy from Hobart and Derwent Bridge via Queenstown. By bus, Kinetic's west-coast service links Strahan to Queenstown and Burnie. Strahan itself is small and walkable, though you'll need a vehicle to head out to the likes of Ocean Beach and Henty Dunes. Bikes can be hired from the Strahan Village hotel.

Cruising from Strahan

Macquarie Harbour and Gordon River adventures

Early each morning Strahan's harbourside is thronged with visitors boarding ships bound for Macquarie Harbour and the Gordon River. The dense rainforest lining the river and the perfection of its reflections make it an unforgettable experience.

Two companies, **Gordon River Cruises** *(gordonrivercruises.com.au; cruises from adult/child $155/75)*, operating *Spirit of the Wild* (aka the Grey Boat), and **World Heritage Cruises** *(worldheritagecruises.com.au; cruises from adult/child $155/70)*, operating the *Harbour Master II* (aka the Red Boat), offer similar itineraries. Both feature options from comfortable seating in spacious downstairs cabins through to fully catered premier experiences on the upper decks. There's plenty of scope for viewing from outdoor decks, and both companies include lunch on the six-hour tours.

TOP TIP

It rains in Strahan, on average, about one in every two days (you can't have all that rainforest without some rain...), so be sure to pack decent wet-weather gear.

HIGHLIGHTS
1 Gordon River Cruises

SIGHTS
2 Morrison's Huon Pine Sawmill
3 West Strahan Beach

ACTIVITIES
4 World Heritage Cruises

SLEEPING
5 Crays
6 Risby Cove
7 Strahan Village
8 Wheelhouse Apartments

EATING
9 Charlotte's at Franklin Manor
10 Coffee Shack
see 6 Risby Cove
see 7 View 42°

ENTERTAINMENT
11 The Ship That Never Was

SHOPPING
see 2 Huon Pine Shop & Gallery

Both cruises cross vast Macquarie Harbour, passing modern salmon farms and historic features such as the 3km-long 'training wall', an 1890s engineering marvel built to maintain the depth of the main channel. Conditions permitting, the boats push through Hells Gates at Macquarie Heads, marked by the Entrance Island lighthouse, and an improbably narrow meeting of the harbour and the Southern Ocean. Tours then head south across the harbour to squeeze into the tannin-darkened Gordon River. A stop at Heritage Landing includes a fully accessible boardwalk into a clearing created when a 2000-year-old Huon pine fell. The final stop is **Sarah Island**, where entertaining guided tours tell the story of the first and most notorious penal colony in Van Diemen's Land.

An alternative to the big boats is a trip aboard the *Stormbreaker,* a 20m ketch operated by **Southwest Expeditions** *(southwestexpeditions.com.au; from adult/child $440/220).* These sailings include an overnight stay aboard the boat on the upper Gordon River, where the *Stormbreaker* picks up rafters at the end of Franklin River trips.

ALL ABOARD

Along with Queenstown, Strahan is a terminus station for the **West Coast Wilderness Railway** (p271). Strahan departures follow the King River to the once-bustling, now-gone port town of Teepookana.

Escape from Sarah Island

Watch Australia's longest-running play

Back in Strahan, continue the convict theme at **The Ship That Never Was** *(roundearth.com.au; adult/child $30/5),* an entertaining 1¼-hour, two-actor performance telling the picaresque tale of a group of convicts who escaped from Sarah Island in 1834 by hijacking a ship they were building. Premiering in 1994, it's the longest-running play in Australia. Nightly performances begin at 5.30pm from September to

Ocean Beach

May. Book ahead by calling 0476 651 089, or email ship@roundearth.com.au.

Nature's Way

From waves to waterfalls

Running in a wave-pounded strip to Strahan's west, **Ocean Beach** is Tasmania's longest beach (40km), stretching uninterrupted from Trial Harbour in the north to Macquarie Heads in the south. It's an evocative place to watch the sun dip into the sea. From Ocean Beach Rd, 6km from town, the **Ocean Beach Trail** is a rail-trail-like shared-use path (4km return) through the coastal bush to a wild stretch of Ocean Beach. Drive on to Macquarie Heads, 14km from town, and you can walk as far along Ocean Beach as you wish. Note that the waves at Ocean Beach are treacherous and swimming isn't recommended. Near town, **West Strahan Beach**, beside the caravan park, has a gently shelving sandy bottom and is a safe swimming beach. Don't be discouraged by the water colour – it's tinted with natural tannin.

Around 14km north of Strahan are the **Henty Dunes**, rising up to 30m off Ocean Beach. From the picnic area, it's a steep, loose climb onto the dunes, which are slowly consuming trees

WHY I LOVE STRAHAN

Andrew Bain, Lonely Planet writer

The editor of a Chicago newspaper travel section once proclaimed Strahan as the best little town in the world. Though decades have passed since that lofty (and, yes, hyperbolic) claim, Strahan itself has changed little, so perhaps it holds. I love that from Strahan it takes little time to hit the sands of Ocean Beach, Tasmania's longest and arguably wildest beach, where, just offshore, the world's largest wave (20m!) was recorded; that the green silence of Takayna/Tarkine is so near; that the West Coast Range beckons my boots; and that the perfect reflections of the Gordon River and, even more intoxicatingly, the furious rapids of the Franklin River, are within easy water reach.

EATING IN STRAHAN: OUR PICKS

Coffee Shack: Strahan's best coffee, home-style baking and toasties in a tin shack opposite the cruise-boat terminal. *6am-2pm* $

Risby Cove: Book ahead for calming harbour views and a short menu reliably featuring local fish, beef and house-made gnocchi. *5.30pm-late* $$$

Charlotte's at Franklin Manor: Fine French dining in one of Strahan's historic guesthouses. A five-course set menu, plus a wine tasting room to extend the evening. *5.30-11pm Tue-Sat* $$$

View 42°: Harbour views and an evening buffet, including a Tasmanian salmon platter and an artisanal meat board. *7-9am & 6-8.30pm* $$$

TASMANIA'S FAMOUS TIMBER

No tree is more emblematic of Tasmania than the shaggy Huon pine. One of the planet's slowest-growing and longest-living trees, a Huon pine can take 2000 years to reach 30m in height, and can live to 3000 years. Prized for its rich, golden hue and rot-resistant oils, it was plundered by loggers and shipbuilders in the 19th century. Today, it's illegal to harvest Huon pine – those lovely Huon pine items you see for sale are made from ethically salvaged timber that washes down the rivers – and one 2000-year-old beauty can be viewed during Gordon River cruises. Huon pine was central to the early settlement of the west coast – Sarah Island was selected as the site for a convict station so that convicts could fell Huon pines for shipbuilding.

ANDREW BAIN/LONELY PLANET

Milling demonstration, Morrison's Huon Pine Sawmill

and even the edges of the picnic area. Wander and explore the dunes to your heart's content, with the tops of tall dead trees poking out from their tops. Sandboards can be hired from Gordon River Cruises (p267) in Strahan if you want to scoot down the dunes.

Go from the emptiness of dunes to the energy of waterfalls with a walk to **Hogarth Falls**. The 40-minute return walk follows fern-lined, platypus-inhabited Botanical Creek from People's Park, off the Esplanade opposite Risby Cove. If nothing else, it might be the first time you've hiked a boardwalk covered in artificial grass.

Sawmilling & Souvenirs

A world of Huon pine

Each afternoon on the return of the Red Boat from the Gordon River (typically 3pm), **Morrison's Huon Pine Sawmill** *(morrisonshuonpine.com.au)*, on Strahan's wharf, offers free milling demonstrations. The sawmill has been operating on this spot since the 1940s, when it relocated from the King River, and is still run by the Morrison family. Alongside the mill is the **Huon Pine Shop & Gallery**, which sells everything from bags of Huon pine woodchips to work-of-art tables costings tens of thousands of dollars.

Queenstown

HISTORIC RAILWAY | MOUNTAIN BIKING | ART

There's a haunting beauty to Tasmania's starkest mining town. Once devoid of trees, with a moonscape of bare hills where rainforest once proliferated, its landscape remains a patchwork of mineral colours, even as the trees have started to return in recent decades. Copper was discovered here in the 1890s, and mining quickly poisoned the land and the rivers. Unexpectedly, the town has always had a hard edge – its gravel-topped football oval is a case in point – but it's a likeable grittiness, and you'll meet a few of Tassie's friendliest locals.

Queenstown's economy was hit hard by the closure of the Mt Lyell Copper Mine in 2014, with a feasibility study into its potential reopening ongoing at the time of writing. Meanwhile, Queenstown continues to reinvent itself as a travellers' destination. Art has come to the fore, headlined by the biennial Unconformity arts festival, alongside a network of mountain bike trails that course down the slopes of Mt Owen, which looms over the town.

GETTING AROUND

Kinetic's west-coast bus connects Queenstown to Strahan and Burnie, with stops in Zeehan and Rosebery, while a service to Hobart runs on Tuesdays and Fridays. Central Queenstown is compact and walkable, but to reach anything beyond, such as Iron Blow Lookout and Nelson Falls, you'll need your own vehicle.

Rails & Rainforest

Ride the West Coast Wilderness Railway

When the **West Coast Wilderness Railway** *(wcwr.com.au)* was built in 1896, the steam train and its tortuous route through remote country was a marvel of engineering. It clings to the steep-sided gorge of the King River, passing through dense rainforest across 40 bridges and on gradients that little other rolling stock could handle. The railway was the lifeblood of Queenstown's Mt Lyell Mining & Railway Co, connecting it to the bustling (and now gone) King River port of Teepookana, and also with Strahan. The original railway closed in 1963, but began operating as a tourist service in 2002, transporting visitors in heritage wood-lined carriages.

Routes offered on the railway change according to such matters as track maintenance work, but at the time of writing, two trips were departing from the 1890s train station in

TOP TIP

One of Queenstown's finest historic treasures is hidden behind doors. Step into the grandiose Empire Hotel (p273) to view its blackwood staircase – in 1904 the timber was sent from Tasmania to Britain, where it was crafted into this staircase, which is now National Trust–listed.

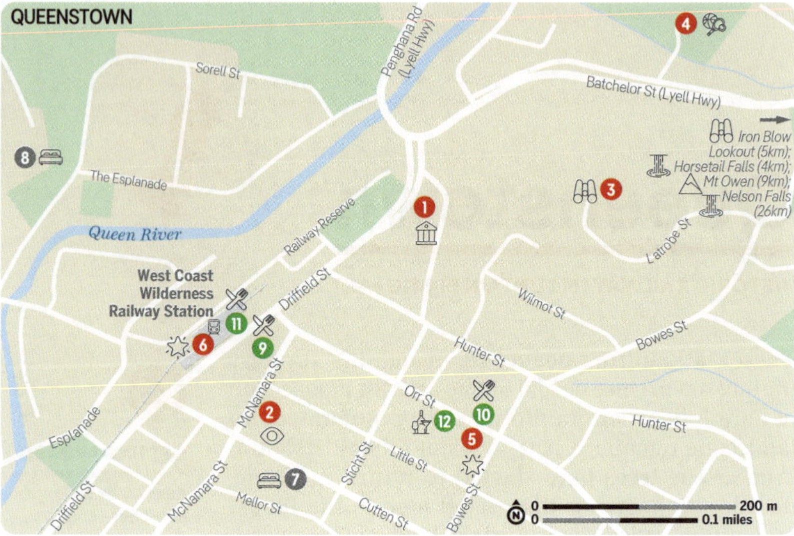

SIGHTS	ACTIVITIES	SLEEPING	
1 Galley Museum	see 2 RoamWild	7 Mt Lyell Anchorage	10 Orange Pete's
2 Paragon Theatre	5 West Coast Ride	8 Penghana	11 Tracks Cafe
3 Spion Kop Lookout	6 West Coast Wilderness Railway	**EATING**	**DRINKING & NIGHTLIFE**
4 The Gravel		9 Empire Hotel	12 Moonscape

Queenstown. The 1½-hour **Lynchford Express** *(adult/child from $50/30)* travels from Queenstown to Lynchford, a former gold-mining town. Disembarking at Lynchford, you can try panning for gold or take a peek at the Lynchford Museum before the return to Queenstown. **Rinadeena, Rack & Rainforest** *(Heritage/Wilderness carriage from $95/130)* is a three-hour rail trip continuing past Lynchford to Rinadeena, making the steep 3km climb on a rack-and-pinion line to Rinadeena Saddle. Its premium Wilderness carriages have a balcony and passengers get a glass of sparkling wine or orange juice along with canapés and a light meal.

Mines & Mountains

Tours around Queenstown

Based out of the Paragon Theatre (p274), **RoamWild** *(roamwild.com.au)* runs a range of immersive tours. Among others, the three-hour Lost Mines tour is a deep look into Queenstown's mining surrounds, allowing you to pan for gold, visit the Mt Jukes mine and even try your hand at rock chip sampling. A 4WD tour onto Mt Owen heads high above Queenstown for views as far as Frenchmans Cap and the peaks of Cradle Mountain-Lake St Clair National Park, while the No Dams tour visits important sites from the epochal Franklin River blockade of the early 1980s.

Unforgettable Scenery Forged by History

Witness the impacts of mining

Queenstown's history is best explored at an excellent local museum and at elevated viewing locations in the stark mountains around town. The **Galley Museum** *(adult/concession $10/5)* is a warren of rooms telling the story of the region's eventful history, from the 14 pubs that once graced its streets (the museum building was one of them) to the 1912 mine disaster that killed 42 men. Nearby, **Spion Kop Lookout** looks out over the town and its ring of mountains, though the view is dominated by the bare circle of Queenstown's unique football oval (p274).

Atop Gormanston Hill (on the eastern outskirts of town, just before the Lyell Hwy follows tight hairpin bends down into Queenstown), a side road leads to a spectacular lookout over the **Iron Blow**. This decommissioned open-cut mine, where Queenstown's mining career first began, is now filled with emerald water. Get an eagle's-eye view from the vertiginous walkway projecting out over the mine pit.

The Biking Revolution

Mountain biking on Mt Owen

Amid Queenstown's rugged landscapes, mountain biking is growing in popularity, and the focus here – in contrast to forested trails elsewhere in Tasmania – are mountain tracks coursing along and down the exposed ridges and slopes of **Mt Owen** *(mtb.westcoasttas.com.au)*. More than 35km of trails include beginner-friendly loops and challenging, plunging descents. As a general rule, the easiest trails are on the lower half of the mountain, while the blacks and blues – the more difficult trails – are high up and require shuttles (from $85), which are operated by RoamWild. Bike hire can be arranged through **West Coast Ride** in the main street.

A Pair of Powerful Waterfalls

Walk to Horsetail and Nelson falls

Pouring in a wispy pattern that gives the waterfall its name, **Horsetail Falls** form a spectacular backdrop to Queenstown, at least immediately after rain. The 50m-high falls on the slopes of Mt Owen are seasonal (though it rains a lot here so seasonal can be a daily thing). After rain, they pour fast and fleetingly, draining a small catchment. From the Gormanston

THE UNCONFORMITY

Beyond its mining-inspired grittiness and railway adventures, Queenstown has an active and involved arts scene. Innovation and creativity come to the fore at **The Unconformity** *(theunconformity.com.au)*, an edgy biennial arts festival partially inspired by the maverick style of Hobart's Dark Mofo. The festival is named after a geological feature, the Haulage Unconformity on nearby Mt Lyell, and since its first incarnation as the Queenstown Heritage and Arts Festival in 2010, the event has instigated a creative reawakening on the west coast. There's a good chance your multi-tasking, mountain-biking shuttle driver could also be an artist inspired by the history and hardscrabble landscapes of the region. Music, theatre and the visual arts all coexist when the festival is held in October on even-numbered years.

EATING & DRINKING IN QUEENSTOWN: OUR PICKS

Moonscape: Wine bar and cafe with a sunny beer garden. Burrata and flatbread pizzas team with craft beers. *3-8.30pm Wed & Thu*

Tracks Cafe: Coffee and breakfast before a railway adventure, or one of its own Mt Lyell Mongrel lagers afterwards. *7.30am-8pm Mon-Sat, 8am-3.30pm Sun* $$

Orange Pete's: Step into the very orange world (orange recliners, orange rusted walls) of the orange-suited Pete for a warm welcome, toastie and coffee. *5.30am-3.30pm* $

Empire Hotel: Hearty pub standards in the hotel dubbed the 'grand old lady of the west coast'. *noon-2pm & 6-8pm* $$

THE GRAVEL

They breed 'em tough out here. So tough, in fact, that Queenstown's historic football oval is known as 'the Gravel'. When laid out in 1880, the oval was covered in gravel to withstand the area's heavy rain. Pollution from the mine also made it difficult for grass to take hold. In 1969 the surface was changed to (slightly) less abrasive silica from the nearby Mt Lyell Copper Mine, but it remains a challenging place to play. Cuts, scrapes and lost skin are all but guaranteed for players. It's the home ground of the Queenstown Crows, playing in West Coast Tasmania's Darwin Football Association. A good time to catch a match here is during the Unconformity festival (p273).

JAX10289/SHUTTERSTOCK

Paragon Theatre

Hill crest, opposite the turning to the Iron Blow (p273), the one-hour return walking track heads along a boardwalk clipped to the slopes and then onto a well-formed path to a lookout platform that seemingly hangs over the waterfall. There are good views down onto Queenstown and out to the town's plateau airstrip.

A further 22km east from the Horsetail Falls car park, past Lake Burbury, 35m-high **Nelson Falls** are reached on an easy 20-minute return walk on a well-graded track through dense rainforest. Through winter and after rain, these falls fan out wide, covering the lookout platform in spray as the river hurries on through the moss-covered valley.

For a more sombre look at nature, spare a few minutes to take a look at the **Queen River** as it flows through Queenstown. Known to some locals as the Pumpkin Soup River, it flows orange through town, a legacy of the mining and mineral days. A good viewing point is along Esplanade, south of the town centre.

Tour the Paragon Theatre

A relic of Queenstown's glory days

Queenstown's Art Deco **Paragon Theatre** *(theparagon.com.au; self-guided tour $7)* was built in 1933 and originally seated 750 theatregoers. Take a self-guided tour through the theatre, ascending into the dress circle and projection room and watching a 15-minute film about the theatre's topsy-turvy history, including a 15-year stint as an indoor cricket centre. At 5pm on weekdays, settle into the leather couches (with knee blankets) for a screening of *Franklin* (2022), a documentary about the environmental battle to save the remote Franklin River from being dammed for a hydroelectric project in the 1980s. Wine, craft beer and snacks are available during screenings.

Beyond Queenstown

Mining relics give way to mountains and Tasmania's tallest waterfall as you journey north from Queenstown.

Places

Zeehan p275
Rosebery p276

If Queenstown had a mining buddy, it was Zeehan, 38km to its north, where the mining boom of the late 19th century was focused on silver. Like so many mining towns, it boomed big, as evidenced by the line of grand buildings along its main street. None is grander than the Gaiety Theatre, where even soprano Nellie Melba was once booked to play. Today, you can step into the theatre (part of a larger museum complex) to watch snippets from the world's first feature film. Continue towards Rosebery – itself still a mining town – and you can turn silver into green by hiking or cycling to the highest waterfall in Tasmania, its flows fed by the west coast's abundant rainfall.

Zeehan

TIME FROM QUEENSTOWN: **40MIN**

Silver sights

Once a self-proclaimed 'Silver City' of 27 pubs and 10,000 people, Zeehan (population now 720) is anchored by the **West Coast Heritage Centre** *(wchczeehan.com.au; adult/concession $25/20)*, housed in the 1894 School of Mines & Metallurgy and a showcase of the town's silver-flecked glory days. Highlights include a vast collection of minerals, the chance to burrow beneath the buildings in an underground mine simulation, and stepping into the **Gaiety Theatre**. At the time of its construction in 1898, the theatre was the grandest building on the west coast and one of Australia's finest theatres. Banjo Paterson read his poems here, and Nellie Melba was booked to perform, though it's believed she took ill and didn't make it. Sit in the theatre's old seats and watch the surviving remnants of one of two B&W silent movies: either *Jewelled Nights* (1926) or *The Story of the Kelly Gang* (1907), which was the world's first feature film.

At one time there were around 380 silver-mining leases around Zeehan, including the Silver Spray Mine, where the 100m-long **Spray Tunnel** was built to operate a tramway from the mine. The tunnel is 3km out of town, along Fowler Rd, past the golf course, and is unusual in that it's shaped a little like a keyhole: wider around its top to allow round, 10-tonne steam boilers to pass through. It's also home to glowworms. The narrow road to the tunnel isn't suitable for caravans or trailers.

GETTING AROUND

Kinetic's daily west-coast bus service between Queenstown and Burnie stops in Zeehan and Rosebery, but if you want to get out of town to Montezuma Falls, Mt Murchison or the Spray Tunnel, you'll need you own wheels.

TASMANIA'S NEXT BIG WALK?

On the heels of the success of the Three Capes Track (p94) on the Tasman Peninsula, Tasmania's next 'iconic walk' project is squarely fixed on the Tyndall Range, a line of mountains reaching to almost 1200m between Queenstown and Rosebery. Proposed to be a three-day, 28km hut-based hike, the trail will run north-south from Lake Plimsoll to the old Lake Margaret Power Station. The two huts along the route are expected to replicate their plush cousins on the Three Capes Track (rather than the more basic Overland Track-style huts). Critics of the proposal note that the wetter, colder, more uncomfortable hiking conditions on the west coast might deter many hikers. The track is slated to open in 2029.

STEVE TODD/SHUTTERSTOCK

Montezuma Falls trail, Rosebery

Rosebery

TIME FROM QUEENSTOWN: **50MIN**

Hike to Tasmania's highest waterfall

The base-metal mining town of Rosebery is more fondly known for its proximity to Tasmania's tallest waterfall, 104m-high **Montezuma Falls**. To see the waterfall, drive 2km south-west out of Rosebery and turn off to Williamsford, another abandoned mining town. The easy three-hour, 11km return walk follows the course of an old forest tramway to the falls. It can also be cycled on a mountain or gravel bike. Venture onto the swing bridge for views of the falls and a forested chasm.

Around 17km southeast of Rosebery, off Anthony Rd, one of Tasmania's most rewarding mountain trails ascends to the summit of the highest peak in the West Coast Range, 1278m **Mt Murchison**. It's a 6km return walk but it shouldn't be underestimated – this is a challenging climb, but it's rewarded with views over Rosebery and nearby Tullah and into the craggy lake-filled innards of the mountain.

EATING IN ZEEHAN: OUR PICKS

Pitstop Cafe: Terrific diner-style cafe, appended by a vintage motorbike workshop, making it a favourite with touring motorcyclists. *9.30am-1.30pm Thu & Fri, to 12.30pm Sun* $

Big Z Cafe & Restaurant: Opened in late 2025 with simple offerings of toasties, burgers and spring rolls. *8am-2pm Tue-Fri & Sun, to 2.30pm Sat* $$

Carol's on Wheels: Food truck serving homemade pies and egg and bacon rolls from among the outdoor locomotives of the Heritage Centre. *7.30am-5pm Mon-Fri* $

Heemskirk Motor Hotel: Straight-up pub grub – parmi, steak burger, roast of the day – at this large pub on Zeehan's outer edge. *noon-10pm Mon-Sat, to 8pm Sun* $$

Places We Love to Stay

$ Budget $$ Midrange $$$ Top End

Stanley

MAP p255

Stanley Seaview Inn $$ Spotless motel rooms and self-contained units – some with views of The Nut – combine with kids' playgrounds, a barbecue area and a bar. Around 2km from central Stanley.

Inlet $$$ Four luxury beach houses with avian titles – Sea Eagle, Pelican, Oystercatcher, Sandpiper – atop the sand dunes of a cattle farm 5km from Stanley. They're ideal for couples and their seclusion all but guarantees a private beach.

Ark $$$ Five luxurious suites feature at this luxury B&B, the relaxing 21st-century incarnation of one of Stanley's most historic buildings. Owners Christer and Rhonda are a mine of local information.

Ship Inn $$$ It's all style and suaveness in this wonderfully restored historic property, formerly the Bayview Hotel, with a seamlessly curated blend of heritage and modernity.

Horizon Deluxe Apartments $$$ You can just about sightsee from the chandelier-lit spa bathtubs at this small collection of luxurious self-contained apartments with the best Nut views in town. Around 2km from central Stanley. Check-in is at the Stanley Seaview Inn.

Smithton

MAP p259

Tall Timbers $$ Set in 8 hectares of landscaped bushland, facilities for the 60-plus wooden cabins include a restaurant, tennis courts and a swimming pool. The lakeside apartments have a bit of extra pizzazz.

Platypus Waters $$ At Smithton's southern edge, this modern, self-contained B&B unit has rural views of Duck River, where, despite the name, you're just as likely to spot Jeremy, the resident platypus.

Arthur River

Arthur River Beach House $$ This absolute waterfront property, looking out onto the Edge of the World, has three bedrooms and a fully equipped kitchen and laundry.

Arthur River Spa Cottage $$ Right on the river's edge, this newly refurbished beach house sleeps up to 10 people. In good weather you'll spend most of your time on the expansive river-facing deck with potbelly fireplace.

Corinna

MAP p265

Corinna Wilderness Village $$$ These off-grid timber cottages – once the homes of gold miners – are nestled deep into the Takayna/Tarkine rainforest on the banks of the Pieman River. Strung along the riverbank, commanding the best real estate, are 10 unpowered camp sites.

Strahan

MAP p268

Crays $$ Central yet secluded, these five large cottages share an on-site BBQ shelter and guest laundry.

Risby Cove $$$ Luxury suites and waterfront corrugated-iron cottages – any more Harbourside and they'd be afloat – inspired in design by beach sheds.

Wheelhouse Apartments $$$ Perched above Strahan, this brace of high-end town houses has wraparound windows framing superb views over Macquarie Harbour.

Bushy Summers $$$ One of several luxury (and luxuriously isolated) former mine workers' holiday shacks in waterfront Lettes Bay, 6km south of Strahan.

Queenstown

MAP p272

Mt Lyell Anchorage $$ This 1890s two-bedroom weatherboard home, and the neighbouring two-bedroom cottage, have been transformed into stylish guesthouses steps from the major Queenstown sights. Heated towel racks are just the tonic after a wet west-coast day.

Penghana $$$ Built in 1898 as the mine manager's residence, this National Trust–owned mansion commands the loftiest and most luxurious position in town. Guests can enjoy two sitting rooms, a shared kitchenette and a wine bar.

Zeehan

Zeehan Bush Camp $$ Glamping-style bell tents (November to April, with shared amenities) and self-contained cabins (year-round) at this leafy spot tucked away behind town.

TOOLKIT

The chapters in this section cover the most important topics you'll need to know about in Tasmania. They're full of nuts-and-bolts information and valuable insights to help you understand and navigate Tasmania and get the most out of your trip.

Mt Oakleigh from the Overland Track (p244)

RYAN HOI/SHUTTERSTOCK

Arriving

Daily flights connect most Australian capitals to Hobart and Launceston, often via Sydney or Melbourne, the latter of which also services regional airports including Devonport and Burnie/Wynyard. The only international connection is a twice-weekly flight from Auckland to Hobart (October to March). The *Spirit of Tasmania* vehicle ferries sail nightly between Devonport and Geelong, Victoria, in both directions, with extra day sailings in summer.

Head for the Exit

Hobart Airport remains a work in progress. Head for the back wall, turn right through the automatic doors, then traverse the vast check-in hall to the luggage carousels at the far end.

Visa/Customs

If arriving internationally, everyone other than Australian and New Zealand citizens requires a visa prior to travelling. Standard Australian customs and quarantine declarations apply on arrival, with some biosecurity caveats particular to Tasmania.

Money

There are no money exchange agencies in Tasmanian airports, though cards are accepted by all businesses and there are ATMs inside and outside security at Hobart and Launceston.

Bike Stations

Both Hobart and Launceston airports have bike stations with tools and pumps for easy disassembly/reassembly of bicycles. Both Qantas and Virgin airlines sell bike boxes.

Transport from Airport/Terminal to City Centre

	Hobart	Launceston	Devonport (Ferry Terminal)
BUS	$22 25min	$15 20min	n/a
TAXI	$44–55 20min	$35–45 15min	$15–20 8min
RIDE-SHARE	$40–45 20min	$32–42 15min	$12–18 8min

BIOSECURITY

Tasmania has strict biosecurity rules to protect its unique environment. Domestic rules are similar to entering Australia from overseas, but without the formal declaration. Throw out any prohibited food items into the quarantine bins provided. Sniffer dogs are active at all ports of entry. Prohibited items most affecting travellers are honey, seafood (including bait), and fresh fruit and vegetables.

If you're bringing your muddy vehicle over on the *Spirit*, wash it first or you'll be obliged to do so at the port, where your car is also searched. See nre.tas.gov.au/biosecurity-tasmania for the full list of banned items.

Getting Around

Having your own vehicle is the best way to see Tasmania: public transport becomes patchy the further you travel from the cities.

TRAVEL COSTS

Car rental per day
$70

Petrol per litre
$1.70–2

Bike/e-bike rental per day
$40/60

EV charging per kWh
$0.30–0.70

Hobart on Foot

If you're just in Hobart for a weekend you can do without a car: the compact city and waterfront areas are easily navigable on foot (not to mention the lack of affordable all-day parking in the city centre). Bicycles, e-bikes and electric scooters can all be hired easily.

Rental Vehicles

Rental cars and vans are big business in Tasmania. Demand and prices spike higher during summer and holiday periods. Watch out for hidden excesses for hitting wildlife, driving at night and driving on unsealed roads. You can usually return your rental to another airport without a one-way penalty.

TIP

Allow extra time to get from A to B. Roads here are mostly single-lane and winding, and mountainous roads always take longer than you think.

THINGS THAT GO JUMP IN THE NIGHT

Most of Tasmania's many nocturnal marsupials seem to like nothing better than to bounce right in front of your headlights. Avoid driving at night if possible; you'll see enough roadkill during the day to understand why. Most rental-car companies in Tasmania have higher excesses for 'single-car collisions' (ie the big dent from the poor pademelon), and bigger animals like wombats and the larger kangaroos can cause serious damage.

DRIVING ESSENTIALS

Drive on the left.

Distances are in kilometres.

50

Speed limit is 50km/h in urban areas, 100km/h on rural roads, 110km/h on some highways and 80km/h on gravel.

Blood alcohol limit is 0.05%.

There are no toll roads in Tasmania.

Intercity Buses

Kinetic buses connect the Midlands and east-coast towns to both Launceston and Hobart several times daily, extending to Devonport and Burnie. There's a daily service between Strahan and Burnie, but only twice-weekly along the Lyell Hwy to Hobart via Derwent Bridge. There are no buses to Mt Field National Park or anywhere in the southwest.

Bikepacking

Tasmania is an excellent place for that long bicycle tour, with plentiful free camping and manageable distances. There's also the excellent Tasmanian Trail bisecting the island north to south and car-free Maria Island. Just be prepared for plenty of hills and any weather, any time. For bike hire try Roll Cycles, Longhaul Tasmania or Hobart Bike Hire.

Bushwalker Shuttles

Fast and convenient, these companies will deliver you directly to your trailhead or mountain-bike (MTB) park. Stove fuel and gas canisters can be supplied. Shuttles are not cheap, but often they're the only way to get out of Cockle Creek, Scotts Peak Dam or Cynthia Bay. Try twe. travel; prices start at $110.

Money

CURRENCY: AUSTRALIAN DOLLAR ($)

Credit & Debit Cards

Visa and Mastercard are widely accepted by all ATMs and EFTPOS machines, the latter predominantly contactless. You'll struggle with Amex or Diners Club outside of expensive hotels. Beware the hidden 'credit-card surcharge' (around 1%), which has become increasingly prevalent. Some cheaper student restaurants and roadside stalls might only accept cash.

Tipping

Similar to mainland Australia and New Zealand, tipping is not part of Tasmanian culture, though it will be readily accepted if offered. Feel free to ignore the 'add tip' pop-up on the EFTPOS machine when paying a bill; however, when paying cash it's customary to 'round the bill up'.

Splitting the Bill

It's quite common for Australians to ask for a split restaurant bill where a group of people who have shared a meal all wish to pay separately. Some restaurants will boldly proclaim 'no split bills', as it's an inconvenience that becomes exponential the more diners involved.

HOW MUCH FOR...

Launceston to Hobart bus fare
$34

Day/annual national parks pass
$48/102

MONA entry
$39

Seven-day trout-fishing licence
$48

HOW TO... Pay Less on Holiday

Travelling off-peak is an obvious money saver (hot tip: winter isn't off-peak when Dark Mofo is happening). Always ask for a discount – for a family, child, group or senior (60+) – and especially if paying with cash. Contact accommodation directly to make bookings, and ask if it's cheaper to stay an extra night. Look for midweek specials, and do your boozing during happy hours. Embrace camping, self-catering, roadside-stall groceries and fishing, and check out the free *Hobart Magazine* for cheap deals.

ARE PRICES HIGHER HERE THAN ON THE MAINLAND?

Yes. You can find the same item in the same supermarket chain in Hobart and it will be $0.50 higher than in Melbourne. Takeaway meals are more expensive, eating out is more expensive, and fuel is definitely more expensive. The excuse is that everything has to be transported across Bass Strait (which is true for fuel and many items), but even local produce is more expensive (except from roadside stalls). Balance this against lower wages and a dearth of cheap accommodation, and the cost of living is suddenly a very big issue for many Tasmanians.

HOBART FOR FREE

Plenty of Hobart's best features are free to stroll around, including the waterfront, Kunanyi/Mt Wellington, weekend and night markets, beaches, parks, the Botanical Gardens, and cycling and mountain-bike trails.

Accommodation

By the Lake

Many Central Plateau lakes (and those along the Lyell Hwy) have bush camp sites right by the foreshore, some close enough to throw a line in from your tent. Prices are minimal to nonexistent, depending on facilities (or lack of) provided, and those outside conservation areas are pet-friendly. Some councils have maximum stay limits, so don't get too cosy.

By the Beers

Tasmania's heritage pubs are a great budget overnight choice for singles or couples: small town, small prices. Expect serviceable rooms oozing character, shared bathrooms down the hall, hearty meals, roaring fires and plenty of interesting locals happy to spin a yarn and impart their venerable knowledge. Important consideration: is there a band playing tonight?

By the Seashore

Tasmania is an island: the coast is where daily life transpires, and where nightly stays often come with a prime waterfront position. Seaside towns like Strahan, Bicheno, Swansea, Penguin and Stanley all have waterfront digs with lulling waves as you fall asleep, and prime ocean views to wake up to.

By the Trees

Tasmania's Parks & Wildlife Service maintains camp sites in spectacular natural locations, ranging from free (eg Cockle Creek) to minimal fees (Fortescue Bay) – a bargain option for families. Some sites require advance booking, but most are first-come, first-served. PWS also offers accommodation in rustic huts (Mt Field), self-contained cabins (Cradle Mountain) and convict-era buildings (Maria Island).

HOW MUCH FOR A NIGHT IN A...

national park camp site (couple)
$13

four-bed dorm bed in Hobart
$38

B&B (double)
$160

By the Many Hundreds

Tasmania's high-end hotels are a stellar option, offering island individuality and charm rather than cookie-cutter corporate sameness. Often this involves occupying a historic building and inserting bedrooms and restaurants into the historic structure, with spectacular architectural results. Hobart's Tasman and Henry Jones hotels are prime examples.

ISLANDS OFF THE ISLAND

Bruny, King and Flinders Islands all have a selection of unique and quirky self-contained holiday cottages scattered across their heartlands. While some will suit couples, many cottages often sleep between six and 10 people, making them ideal for groups or families. There's usually a minimum stay of three nights, and in all cases you should book well ahead. You'll need to have your own wheels and be ready to do some cooking, but that's all part of the fun. Check out brunyisland.org.au, flindersislandtravel.com.au or kingisland.org.au.

CLOCKWISE FROM TOP LEFT: SHANA ESPINOZA/SHUTTERSTOCK, NDSIGN/SHUTTERSTOCK, KHARKHAN OLEG/SHUTTERSTOCK, HDDIGITAL/SHUTTERSTOCK

Family Travel

Tasmania is a terrific place to bring the family, with its unpretentious vibe and uncrowded cities and wilderness. Distances are short, towns are safe and there's plenty of nature, wildlife, bushwalks, bike rides, beaches and fishing to entice the kids away from the screens. This is your chance to unplug, recharge and reconnect. Just don't expect theme parks.

Hobart for Kids

Sandy Bay's Long Beach (p67) is a top spot for a family picnic. The waves are benign and there's plenty of shady grass, plus a fenced playground, toilets, BBQs and change tables. Drive up Kuynanyi/Mt Wellington (p70) in search of winter snowballs and year-round lunar vibes. Raining? Head to the free Tasmanian Museum & Art Gallery (p52), with displays for every age.

Discounts

Always check for family tickets or at least half-price or child discounts for entry into sites. Parks & Wildlife Service camp sites are either free for kids or offer low family rates, and your Parks Pass can cover a vehicle of up to eight people. Most pubs and middle-tier restaurants offer discounted kids' meals (albeit a limited selection) and transport usually has kids' concessions.

Car Seats

Infants to seven-year-olds must travel in an approved child-restraint car seat in Tasmania. If arriving by air, ensure you ask for one when making your rental car booking (or BYO). The same rule applies to taxis and rideshares.

Change Tables

Many newer public toilet blocks here provide baby-change facilities (including nappy disposal) in non-gendered accessible bathrooms. Look for them next to kids' playgrounds, beaches, car parks and office buildings. Change tables are uncommon in men's bathrooms.

BEST FAMILY ATTRACTIONS

West Coast Wilderness Railway (p271)

Who doesn't love a train ride? Especially through wild West Coast rainforest.

Cataract Gorge (p194)

Chairlifts are always cool: Launceston's Cataract Gorge has a beauty.

Hastings Caves & Thermal Springs (p116)

Southern underground adventures and a naturally heated swimming pool.

Port Arthur Historic Site (p98)

The kids won't leave this place feeling anything but blessed.

Trowunna Wildlife Sanctuary (p227)

Meet some Tasmanian devils at this northwest wildlife park.

FAMILY TRAVEL ON A BUDGET

Embrace camping: if you're not paying much for accommodation, you'll have more money for tours, boat trips and admissions. Many national park camp sites are free; others have a nominal charge.

Get outside in the long summer days, exploring, bushwalking, fishing and beachcombing.

Book a cottage for a whole week, using it as a base. Weekly deals are cheaper and cottages usually cater for families, maybe even with a few wholesome board games for when the weather turns nasty.

Self-cater, taking advantage of roadside stalls, fisher co-ops and bulk wholefood shops.

Health & Safe Travel

SWIMMING

Be very wary of swimming at unpatrolled beaches, even if the waves look benign – and always swim between the flags at patrolled beaches. If you can't swim, don't get in the water! Most Australian kids have swimming lessons from an early age, but every summer foreign tourists drown in Australian waters because they don't recognise the dangers.

Cold Weather

Tasmania's weather is extremely changeable. If you are venturing into the mountains, you need to be prepared for horrible weather, anytime of year. A rule of thumb is you lose 1°C with every 100m gain in altitude. This puts the lookout atop Kunanyi/Mt Wellington at least 12°C colder than downtown Hobart, without taking wind-chill into consideration – which is considerable.

Snakes

Tasmania has three species of snake and they're all venomous. Luckily the antivenom is the same for all three. Look out for tiger snakes (without obvious stripes), lowland copperheads and the smaller white-lipped snakes – though usually only the first two are a problem. Always carry a snake bandage when bushwalking and know how to use it.

SUN SMART

Tasmania's summer UV index reaches extreme levels due to the sun's angle, clear air and reflections. Use SPF50 or SPF50+ sunscreen.

BUSHFIRE DANGER LEVELS

No Rating Minimal risk.	**Moderate** Plan and prepare; most fires can be controlled.	**High** Be ready to act; fires can be dangerous.	**Extreme** Take action now; fires will spread quickly and be extremely dangerous.	**Catastrophic** Leave risk areas immediately or you might not survive.

Healthcare

Tasmania's public healthcare system is strained from years of underfunding, understaffing and the post-pandemic hangover of burnt-out professionals leaving the industry. Ambulance wait times in Hobart are the worst in Australia, to the point that you're better off getting a taxi. This is one state where it pays to have private health cover.

OTHER NASTIES

Leeches Venture into wet buttongrass or rainforest and you'll come across these bloodsuckers. They're not dangerous, just unpleasant, and can be dissuaded by wearing gaiters sprayed with DEET.

Jack Jumpers Not the local basketball team, but the evil ant they're named after. They inflict a painful bite that causes a severe allergic reaction in 3% of people.

CLOCKWISE FROM TOP LEFT: NEW AFRICA/SHUTTERSTOCK, SAVVAPANF PHOTO/SHUTTERSTOCK

Food, Drink & Nightlife

When to Eat

Breakfast (6.30am to 9am) Cereal, or smashed avo (avocado) on toast with fetta and a poached egg. Coffee.

Lunch (noon to 2.30pm) Wraps, pies, sushi or 'lunch specials' – rice or noodles with two or three curries or stir-fries.

Dinner (5.30pm to 8.30pm) Hearty cooked meal in winter; fish or salads in summer. Roast meat of the day on Sundays.

Where to Eat

Pubs Serving everything from basic burgers, parmis, steak and fish and chips to meze plates, seafood chowder, crumbed scallops and kids' meals.

Cafes Early openers for coffee, breakfasts and light lunches. Usually close by 3pm.

Restaurants Proper dining; open for evening meals and lunches on the weekend.

Food trucks Found at markets and, increasingly, at craft brew pubs and outdoor bars.

Small bars It's about the vinyl, the vibe, the cocktails and that delicate thing you're gnawing on.

MENU DECODER

BYO You can bring your own alcohol (sometimes only wine, not beer); you'll pay corkage.

Corkage The financial charge for BYO; can be per person or per bottle.

Curried scallop pie Southern Tasmanian delicacy, with scallops in a white/curry sauce inside pastry. Unbeatable.

Feed-me menu It's degustation baby, just a different name.

Meze, mame zala, tapas Small delectable plates to share.

Parmi or **Parma** Usually a chicken parmigiana; ie a crumbed schnitzel ('schnitty') with tomato, ham and melted cheese on top.

Reef and beef or **Surf and turf** Steak with prawns or scallops on top.

Oyster shooter An oyster in a shot glass of spirit (pictured above). Down it in one.

Seniors meal Kid-sized meal for old timers. Usually fried.

HOW TO... Order Coffee & Breakfast

Cafe waiters will usually ask for your drinks order first (coffee, tea, juice) so you can kick your brain into gear while perusing the menu.

Flat white Australia's most popular coffee style is steamed milk poured over an espresso shot in a 200ml cup.

Latte Similar to the flat white, but served in a glass with more foam in the milk.

Long black Resembling an Americano, it's a double shot of espresso over hot water in a 200ml cup.

English breakfast Not black pudding but black tea, hopefully in a pot, with milk on the side if you need it.

Popular breakfasts:

Egg-and-bacon roll The good stuff inside a roll, bagel, wrap (pictured left) or pide bread.

Pancakes Enjoyed by both kids and grown-ups, with sweet and savoury options.

Full vegetarian Mushroom stack, fried haloumi (cheese), beans, chickpeas and other pan-fried veggie delights.

CLOCKWISE FROM TOP LEFT: LISA TOP/SHUTTERSTOCK, MARK READ/LONELY PLANET, LAREK/SHUTTERSTOCK

HOW MUCH FOR A...

coffee
$5

pint of craft beer
$14

glass of wine
$13

egg-and-bacon roll
$12

pub parmi
$32

fine-dining meal for two (with drinks)
$200

fish and chips for one (takeaway)
$18

HOW TO... Order Craft Beer

If you're new to craft beer, 'paddle' – usually four sma glasses (100–140ml) of beer served c a wooden tray (pictured right), with a sample of the house offerings.

Weiss, weizen, witbier Light-coloured and light-tasting beer made from wheat. 5% alcohol by volume (ABV)

Lager, draught, export Classic no-nonsense, easy-drinking Aussie beer served ice cold. Around 5% ABV

Pale ale Light in colour but not alcohol, pale ales typically are more fruity, hoppy and bitter than lagers. 4–6% ABV

IPA Indian pale ale; extra hops and extra bitterness. 5–6% ABV

XPA Extra pale ale; more an American style with extra hops and extra alcohol. 5–7% ABV

Hazy The current fad; cloudy pale ales with lots of fruit. 5–7% ABV

Session ale Made to drink all afternoon, with a lower alcohol content. Around 3.5% ABV

Red, amber ale Beautiful, copper-coloured full-bodied ale in the English/Irish tradition. 5% ABV

Sour A good sour beer is lip-puckering and dark red in colour, yet can be quite refreshing. 3–5% ABV

Stout Dark, thick and wintry (Guinness is a stout), with overtones of chocolate, burnt caramel or Christmas pudding. Strong stuff. 5–8% ABV

Beer Glasses

Regular Tasmanian beer-glass sizes are the pint (568ml), 10-ounce (285ml) and occasionally schooner (425ml). Specify glass size then beer; eg 'Pint of Harbour Master, thanks mate!'

A NIGHT OUT IN HOBART

Hobart's younger drinkers are 10,000 leagues removed from the rum-addled whalers of the past, but the general intentions remain true: drink a bit, relax a lot, and maybe get lucky and take someone home. Salamanca Place, the waterfront and North Hobart are the main drinking and nocturnal hubs.

Locals will meet after work on a Friday for a couple of wind-down drinks in a raucous bar or pub where office workers, 'tradies' (tradespeople) and students bump elbows. Groups split into smaller shouts (rounds of drinks), so everyone doesn't get hammered too early by the obligation of getting a round. They'll be drinking outside, under the warmth of heaters or around firepits, or in the lingering summer twilight under the ever-watchful gaze of Kunanyi/Mt Wellington.

There'll be a restaurant nearby that's quieter than the pub, or maybe a separate bistro or dining area upstairs, away from the noise. Depending on the restaurant, the size of the group and their current lubrication levels, they might start with a cocktail or switch to sharing a bottle of wine or two. The next decision is whether to order individual meals or a selection of grazing plates to share. When it's time for the bill, everyone pays separately, or the total is divided equally and everyone pays the same.

By now some people will peel off home; others might kick on looking for a small bar to have one last drink before calling it a night.

Responsible Travel

Climate Change & Travel

It's impossible to ignore the impact we have when travelling; Lonely Planet urges all travellers to engage with their travel carbon footprint, which will mainly come from air travel. While there often isn't an alternative, travellers can look to minimise the number of flights they take, opt for newer aircrafts and use cleaner ground transport, such as trains. One proposed solution – purchasing carbon offsets – unfortunately does not cancel out the impact of individual flights. While most destinations will depend on air travel for the foreseeable future, for now, pursuing ground-based travel where possible is the best course of action.

The **UN Carbon Offset Calculator** shows how flying impacts a household's emissions

The **ICAO's carbon emissions calculator** allows visitors to analyse the CO^2 generated by point-to-point journeys

Get It From the Source

Support local farmers and minimise food miles by buying from roadside stalls, local co-ops and farmers markets. BYO bags, reuse containers and gather your organic goodness in bulk from wholefood shops.

Pound the Pavement

Save the car for getting from A to B and use your legs once you get there. Most Tasmanian cities are easily navigable on foot, and you won't need to worry about scorching temperatures or cloying humidity.

On Yer Bike

Get onto two wheels for some exercise, family fun and positive environmental vibes. Tasmania is a great place to ride a bike, be it on the road, cross-country touring, or hell-for-leather downhill shredding.

Recycle Rewards

Generating a few empty bottles and cans in your leisure time? In 2025 Tasmania introduced a recycling refund scheme for eligible empties ($0.10 per item): see recyclerewards.com.au for details and locations.

They may look cute, furry and hungry, but Tasmania's native critters are still wild animals and have not evolved to eat your food – even if they think they want to.

Be like the omnipresent bumper sticker and 'Keep Tassie Wild': volunteer with **Wildcare** *(wildcaretas.org.au)*, a cooperative of local community groups across the island involved in various restorative and sustainable outdoor projects.

DON'T BURN IT

Roaring log fires are tempting when camping, but most of Tasmania's national parks are fuel-stove only. These ecosystems are unique and fragile, having evolved without a fire resilience, unlike their mainland counterparts.

FORAGE FOR BUSH TUCKER

Take one of the excellent Kipli Takara (p78) bush tucker foraging tours at Piyura Kitina/Risdon Cove, where you learn about Tasmanian Aboriginal culture while you're identifying and sampling bush foods.

Minimal Impact

When bushwalking, take out whatever you brought in with you, including all rubbish, and stick to established paths. Get acquainted with the Minimal Impact Code developed by the **Hobart Walking Club** *(hobartwalkingclub.org .au/resources/minimal-impact-code).*

Fish Responsibly

Know where marine reserves are and if fishing season is open. See fishing.tas.gov.au for coastal fish bag limits, and ifs.tas.gov.au for inland angling information, including licences, maps and access information for the Highland Lakes.

Drones are banned in all Tasmanian national parks and conservation reserves.

Launceston Town Hall's Recycle Hub takes batteries, iPhones, bread tags and coffee pods, among other items.

Bottle Your Own Water

There's no reason to buy bottled water in Tasmanian. Tap water is Australia's best, and shops around the island will sell you a reusable water bottle that can be refilled almost anywhere.

Ship or Plane?

Even the most efficient cruise ship emits roughly 500kg of CO_2 per passenger on a 2000km ocean journey (eg Sydney to Hobart return). By air, the same passenger's CO_2 emissions are around 260kg.

RESOURCES

slt.org.au
Sustainability info for making informed decisions in Tasmania.

parks.tas.gov.au
Parks & Wildlife Service camp sites, rules and alerts.

tacinc.com.au
Tasmanian Aboriginal protocols, dual-naming and palawa kani language.

LGBTIQ+ Travellers

In less than 30 years Tasmania has progressed from having some of the most outmoded anti-homosexual laws in the Western world to the most progressive and anti-discriminatory. Gay, transgender and nonbinary rights are now enshrined in law, and Tasmania leads other Australian states in protecting the rights of intersex people. However, attitudes can still be stuck in the past when you get further away from the cities.

Taspride

Tasmania's premier rainbow celebration is held in its biggest city over the February long weekend. The annual Pride March departs North Hobart bound for Franklin Sq, where the Party in the Park takes over. Other regular events include a river cruise, art exhibitions, fireworks, a handbag throw, a cake-baking competition, the Queer History Walk and picnics around town. Local businesses and Hobart City Council get behind the events, with rainbows popping up everywhere. Spin-off events often take place nearby in the Huon Valley and New Norfolk. See taspride.com.

QUEER SPORTS

Both Hobart and Launceston have member clubs in the Queer Sporting Alliance, which promotes inclusiveness in community basketball, netball and other sports. No experience (or even sporting ability) is required, and anyone too good is given a 'rainbow card' to limit their scoring. Games are often accompanied by queer DJs and raucous cheering. Fun! See queersportingalliance.com.

Queer History Walk

Coinciding with Hobart's Taspride festival, this thought-provoking walk led by gay rights activist Rodney Croombe and transgender campaigner Martine Delaney visits historically significant sites around Salamanca and the waterfront, revealing the city's rich queer history from convict times to the present. Croombe, a trained historian, was at the forefront of the gay rights protests at Salamanca Markets in 1988. See taspride .com/headline-events.

A TWIST OF LEMONS

This relaxed social group offering a safe place for queer women (18+), diversity and allies meets on the last Friday of every month at North Hobart's Room for a Pony (p78). Singles and couples all welcome; predilection for cocktails useful but not mandatory *(facebook.com/atwistoflemons)*.

DIVERSITY, NORTH & SOUTH

Diversity Launceston Originally an inclusive Facebook page for LGBTIQ+ Launceston, now a de-facto queer news group for the rest of the island. **Far South Pride** Located in Geeveston. **North West Pride** Centred on Burnie. **Bag of Quilting** Role-playing board-game group meeting monthly in the Huon Valley. **Friendz** LGBTIQ+ social group meeting weekly around the Huon Valley and Hobart.

The Yellow Line

Embedded in the footpath outside Hobart's Parliament House are two backlit lightboxes known as the 'Yellow Line' that commemorate the gay rights protests at Salamanca Markets in 1988 and the formal apology issued years later.

ROBERT RED2000/SHUTTERSTOCK

Accessible Travel

The Tasmanian government's *Disability Strategy 2025–27* seeks to improve the level of inclusion and access to all public facilities across the island, including buildings, websites and employment opportunities. Most local councils work with disability groups to create inclusive access plans that might include beach mats, accessible toilets and wheelchair ramps.

Easy Hobart

Central Hobart is easily traversed on wheels, especially the level, step-free waterfront precinct. Salamanca Market also actively encourages visitors with mobility issues.

Airport

Most of Tasmania's airports are single level with good wheelchair accessibility, including Hobart. Launceston has lifts available to departure/arrival gates and also runs a 'Hidden Disability' programme, recognising the international sunflower lanyard protocol.

Accommodation

Accessible accommodation in Tasmania is a mixed bag, so it's best to do some homework. The wheeliegoodguide.com.au is a good starting place. Many smaller B&Bs and older-style hotels and pubs may not be suitable.

SMALL-TOWN ACCESSIBILITY

At Wynyard, the local yacht club runs an inclusive 'Sailability' programme. In Bicheno, the local surf-lifesaving club provides a beach wheelchair for visitors.

Travel Without Limits

Australia's only dedicated accessible-travel magazine, travelwithoutlimits.com.au is a great place to find inspiration and tips of what to see and do and how to do it in Tasmania.

Outdoor Access

Tasmania's Parks & Wildlife Service has many accessible sites around the state suitable for wheelchair access (eg Pine Lake; p134), and offer all-terrain wheelchairs at Cradle Mountain, Mt Field and Freycinet visitor centres.

TRANSPORT

Tasmanian car-rental companies usually have a few hand-operated vehicles; book in advance. Tourist buses around Hobart like Red Decker and the Kunanyi/Mt Wellington Explorer offer wheelchair access, as do some Kinetic intercity and Metro bus services.

RESOURCES

facebook.com/wheelchairfriendlytamania Recommendations for wheelchair-friendly access to restaurants, sights and accommodation in Tasmania.

wheeliegoodguide.com.au Searchable lists per Tasmanian region of wheelchair-friendly venues.

Vacayit Free app for travellers who are blind and with visual impairments, with around 50 audio guides on Tasmania.

discovertasmania.com.au/planning/accessible-travel Audio guides (Vaycayit) and loads of useful information for accessible travel on the island.

The most picturesque wheelchair-accessible track on the island is the easy 1.4km loop through temperate rainforest to the ethereal, fern-fringed Russell Falls in Mt Field National Park. Allow 25 minutes at a gentle pace.

Great Overnight Walks of Tasmania

Tasmania's Parks & Wildlife Service actively promotes its 60 Great Short Walks, but there's no formal classification of the island's excellent overnight walks, which offer some of the best bushwalking in the country.

When to Go

Summer is prime-time walking season in Tasmania, with longer days and milder daytime temperatures than on the mainland. February and March deliver the most stable weather, though you can walk any time of year if you're prepared. Alpine conditions are demanding in winter, though a snowy Overland Track in low golden sunlight is a truly magical experience. Hobart and Launceston have plenty of outdoors shops so you can make sure you're properly kitted-out.

Essential Ambles

Overland Track (p244) Tasmania's premier long-distance trail (65km, six days) is also your best introduction to long-distance wilderness walking. Don't miss side trips to Cradle Mountain, Mt Ossa, Pine Valley and Barn Bluff.

Three Capes Track (p94) Spectacular 46km, four-day walk taking in Capes Pillar and Hauy, with a boat trip to see Cape Raoul. Look forward to architect-designed huts, endless ocean views and the highest sea cliffs in the country.

Freycinet Peninsula Circuit (p161) Easygoing low-level circuit of the peninsula (27km, two to three days) containing Tasmania's most photogenic beach.

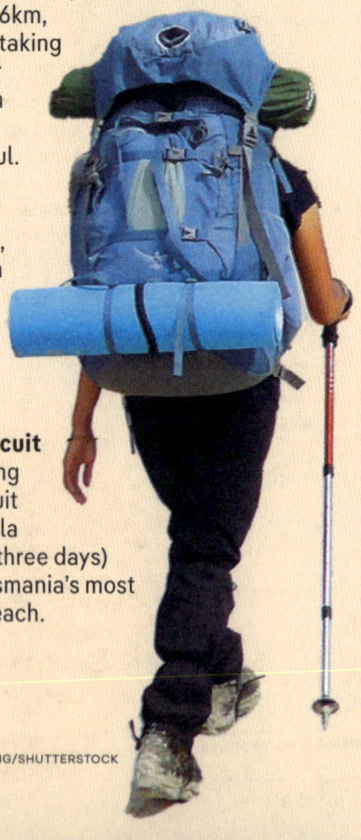

4 SEASON BACKPACKING/SHUTTERSTOCK

Intermediate Walks

South Coast Track (p121) This 85km (seven- to nine-day) hut-less walk along Tasmania's southern coastline will test your gear and camping expertise on a well-defined, mostly low-level trail. Expect brilliant beaches, unbridged rivers and plenty of mud.

Walls of Jerusalem (p227) The compact Walls can be explored in a weekend or longer, with its varied lakes and peaks great for honing your navigational skills. Approachable from many directions, the shortest, easiest route is four hours (12km) from the west.

Frenchmans Cap (p140) Excellent southwest 42km, three-day return trek to a commanding peak with sheer 400m cliffs – or a more-demanding off-track circuit (49km, five days) via the Franklin River.

Hard Going

Mt Anne Circuit (p121) Classic 22km, three- to five day circuit to the Southwest's highest peak. You'll need a good head for heights for the summit and the traverse of Mt Lot.

Western Arthur Range Traverse (p121) Difficult but sensational traverse of the Western Arthur Range, basking in some of the worst weather in Tasmania! It's a week-long 52km loop from Scotts Peak Dam.

Eastern Arthur Range Traverse (p121) The most exciting, challenging and eye-popping walking in Tasmania leads to Federation Peak, the bushwalker's Holy Grail, across a skyline traverse of the Eastern Arthur Range. Allow a week or more; 72km.

GUIDEBOOKS

John and Monica Chapman publish several excellent old-school bushwalking guidebooks, including *Cradle Mountain Lake St Clair* (including Walls of Jerusalem) and *South West Tasmania*. These invaluable resources are loaded with route descriptions, distances, maps, side trips and scientific and historical insights. See john.chapman.name.

Nuts & Bolts

OPENING HOURS

There is no late-night shopping in Tasmanian cities, except for supermarkets.

Banks 9.30am to 4pm Monday to Thursday, to 5pm Friday

Cafes 7am to 3pm

Post offices 9am to 5pm Monday to Friday; some open Saturday morning in cities

Pubs and bars Mostly noon to 11pm

Restaurants Lunch noon to 2.30pm, dinner 5.30pm to 8.30pm

Shops 9am to 5.30pm Monday to Friday, to 5pm Saturday, 10am to 4pm Sunday

Supermarkets 7am to 10pm in the south, from 6am in the north.

Daylight Savings

Clocks go forward one hour on the first Sunday in October and revert on the first Sunday in April.

GOOD TO KNOW

Time Zone
GMT +10

Country calling code
+61

Emergency number
000

Population
570,000

Drinking & Smoking

Alcohol and tobacco products can only be sold to people aged 18 or older.

Weights & Measures

The metric system is used for all distances, weights, temperatures, areas etc.

Electricity

230V/50Hz

PUBLIC HOLIDAYS

New Year's Day 1 January

Australia Day 26 January

Hobart Regatta Day 2nd Monday in February (southern Tasmania)

Launceston Cup Last Wednesday in February (Launceston only)

King Island Show 1st Tuesday in March (King Island only)

Eight Hour Day 2nd Monday in March

Easter March/April (Good Friday to Easter Tuesday inclusive)

ANZAC Day 25 April

Kings's Birthday 2nd Monday in June

Burnie Show 1st Friday in October (Burnie only)

Launceston Show 2nd Thursday in October (Launceston only)

Hobart Show 3rd Thursday in October (southern Tasmania)

Flinders Island Show 3rd Friday in October (Flinders Island only)

Recreation Day 1st Monday in November (northern Tasmania)

Devonport Show Last Friday in November (Devonport only)

Christmas Day 25 December

Boxing Day 26 December

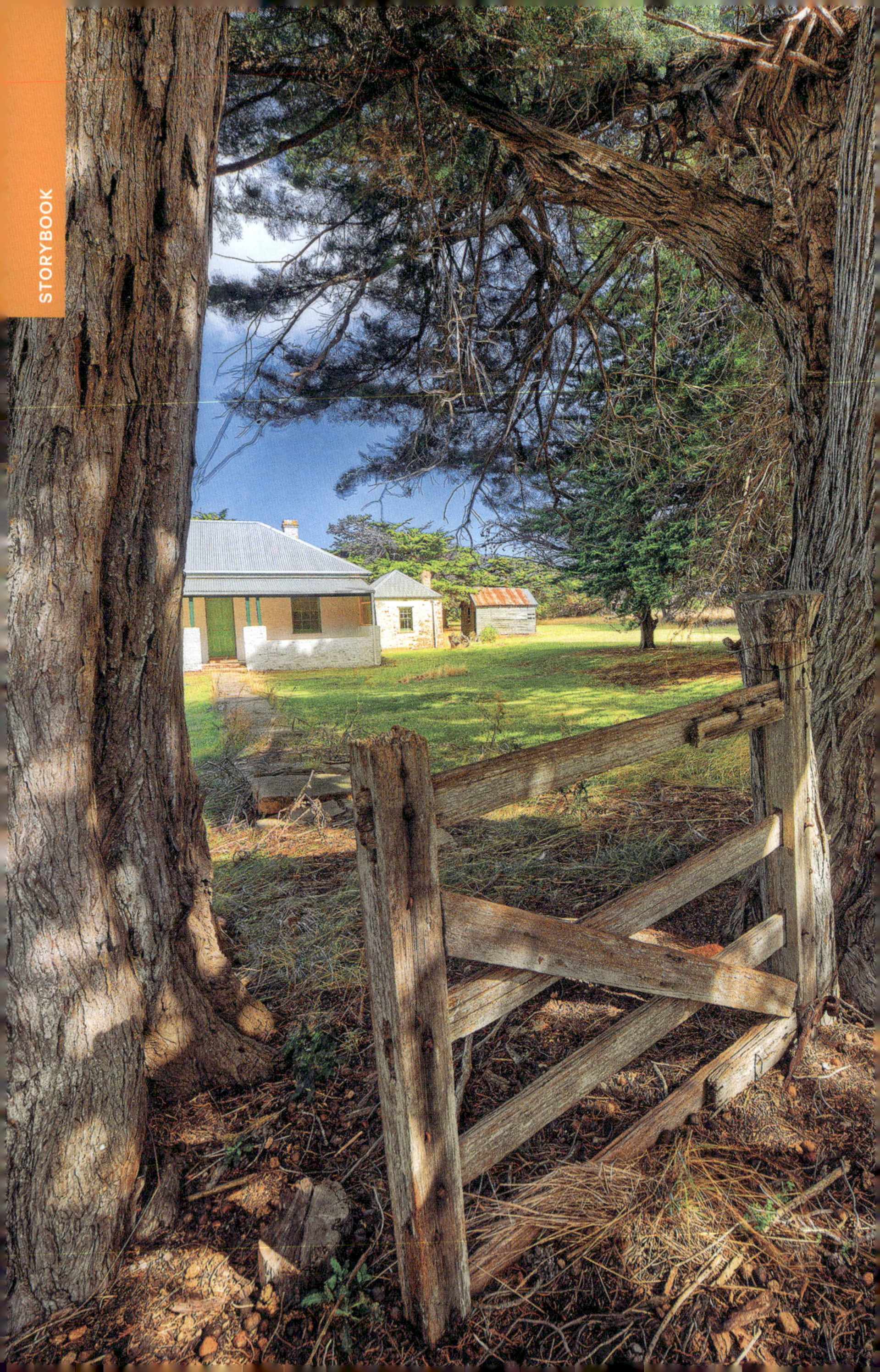

THE TASMANIA

STORYBOOK

Our writers delve deep into different aspects of Tasmanian life

Wybalenna (p180), Flinders Island

SOUTHERN LIGHTSCAPES-AUSTRALIA/GETTY IMAGES

A HISTORY OF LUTRUWITA/ TASMANIA IN 15 PLACES

Cruel and uncompromising, the history of Tasmania is not an easy read, following an all-too-familiar path of what happens when a European naval power encounters an ancient, Indigenous culture. Even today, the future of the island is a delicate balancing act between nature and development – about which debates are endless.

AS YOU TRAVERSE vast Bass Strait on the *Spirit of Tasmania* ferry, it's hard to imagine that Tasmania was once connected to mainland Australia by dry land, when sea levels were lower. But those orange-lichen-encrusted boulders at Wilsons Promontory in Victoria are just like Bicheno's! Aboriginal peoples migrated to the island via several routes, and while facts are scarce, they were definitely living here at least 40,000 years ago.

The 'heroic era' saw the Dutch come for a look but leave empty-handed. French and British explorers arrived in the late 18th century, with sealers and whalers hot on their heels. Britain, spooked by the French interest, established a colony at what is now Hobart in 1803. The French left plenty of names behind.

Colonisation of 'Van Diemen's Land' had a devastating impact on the Palawa (Tasmanian Aboriginal people), culminating in the Black War (1824–31) and their banishment to Flinders Island. Simultaneously, British colonial expansionism used convict labour to get things built. The wholesale shipping of convicts to Australia, usually for life, was called 'Transportation'. It ceased in 1853, and three years later the island was renamed 'Tasmania' and granted self-governance, with federation into the Commonwealth of Australia following in 1901.

1. Flinders Island

ACROSS THE LAND BRIDGE

Around 40,000 years ago a land bridge connected Tasmania to the Australian mainland. Aboriginal peoples made their way down through the Kent Islands and Flinders Island to Tasmania's east coast. Not a lot is known about these early migrations, though artefacts that date back 27,000 years found on offshore islands and in Southwest caves indicate habitation. Sea levels rose around 12,000 years ago, cutting Tasmania off from the mainland. Sealers arrived on these islands in 1796, taking Aboriginal women from mainland Tasmania. Many contemporary Tasmanian Aboriginal people trace their lineage back to these Flinders Island women.

For more on Flinders Island, see p180.

2. Maria Island

OFFSHORE EDIBLES

Despite some problems with diseased, toxic parrot fish around 3500 years ago, the Palawa, now widely established across Tasmania, took to the sea in bark canoes around 3000 years ago. This enabled offshore islands to become seasonal hunting and fishing grounds, including Robbins Island and Hunter Island in the northwest and Maria Island off the east coast. Shoreline hunting and gathering also increased: oysters, abalone and crayfish boosted the size and number of middens as the Palawa population increased. Later, around 700 years ago, catamarans allowed further ocean expeditions to hunt seals and birds in places like Maatsuyker Island.

For more on Maria Island, see p148.

3. West Coast

EUROPEAN NAMING RIGHTS

The first recorded sighting of Tasmania by a European was in 1642 when Dutch explorer Abel Tasman, on a voyage south from Batavia (Jakarta), spied the mountains of the west coast near what is now Zeehan. Tasman named the land 'Van Diemen's Land' after the governor of the Dutch East Indies, and continued south around the bottom of the island. Strong winds blew his ships (*Heemskerck* and *Zeehan*) across 'Storm Bay' to Marion Bay, where a sailor swam ashore and planted the Dutch flag. There is no record of interaction with the Palawa. Matthew Flinders subsequently named Tasman's west-coast mountains after Tasman's two ships.

For more on the west coast, see p248.

4. Hobart

BIRTH OF A CITY

The NSW Governor Captain Philip King, nervous about French explorers charting the eastern coastline, dictated that a colony should be established on the River Derwent. In 1803 Lieutenant John Bowen set up shop at Piyura Kitina/Risdon Cove on the river's eastern shore, but fresh water was scarce: Bowen relocated across the river to Sullivans Cove, site of present-day Hobart. On Mouheneener country, relations with the tribe were tense but evenly poised, until an influx of settlers from Norfolk Island provided the colonials with a distinct advantage. The ensuing Black War and disease drastically depleted the original inhabitants.

For more on Hobart, see p44.

Sarah Island penal colony ruins (p268), west coast

MARIE JENSEN/SHUTTERSTOCK

5. George Town

STAY OR GO?

William Paterson established a garrison at Outer Cove on the eastern shore of Kanamaluka/River Tamar in 1804, though several weeks later most residents decided the western shore looked nicer. By 1806 they'd moved further upriver and founded (rather humbly) Patersonia, where Launceston sits today. Colony supremo Lachlan Macquarie told them to go back to Outer Cove, which he renamed George Town, after the British King. Most settlers of Patersonia (now renamed Launceston, in honour of NSW Governor King's English birthplace) decided not to go, but the need for an army to protect the river mouth ensured George Town has been populated ever since.

For more on George Town, see p208.

6. Sarah Island

A CONVICT HELL

Tasmania's first convict penitentiary was one of its worst, with regular floggings and rampant disease caused by malnutrition. These days Sarah Island might seem idyllic, but in 1821 the Macquarie Harbour Penal Station was a terrifying destination for those convicts who survived the rugged boat journey through the harbour's infamous 'Hells Gates'. One convict stabbed two others in the hope he would be hanged; others tried escaping, including the infamous cannibal Alexander Pearce. The island features in classical Australian literature such as *For the Term of His Natural Life* (Clarke) and *Gould's Book of Fish* (Flanagan).

For more on Sarah Island, see p268.

7. Port Arthur Historic Site

WORLD HERITAGE GRAVEYARD

The British began transporting criminals to remote Port Arthur in 1833, putting them to work expanding the settlement. The convicts cut timber and used it to build boats. Conditions were harsh and many prisoners ended up buried in unmarked graves on the Isle of the Dead across the bay. Transportation ended in 1853, but Port Arthur remained a prison and an asylum until 1877. Considered one of the finest examples of 19th-century convict settlements worldwide, it's now a UNESCO World Heritage Site. In 1996 a lone gunman killed 35 people here, sparking strict gun controls Australia-wide.

For more on Port Arthur, see p98.

8. Wybalenna

PALAWA IN EXILE

In an effort to end the Black War between the colonists and Tasmania's original inhabitants, lay preacher George Augustus Robinson attempted to negotiate a peace treaty by undertaking 'friendly missions' among the tribes. He promised a safe haven, food and a place to practise their own culture on Flinders Island. By 1834 he'd coaxed 134 Palawa to Wybalenna, a makeshift camp near Port Davies. This effectively ended the Black War, but when Robinson moved on, conditions at Wybalenna turned squalid, the Aboriginal people dying from disease and prevented from practising their culture. In 1847 the 47 survivors were relocated to Oyster Cove near Kettering.

For more on Wybalenna, see p180.

9. Cradle Mountain

MOUNTAINOUS VISION

During an exploratory trip to Cradle Mountain in 1909, Gustav Weindorfer was stunned by the area's sheer natural beauty. He and his wife, Kate, bought land and built a rough cabin they named Waldheim ('forest home') to accommodate paying guests. Realising the conservation value of the area, the couple campaigned relentlessly for a national park, which was eventually gazetted in 1922. Parks & Wildlife, after removing the original Waldheim, which had fallen into disrepair after Gustav's death, recreated the original rough wooden cabins after a public outcry. Today, Cradle Mountain is the start of Tasmania's most famous multiday hike, the Overland Track.

For more on Cradle Mountain, see p240.

10. Lake Pedder

DROWNING THE WILDERNESS

By the 1950s bushwalking clubs began exploring the Southwest wilderness, and photographers captured exquisite images of Lake Pedder and its unique pink quartzite beach. Lake Pedder was protected by an Act of Parliament in 1955, which was revoked 12 years later by progress-driven politicians committed to damming the nearby the Serpentine and Huon Rivers. There was public outcry, environmental groups rallied and protests continued until 1972, when inundation caused by the dams began. Tasmania's first major conservation battle was unsuccessful (the pink quartzite beach now lies under 15m of water), but it set the framework for conservation battles to come.

For more on Lake Pedder, see p120.

11. Franklin River

SAVING THE WILDERNESS

If the flooding of Lake Pedder was a low point for Tasmanian environmentalists, it was also a wake-up call. Knowing the state-owned Hydroelectric Commission (HEC) was surveying other Southwest sites, smaller groups involved in the Pedder protests amalgamated and were ready when news broke of the Gordon-below-Franklin project in 1978. Environmentalists knew public support was needed, not just in Tasmania but across Australia and internationally. The Tasmanian Wilderness Society's media-savvy No Dams campaign and televised Franklin blockade was one of Australia's biggest environmental battles. It ultimately swung a Federal election and saw a 1983 High Court ruling protect the river.

For more on the Franklin River, see p137.

12. Berriedale

THE MONA EFFECT

In 1956 Italian immigrant Claudio Alcorso planted vines on a Berriedale headland overlooking the River Derwent 11km north of Hobart, establishing Moorilla Estate.

Isle of the Dead (p99), Port Arthur Historic Site

After Claudio died, David Walsh – a mathematician, gambler, art collector and professional rogue – bought the winery in 1995 to house his art collection. Walsh fell in love with the winery and created his Moorilla Museum of Antiquities nearby. When nobody came, Walsh shuttered the old museum and in 2011 opened his new, shocking and totally immersive Museum of Old and New Art (MONA), taking a blowtorch to the art establishment and fuelling Tasmania's economy: 'the MONA effect'.

For more on MONA, see p76.

13. Derby

FROM TIN TO MTB TRAILS

Tin was discovered in northeast Tasmania in 1874 and the brothers Krushka founded a mine in what is now Derby. The lucrative Briseis mine was the lifeblood of the town for the next 70 years, even surviving two devastating floods in 1929. After the mine closed in 1948, the town fell into a steady decline until 2015, when the Blue Derby Mountain Bike Trails opened and Derby's fortunes took a major U-turn. Over 125km of world-class trails were constructed as a joint venture between state and local governments, and Derby is now revered worldwide as a mountain-biking nirvana.

For more on Derby, see p175.

14. Launceston

CITY OF GASTRONOMY

For too long outshone by big-brother Hobart to the south, Launceston finally had its moment in the sun in 2021 when the city was named a UNESCO City of Gastronomy – one of only 36 such cities around the world at the time (now 50). The accolade acknowledged the city's prime position at the head of the Tamar Valley Wine Region; its burgeoning cafe, restaurant, craft-beer and food-market scenes; and Launceston's inexorable ties to the fertile farmlands and productive oceans of Tasmania's north. 'Paddock-to-plate' gourmet culture is what it's all about: Saturday-morning Harvest Market is where it all comes together.

For more on Launceston, see p190.

15. Takayna/Tarkine

LARGELY UNPROTECTED RAINFOREST

With Aboriginal petroglyphs, middens and hut sites dating back 6000 years and Australia's largest tract of temperate rainforest, it's unbelievable that the Takayna/Tarkine area of the wild northwest coast is largely unprotected by laws. The inaccessible Savage River National Park covers only 10% of Takayna/Tarkine's estimated 495,000 hectares, and while environmental groups have been calling for a national park covering the whole region, logging and mining industries are competing for access. Local councils must try to balance these competing interests, preserving the area's scenic beauty and encouraging tourism, while at the same time remaining sympathetic to development proposals.

For more on Takayna/Tarkine, see p248.

MEET THE TASMANIANS

From marriages built to last and fundamental happiness to slender pay packets and disappointing cricket, CHARLES RAWLINGS-WAY introduces his people.

LET'S START WITH some facts. Tasmania's population is growing at the slowest rate of any Australian state, at a mere 0.2% annually. The island also has Australia's lowest life expectancy (80.3 for men, 84.3 for women); lowest literacy rates (50% of locals have inadequate reading skills); highest smoking rates (12% of people here have at least one daily dart); lowest median weekly household income ($1208.00); and (critically) the lowest winning percentage of any state in the history of the Sheffield Shield domestic cricket competition (24.88%). I could go on, but the point has been made: Tasmanians have some issues to contend with.

At its most limiting, this societal backdrop breeds suspicion of those who are seen to be too ambitious, and an innate kind of hyper-modesty: there are plenty of bushels in Tasmania with people's lights hidden under them. But at best, living on this southern island equips islanders with hard-wired resilience and the kind of dogged persistence that can take them all the way to the top.

Yes, living here presents some challenges. But there are so many positives. Hearteningly, given the 19th-century assertion that the Palawa (Tasmanian Aboriginal) people were essentially extinct, just over 5% of Tasmanians now identify as Aboriginal – the highest percentage of any Australian state. Tasmania also has Australia's lowest divorce rate at 2%, well below Queensland where 2.6% of marriages dissolve in the humidity. It's true that overall household income may be slim down south, but Tasmanian wage growth is heading north, leading the nation at 3.9%. Tasmania also has the highest percentage of people who don't align themselves with a particular religion (50%) – which, depending on which way your spiritual compass is pointing, is either a shame or a blessing.

But beyond all the stats and demographics, this island is a happy and friendly place. Recent surveys have crowned Tasmania as Australia's top state when it comes to residents' wellbeing, personal safety and sense of community connection and belonging. Small-town friendliness, openness and unpretentiousness are the norm here – locals will readily greet strangers with a cheery 'Good morning' on the street. And beyond the streets, the access to nature that Tasmanians enjoy is unmatched in any Australian city – beaches, mountains, forests, rivers and lakes, all within an easy drive of the major hubs. The food and drink here are also sublime, and if a slow-growing population means you can get a seat at your chosen restaurant without booking three weeks in advance, all the better.

Tasmanians certainly are a resilient and persistent bunch, and they also know that they're living in a very special place and are extremely happy to be here.

Born on the Island

Around 80% of Tasmanians are born in Australia, and the vast majority of these folks are born on the island. Overseas-born players include 3.5% from the UK, 1.2% from China, 1.1% from Nepal and 1.1% from India.

Pictured clockwise from top left: Launceston local (p186); Tasmanian farmer; Musician, Queenstown (p271); Palawa (Tasmanian Aboriginal person)

CLOCKWISE FROM TOP LEFT: ULRIKA/GETTY IMAGES, PIXDELUXE/GETTY IMAGES, SLOVEGROVE/SHUTTERSTOCK, THURTELL/GETTY IMAGES

BACK IN TASMANIA

I have a conflicted relationship with Tasmania. I wasn't born here – I'm technically a Devonian. But I moved to Hobart when I was three and stayed until I was 27 (on and off – there was some backpacking in there, too). Now, in what I've come to accept is middle age, I've returned with my family to live on the island again, and I'm conflicted between the Tasmania I once knew and the Tasmania I see today. Why have all those old pubs closed? What's happened to the winter-long snow on Kunanyi? Why are houses so expensive? Why can I still not get a pizza after 10pm? Time runs its race: some things change; some things refuse to. The trick with Tasmania, as with middle age, is to accept its flaws and live in the moment – to mourn the boarded-up pub as you drink in the crowded craft-beer bar. And of course, one thing remains constant: hot damn this cold island is beautiful.

ARE YOU OUT THERE, THYLACINE?

The tragic tale of the Tasmanian tiger. By Charles Rawlings-Way

THE STORY OF the thylacine, aka the Tasmanian tiger, has two different endings. Ending one says that thylacines were hunted to extinction in the early 20th century. Ending two says that thylacines still survive, deep in the Tasmanian wilderness. Scientists ridicule such suggestions, but sightings continue, and the tale of the thylacine is endlessly captivating.

A Tiger in Tasmania?

Thylacinus cynocephalus, the thylacine, was a striped, nocturnal dog-like predator that was widespread in Tasmania 200 years ago – and before that on mainland Australia and in Papua New Guinea. When Tasmania was isolated by rising sea levels at the end of the last Ice Age 12,000 years ago, the thylacine became the apex predator on its own island paradise. Some Palawa (Tasmanian Aboriginal) clans hunted thylacines for food; others revered them, weaving them into Dreaming stories and local lore. Either way, the island's ecology maintained a harmonious balance for thousands of years and thylacines thrived. Meanwhile on the mainland, thylacine numbers dwindled due to a warming climate and the arrival of dingoes around 5000 years ago. But there were no dingoes in Tasmania, and the island remained a tad chilly. These lean marsupial hounds – measuring up to 1.8m long nose-to-tail and 60cm high, with their distinctive wide jaws and black-striped hind quarters – had a good life in Tasmania. Then in 1803, everything changed.

Bounty Hunted

It took a few decades for Europeans to get busy farming Tasmania's fertile Midlands and lush southern valleys, but from the 1830s onwards, land was systematically cleared, ploughed and seeded in the British agrarian tradition. The Midlands became the new colony's food bowl, and unfortunately for the thylacine, sheep farming was equally successful here. Docile, slow-moving sheep were unaccustomed to being hunted, and thylacines weren't stupid. It was much easier to drag down a ewe or two in an open paddock than chase a wallaby through the dense undergrowth. Feral dogs probably killed as many sheep as thylacines did, but by 1888 the Tasmanian government had had enough. A bounty was placed on the thylacine's head: £1 for a dead adult and 10 shillings for a pup. At least 2184 bounties were paid by the government (any many more by private land holders), until the problem was deemed resolved in 1909, and bounties ceased. But the damage had been done. With their breeding numbers decimated, their habitat increasingly fragmented and introduced diseases also taking a toll, the last known thylacine, a lonely specimen called Benjamin, died in Hobart's old Beaumaris Zoo in 1936.

Did You Just See That?

The thylacine was officially declared extinct in 1986, the requisite 50 years after Benjamin died. But sightings have continued across the decades since. Many scientists agree that, given Tasmania's vast tracts of untouched forest, shy thylacines probably survived in low numbers as recently as the 1980s. Many sightings, some of them by entirely credible and trustworthy figures, lend weight to this theory. Of particular note are sightings by park rangers Hans Naarding in 1982 at Togara in the remote northwest; and Charles Beasley in 1995 at Pyengana in the northeast. But given the thylacine's shrunken gene pool and the endless encroachment of roads, people and technology into their habitat – not to mention the glaring absence of a single verifiable thylacine image, scat, footprint or carcass – the consensus now is that the thylacine has gone the way of the dodo.

De-extinction Dollars

But still, sightings and thylacine intrigue persist. The species has become an icon of Tasmania, its noble image adorning everything from government letterheads and licence plates to council logos and beer labels. Is this a societal attempt to absolve the shame of the thylacine's extinction? Or wishful thinking that the tiger will rise, Lazarus-like, from the wilderness? Several other Australian marsupials have done this: the mahogany glider was rediscovered in Queensland in 1989 after being presumed extinct for more than 100 years; while in 1973, the bridled nail-tail wallaby also remerged in Queensland after 50 years of extinction. Not to mention the Tammar wallaby, declared extinct in South Australia in the 1920s but rediscovered on an island in New Zealand in 2001! But none of these were as large as the thylacine, nor as limited in geographic boundaries.

The thylacine may never be rediscovered in the wild, but recently, Hollywood dollars have been laid on the table in an effort to 'de-extinct' the species through genetic engineering. Actor Leonardo DiCaprio's organisation Re:wild is collaborating with Texan company Colossal Biosciences, backed by actor-investors Chris, Liam and Luke Hemsworth, in developing cloning technology that could 'edit' the DNA of a similar species, such as the diminutive fat-tailed dunnart, to recreate a thylacine – a tantalising prospect.

The demise of the thylacine is a tragic tale of human ruthlessness and stupidity – but it's also a story of human hope. Will the Tasmanian tiger's script have a Hollywood ending?

Read, Watch, Listen: the Thylacine in Popular Culture

Thylacine (Monique Brumby, 1997) Hobart-raised singer-songwriter Brumby recorded her debut album in Melbourne – perhaps feeling a little endangered herself in the big smoke.

Thylacine (David Owen, 2003) Owen's book is a rigorous dissertation of the creature's life and times, sidestepping mythology and sticking to the facts.

The Hunter (director Daniel Nettheim, 2011) Willem Defoe plays a fly-in-fly-out hunter of rare species, sent to Tasmania to snare the DNA of the last thylacine.

Hunt for Truth: Tasmanian Tiger (Tim Noonan, 2024) Noonan's emotion-charged documentary takes him into the jungles of Papua New Guinea in search of the elusive 'stripy dog'.

TASMANIAN WOMEN

Women from Tasmania are among the hardiest on Earth and their tumultuous history shows us why. By Sue Williams

WOMEN FROM TASMANIA, the island state of Australia, have punched above their weight since the beginning of time. Is it because their comparative isolation breeds in them new levels of determination and resilience? That's certainly a factor, but we need to look no further than their turbulent history to really understand why they so consistently overachieve. From the start, our First Nations sisters had the odds stacked against them, with one of the most brutal colonial regimes ever seen, which decimated the population, through violence, murder, disease and land grabs, and which directly led to the bloody years of the Black War (1824–31).

First Nations Women

One of Tasmania's most celebrated heroines is Truganini (1812–76), a palawa (Aboriginal Tasmanian) woman who grew up in traditional culture – until the Europeans arrived. By the age of 17, her mother had been murdered by sailors, her uncle shot by a soldier, her sister abducted by sealers and her fiancé slain by loggers.

Truganini became a guide, teaching others, both Indigenous and non-Indigenous, her language and customs. After a period incarcerated at the Friendly Mission's Wybalenna settlement on Flinders Island, where First Nations people were sent to be 'civilised and Christianised', she was forced to return to Oyster Cove Station in 1847, south of Hobart. Today, Truganini is seen by both black and white as a symbol of the struggles, courage and rights of First Nations people, and Oyster Cove Station –

Pictured clockwise from top left: Elizabeth Blackburn; Fanny Cochrane Smith; Alannah Hill; Mary Reibey

where 47 Aboriginal people lived – is a historic site, with an annual putalina festival of remembrance open to all each January. Many also visit the cemetery and chapel at Wybalenna.

At the time of her death, Truganini was incorrectly thought by many to be the last 'true' Palawa. In fact, Truganini was outlived by other Aboriginal Tasmanian women who were taken by sealers to both the Bass Strait Islands and Kangaroo Island in the early 19th century. Also outliving Truganini was Fanny Cochrane Smith (1834–1905), who after the death of Truganini, claimed the title of the 'last Tasmanian' – despite having 11 children. She is the only Aboriginal person to be recorded singing in an Indigenous Tasmanian language, which can now be heard at the Tasmanian Museum and Art Gallery.

Another significant Indigenous figure was Aboriginal leader Tarenorerer (1800–31), who, from 1828, trained her warriors to use firearms against the Europeans. She ended up exiled to Gun Carriage Island, where she died of influenza. Dolly Dalrymple (1808–64), too, was an Indigenous woman of note. Her mother's kidnapper sold her to a sealer for one guinea, but she was later given a government land grant at Perth, south of Launceston, for her bravery in holding off a six-hour attack on her hut.

Early European Women

There was no shortage of courage among the European women brought over to Tasmania, either. The toughest and smartest could usually be found among the convicts, shipped over from Britain for often trivial crimes, usually committed because of poverty. Many were forced to live in correctional centres known as female factories, where they worked as cooks, hospital attendants, seamstresses, cleaners and launderers.

The most infamous centre is the Cascades Female Factory, which operated in Hobart from 1828 to 1856 and, at its peak, held 1200 women and children. It's now World Heritage–listed and is both a fascinating and disturbing place to visit. Notable convicts include Betty King (1765–1856), transported for stealing five handkerchiefs, who was said to be the first European woman to set foot on Australia when she was carried ashore as a rehearsal for the officers' wives. She came to live in Van Diemen's Land after her sentence and was also the last survivor of the First Fleet. There's a monument to her at Lawitta.

Mary Reibey (1777–1855) was the most successful female convict of her generation, becoming a wealthy businesswoman upon the death of her husband, Thomas, with vast landholdings in both Tasmania and NSW. Learn about her astonishing story, and find out why her face appears on the $20 note, during a visit to Entally House (p199), near the village of Hadspen in northern Tasmania.

Women of Achievement

Tasmanian women have often excelled. Dame Enid Lyons (1897–1981) was the first woman to be elected to Federal Parliament and the first to serve in the Cabinet. She had a good role model: her husband Joseph was a former Tasmanian premier and Australian prime minister. Following on was Jocelyn Newman (1937–2018), a Tasmanian senator for 15 years, a minister in the Howard government and a strong advocate for social-security reform.

In medicine, Elizabeth Blackburn (b 1948) won the Nobel Prize in 2009 for her astonishing discoveries in the field of genetics and cancer, while Shirley Jeffrey (1930–2014) was an internationally renowned marine biochemist, specialising in micro-algal research. She was dubbed the 'Mother of Chlorophyll C' and helped provide the basis for the development and growth of aquaculture.

Today's Heroines

Tasmania has a wealth of present-day heroines who have inspired the rest of Australia, and often the world. Probably the best-known Tasmanian on Earth is Mary Donaldson (b 1972), today more correctly referred to as Queen Mary of Denmark. Then there's the 2021 Australian of the Year Grace Tame (b 1994), an outspoken advocate for the survivors of sexual assault; fashion designer Alannah Hill (b 1962); and the late, globally celebrated fantasy writer Sara Douglass (1957–2011).

All are part of a long line of Tasmanian over-achievers who despite – or perhaps because of – their start on a tiny island at the bottom of the globe have had an outsized impact on us all.

Western Arthur Range Traverse (p121)

JIRI VIEHMANN/SHUTTERSTOCK

THE TASMANIAN LANDSCAPE

Wild, rugged and diverse, what makes this mountainous island so unique and celebrated by hikers, scientists and artists alike? By Steve Waters

Gondwanaland

While admiring the changing of the fagus (deciduous beech trees) on Mt Field's Tarn Shelf, or on the steep slopes of Crater Lake in Cradle Mountain-Lake St Clair National Park, take a moment to reflect on this echo from the supercontinent Gondwanaland. Some 250 million years ago Australia was thought to be part of a supercontinental landmass along with Antarctica, Africa, India, South America, Madagascar, New Zealand and New Guinea. Around 165 million years ago (thanks to shifting plate tectonics), the supercontinent began breaking up. Australia and Antarctica were the last of the continents to pull apart some 45 million years ago, which is why Tasmania has more in common geologically with Antarctica than it does with the rest of the Australian mainland. And while our fagus *(Nothofagus gunnii)* is found only in Tasmania, the fact that other *Nothofagus* species are found only in other southern hemisphere locales, predominantly New Zealand, Patagonia and New Guinea, gives credence to the Gondwanaland theory. Fossil records found across the southern hemisphere, including in Antarctica, reveal a commonality of plant types; one fossil of the giant conifer *Fitzroya tasmanensis* was found near Cradle Mountain, though the tree now only grows in Chile.

Glaciation

Unlike on the Australian mainland, glaciers are responsible for most of the rugged scenery seen in Tasmania's Southwest, west coast and central plateau, though apart from on Ben Lomond, there's no evidence of glaciation in Tasmania's east. There have been several glacial eras in Tasmania, the oldest roughly one million years ago, with the last glaciers disappearing around 14,000 ago. At one point the Central Plateau was covered by a permanent ice cap – something you could well imagine if you step out of your car in winter underdressed. The cirques, tors and hanging valleys of the Arthur Range in the Southwest are classic examples of glaciation.

Sub-Antarctic Islands

While glaciation is also evident in lakes and tarns on World Heritage–listed Macquarie Island, some 1500km south of Tasmania and halfway to Antarctica, it's seismic activity that was a more obvious instrument of the island's creation. Administered by Tasmania (postcode 7151!), windswept Macquarie is the only place on the planet where the Earth's mantle rises

above sea level (known as an ophiolite). Both the island and the waters surrounding it are important habitat for marine creatures and are protected as conservation areas. Roughly 3.5 million seabirds nest on the island, including four species of albatross, and it's the only breeding site of the royal penguin. It's also home to significant numbers of fur seals, and orca and southern right whales are frequent visitors. The only permanent settlement is an Australian scientific research station.

Glaciers are still present on Heard Island, one of the remotest places on Earth, over 4000km southwest of Perth in the Southern Ocean. Once covering 80% of this uninhabited island, glaciers are now retreating in the face of climate change. The island is home to Big Ben, one of Australia's two active volcanoes (the other is on nearby McDonald Island). Macquarie Island is also topped by Australia's tallest mountain outside of Antarctica, Mawson Peak (2745m). The island is administered by the Australian Antarctic Division at Kingston.

Dolerite

While most mountains of Southwest Tasmania consist of quartzite, when Gondwanaland began breaking up there was a massive upthrust of molten magma that cooled just below the Earth's surface, forming the igneous rock dolerite. Several more million years of erosion resulted in the blocky, geometric 'fluted' columns you see around the island today. Tasmania has the largest deposits of dolerite worldwide, from the Tasman Peninsula's towering sea cliffs to the lofty peaks of the Overland Track. And if you thought the Organ Pipes at Kunanyi/Mt Wellington were impressive, check out the nearby Lost World amphitheatre.

Diverse Ecosystems

Temperate rainforest Myrtle beech rainforests require an annual rainfall of 1500mm, restricting them mostly to the western side of the island and wetter gullies in the southeast. These forests grow very slowly and are susceptible to fire and climate change. Species include sassafras and celerytop, king billy and huon pines (none are actual pines) and leatherwood. Huon pine's natural oiliness made it a desirable wood for boat-building, and these slow-growing trees (some live for over 2000 years) were almost logged to extinction. The few remaining Southwest copses are now protected. Rainforest habitat is easily experienced at Mt Field National Park on the Russell Falls walk, at Myrtle Forest, Collinsvale near Hobart, on the Franklin River Nature Trail and on any of the longer walks in the World Heritage Area national parks.

Alpine Usually found only above 1000m, these rocky herb fields contain a rich repository of fragile endemic flora, among them the Gondwanaland-remnant deciduous beech *(Nothofagus gunnii)* as well as cushion plants, scoparia (the prickly bushwalkers' lament), richea and the Dr Seuss–like pandani. The summit of Kunanyi/Mt Wellington, the Hartz Mountains, higher sections of Mt Field and around the Cradle Plateau are the most easily accessed alpine habitats.

Wet sclerophyll The domain of tree ferns and towering eucalypts like gumtopped stringybark *(Eucalyptus delegatensis)* receives between 1000mm and 1500mm of rainfall per annum and is commonly found midway up mountain slopes across the island. You'll pass through this habitat on most west-coast drives, during the ascent of the Great Western Tiers from Deloraine to the Central Plateau and on Kunanyi's southern flanks beyond Fern Tree.

Dry sclerophyll Lower, more open eucalypt forest predominantly found along the east coast and Tasman Peninsula, with she-oaks, wattles, peppermints and Tasmanian blue gum *(Eucalyptus globulus),* the state's floral emblem.

Coastal heath Salt tolerant and wind stunted, these shrubs include banksias, wattles, tea trees, hakeas and grass trees. You'll find them anywhere near the coast with sandy soils, including in the dunes behind Seven Mile Beach, on the Alum Cliffs between Taroona and Kingston, and on the exposed capes of the Tasman Peninsula.

Sedgelands Tasmania has several types of grasslands, but walkers will commonly come across the wet buttongrass plains of the Southwest. Paths through these swampy areas erode quickly, turning to gaiter-sucking mud holes. Frenchmans Cap and the South Coast Track, once notorious for boot-stealing bog, have mostly been rerouted onto boardwalks. Sundews, sphagnum moss and native orchids can be found around the edge of bogs.

Giant kelp forests It's not only above ground that Tasmanian habitats are both unique and vulnerable to climate change. Giant kelp *(Macrocystis pyrifera)* forests were once found all along the east coast. In 2012 rising sea temperature was recognised as a serious threat. Ten years later the kelp forests were almost entirely gone, with only a few isolated patches remaining: bad news for species like weedy sea dragons, rock lobsters and abalone. Luckily, giant kelp can grow up to 10m a year, and now a multi-agency project is working on reseeding the forests.

GIANT KELP CAN GROW UP TO 10M A YEAR, AND NOW A MULTI-AGENCY PROJECT IS WORKING ON RESEEDING THE FORESTS

Kelp forest

IGOR KRUGLIKOV/SHUTTERSTOCK

Horizontal scrub Not a separate ecosystem but an explorer's nightmare that still causes grief to bushwalkers today, *Anodopetalum biglandulosum* forms a tangled mat of impenetrable branches that grow upright from a horizontal trunk. Typically found in wetter forests and near creek systems. Think twice before going off-track in the Southwest.

Landscape Art

If hiking the sodden Tasmanian landscape doesn't excite you, but you're still interested in discovering its beauty, track down some of these artists' work.

John Glover (1767–1849) He was among the first European artists to successfully capture the clear, harsh Tasmanian sunlight. His paintings hang in state galleries and libraries across the country. Australia's premier landscape art prize is named after him.

Max Angus (1914–2017) This revered Tasmanian landscape painter was as prolific as he was long-lived. A selection of his iconic watercolours can be viewed at TMAG in Hobart.

Olegas Truchanas (1923–72) It was this Lithuanian immigrant's photographs of Lake Pedder (before the dam) and the Southwest that really alerted the general populace to the beauty of the World Heritage area. The classic book *The World of Olegas Truchanas* is out of print but routinely appears in secondhand bookshops and on the internet. Truchanas tragically drowned in the Gordon River while trying to replace slides lost in the Hobart 1967 bushfire.

Peter Dombrovskis (1945–96) An admirer of Truchanas, Dombrovskis also took large-format photographs of the Southwest, in particular the Arthur Ranges and the Franklin River. His 'Morning Mist on Rock Island Bend' became the iconic photograph of the No Dams campaign. Look for his book *Wild Rivers*, co-authored with Bob Brown.

Grant Dixon and Rob Blakers The calendars of these contemporary Tasmanian landscape photographers capture the beauty of Tasmania's wild places, including Takayna/Tarkine, Cradle Mountain, the Southwest and the west coast.

Bill Wilkinson The latest edition of Wilkinson's lifelong work *The Abels* is a love song to Tasmania's wild mountains and the rare and fragile environments they inhabit.

Kit Hiller You'll see Hiller's iconic square linocuts of Tasmanian birds and scenery in gift- and bookshops across the island.

Olivia Hickey A multimedia artist by trade, Hickey also produces exquisite jewellery, including pieces depicting ferns and fagus.

See wildislandtas.com.au for more Tasmanian landscape artists.

TASMANIA'S AGRARIAN REVOLUTION

Producers and restaurateurs have transformed the Apple Isle into the abundant isle. By Andrew Bain

IT'S EASY TO take the abundance of Tasmania's famously fresh produce for granted. The lush red soils across the state's north are as fertile as any on the planet, the world's cleanest air (officially certified by the weather station at Cape Grim) purifies the island, oyster racks stripe the shallows of bays and lagoons, and fresh ocean catches arrive daily into docks around the island.

It looks like a cornucopia, and yet there was a time, not so long ago, when sourcing much of this produce was only marginally less difficult than sighting a thylacine. Chefs in search of produce would head down backroads, following directions or tips to properties that might have fruit from a tree or two of this, or vegetables from a bush or three of that, even if only for a few days in season. How times have changed.

Pioneers of Produce

The secret to Tasmania's celebrated produce begins from the ground up. Running across the state's north is a rich band of chocolate-red soil laid out millions of years ago by ancient (and now extinct) volcanoes

Curried scallop pie, Richmond Bakery (p84)

such as Table Cape. Abundant in nutrients, this is where Australia's first black truffles were scratched from the ground (in aptly named Red Hills) by Tim Terry in 1999 and where so much of the state's prime produce continues to sprout.

At around the same time, another pioneer of Tasmanian premium produce was beginning to forge a stand-alone reputation for the quality of its product. After decades of turning out commodity cheeses, King Island Dairy switched to the production of triple cream bries, cheddars and other speciality fromages, establishing such a reputation that it briefly commanded more than 25% of the Australian speciality cheese market. In effect, it had turned the disadvantage of isolation and distance into the advantage of premium exports. How else, after all, could a small island with a low population and high costs compete except to aim for the high end of taste town?

It was a model that would permeate throughout Tasmania, with the cost of shipping to mainland and international markets fuelling an inexorable shift towards high-quality, high-price produce and products. In chasing the premium market, Tasmania shed its monocultural moniker of the Apple Isle to overflow with an almost inexhaustible bounty of goodies, from cherries and berries to olives, hazelnuts, garlic, saffron, wasabi, leatherwood honey, kimchi, avocadoes, truffles, pickled onions, ginseng, oysters, scallops, abalone, crayfish and some of the country's most prized meat labels.

Pickled produce, Agrarian Kitchen (p84)

FROM LEFT: SUTHIKAIT TEERAWATTANAPHAN/SHUTTERSTOCK, STEVE WATERS/LONELY PLANET

Such Good Taste

Tasmania might still claim the humble scallop pie as its signature food item (albeit a little tongue in cheek at times), but these days the curried bakery item is as much a novelty piece, eclipsed by the restaurants bringing fresh local produce to the fore.

They're the very ingredients that were still difficult to find when the likes of the Tetsuya's-trained Rodney Dunn (owner of the Agrarian Kitchen) and Luke Burgess (chef/owner of Hobart's now-defunct Garagistes restaurant) arrived in the state in around 2008, unknowingly helping to set in motion the emergence of modern Tassie cuisine.

Like so much else in the state, however, it was the 'MONA effect' that really set the local dining table. When the subterranean art gallery opened in Hobart in 2011, savvy visitors arrived wanting complementary experiences – premium dining high among them. Restaurants such as Franklin and Ethos burned brightly (if briefly) in Hobart, while Launceston fell under the spell of the likes of Stillwater and Black Cow Bistro.

As things settled, restaurants came and went, but always the quality remained, with gastronomy soon rivalling bushwalking trails as one of Tasmania's greatest visitor lures. In 2021, UNESCO anointed Launceston as a City of Gastronomy – one of just 50 in the world and only the second in Australia (alongside Bendigo in Victoria). And in 2023 *Gourmet Traveller* named five Tasmanian restaurants – Peppina (Hobart), Fico (Hobart), Institut Polaire (Hobart), Stillwater (Launceston) and Van Bone (Marion Bay) – in its annual list of the country's finest eateries. It equated to more than 5% of the total list, from a state with just 2% of the national population. Cheers to that.

Saint John (p198), Launceston
NESS VANDERBURGH/LONELY PLANET

TASMANIA – UNDER THE INFLUENCE

Tasmanian beer and whisky from colonial to contemporary times. By Brett Atkinson

FROM 1804 TO 1813, the fledgling island colony of Van Diemen's Land was split into two distinct counties along the 42nd parallel. Travel north of the region that's now the Midlands town of Ross, and you were in Cornwall, centred on Launceston and the Bass Strait port of George Town. To the south, Hobart, first settled in 1803, was the commercial and administrative hub of the county of Buckingham. Control of all of Tasmania was ceded to Hobart in 1813, but echoes of the state's initial division still linger in sports rivalries and the very important subject of beer.

Hobart's Cascade Brewery – established in 1824 – flew the flag for southern drinkers, while Launceston's Boag's – established in 1881 – was the brew of choice for northerners. Until the last couple of decades, this hoppy north–south divide was unconditional. Draw a west–east line from Strahan through Ross to Bicheno, and you'd struggle to find a northern pub serving Cascade. Down south, asking for a Boag's would potentially elicit confusion and ridicule. Now, things are (slightly) less definitive, but Hobart folk and Launceston residents still take pride in their regional beers, despite both breweries now being owned by multinational brewing conglomerates.

Australia's Oldest Brewery

Harnessing the crisp and pure waters of the Hobart Rivulet on the slopes of Kunanyi/Mt Wellington, Cascade Brewery is Australia's oldest brewery, and was just one of several making beer for the new settlement in the early 19th century. By 1850, more than 40 breweries called Hobart home, and beers from Launceston were being praised by *The Australian* newspaper in Sydney as being superior to anything brewed in New South Wales. The malting of Tasmanian barley and the development of hop farms around Bushy Park in the Derwent Valley from 1867 ensured brewing became an essential part of the Tasmanian economy, and Tasmanian hops continue to be a mainstay of the Australian brewing industry. Visit in April for the Derwent Valley's annual Fresh Hop Festival celebrating the Tasmanian hop harvest.

Crafty Beginnings

Throughout the 20th century, consolidation of breweries led to the inevitable north vs south duopoly of Boag's vs Cascade, and it wasn't until early in the 21st century that diversity, craft and independence bubbled up again in Tasmanian brewing. Five breweries, all established between 2005 and 2009, are Tasmania's craft-beer pioneers,

SAINT JOHN

and all are still producing beers today. Moo Brew's launch in 2005 has expanded to include Manky Sally's, a dive bar meets taproom on Hobart's Salamanca Place, while New Norfolk's Two Metre Tall continues its innovative focus, beginning in 2008, on farmhouse ales and wild-fermented brews. Iron House Brewing combines beachy east-coast views with approachable summer-friendly beers, and Evandale's Van Dieman Brewing crafts barrel-aged and wild-fermented beers from its own fields of hops, barley and wheat. Since 2008, Willie Simpson at Seven Sheds has focused on mead and interesting English-style ales, best enjoyed overlooking his compact hop farm in the Cradle Country hamlet of Railton. Opened in 2011 in an 1840s sailmaker's cottage, Preachers in Hobart's Battery Point neighbourhood soon became the city's best place for discovering Tasmanian craft beers. More than a decade on, the raffish and unpretentious bar is still an essential Hobart experience, and your best opportunity for trying beers from around the state.

Modern Craft Beer & Cider

Inspired by these brewing trailblazers there are now craft breweries all around Tasmania. North Hobart – aka 'NoHo' – is the state capital's hoppy hub, with industrial-style taprooms at Deep South, Overland and T-Bone all channelling a relaxed vibe equal to international craft-beer hot spots like Portland or Wellington. Hobart Brewing Co's sprawling beer garden near the harbour is perfect on a sunny day, while Fox Friday's impressive central Hobart beers are now also being served at its interstate taprooms in Melbourne and Perth. In Launceston, Du Cane Brewing, Tandy's Alehouse and Saint John Craft Beer Bar are crafty hangouts in Boag's country, and the annual Launceston BeerFest NYE is a fine way to celebrate New Year's Eve. Craft cider is also growing in popularity, especially around Tasmania's apple-growing region of the Huon Valley. Both Pagan Cider in Cygnet and Huonville's Willie Smith's Apple Shed have popular cellar doors. Visit in summer for food trucks at Pagan and a seasonal restaurant at Willie Smith's. Near Launceston, Brady's Lookout Cider, named after a bushranger's hideout in the Tamar Valley, is Tasmania's only producer of traditional bottle-conditioned ciders.

A 150-Year Wait for Whisky

From the earliest days of the colony, whisky distilling was also popular in Tasmania. But an 1838 observation from Lady Jane Franklin, wife of Governor Sir John Franklin, plunged the Tasmanian whisky scene into stasis for more than 150 years. After hearing his wife opine, 'I would prefer barley be fed to pigs than it be used to turn men into swine', Sir John promptly outlawed the distilling of spirits in 1839. That remained the status quo until Hobart surveyor Bill Lark successfully lobbied for a change in the laws. After recognising Tasmania's natural advantages for whisky production – including premium barley and crystal-clear water – while on a 1989 trout-fishing trip in the Central Highlands, Lark established the Lark Distillery with his wife Lyn in the heritage town of Richmond north of Hobart following 1992's change in legislation.

Whisky's Exponential Growth

The first release of Lark Distillery single malt whisky followed in 1998, and proved to be the catalyst for an industry making up for lost time. By 2000, there were six distilleries dotted around the state, and by the end of 2023, more than 70, some also producing gin and other spirits while they waited for their whisky to mature for commercial release. The Lark empire now includes The Still, a whisky tasting room in the Art Deco former premises of Hobart's *Mercury* newspaper, and the Lark Distillery at historic Pontville north of Hobart. Three decades after the overdue shakeup of the state's distilling laws, Tasmanian whisky is consistently awarded around the world, and small-scale artisans like Flinders Island's Furneaux Distillery and Waubs Harbour Whisky in Bicheno are producing outstanding single malts infused with a strong sense of place inspired by Tasmania's remote southern location.

INDEX

Map Pages **000**

Map Pages **000**

T

U

V

W

Z

Map Pages **000**

"The kids loved venturing into Hastings Caves (p116)...but it was much harder to get them out of the Thermal Springs afterwards."

CHARLES RAWLINGS-WAY

"Hitting the west coast during heavy rain to find Nelson, Horsetail and Montezuma falls pumping unseasonably with water."

ANDREW BAIN

FROM LEFT: AVANT VISUAL/SHUTTERSTOCK, REINDO/SHUTTERSTOCK

THIS BOOK

The 11th edition of Lonely Planet's *Tasmania* guidebook was written and researched by Andrew Bain and Charles Rawlings-Way. The previous edition was written by Brett Atkinson and Steve Waters. This guidebook was produced by the following:

Destination Editor Jessica Lockhart

Coordinating Editor Andrea Dobbin

Cartographer David Connolly

Production Editor Kathryn Rowan

Image Researcher Hannah Blackie

Assisting Editors Peter Cruttenden, Melanie Dankel, Kate James, Jenna Myers

Cover Researcher Sam Ubinas

Thanks Darren O'Connell

MIX
Paper | Supporting responsible forestry
FSC™ C021741

Paper in this book is certified against the Forest Stewardship Council™ standards. FSC™ promotes environmentally responsible, socially beneficial and economically viable management of the world's forests.

Published by Lonely Planet Global Limited
CRN 554153
11th edition – Oct 2026
ISBN 978 1 83869 965 9

10 9 8 7 6 5 4 3 2 1
Printed in China